Oh My Goddess!

ああっ女神さまっ

Miss Keiichi

Oh My Goddess!

ああっ女神さまっ

Miss Keiichi

STORY AND ART BY

Kosuke Fujishima

TRANSLATION BY

Dana Lewis & Toren Smith

LETTERING AND TOUCH-UP BY

Susie Lee & PC Orz

DARK HORSE COMICS®

PUBLISHER
Mike Richardson

SERIES EDITORS
Dave Chipps & Rachel Penn

COLLECTION EDITOR
Chris Warner

COLLECTION DESIGNER
Amy Arendts

ART DIRECTOR
Mark Cox

English-language version produced by Studio Proteus
for Dark Horse Comics, Inc.

OH MY GODDESS!: Miss Keiichi

This volume collects issues seven through twelve of the Dark Horse comic book series *Oh My Goddess! Part V.*

Published by
Dark Horse Comics, Inc.
10956 SE Main Street
Milwaukie, OR 97222

www.darkhorse.com

To find a comics shop in your area, call the Comic Shop
Locator Service toll-free at 1-888-266-4226

First edition: February 2001
ISBN: 1-56971-522-X

1 3 5 7 9 10 8 6 4 2
Printed in Canada

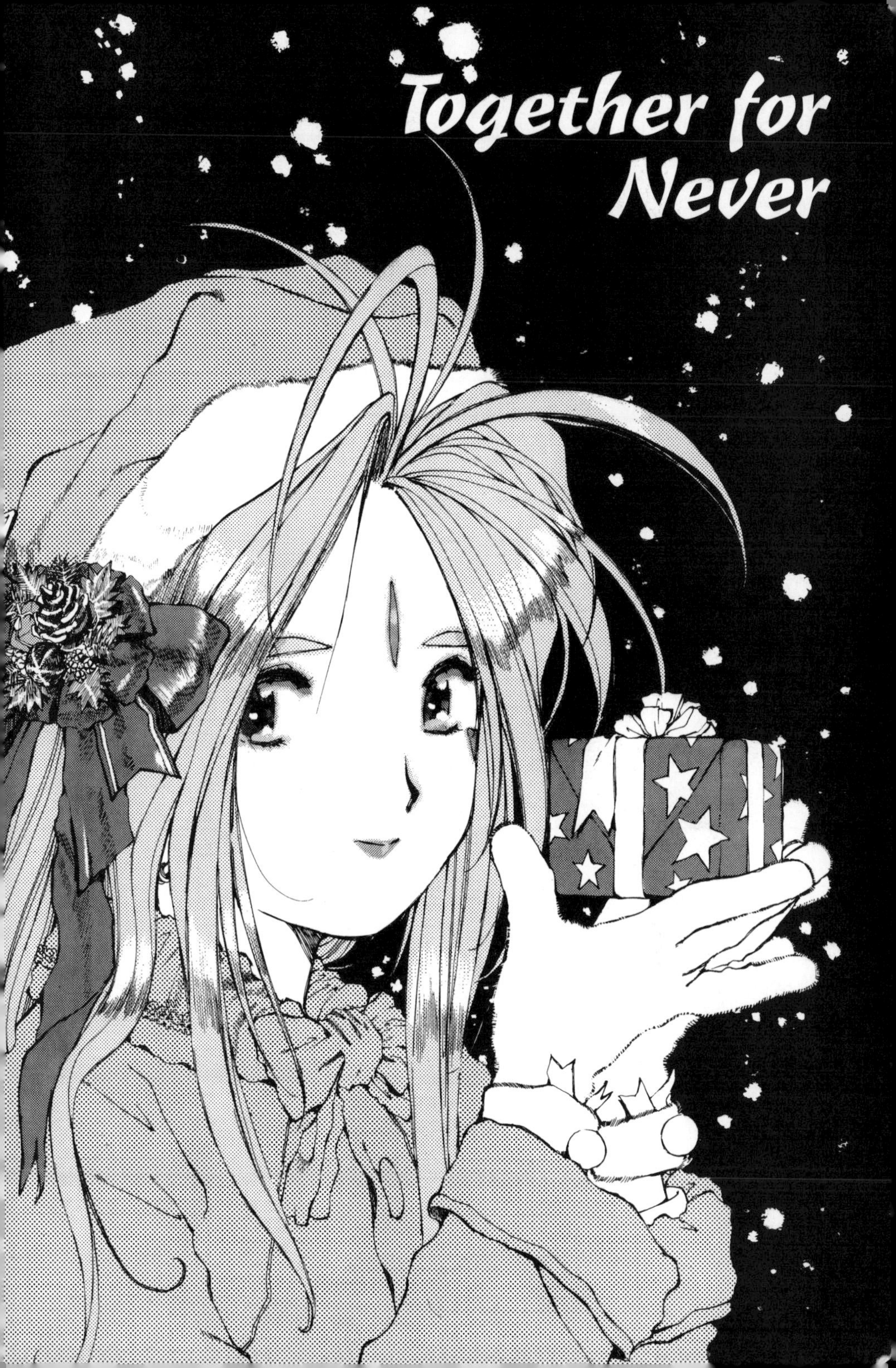
Together for
Never

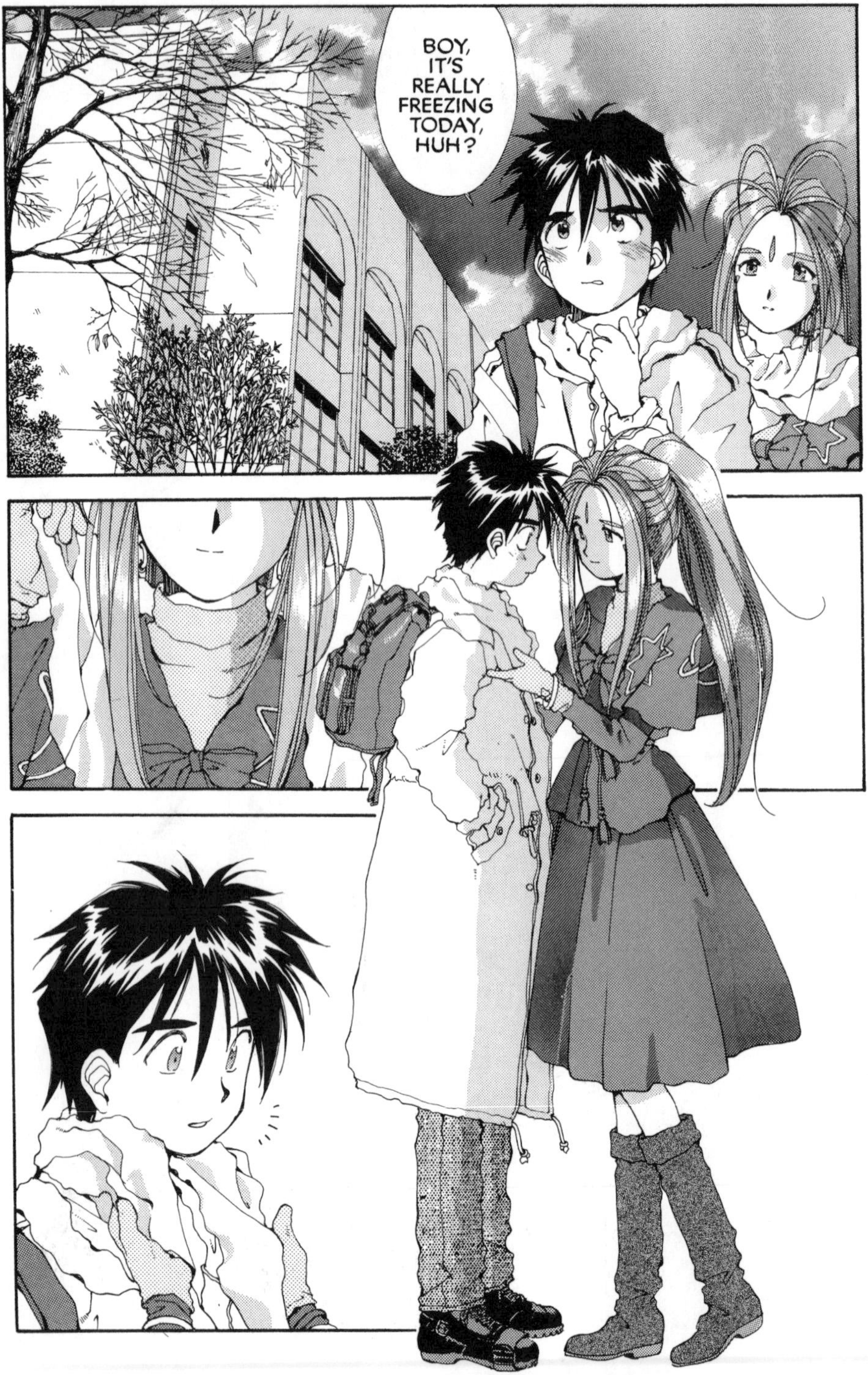
BOY, IT'S REALLY FREEZING TODAY, HUH?

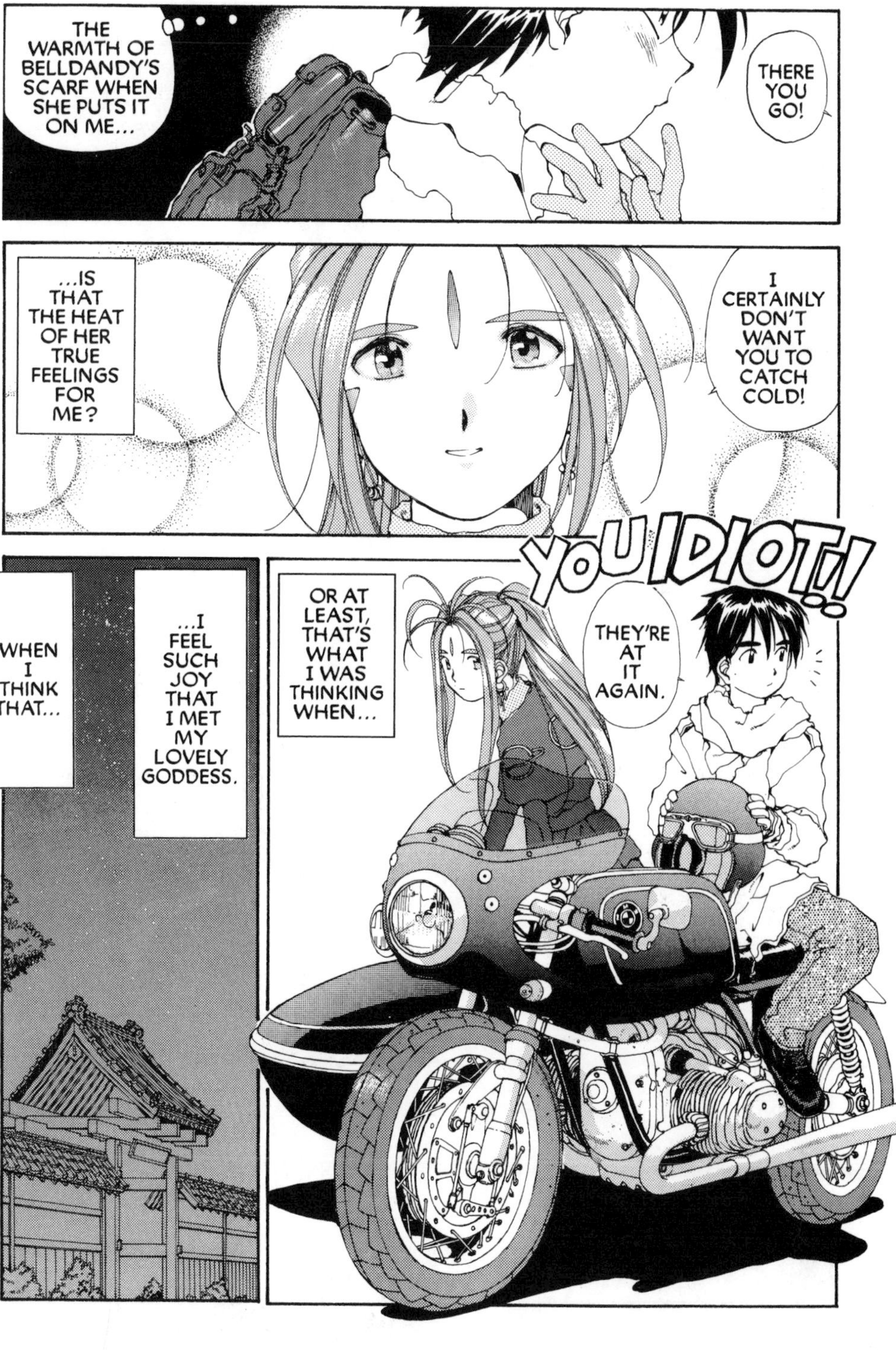
THE WARMTH OF BELLDANDY'S SCARF WHEN SHE PUTS IT ON ME...
THERE YOU GO!
...IS THAT THE HEAT OF HER TRUE FEELINGS FOR ME?
I CERTAINLY DON'T WANT YOU TO CATCH COLD!
WHEN I THINK THAT...
...I FEEL SUCH JOY THAT I MET MY LOVELY GODDESS.
OR AT LEAST, THAT'S WHAT I WAS THINKING WHEN...
YOU IDIOT!!
THEY'RE AT IT AGAIN.

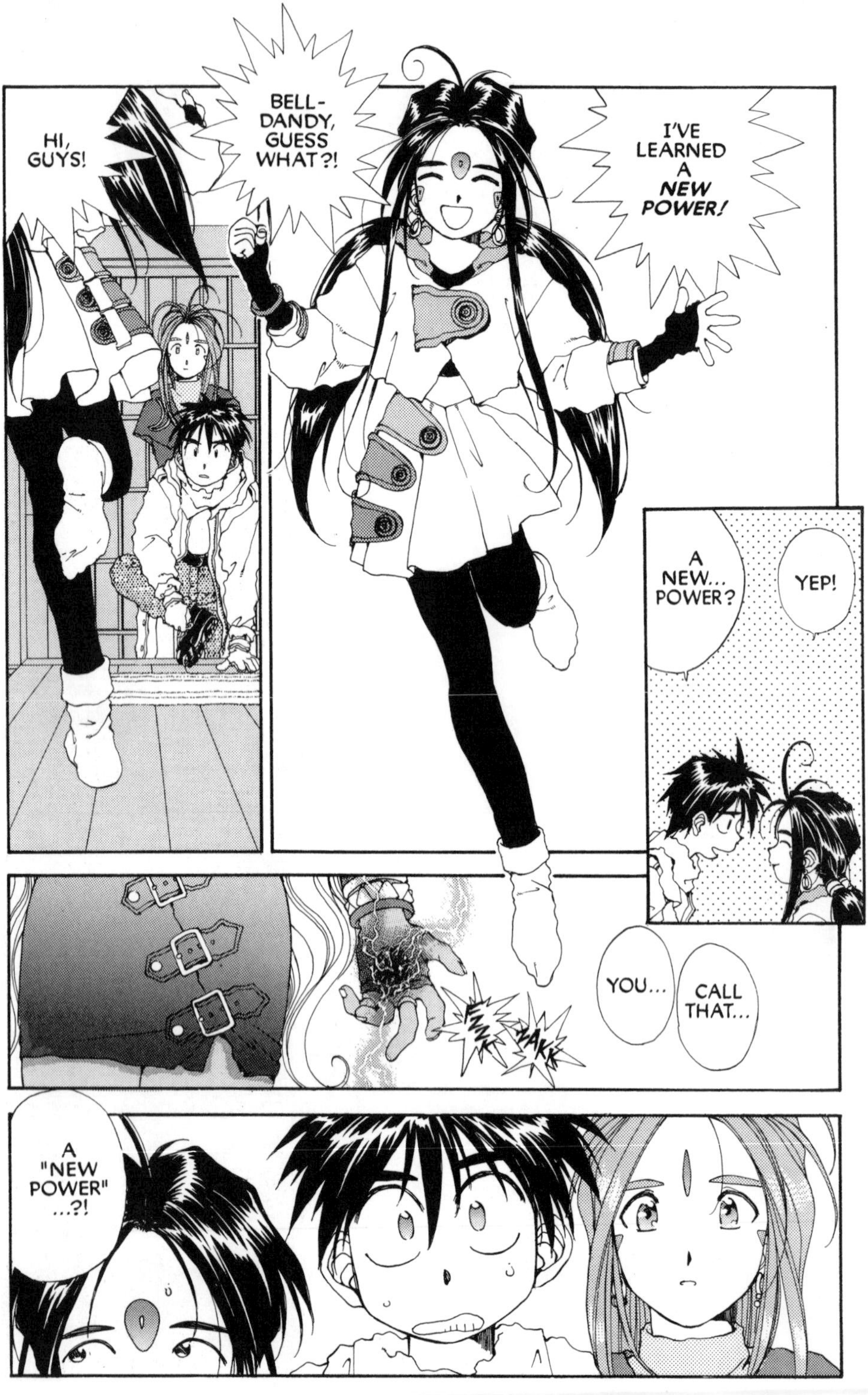
HI, GUYS!
BELL-DANDY, GUESS WHAT?!
I'VE LEARNED A *NEW POWER!*
A NEW... POWER?
YEP!
YOU...
CALL THAT...
A "NEW POWER" ...?!

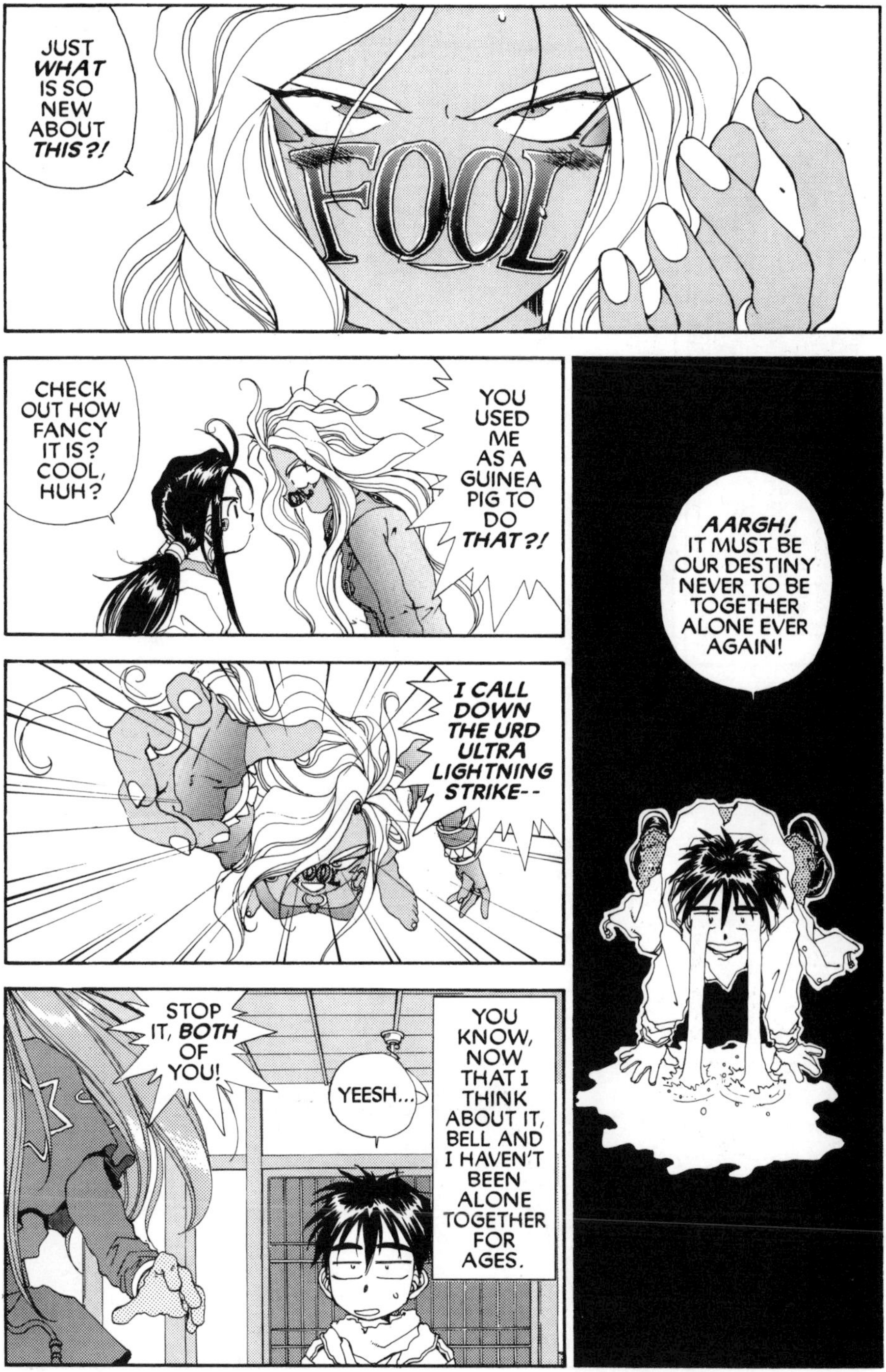
JUST *WHAT* IS SO NEW ABOUT *THIS?!*
FOOL
CHECK OUT HOW FANCY IT IS? COOL, HUH?
YOU USED ME AS A GUINEA PIG TO DO *THAT?!*
I CALL DOWN THE URD ULTRA LIGHTNING STRIKE--
STOP IT, *BOTH* OF YOU!
YOU KNOW, NOW THAT I THINK ABOUT IT, BELL AND I HAVEN'T BEEN ALONE TOGETHER FOR AGES.
YEESH...
AARGH! IT MUST BE OUR DESTINY NEVER TO BE TOGETHER ALONE EVER AGAIN!

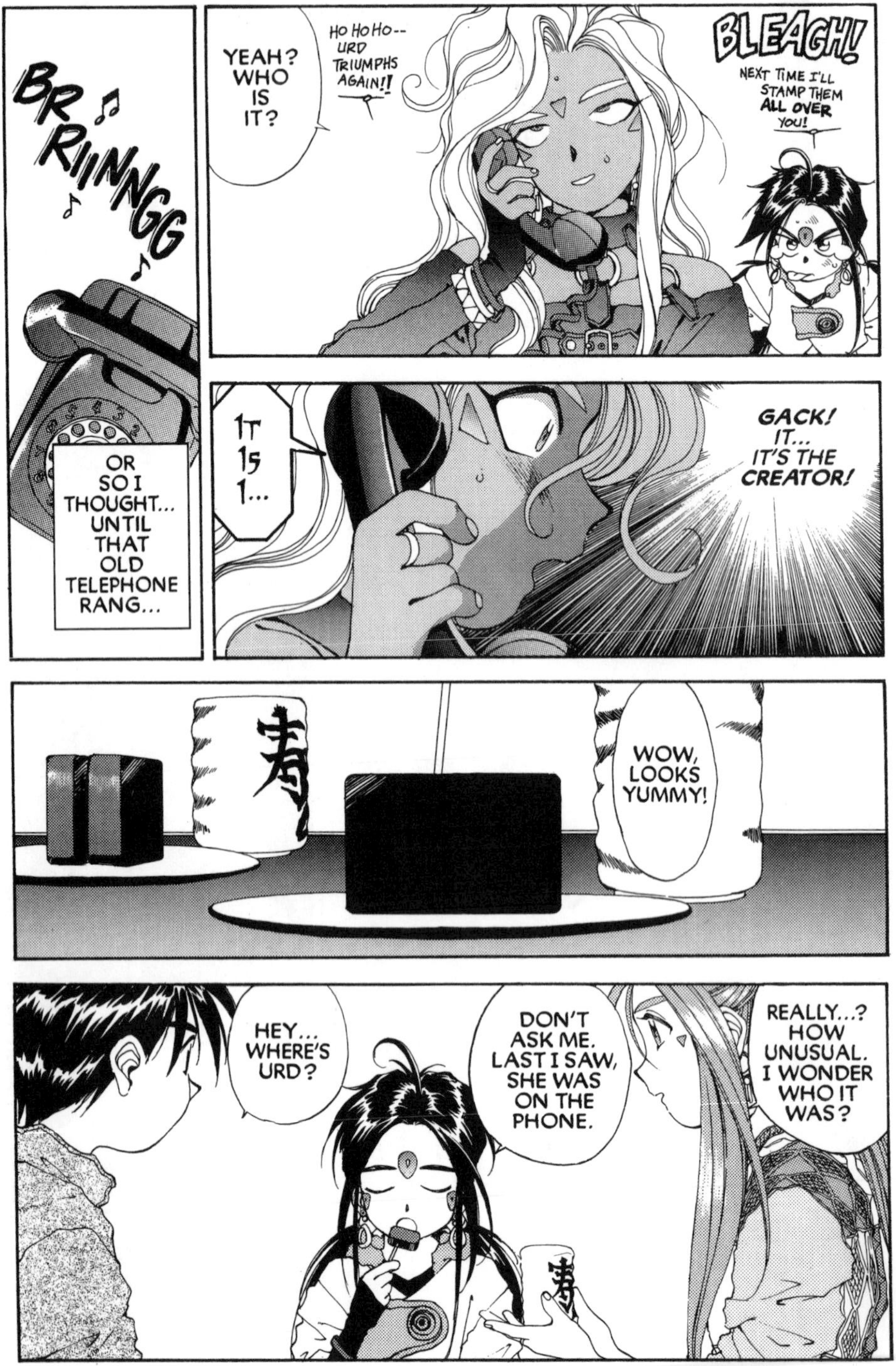
BRRIINNGG
OR SO I THOUGHT... UNTIL THAT OLD TELEPHONE RANG...
YEAH? WHO IS IT?
HO HO HO-- URD TRIUMPHS AGAIN!!
BLEAGH!
NEXT TIME I'LL STAMP THEM ALL OVER YOU!
IT IS I...
GACK! IT... IT'S THE CREATOR!
WOW, LOOKS YUMMY!
HEY... WHERE'S URD?
DON'T ASK ME. LAST I SAW, SHE WAS ON THE PHONE.
REALLY...? HOW UNUSUAL. I WONDER WHO IT WAS?

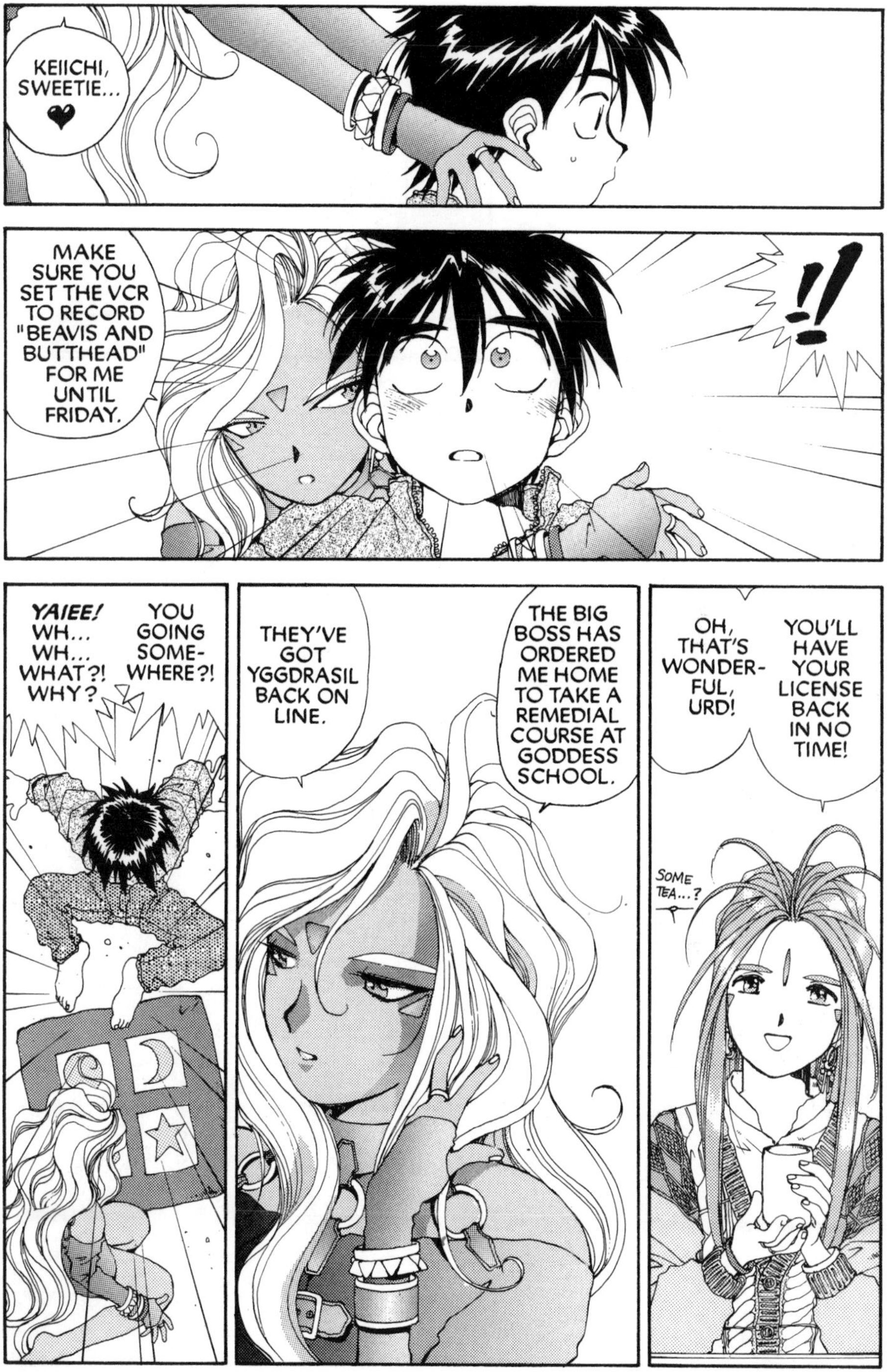
KEIICHI, SWEETIE...
MAKE SURE YOU SET THE VCR TO RECORD "BEAVIS AND BUTTHEAD" FOR ME UNTIL FRIDAY.
!!
YAIEE! WH... WH... WHAT?! WHY?
YOU GOING SOME-WHERE?!
THEY'VE GOT YGGDRASIL BACK ON LINE.
THE BIG BOSS HAS ORDERED ME HOME TO TAKE A REMEDIAL COURSE AT GODDESS SCHOOL.
OH, THAT'S WONDER-FUL, URD!
YOU'LL HAVE YOUR LICENSE BACK IN NO TIME!
SOME TEA...?

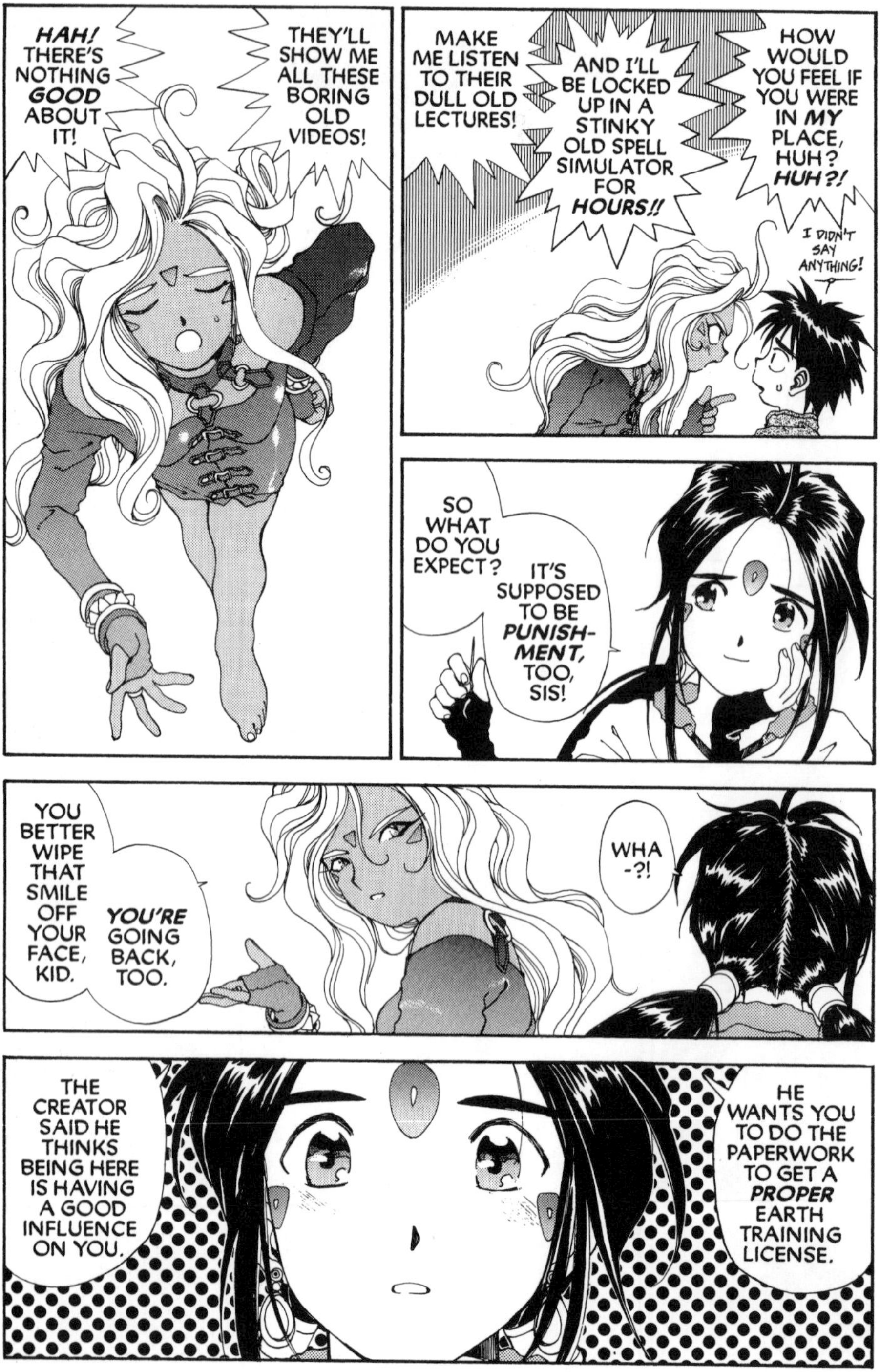
HAH! THERE'S NOTHING GOOD ABOUT IT!
THEY'LL SHOW ME ALL THESE BORING OLD VIDEOS!
MAKE ME LISTEN TO THEIR DULL OLD LECTURES!
AND I'LL BE LOCKED UP IN A STINKY OLD SPELL SIMULATOR FOR HOURS!!
HOW WOULD YOU FEEL IF YOU WERE IN MY PLACE, HUH? HUH?!
I DIDN'T SAY ANYTHING!
SO WHAT DO YOU EXPECT?
IT'S SUPPOSED TO BE PUNISHMENT, TOO, SIS!
YOU BETTER WIPE THAT SMILE OFF YOUR FACE, KID.
YOU'RE GOING BACK, TOO.
WHA-?!
THE CREATOR SAID HE THINKS BEING HERE IS HAVING A GOOD INFLUENCE ON YOU.
HE WANTS YOU TO DO THE PAPERWORK TO GET A PROPER EARTH TRAINING LICENSE.

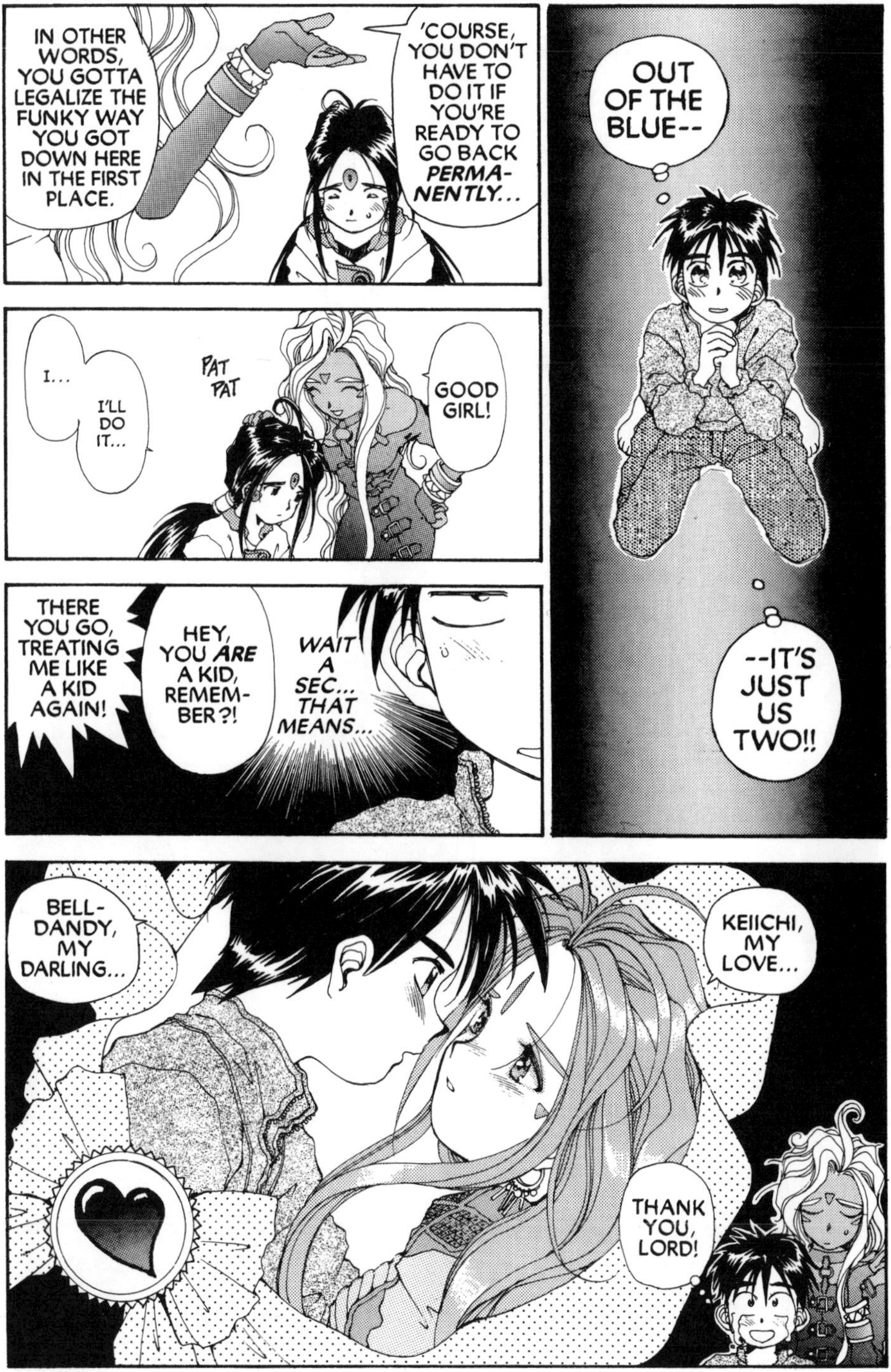
IN OTHER WORDS, YOU GOTTA LEGALIZE THE FUNKY WAY YOU GOT DOWN HERE IN THE FIRST PLACE.
'COURSE, YOU DON'T HAVE TO DO IT IF YOU'RE READY TO GO BACK *PERMANENTLY*...
I... I'LL DO IT...
PAT PAT
GOOD GIRL!
THERE YOU GO, TREATING ME LIKE A KID AGAIN!
HEY, YOU *ARE* A KID, REMEMBER?!
WAIT A SEC... THAT MEANS...
OUT OF THE BLUE--
--IT'S JUST US TWO!!
BELLDANDY, MY DARLING...
KEIICHI, MY LOVE...
THANK YOU, LORD!

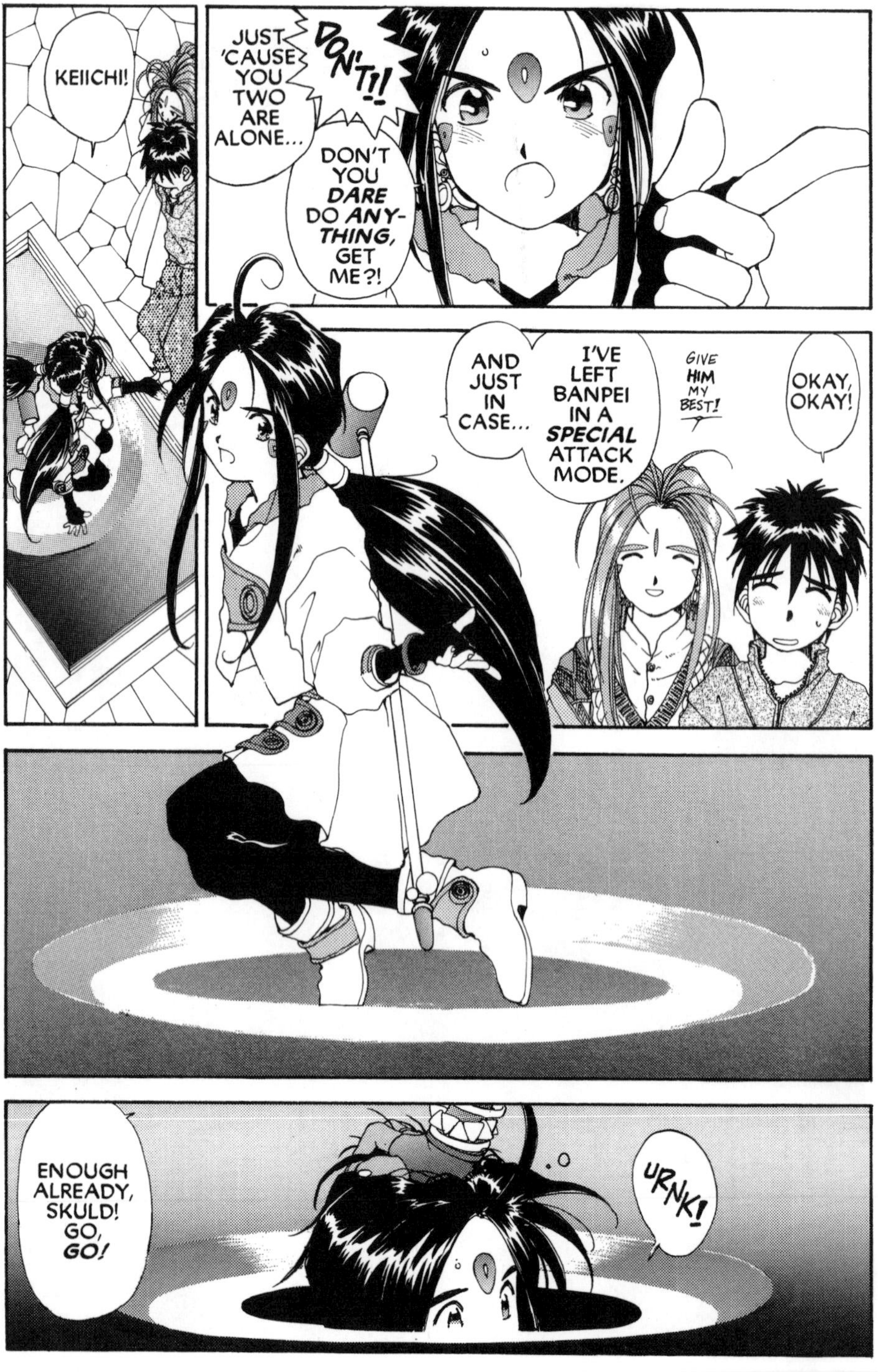
KEIICHI!
JUST 'CAUSE YOU TWO ARE ALONE...
DON'T!!
DON'T YOU DARE DO ANY-THING, GET ME?!
AND JUST IN CASE...
I'VE LEFT BANPEI IN A SPECIAL ATTACK MODE.
GIVE HIM MY BEST!
OKAY, OKAY!
ENOUGH ALREADY, SKULD! GO, GO!
URNK!

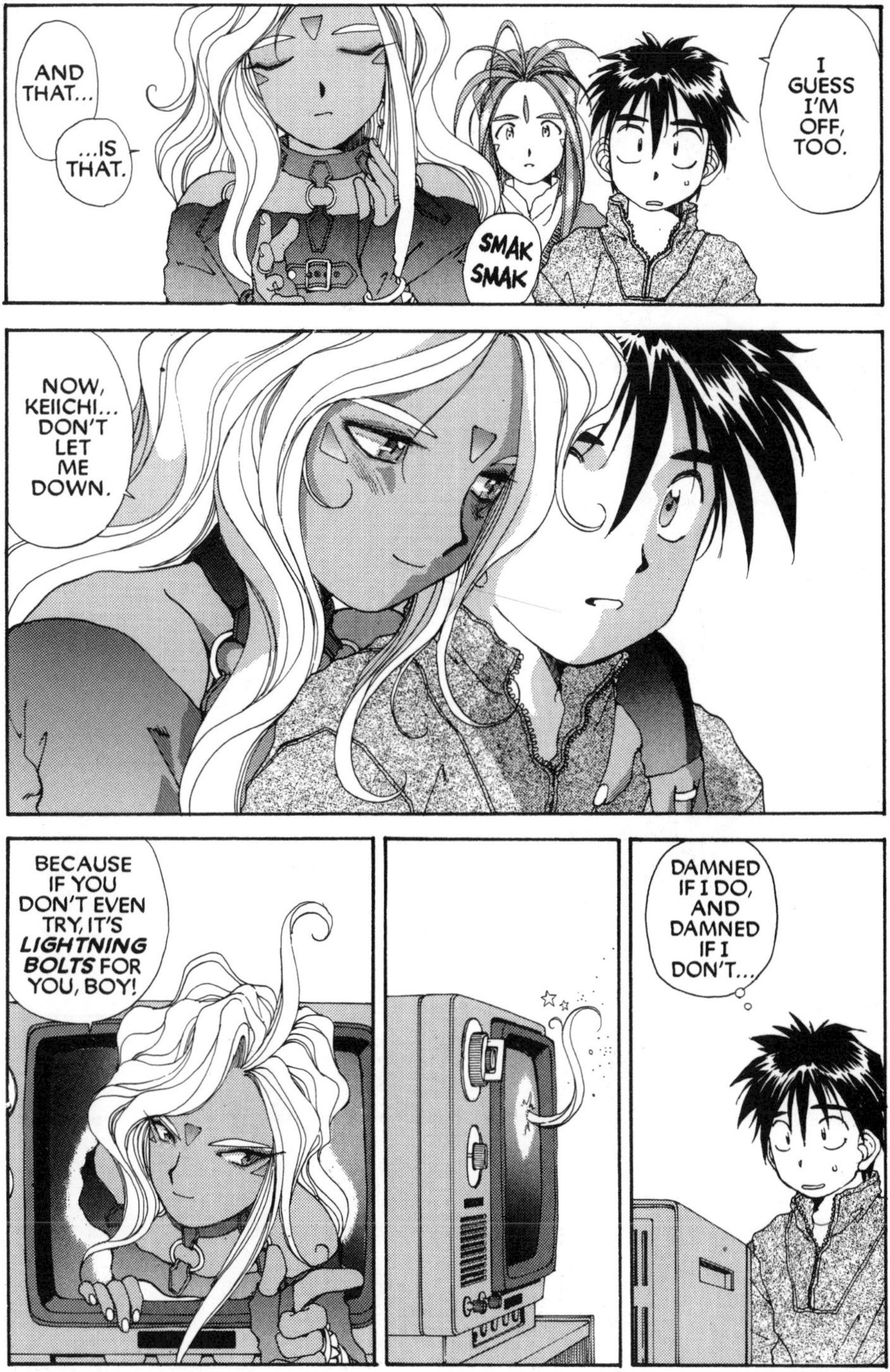
AND THAT...
...IS THAT.
SMAK SMAK
I GUESS I'M OFF, TOO.
NOW, KEIICHI... DON'T LET ME DOWN.
BECAUSE IF YOU DON'T EVEN TRY, IT'S *LIGHTNING BOLTS* FOR YOU, BOY!
DAMNED IF I DO, AND DAMNED IF I DON'T...

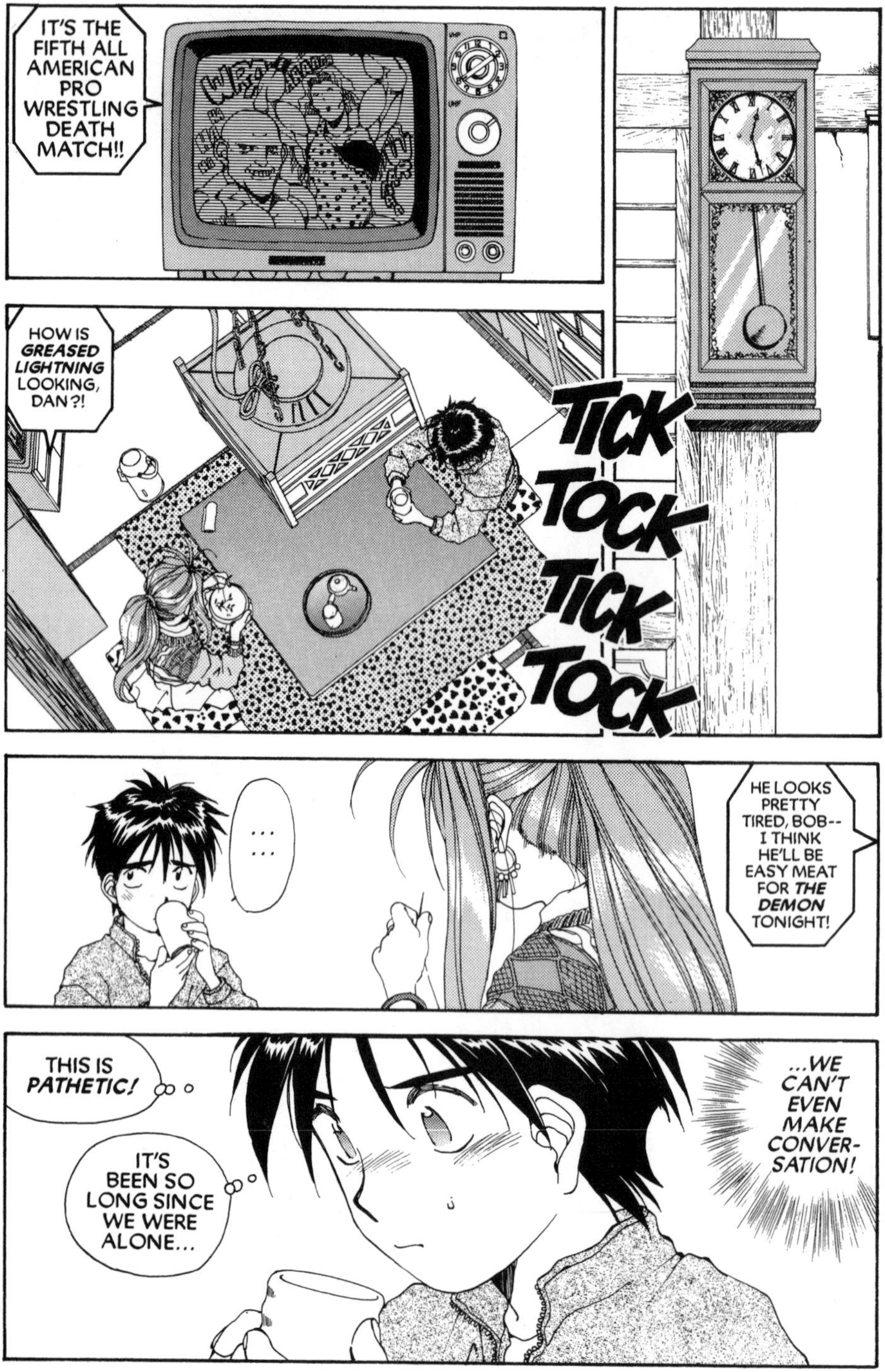
IT'S THE FIFTH ALL AMERICAN PRO WRESTLING DEATH MATCH!!
HOW IS ***GREASED LIGHTNING*** LOOKING, DAN?!
TICK TOCK TICK TOCK
...
HE LOOKS PRETTY TIRED, BOB-- I THINK HE'LL BE EASY MEAT FOR ***THE DEMON*** TONIGHT!
THIS IS ***PATHETIC!***
IT'S BEEN SO LONG SINCE WE WERE ALONE...
...WE CAN'T EVEN MAKE CONVER-SATION!

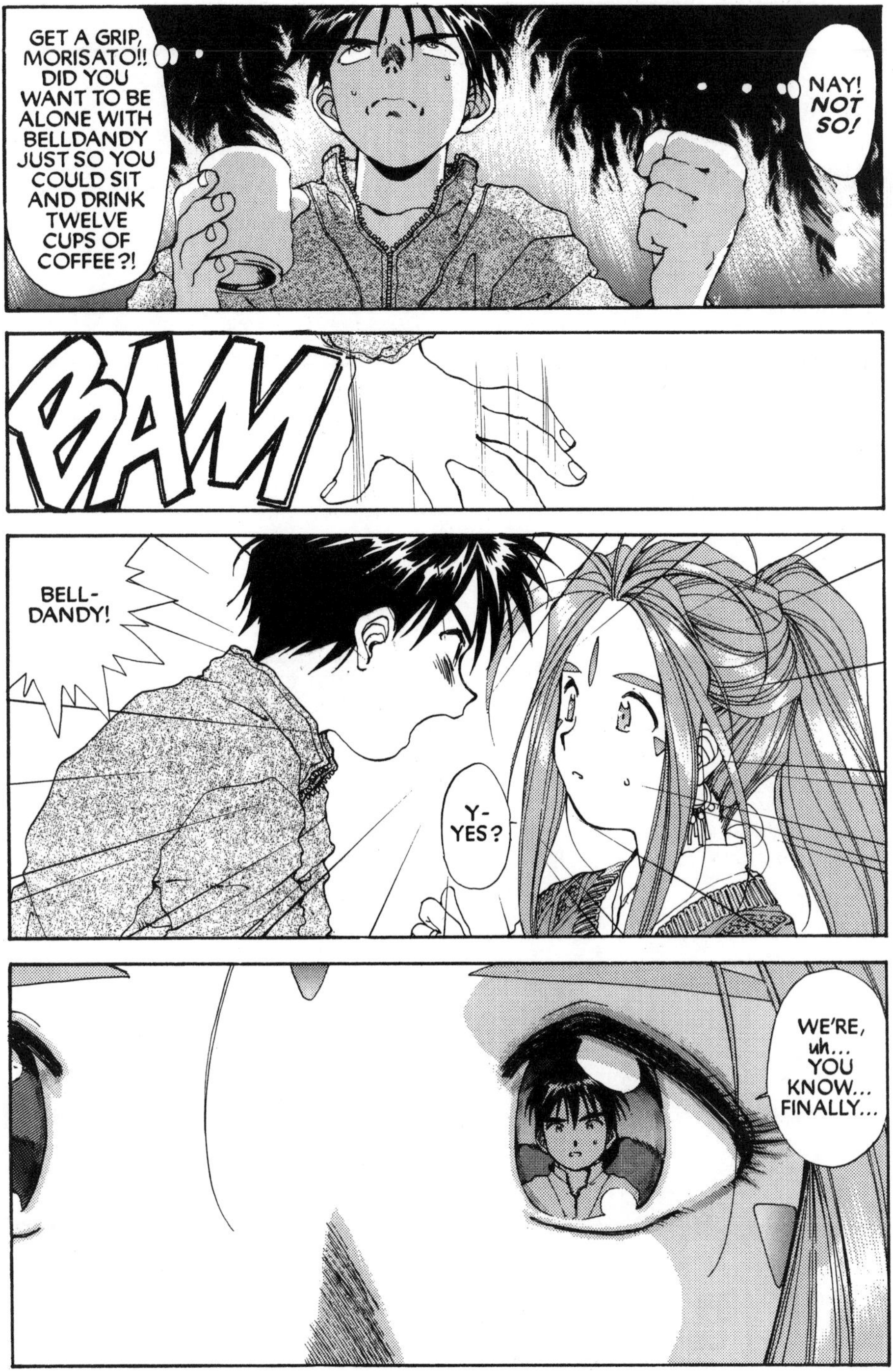
GET A GRIP, MORISATO!! DID YOU WANT TO BE ALONE WITH BELLDANDY JUST SO YOU COULD SIT AND DRINK TWELVE CUPS OF COFFEE?!
NAY! *NOT SO!*
BAM
BELL-DANDY!
Y-YES?
WE'RE, uh... YOU KNOW... FINALLY...

...ALL ALONE...!

!?

...!

?

SO... UH, COULD I... HAVE SOME MORE COFFEE?

DAMN... FORGOT ABOUT HIM.

WELL, OF COURSE!

SO... UM... G'NIGHT.

GOOD NIGHT, KEIICHI.

KEIICHI'S SHOP

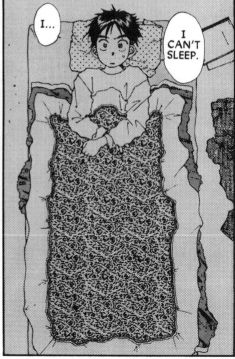

I...

I CAN'T SLEEP.

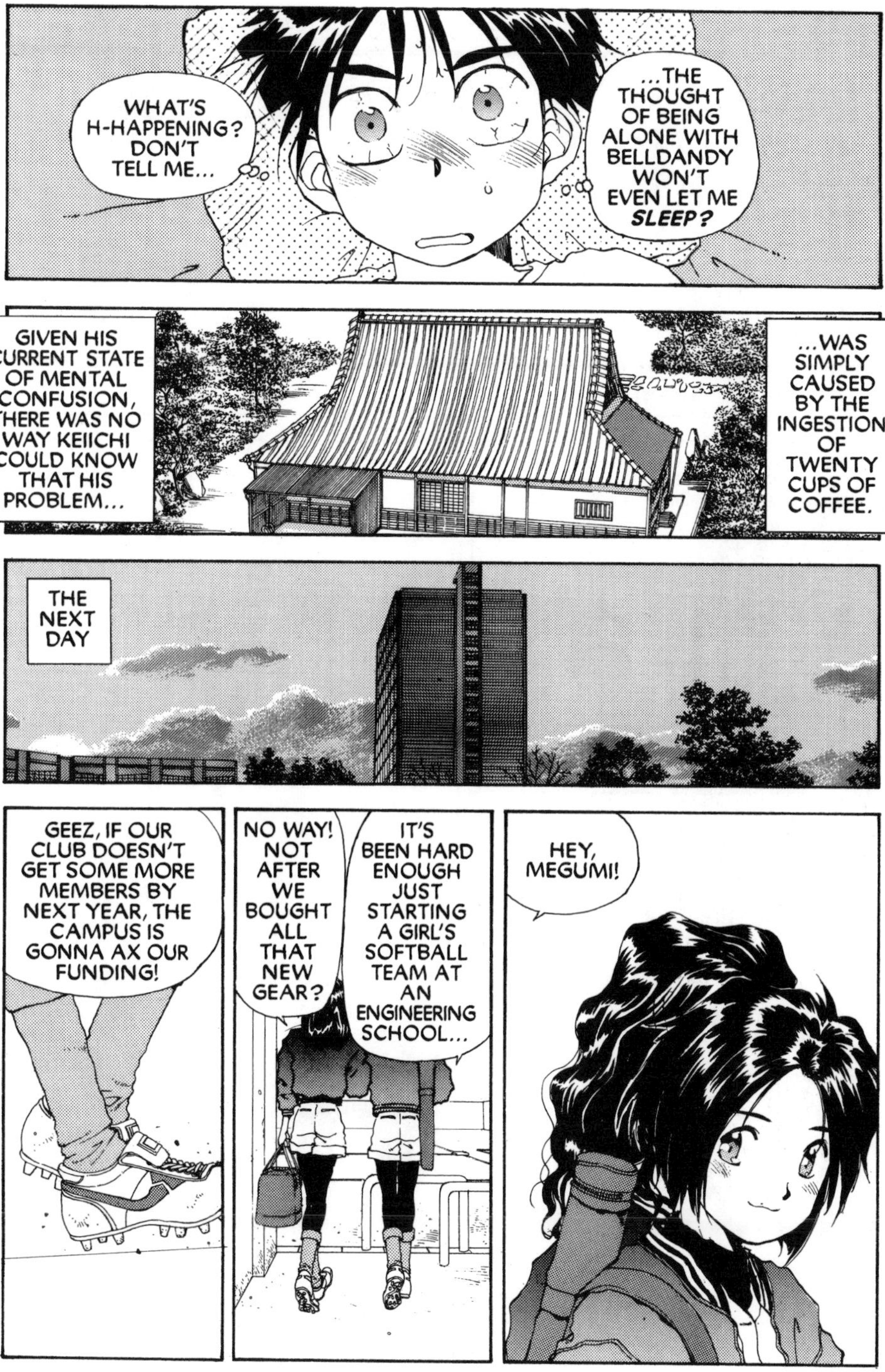
WHAT'S H-HAPPENING? DON'T TELL ME...
...THE THOUGHT OF BEING ALONE WITH BELLDANDY WON'T EVEN LET ME SLEEP?
GIVEN HIS CURRENT STATE OF MENTAL CONFUSION, THERE WAS NO WAY KEIICHI COULD KNOW THAT HIS PROBLEM...
...WAS SIMPLY CAUSED BY THE INGESTION OF TWENTY CUPS OF COFFEE.
THE NEXT DAY
GEEZ, IF OUR CLUB DOESN'T GET SOME MORE MEMBERS BY NEXT YEAR, THE CAMPUS IS GONNA AX OUR FUNDING!
NO WAY! NOT AFTER WE BOUGHT ALL THAT NEW GEAR?
IT'S BEEN HARD ENOUGH JUST STARTING A GIRL'S SOFTBALL TEAM AT AN ENGINEERING SCHOOL...
HEY, MEGUMI!

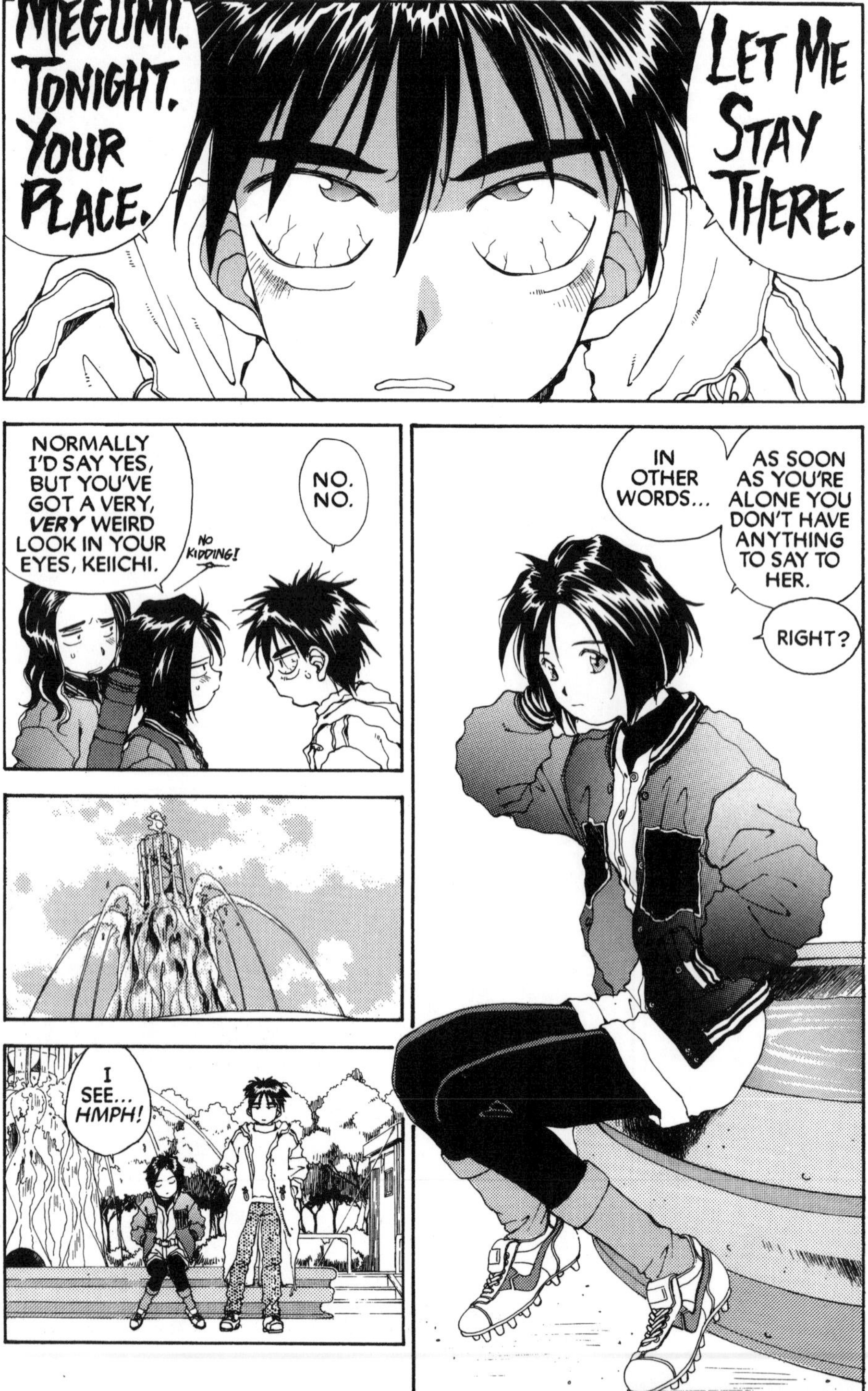
MEGUMI. TONIGHT. YOUR PLACE.
LET ME STAY THERE.
NORMALLY I'D SAY YES, BUT YOU'VE GOT A VERY, *VERY* WEIRD LOOK IN YOUR EYES, KEIICHI.
NO KIDDING!
NO. NO.
I SEE... *HMPH!*
IN OTHER WORDS...
AS SOON AS YOU'RE ALONE YOU DON'T HAVE ANYTHING TO SAY TO HER.
RIGHT?

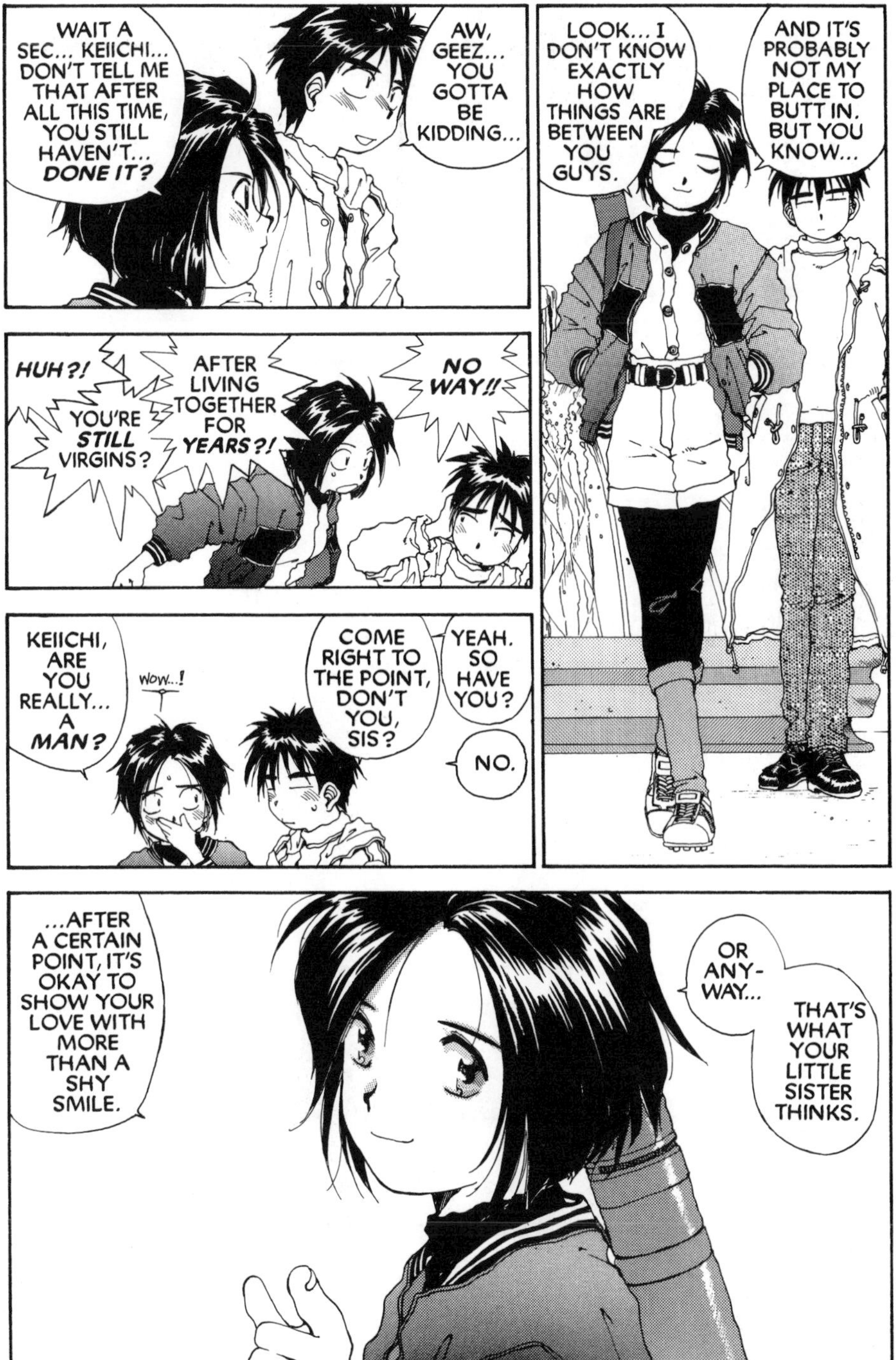
WAIT A SEC... KEIICHI... DON'T TELL ME THAT AFTER ALL THIS TIME, YOU STILL HAVEN'T... DONE IT?
AW, GEEZ... YOU GOTTA BE KIDDING...
HUH?!
YOU'RE STILL VIRGINS?
AFTER LIVING TOGETHER FOR YEARS?!
NO WAY!!
KEIICHI, ARE YOU REALLY... A MAN?
WOW...!
COME RIGHT TO THE POINT, DON'T YOU, SIS?
YEAH. SO HAVE YOU?
NO.
LOOK... I DON'T KNOW EXACTLY HOW THINGS ARE BETWEEN YOU GUYS.
AND IT'S PROBABLY NOT MY PLACE TO BUTT IN. BUT YOU KNOW...
...AFTER A CERTAIN POINT, IT'S OKAY TO SHOW YOUR LOVE WITH MORE THAN A SHY SMILE.
OR ANYWAY...
THAT'S WHAT YOUR LITTLE SISTER THINKS.

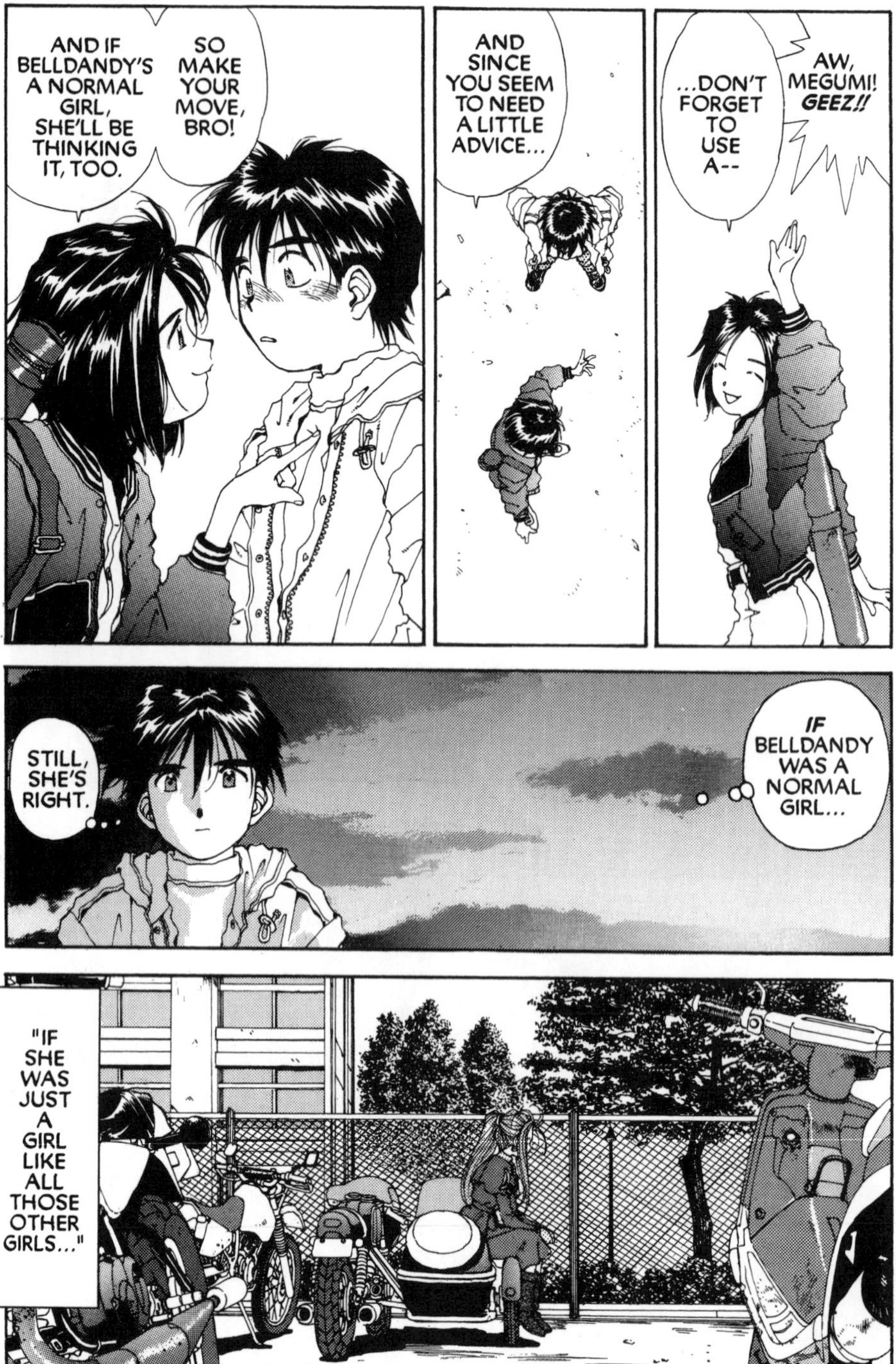
AND IF BELLDANDY'S A NORMAL GIRL, SHE'LL BE THINKING IT, TOO.
SO MAKE YOUR MOVE, BRO!
AND SINCE YOU SEEM TO NEED A LITTLE ADVICE...
...DON'T FORGET TO USE A--
AW, MEGUMI! GEEZ!!
STILL, SHE'S RIGHT.
IF BELLDANDY WAS A NORMAL GIRL...
"IF SHE WAS JUST A GIRL LIKE ALL THOSE OTHER GIRLS..."

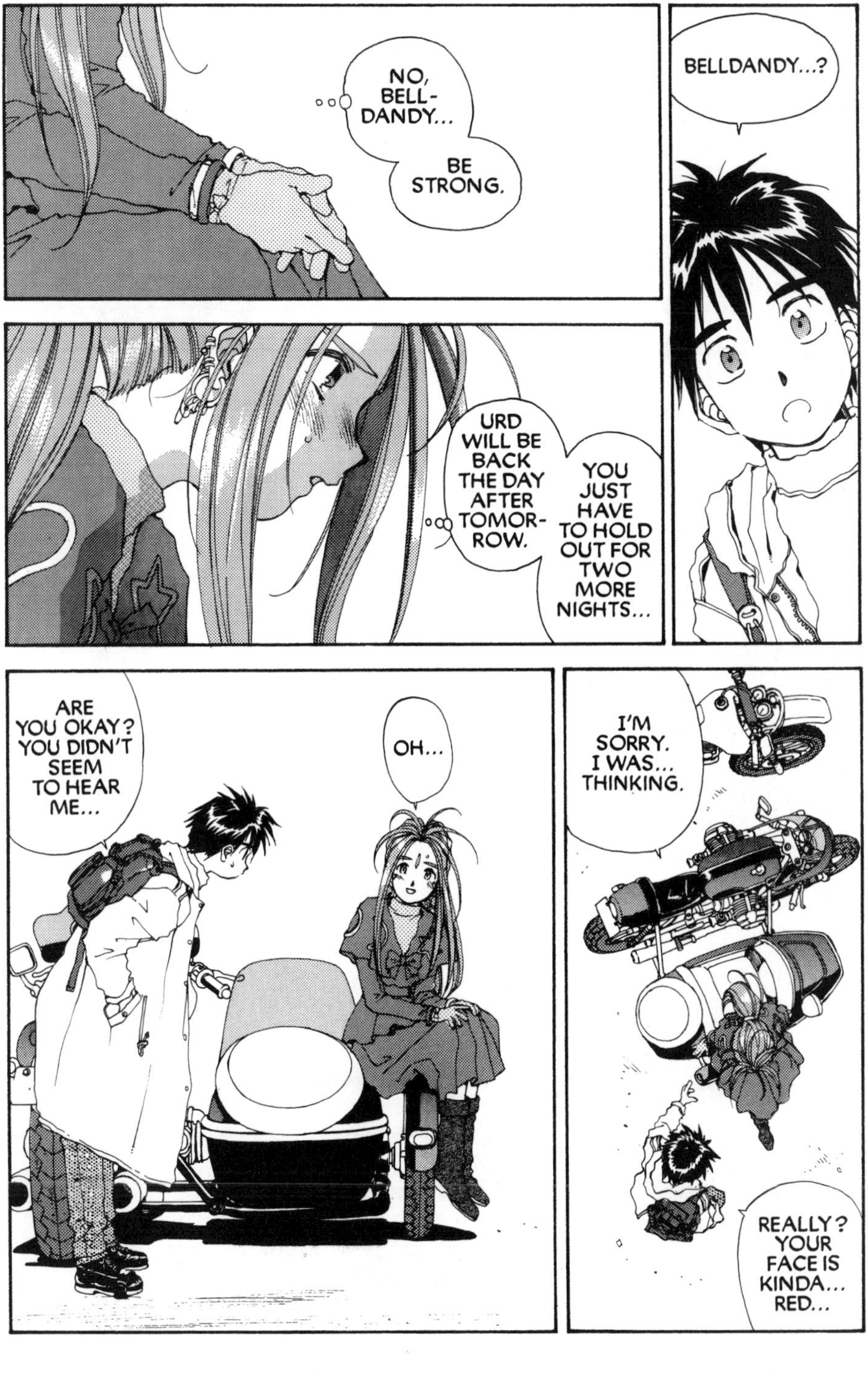
NO, BELL-DANDY...
BE STRONG.
URD WILL BE BACK THE DAY AFTER TOMOR-ROW.
YOU JUST HAVE TO HOLD OUT FOR TWO MORE NIGHTS...
BELLDANDY...?
ARE YOU OKAY? YOU DIDN'T SEEM TO HEAR ME...
OH...
I'M SORRY. I WAS... THINKING.
REALLY? YOUR FACE IS KINDA... RED...

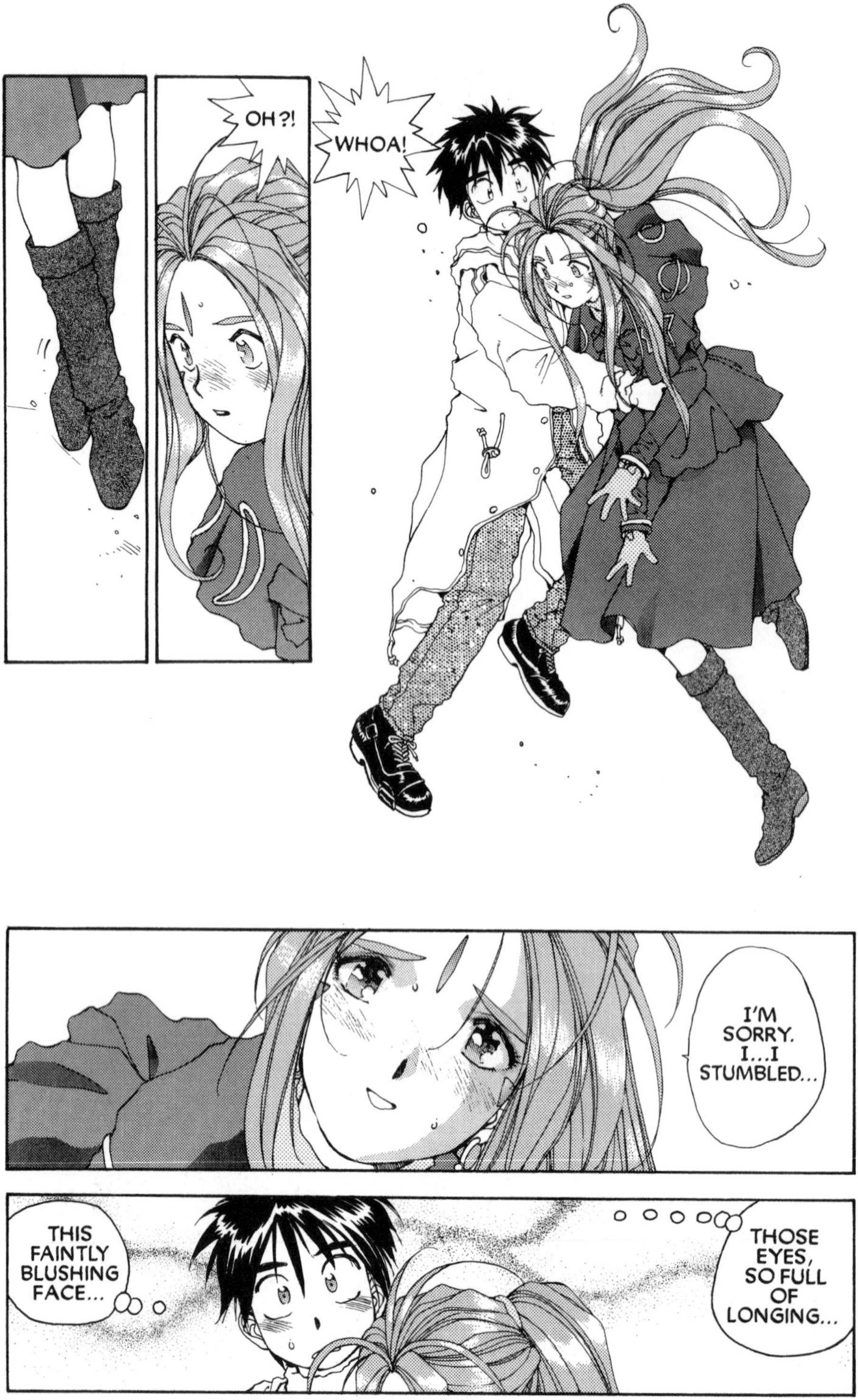
OH?!
WHOA!
I'M SORRY. I...I STUMBLED...
THIS FAINTLY BLUSHING FACE...
THOSE EYES, SO FULL OF LONGING...

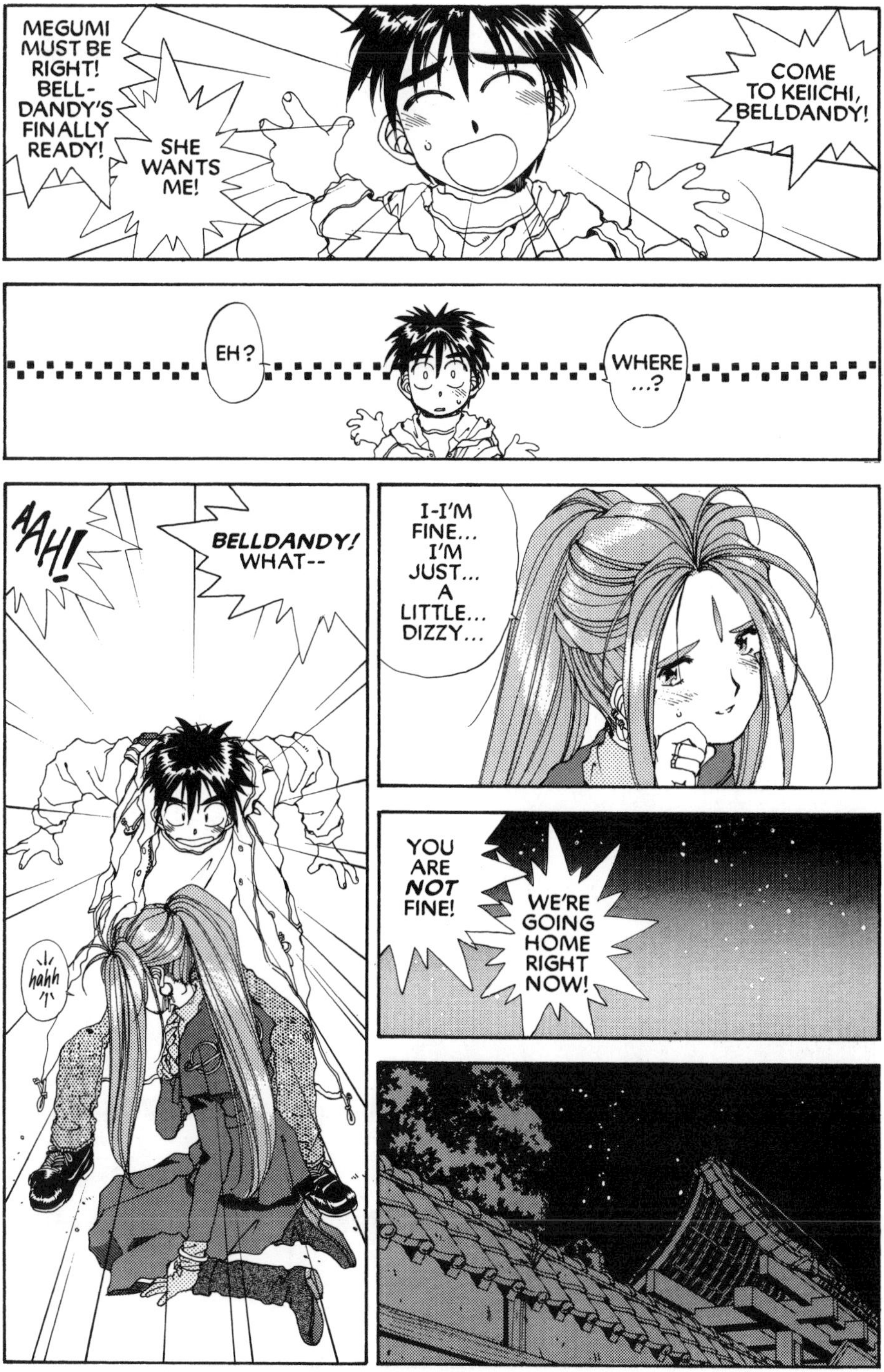
MEGUMI MUST BE RIGHT! BELL-DANDY'S FINALLY READY!
SHE WANTS ME!
COME TO KEIICHI, BELLDANDY!
EH?
WHERE ...?
AAH!
BELLDANDY! WHAT--
hahh
I-I'M FINE... I'M JUST... A LITTLE... DIZZY...
YOU ARE NOT FINE!
WE'RE GOING HOME RIGHT NOW!

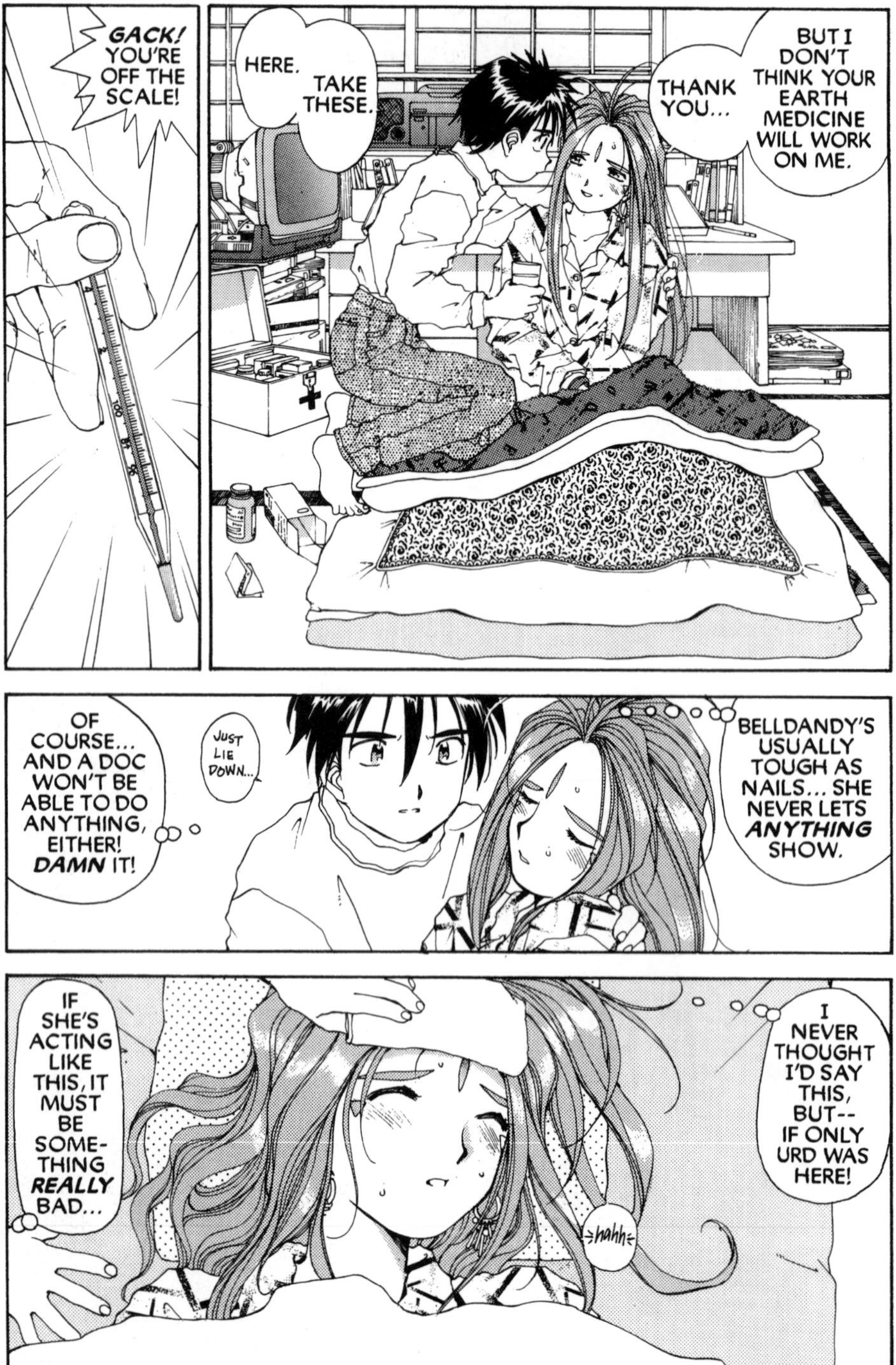
GACK! YOU'RE OFF THE SCALE!
HERE.
TAKE THESE.
THANK YOU...
BUT I DON'T THINK YOUR EARTH MEDICINE WILL WORK ON ME.
OF COURSE... AND A DOC WON'T BE ABLE TO DO ANYTHING, EITHER! DAMN IT!
JUST LIE DOWN...
BELLDANDY'S USUALLY TOUGH AS NAILS... SHE NEVER LETS ANYTHING SHOW.
IF SHE'S ACTING LIKE THIS, IT MUST BE SOME-THING REALLY BAD...
hahh
I NEVER THOUGHT I'D SAY THIS, BUT-- IF ONLY URD WAS HERE!

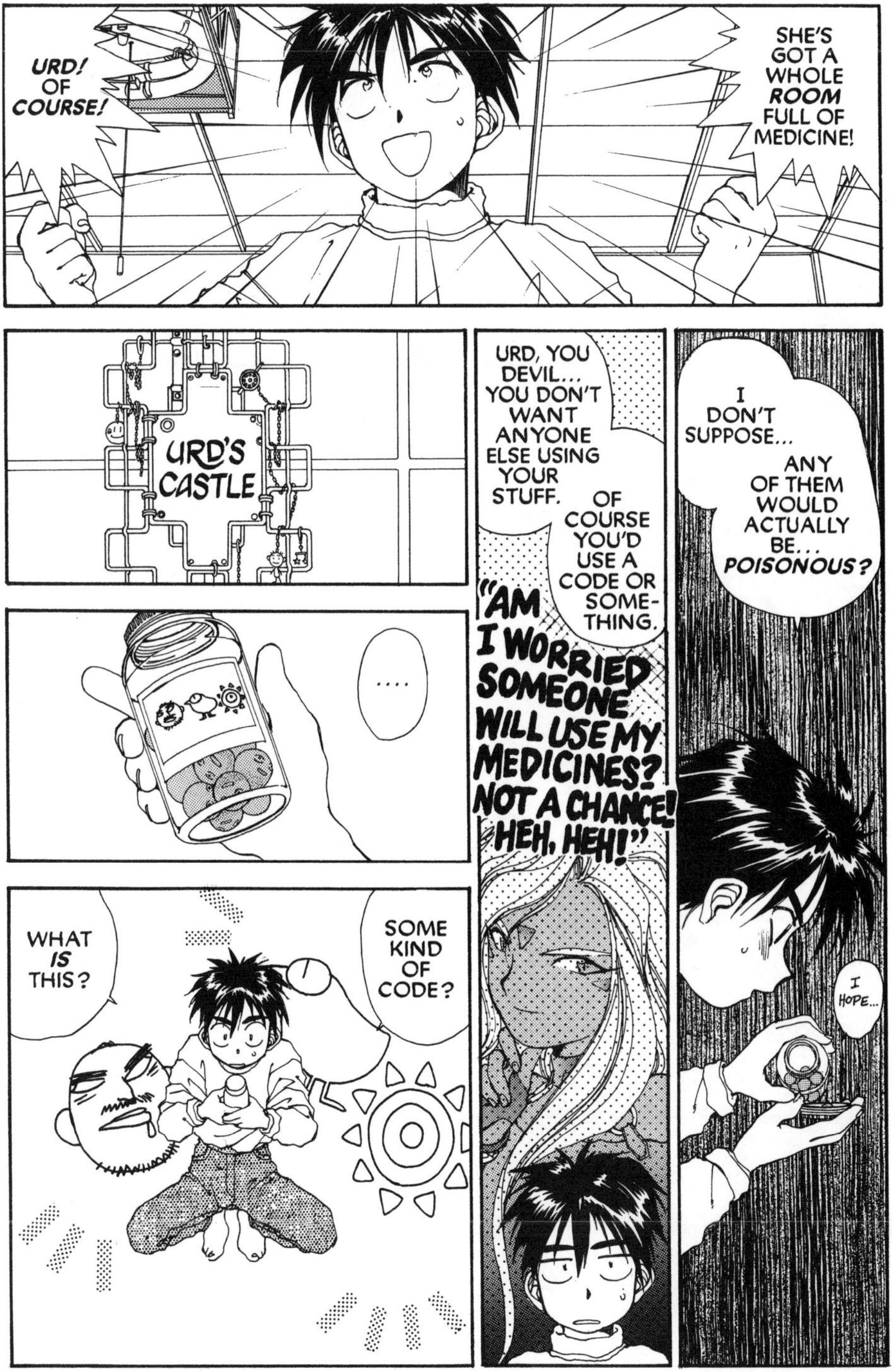
URD! OF COURSE!
SHE'S GOT A WHOLE ROOM FULL OF MEDICINE!
URD'S CASTLE
....
WHAT IS THIS?
SOME KIND OF CODE?
URD, YOU DEVIL... YOU DON'T WANT ANYONE ELSE USING YOUR STUFF.
OF COURSE YOU'D USE A CODE OR SOME-THING.
"AM I WORRIED SOMEONE WILL USE MY MEDICINES? NOT A CHANCE! HEH, HEH!"
I DON'T SUPPOSE...
ANY OF THEM WOULD ACTUALLY BE... POISONOUS?
I HOPE...

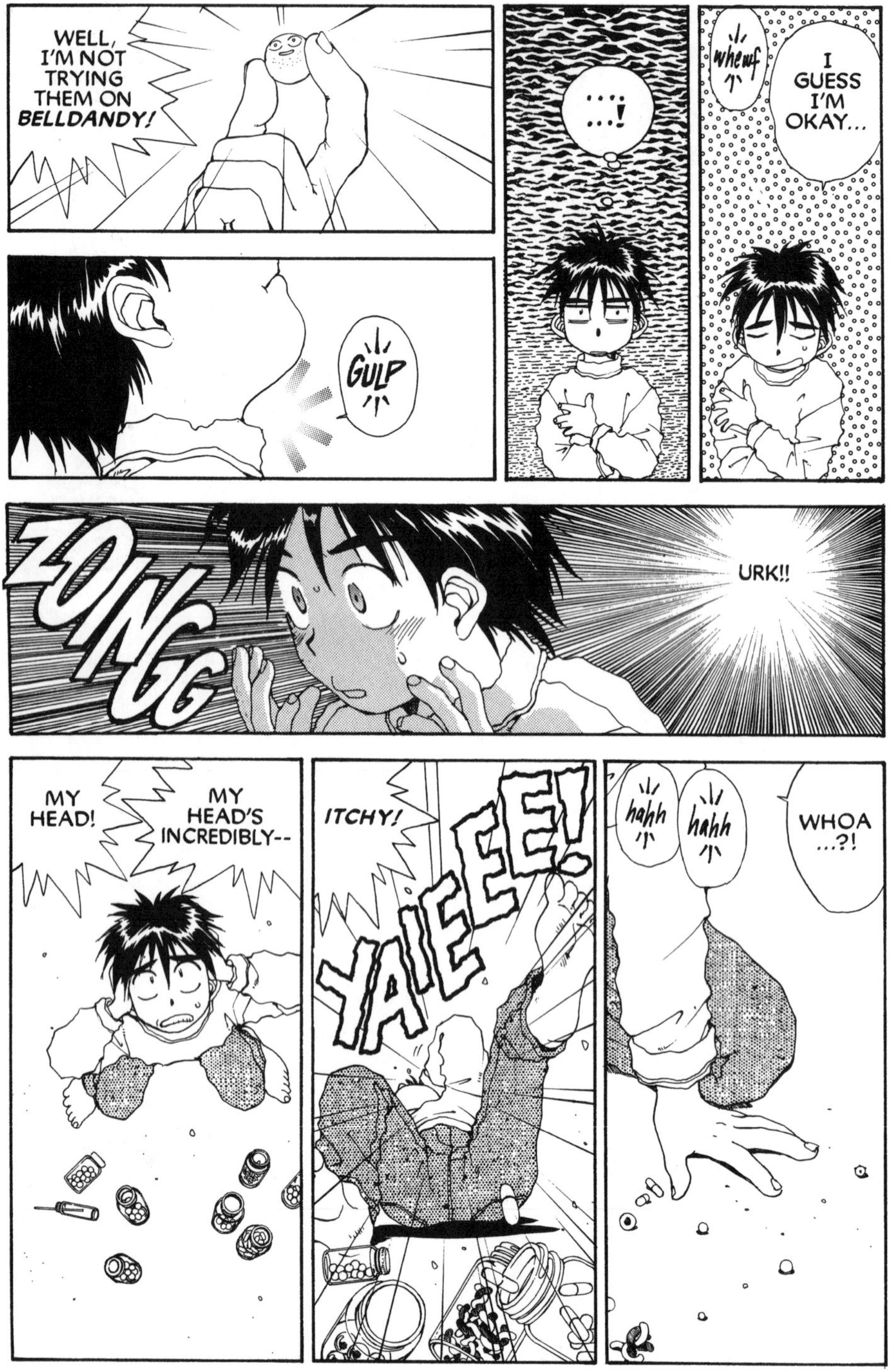
WELL, I'M NOT TRYING THEM ON *BELLDANDY!*
GULP
...!
whew
I GUESS I'M OKAY...
ZONGG
URK!!
MY HEAD!
MY HEAD'S INCREDIBLY--
ITCHY!
YAIEEE!
hahh
hahh
WHOA ...?!

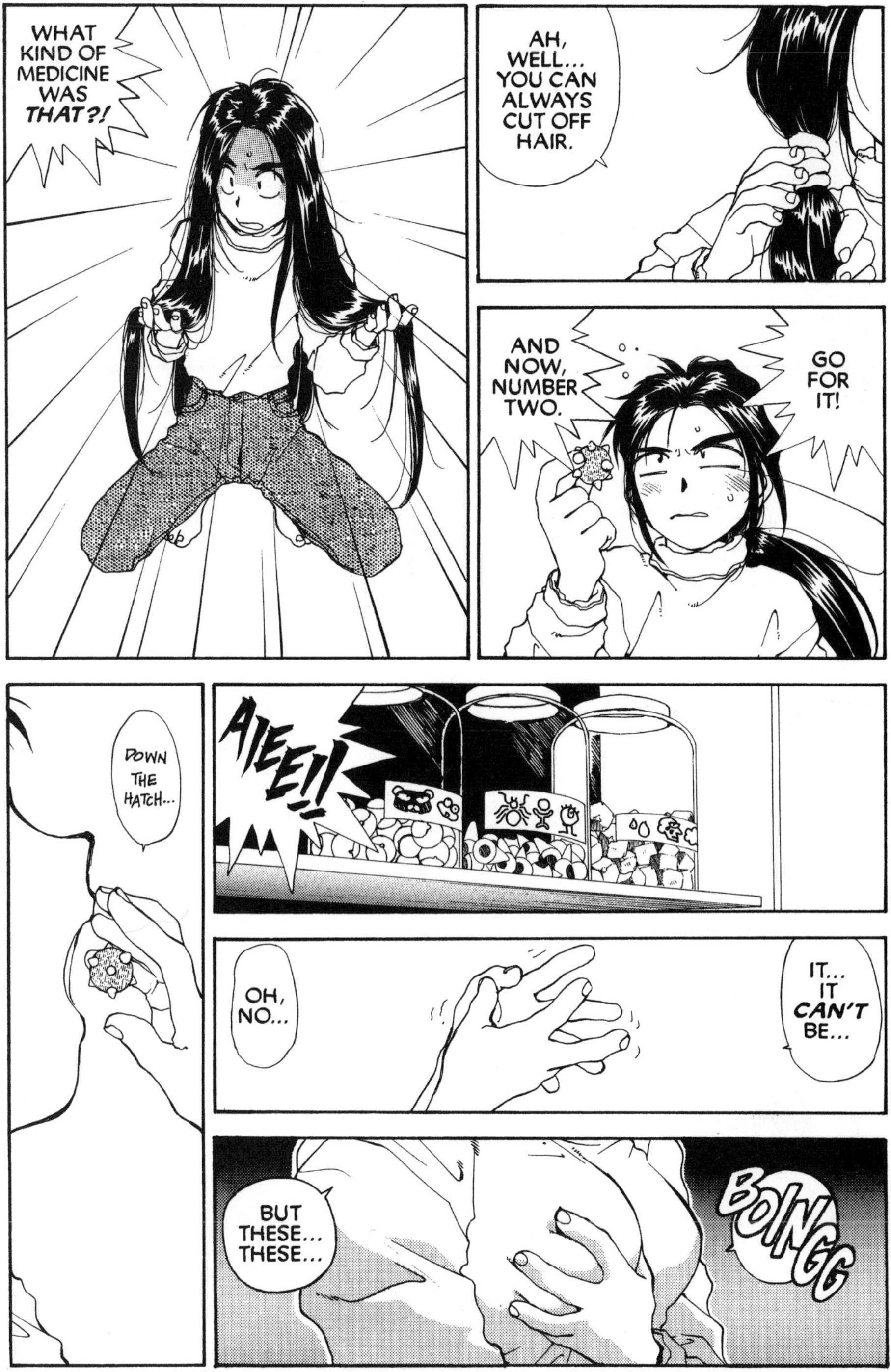
WHAT KIND OF MEDICINE WAS THAT?!
AH, WELL... YOU CAN ALWAYS CUT OFF HAIR.
AND NOW, NUMBER TWO.
GO FOR IT!
DOWN THE HATCH...
AIEEE!!
OH, NO...
IT... IT CAN'T BE...
BUT THESE... THESE...
BOINGG

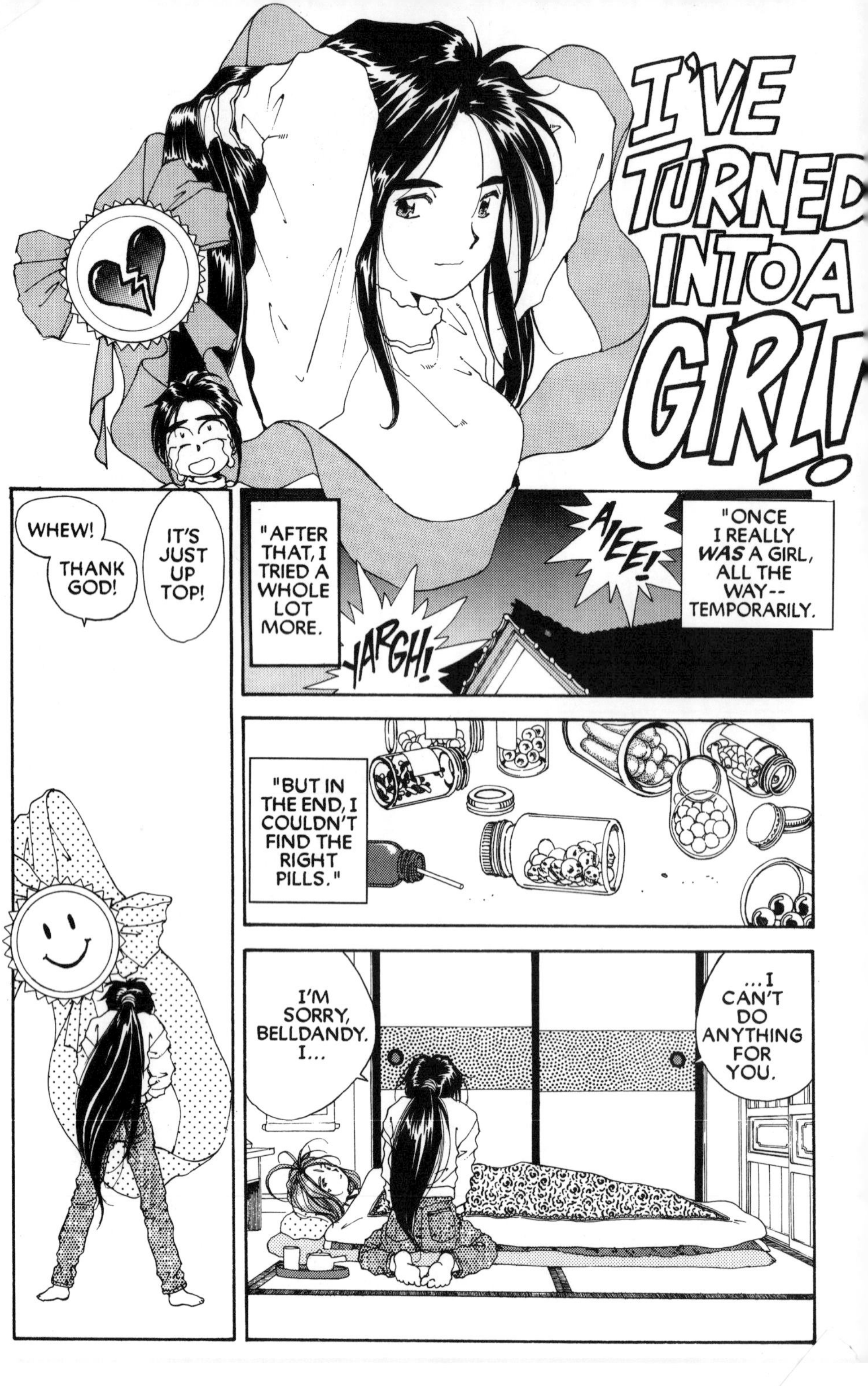
I'VE TURNED INTO A GIRL!
WHEW!
THANK GOD!
IT'S JUST UP TOP!
"AFTER THAT, I TRIED A WHOLE LOT MORE.
AIEE!
"ONCE I REALLY *WAS* A GIRL, ALL THE WAY-- TEMPORARILY.
YARGH!
"BUT IN THE END, I COULDN'T FIND THE RIGHT PILLS."
I'M SORRY, BELLDANDY. I...
...I CAN'T DO ANYTHING FOR YOU.

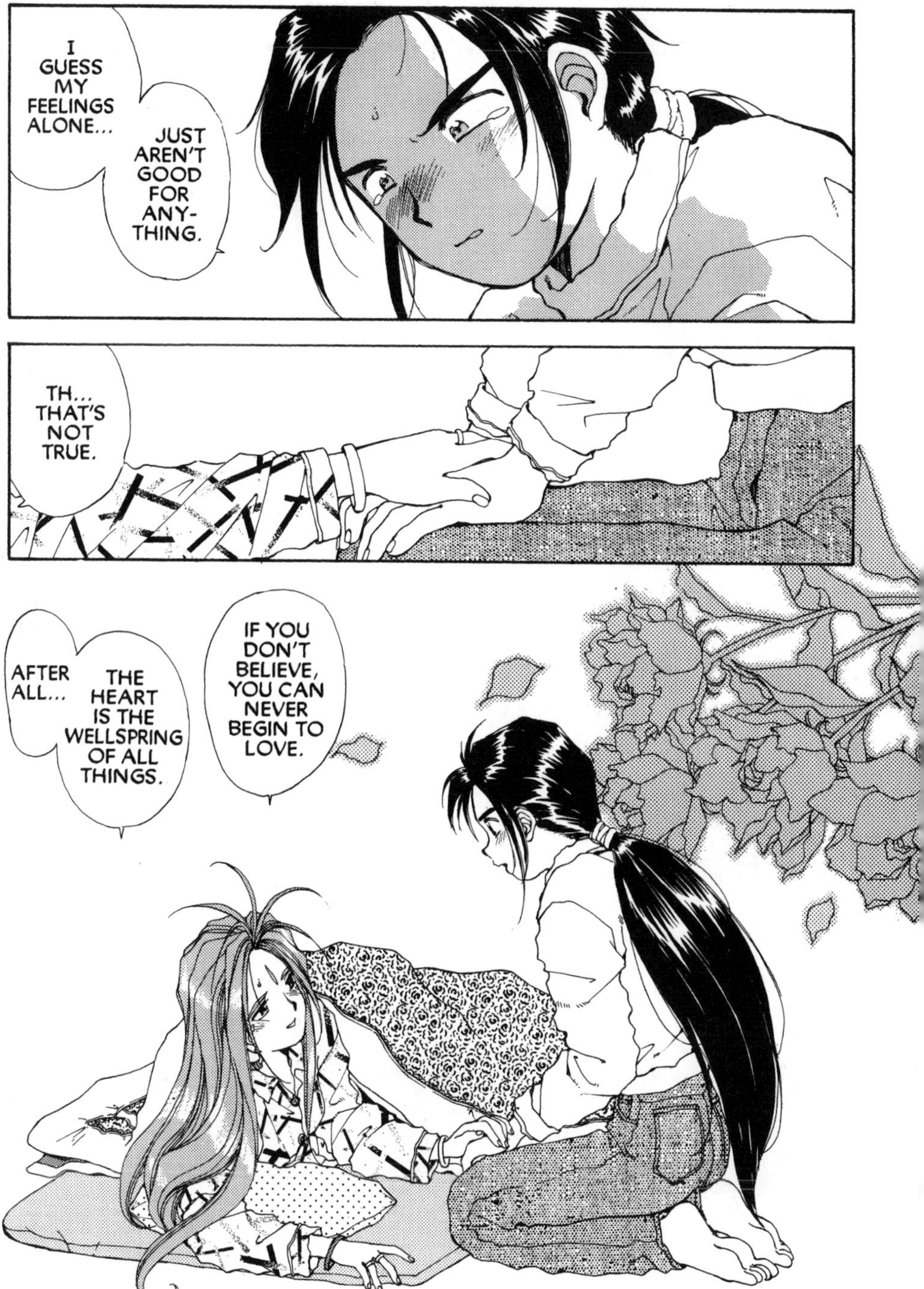
I GUESS MY FEELINGS ALONE...
JUST AREN'T GOOD FOR ANY-THING.
TH... THAT'S NOT TRUE.
AFTER ALL...
THE HEART IS THE WELLSPRING OF ALL THINGS.
IF YOU DON'T BELIEVE, YOU CAN NEVER BEGIN TO LOVE.

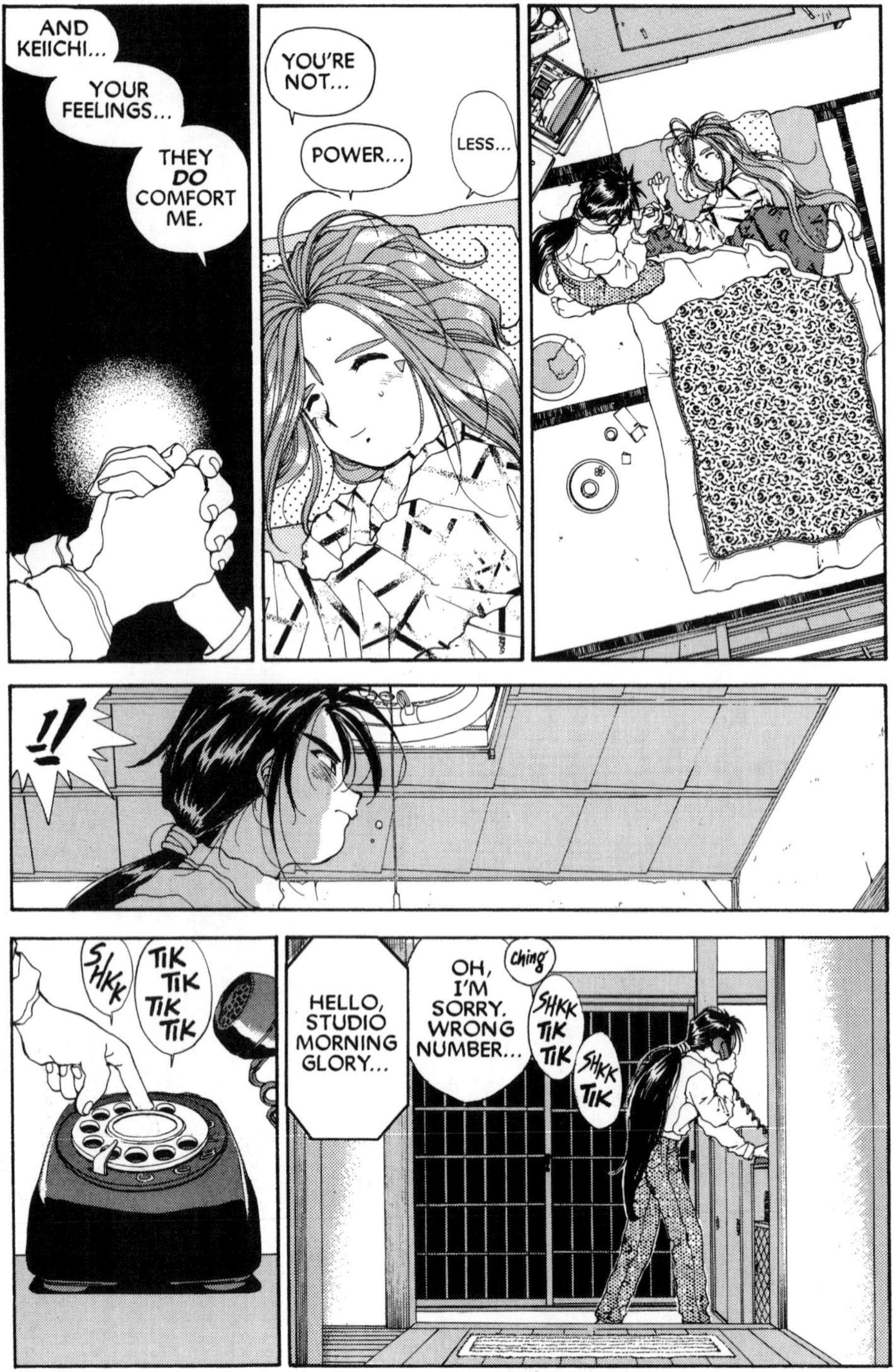
AND KEIICHI...
YOUR FEELINGS...
THEY DO COMFORT ME.
YOU'RE NOT...
POWER...
LESS...
!!
SHKK
TIK TIK TIK TIK
HELLO, STUDIO MORNING GLORY...
OH, I'M SORRY. WRONG NUMBER...
ching
SHKK TIK TIK
SHKK TIK

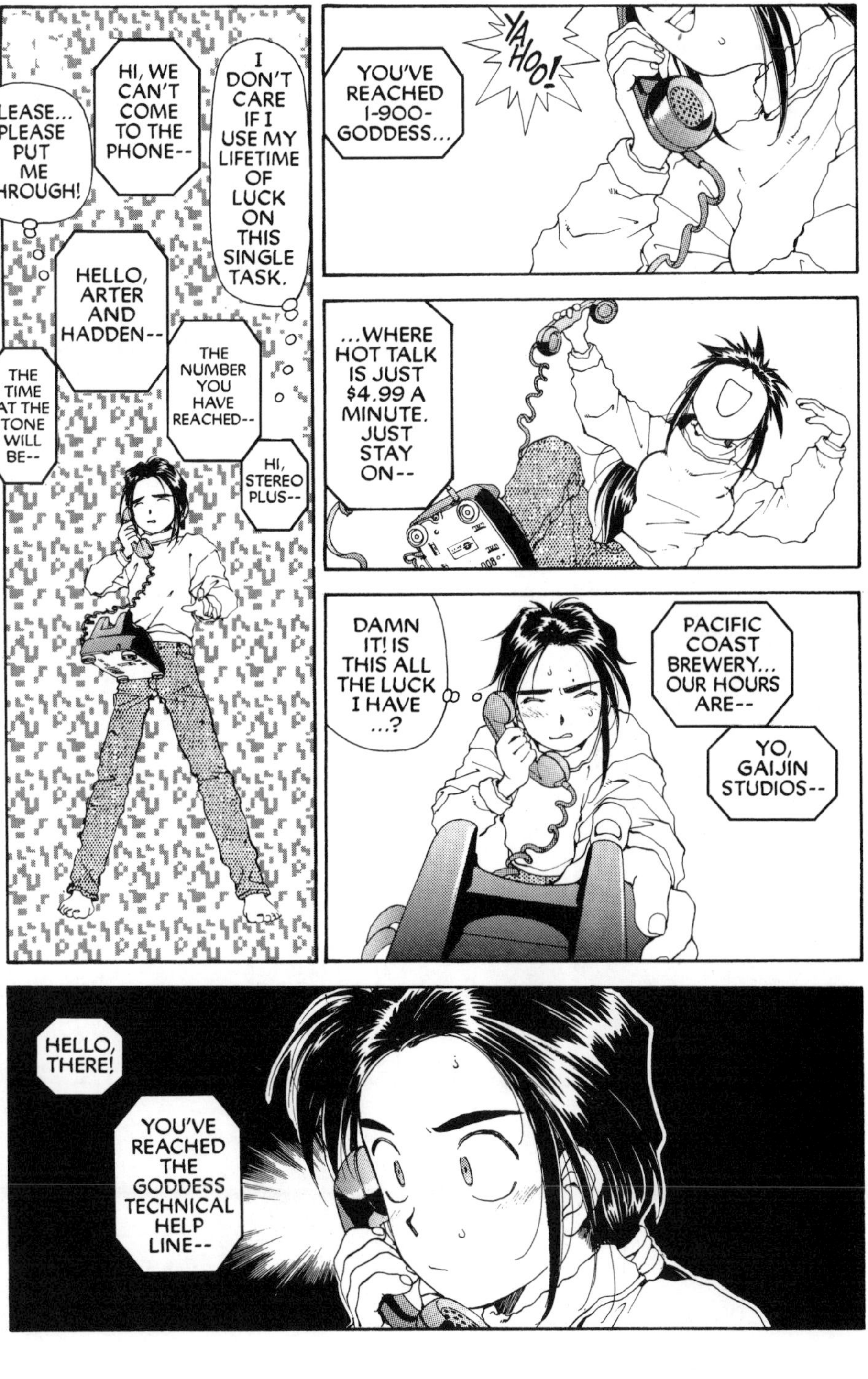
PLEASE... PLEASE PUT ME THROUGH!
HI, WE CAN'T COME TO THE PHONE--
I DON'T CARE IF I USE MY LIFETIME OF LUCK ON THIS SINGLE TASK.
HELLO, ARTER AND HADDEN--
THE TIME AT THE TONE WILL BE--
THE NUMBER YOU HAVE REACHED--
HI, STEREO PLUS--
YOU'VE REACHED 1-900-GODDESS...
YAHOO!
...WHERE HOT TALK IS JUST $4.99 A MINUTE. JUST STAY ON--
DAMN IT! IS THIS ALL THE LUCK I HAVE ...?
PACIFIC COAST BREWERY... OUR HOURS ARE--
YO, GAIJIN STUDIOS--
HELLO, THERE!
YOU'VE REACHED THE GODDESS TECHNICAL HELP LINE--

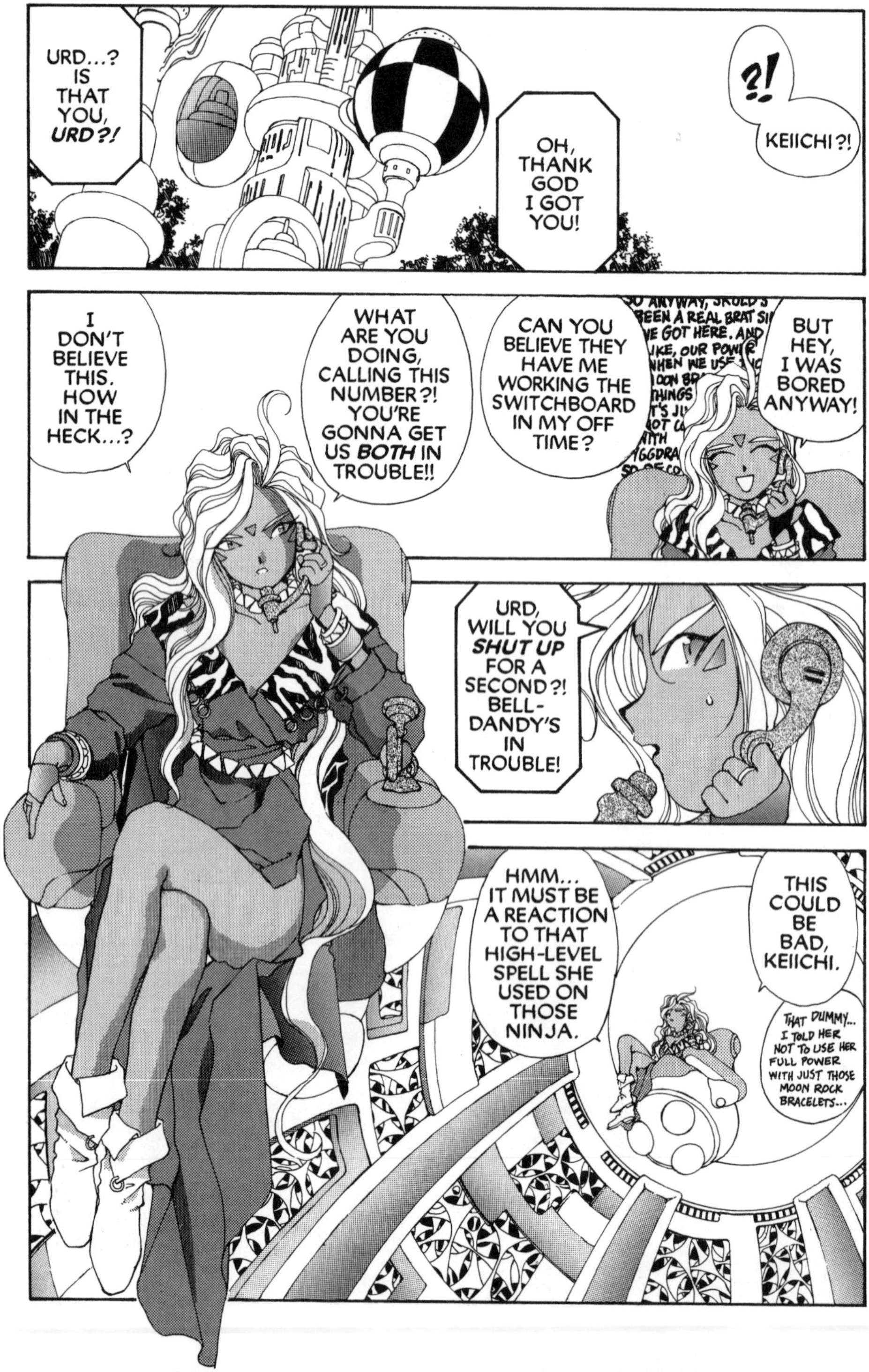
URD...? IS THAT YOU, *URD?!*
OH, THANK GOD I GOT YOU!
?!
KEIICHI?!
I DON'T BELIEVE THIS. HOW IN THE HECK...?
WHAT ARE YOU DOING, CALLING THIS NUMBER?! YOU'RE GONNA GET US *BOTH* IN TROUBLE!!
CAN YOU BELIEVE THEY HAVE ME WORKING THE SWITCHBOARD IN MY OFF TIME?
BUT HEY, I WAS BORED ANYWAY!
URD, WILL YOU *SHUT UP* FOR A SECOND?! BELL-DANDY'S IN TROUBLE!
HMM... IT MUST BE A REACTION TO THAT HIGH-LEVEL SPELL SHE USED ON THOSE NINJA.
THIS COULD BE BAD, KEIICHI.
THAT DUMMY... I TOLD HER NOT TO USE HER FULL POWER WITH JUST THOSE MOON ROCK BRACELETS...

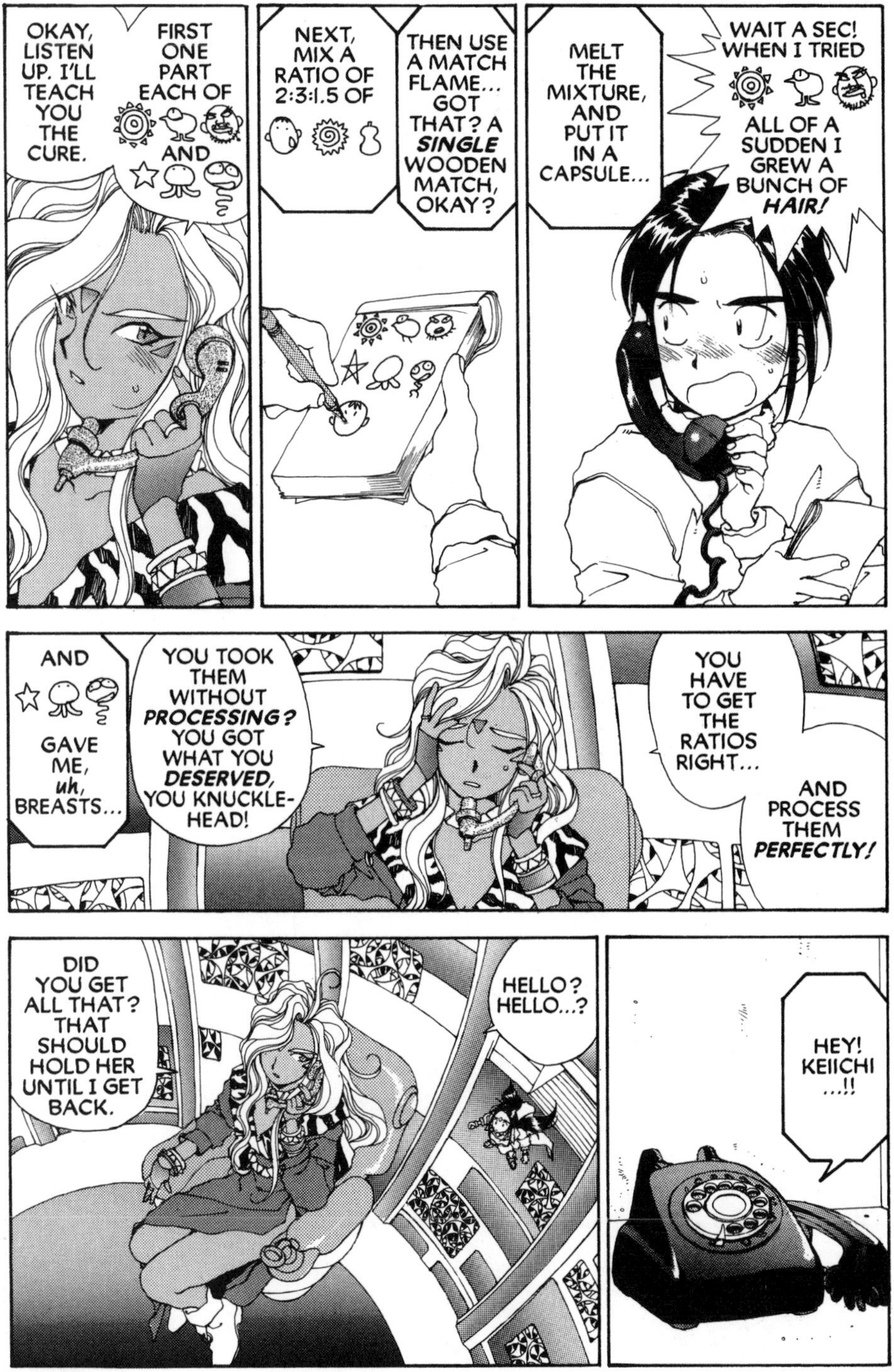
OKAY, LISTEN UP. I'LL TEACH YOU THE CURE.
FIRST ONE PART EACH OF AND
NEXT, MIX A RATIO OF 2:3:1.5 OF
THEN USE A MATCH FLAME... GOT THAT? A *SINGLE* WOODEN MATCH, OKAY?
MELT THE MIXTURE, AND PUT IT IN A CAPSULE...
WAIT A SEC! WHEN I TRIED ALL OF A SUDDEN I GREW A BUNCH OF *HAIR!*
AND GAVE ME, *uh*, BREASTS...
YOU TOOK THEM WITHOUT *PROCESSING?* YOU GOT WHAT YOU *DESERVED,* YOU KNUCKLE-HEAD!
YOU HAVE TO GET THE RATIOS RIGHT...
AND PROCESS THEM *PERFECTLY!*
DID YOU GET ALL THAT? THAT SHOULD HOLD HER UNTIL I GET BACK.
HELLO? HELLO...?
HEY! KEIICHI ...!!

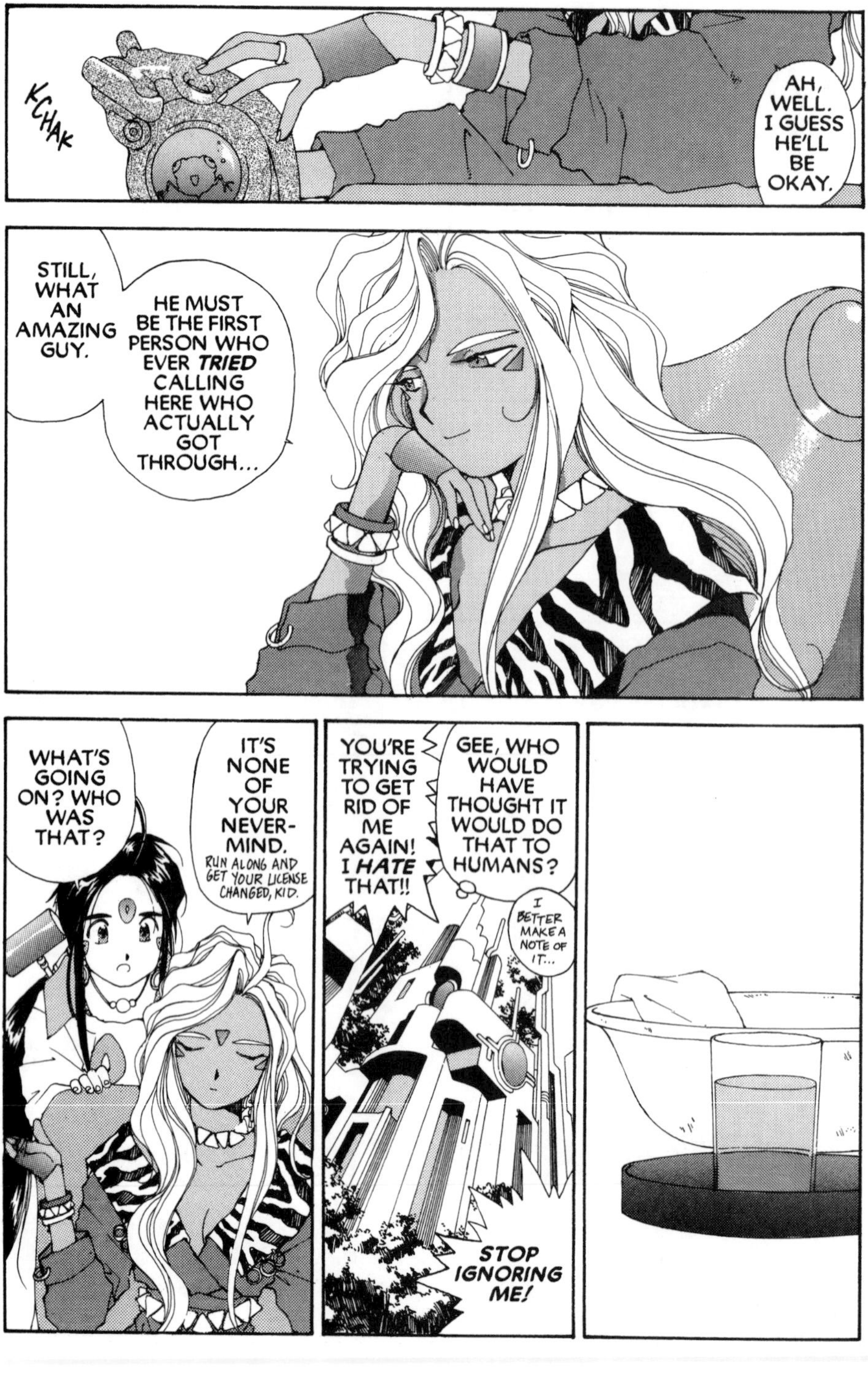
KCHAK
AH, WELL. I GUESS HE'LL BE OKAY.
STILL, WHAT AN AMAZING GUY.
HE MUST BE THE FIRST PERSON WHO EVER *TRIED* CALLING HERE WHO ACTUALLY GOT THROUGH...
WHAT'S GOING ON? WHO WAS THAT?
IT'S NONE OF YOUR NEVER-MIND.
RUN ALONG AND GET YOUR LICENSE CHANGED, KID.
YOU'RE TRYING TO GET RID OF ME AGAIN! I *HATE* THAT!!
GEE, WHO WOULD HAVE THOUGHT IT WOULD DO THAT TO HUMANS?
I BETTER MAKE A NOTE OF IT...
STOP IGNORING ME!

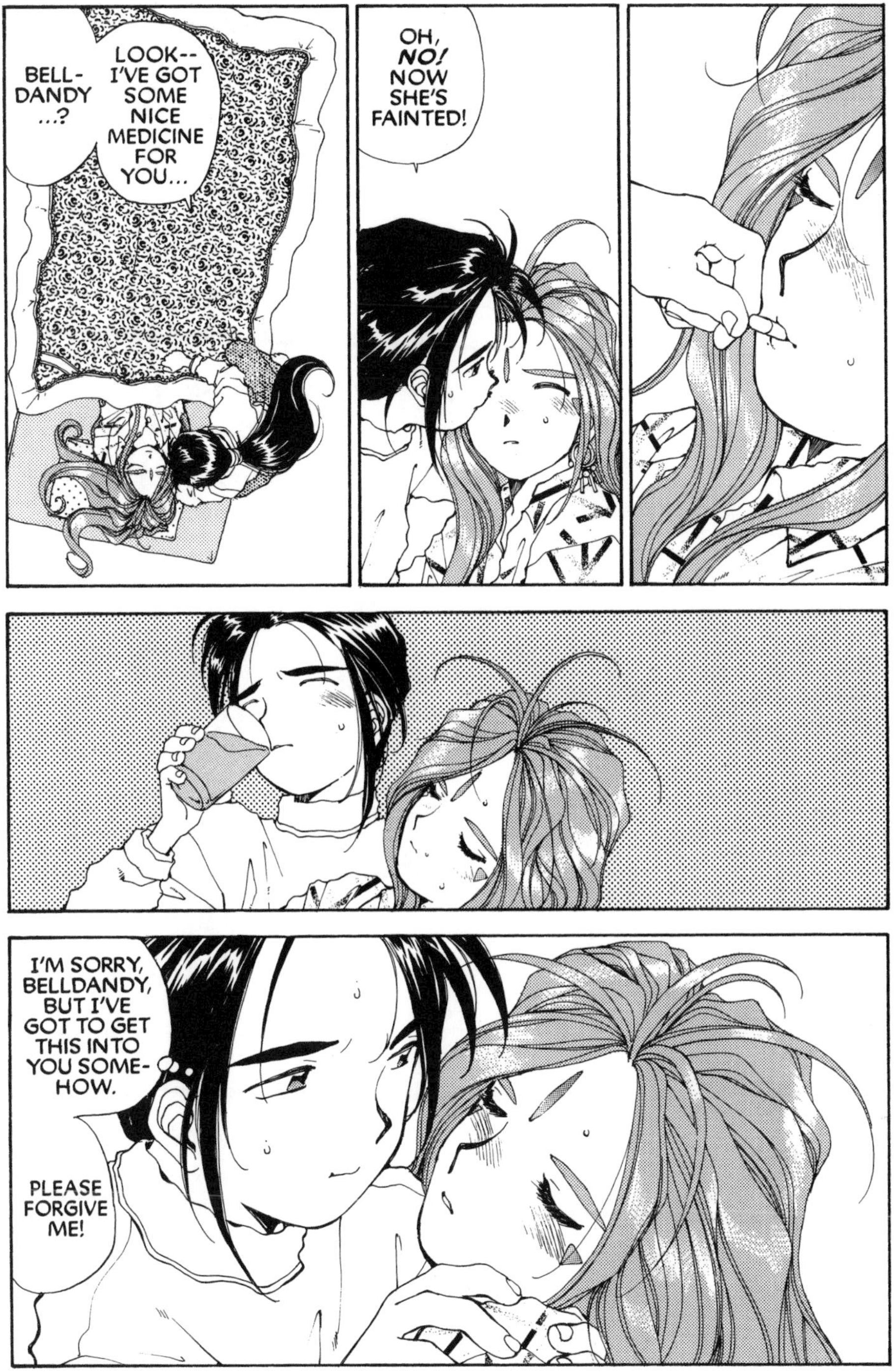
BELL-DANDY ...?
LOOK-- I'VE GOT SOME NICE MEDICINE FOR YOU...
OH, ***NO!*** NOW SHE'S FAINTED!
I'M SORRY, BELLDANDY, BUT I'VE GOT TO GET THIS INTO YOU SOME-HOW.
PLEASE FORGIVE ME!

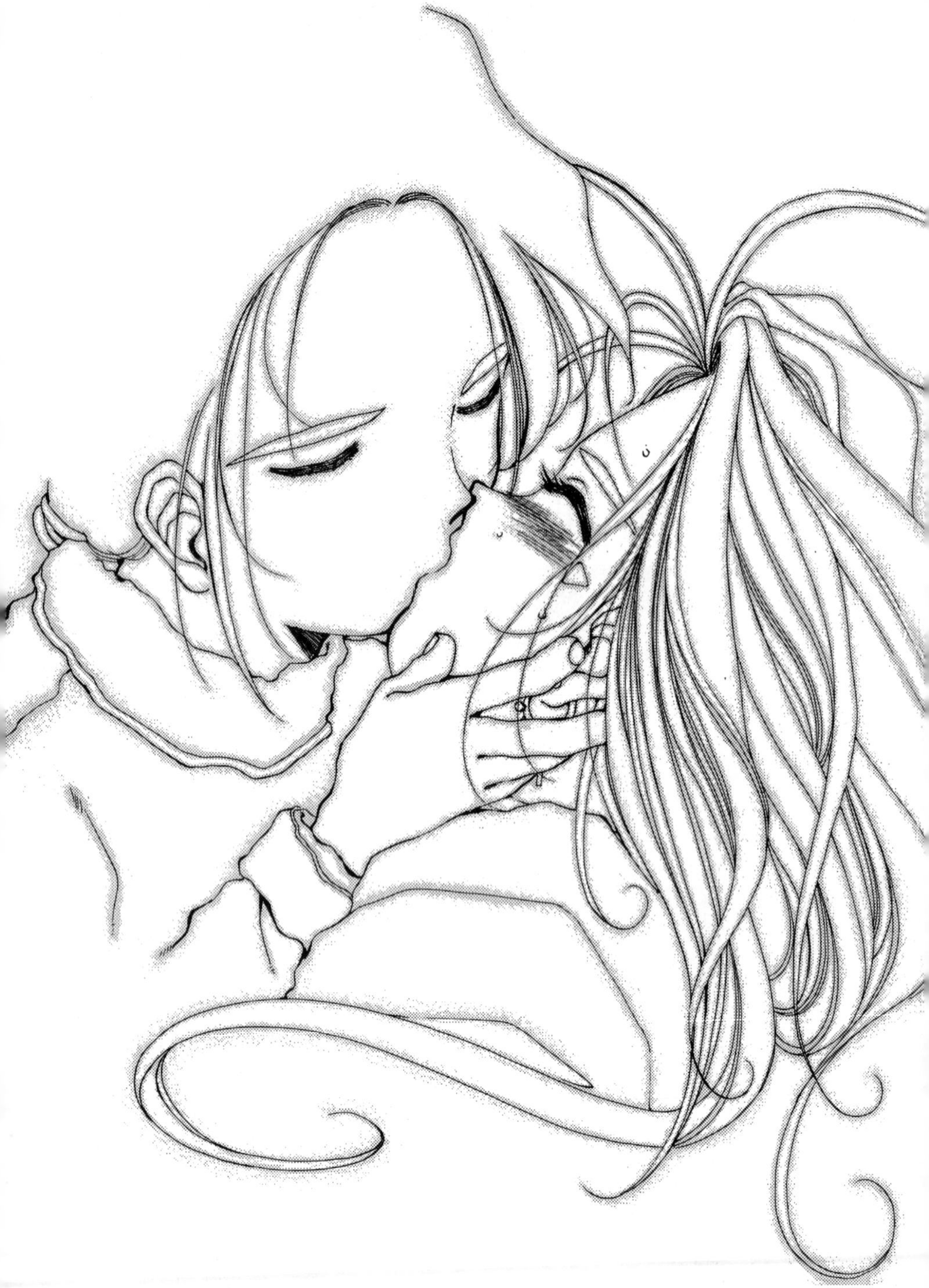

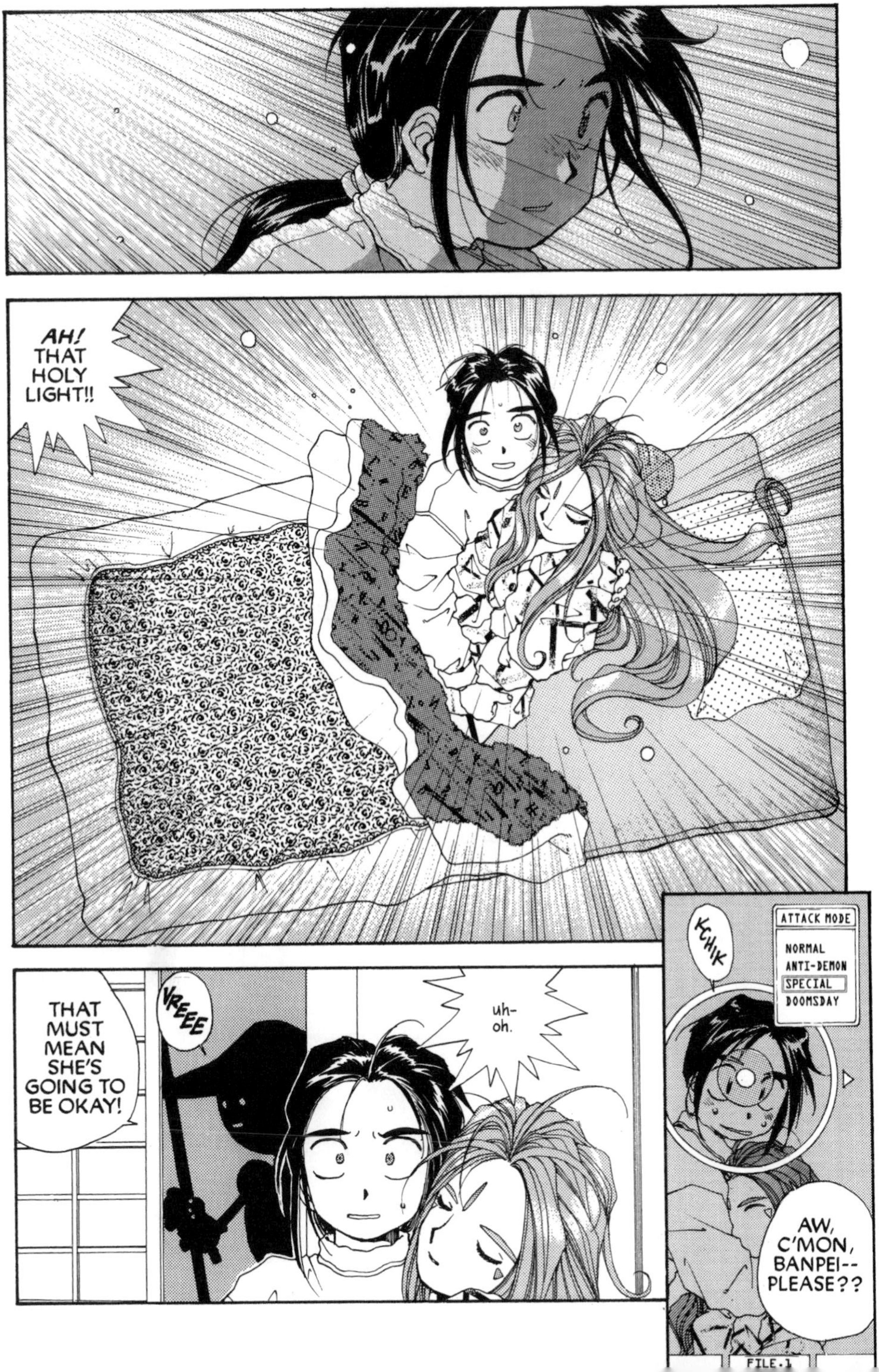
AH! THAT HOLY LIGHT!!
THAT MUST MEAN SHE'S GOING TO BE OKAY!
VREEE
uh-oh.
KCHIK
ATTACK MODE
NORMAL
ANTI-DEMON
SPECIAL
DOOMSDAY
AW, C'MON, BANPEI-- PLEASE??
FILE.1

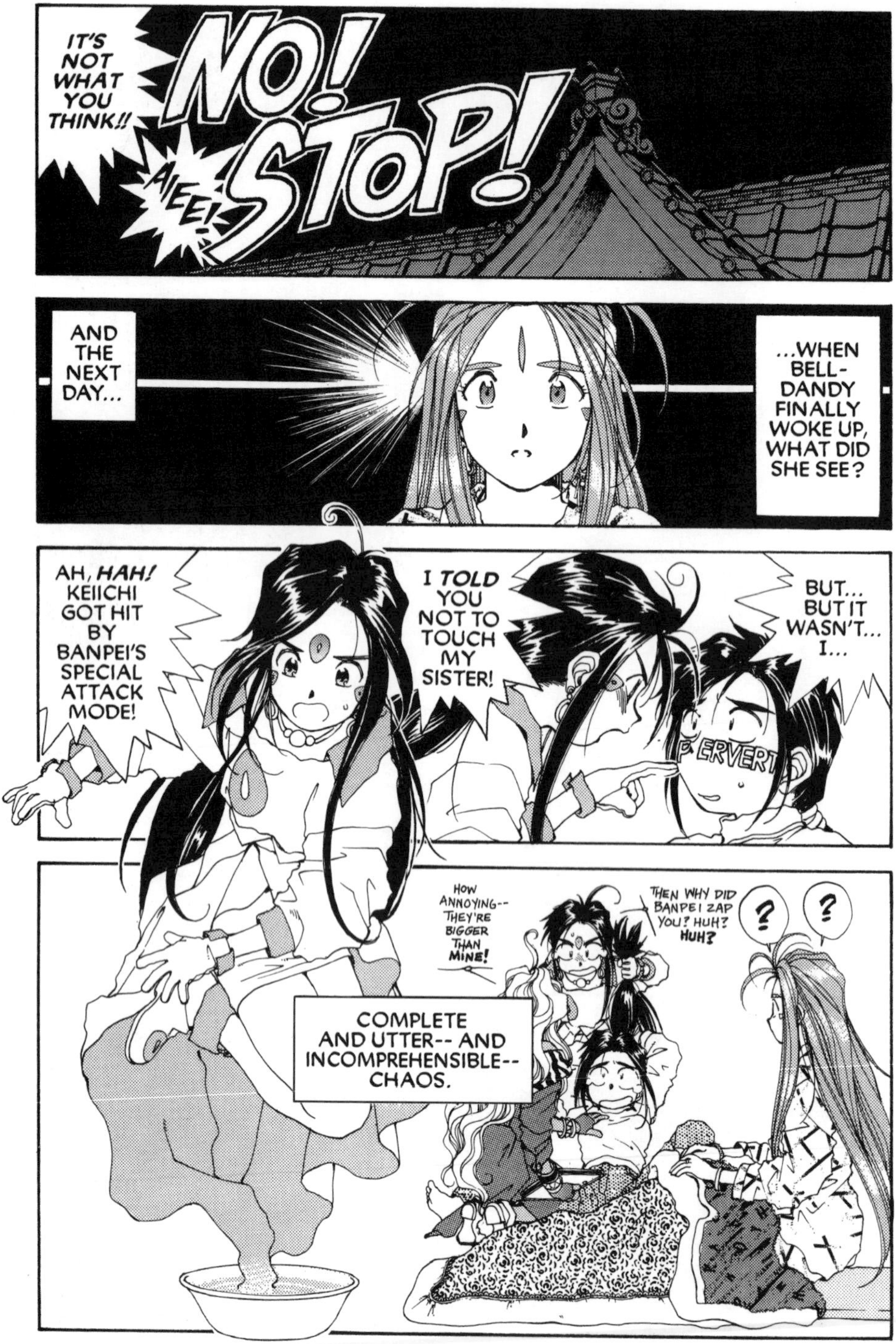
IT'S NOT WHAT YOU THINK!!
NO! STOP!
AIEEE!
AND THE NEXT DAY...
...WHEN BELL-DANDY FINALLY WOKE UP, WHAT DID SHE SEE?
AH, *HAH!* KEIICHI GOT HIT BY BANPEI'S SPECIAL ATTACK MODE!
I *TOLD* YOU NOT TO TOUCH MY SISTER!
PERVERT
BUT... BUT IT WASN'T... I...
HOW ANNOYING-- THEY'RE BIGGER THAN **MINE!**
THEN WHY DID BANPEI ZAP YOU? HUH? **HUH?**
?
?
COMPLETE AND UTTER-- AND INCOMPREHENSIBLE-- CHAOS.

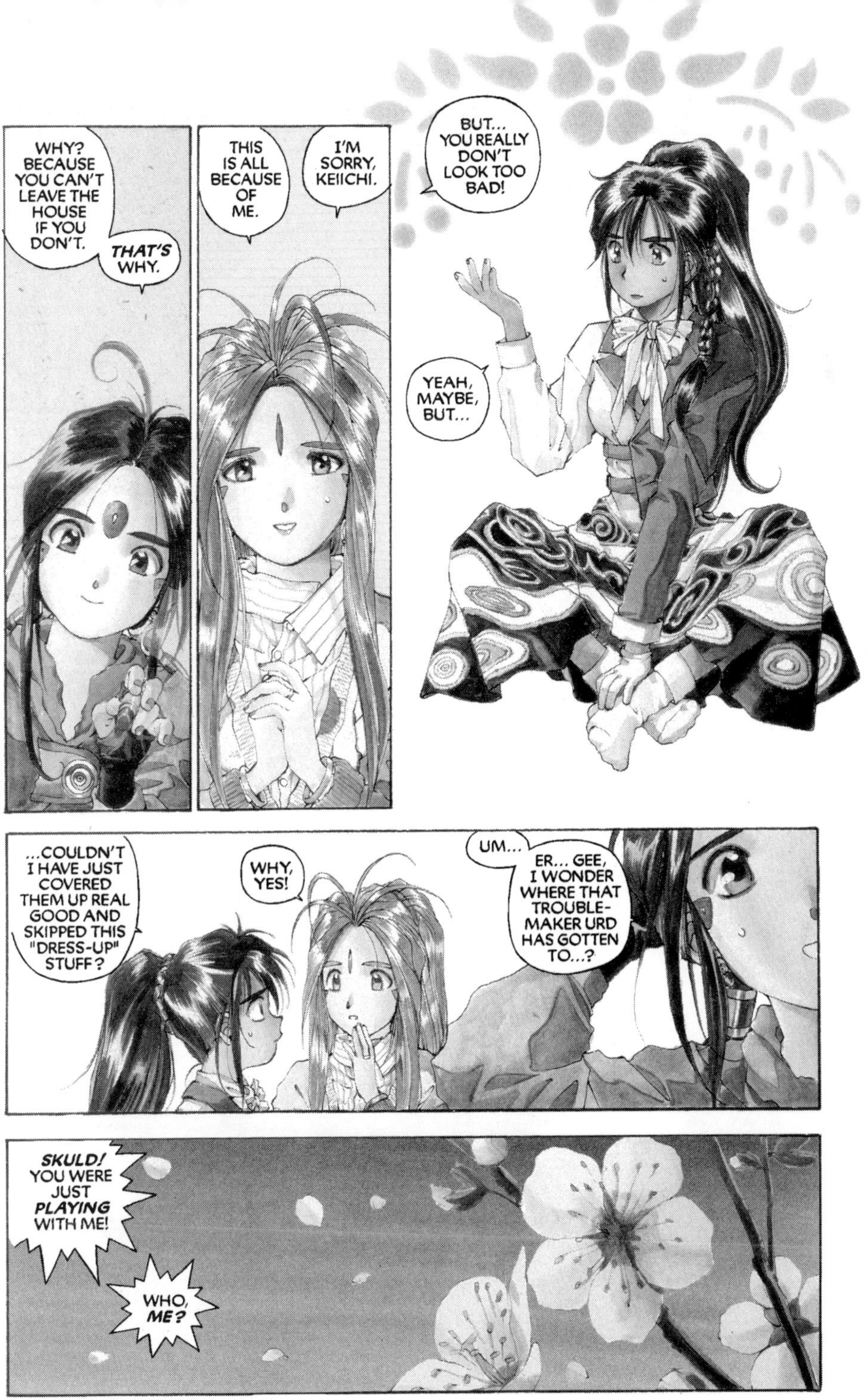
WHY? BECAUSE YOU CAN'T LEAVE THE HOUSE IF YOU DON'T.
THAT'S WHY.
THIS IS ALL BECAUSE OF ME.
I'M SORRY, KEIICHI.
BUT... YOU REALLY DON'T LOOK TOO BAD!
YEAH, MAYBE, BUT...
...COULDN'T I HAVE JUST COVERED THEM UP REAL GOOD AND SKIPPED THIS "DRESS-UP" STUFF?
WHY, YES!
UM...
ER... GEE, I WONDER WHERE THAT TROUBLE-MAKER URD HAS GOTTEN TO...?
SKULD! YOU WERE JUST *PLAYING* WITH ME!
WHO, *ME?*

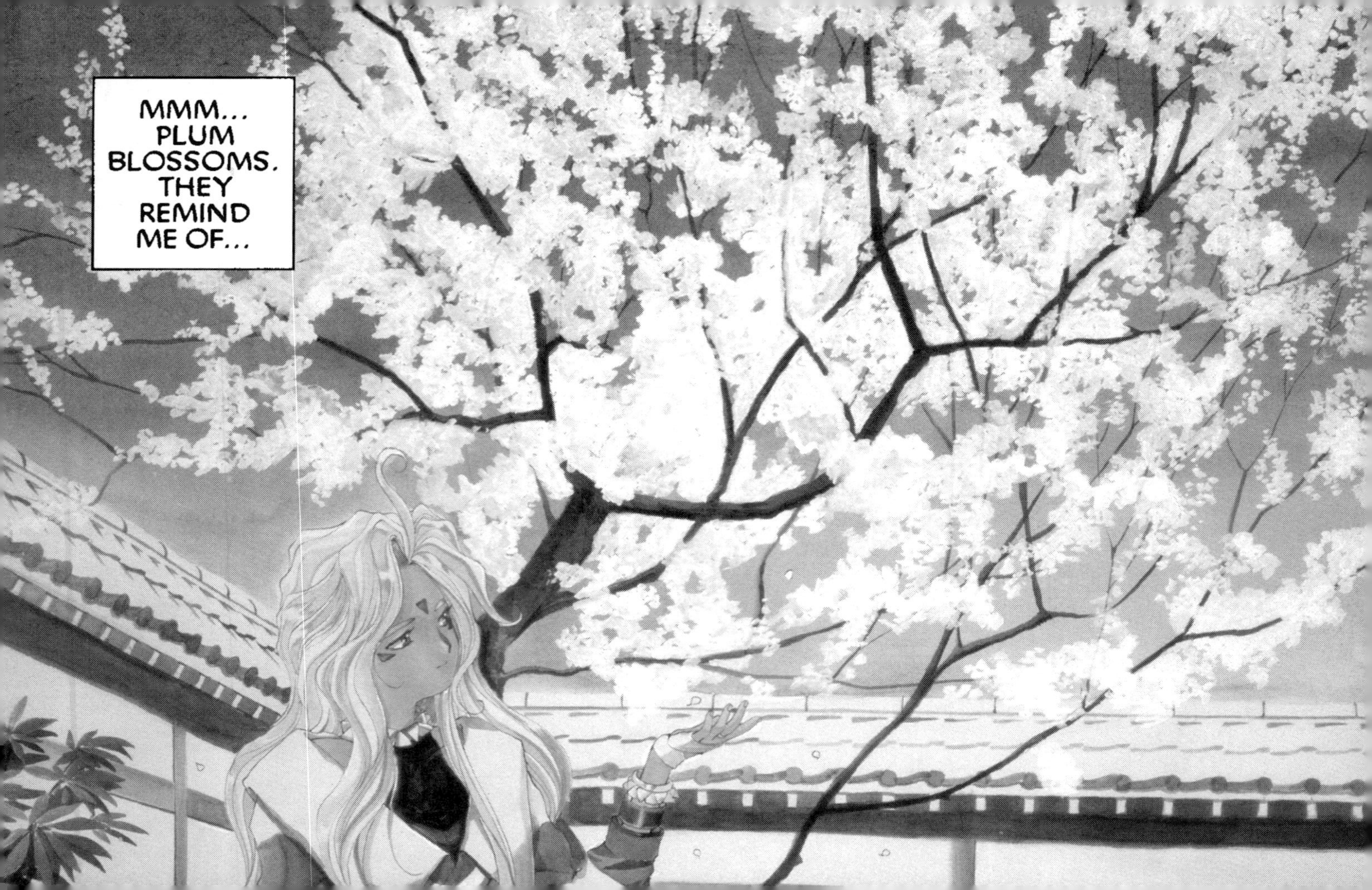
MMM... PLUM BLOSSOMS. THEY REMIND ME OF...

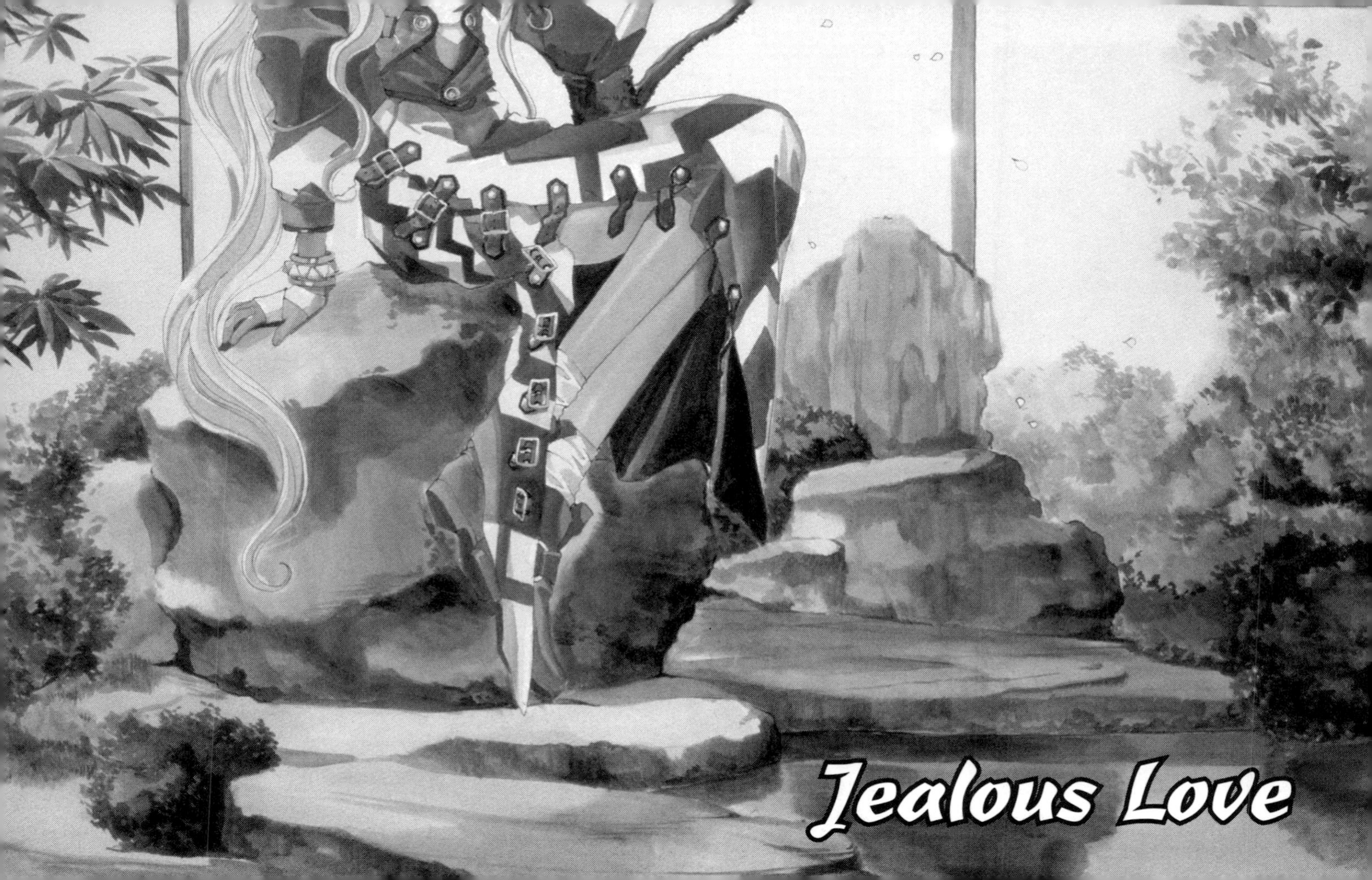
Jealous Love

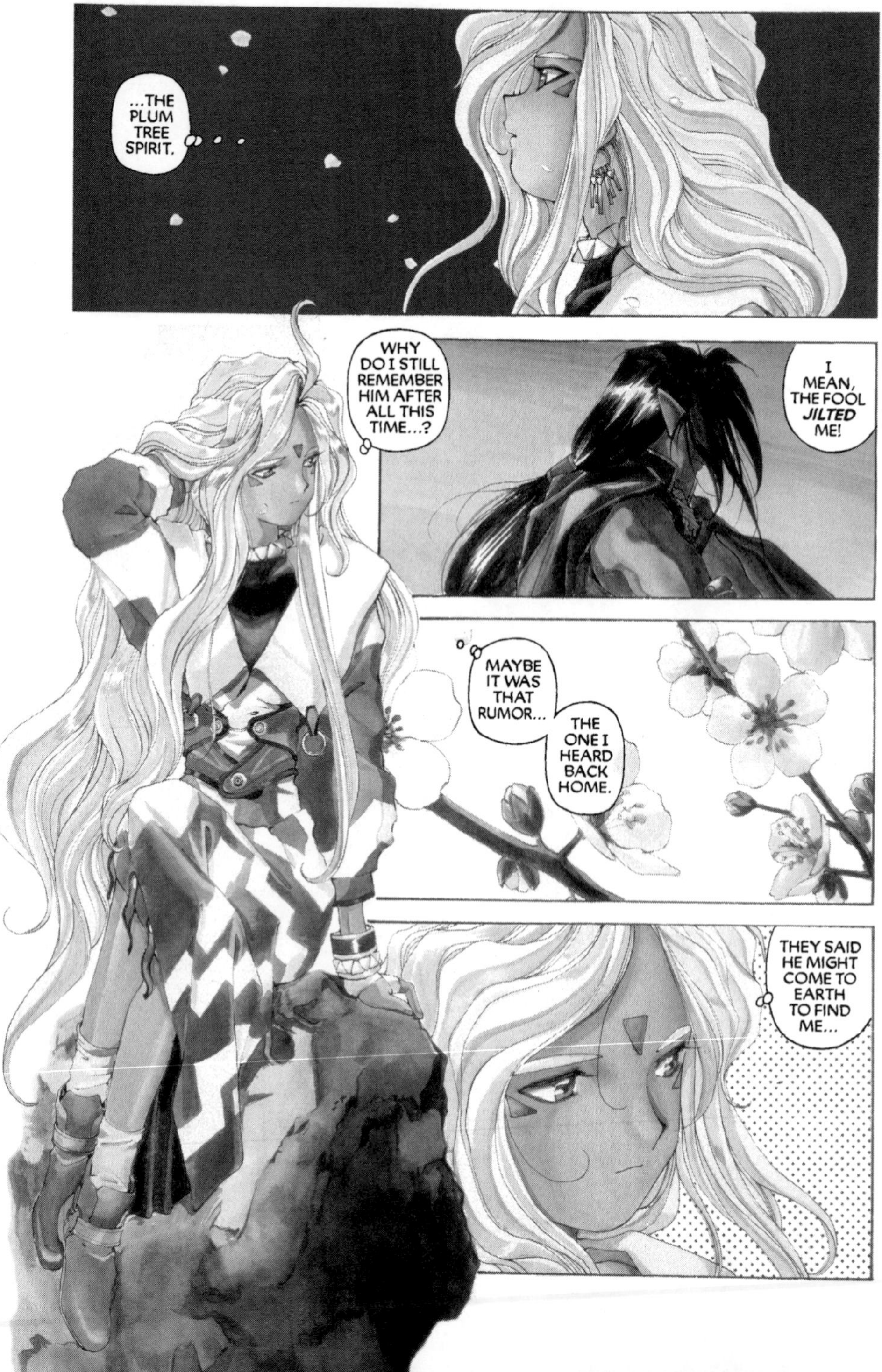
...THE PLUM TREE SPIRIT.
WHY DO I STILL REMEMBER HIM AFTER ALL THIS TIME...?
I MEAN, THE FOOL *JILTED* ME!
MAYBE IT WAS THAT RUMOR...
THE ONE I HEARD BACK HOME.
THEY SAID HE MIGHT COME TO EARTH TO FIND ME...

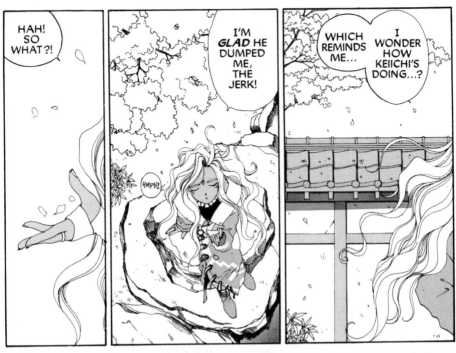

HAH! SO WHAT?!

I'M *GLAD* HE DUMPED ME, THE JERK!

HMPH!

WHICH REMINDS ME...

I WONDER HOW KEIICHI'S DOING...?

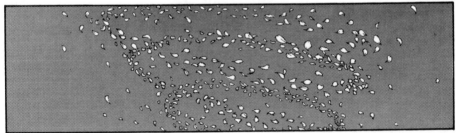

≋*mmph!*≋

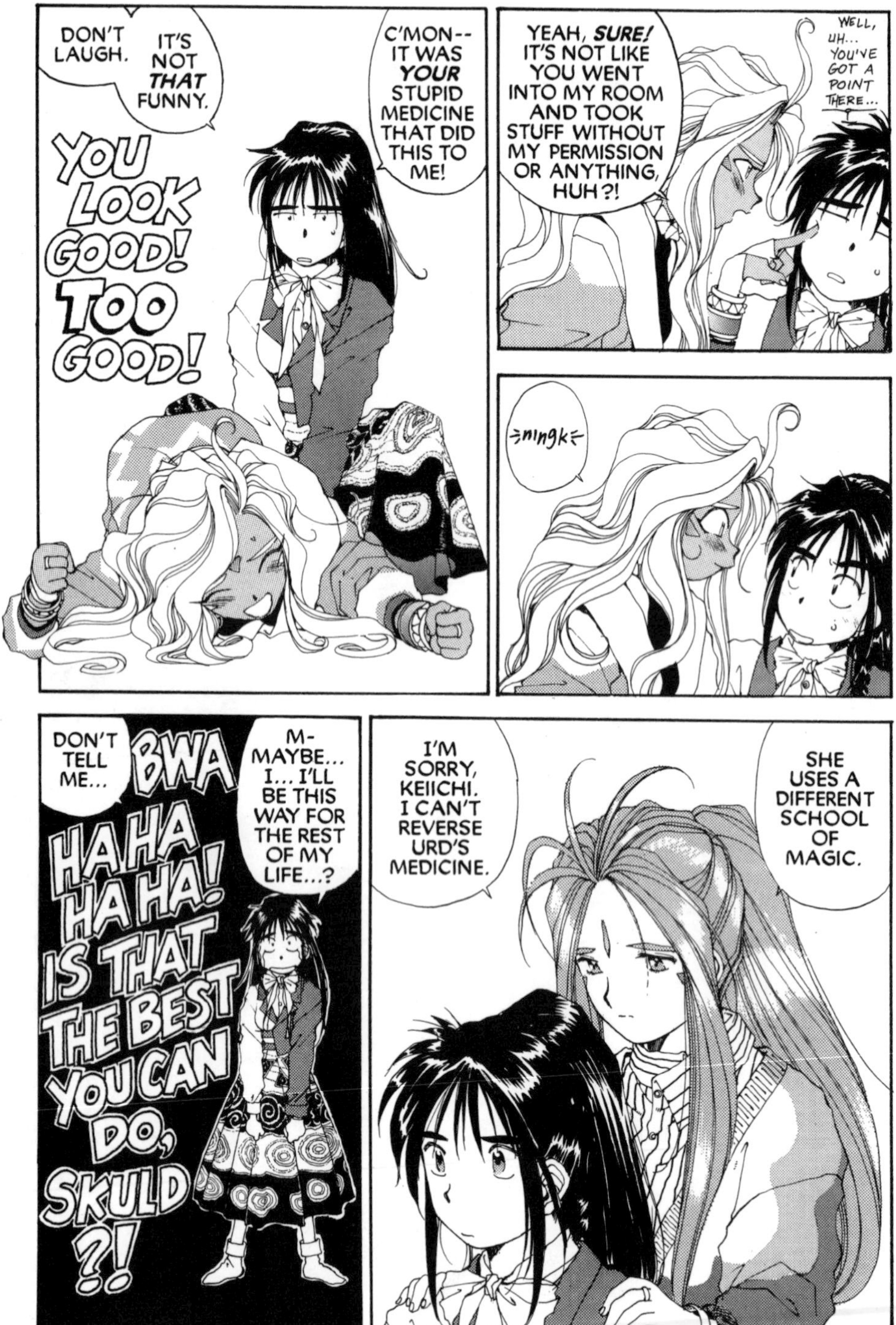
DON'T LAUGH.
IT'S NOT THAT FUNNY.
YOU LOOK GOOD! TOO GOOD!
C'MON-- IT WAS YOUR STUPID MEDICINE THAT DID THIS TO ME!
YEAH, SURE! IT'S NOT LIKE YOU WENT INTO MY ROOM AND TOOK STUFF WITHOUT MY PERMISSION OR ANYTHING, HUH?!
WELL, UH... YOU'VE GOT A POINT THERE...
≡ningk≡
DON'T TELL ME...
BWA HA HA HA HA! IS THAT THE BEST YOU CAN DO, SKULD?!
M-MAYBE... I... I'LL BE THIS WAY FOR THE REST OF MY LIFE...?
I'M SORRY, KEIICHI. I CAN'T REVERSE URD'S MEDICINE.
SHE USES A DIFFERENT SCHOOL OF MAGIC.

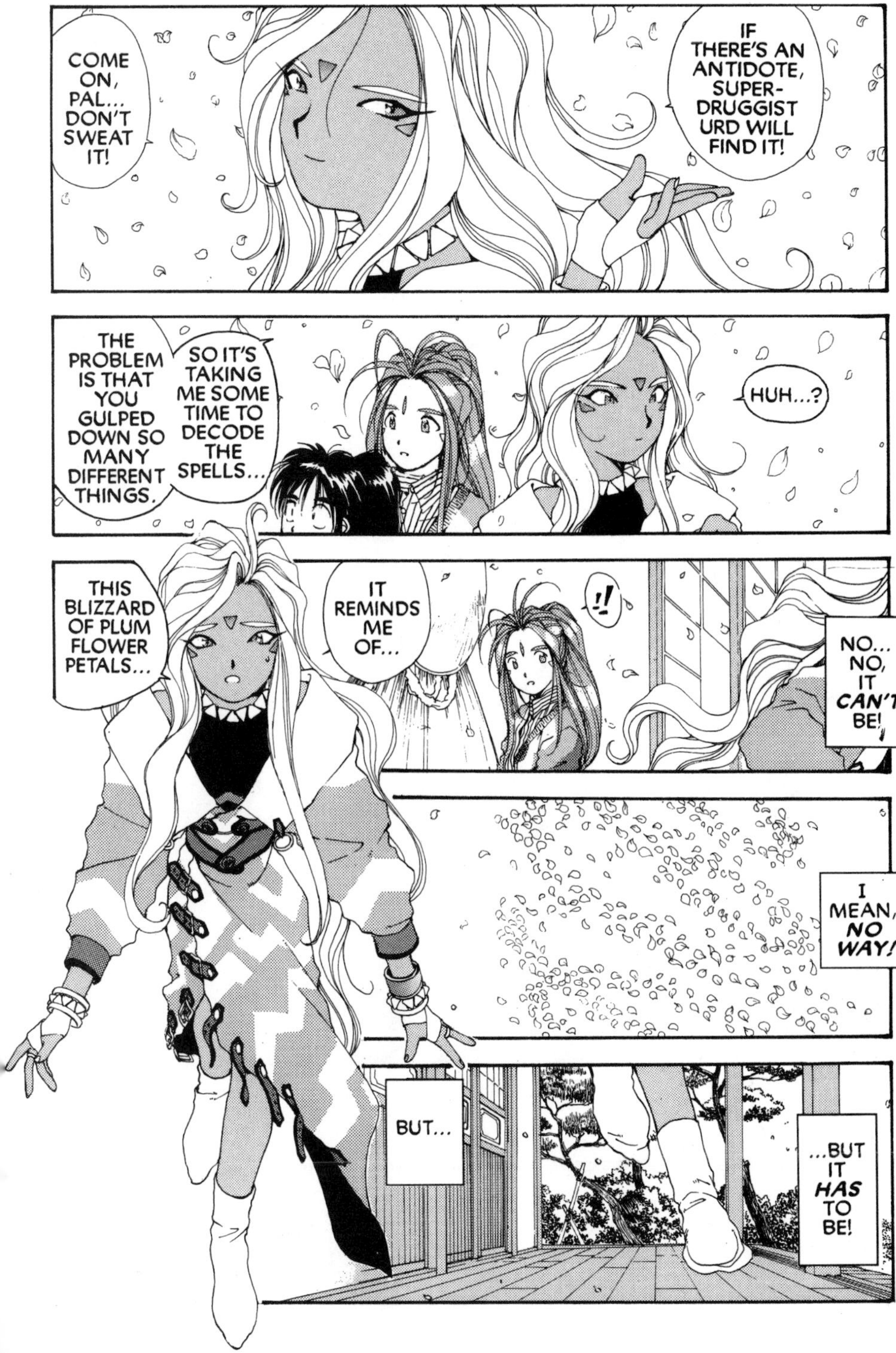
COME ON, PAL... DON'T SWEAT IT!
IF THERE'S AN ANTIDOTE, SUPER-DRUGGIST URD WILL FIND IT!
THE PROBLEM IS THAT YOU GULPED DOWN SO MANY DIFFERENT THINGS.
SO IT'S TAKING ME SOME TIME TO DECODE THE SPELLS...
HUH...?
THIS BLIZZARD OF PLUM FLOWER PETALS...
IT REMINDS ME OF...
!!
NO... NO, IT *CAN'T* BE!
I MEAN, *NO WAY!*
BUT...
...BUT IT *HAS* TO BE!

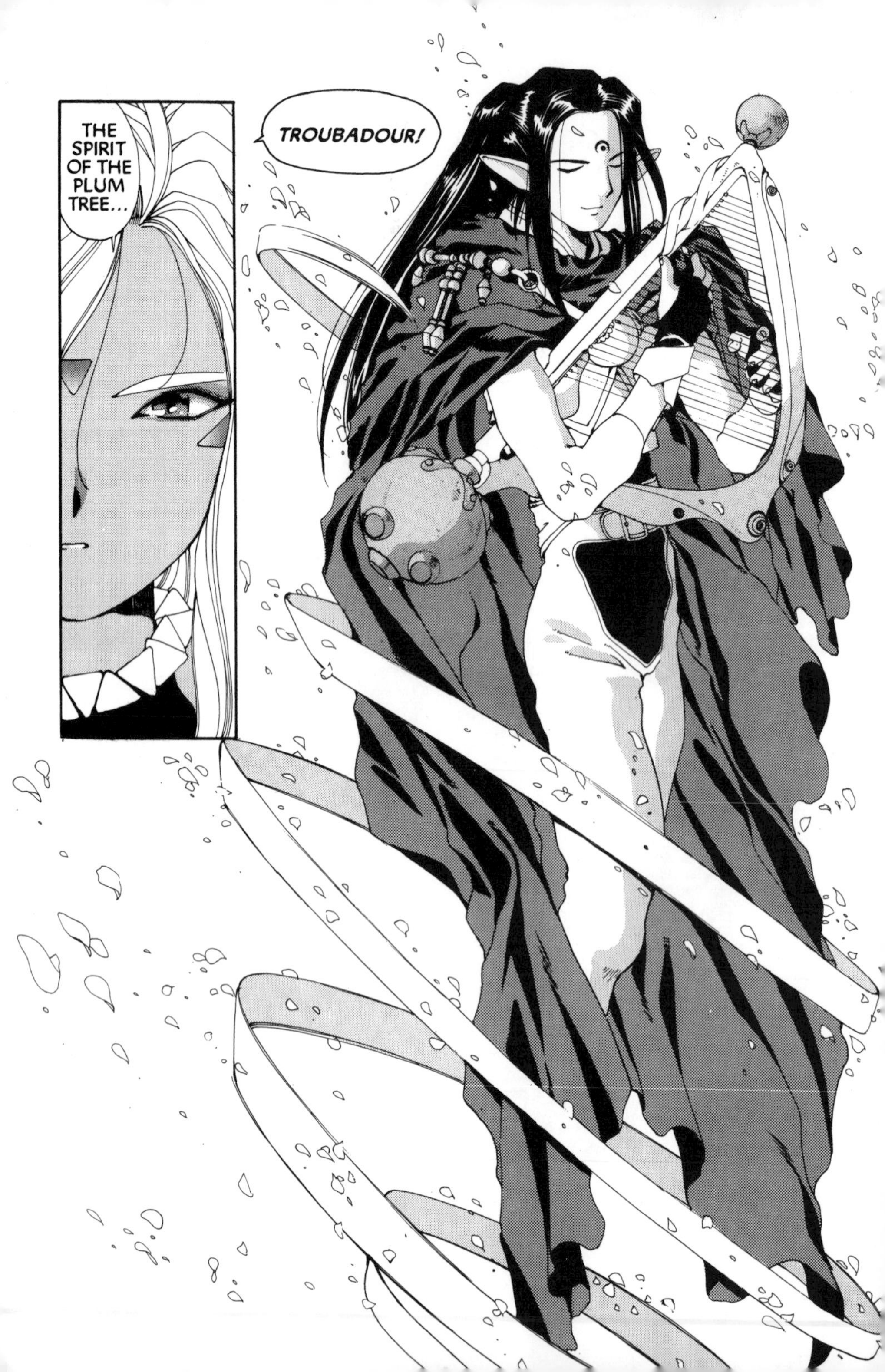
THE SPIRIT OF THE PLUM TREE...
TROUBADOUR!

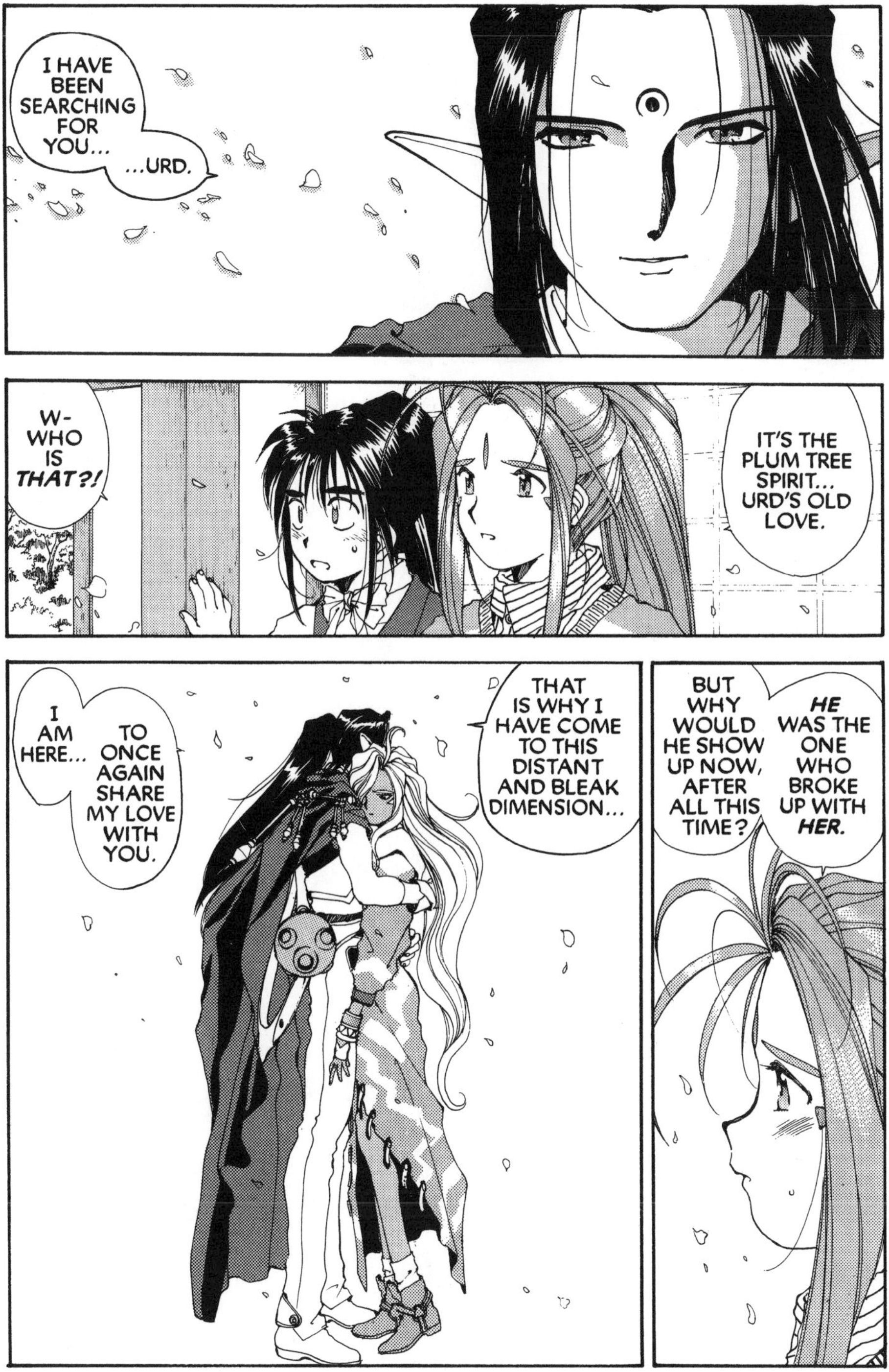
I HAVE BEEN SEARCHING FOR YOU... ...URD.
W- WHO IS *THAT?!*
IT'S THE PLUM TREE SPIRIT... URD'S OLD LOVE.
I AM HERE... TO ONCE AGAIN SHARE MY LOVE WITH YOU.
THAT IS WHY I HAVE COME TO THIS DISTANT AND BLEAK DIMENSION...
BUT WHY WOULD HE SHOW UP NOW, AFTER ALL THIS TIME? ***HE*** WAS THE ONE WHO BROKE UP WITH ***HER.***

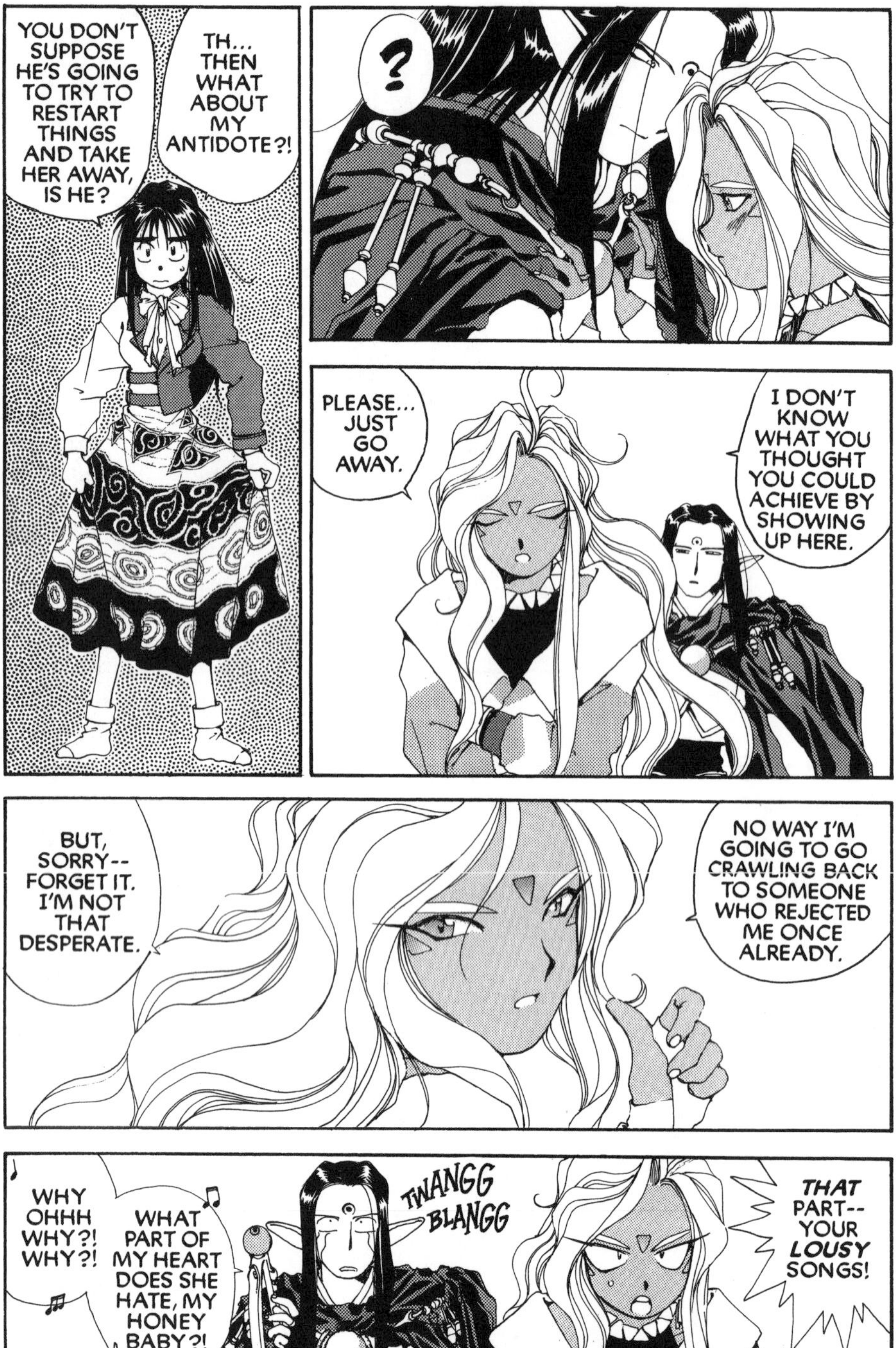
YOU DON'T SUPPOSE HE'S GOING TO TRY TO RESTART THINGS AND TAKE HER AWAY, IS HE?
TH... THEN WHAT ABOUT MY ANTIDOTE?!
?
PLEASE... JUST GO AWAY.
I DON'T KNOW WHAT YOU THOUGHT YOU COULD ACHIEVE BY SHOWING UP HERE.
BUT, SORRY-- FORGET IT. I'M NOT THAT DESPERATE.
NO WAY I'M GOING TO GO CRAWLING BACK TO SOMEONE WHO REJECTED ME ONCE ALREADY.
WHY OHHH WHY?! WHY?!
WHAT PART OF MY HEART DOES SHE HATE, MY HONEY BABY?!
TWANGG BLANGG
THAT PART-- YOUR LOUSY SONGS!

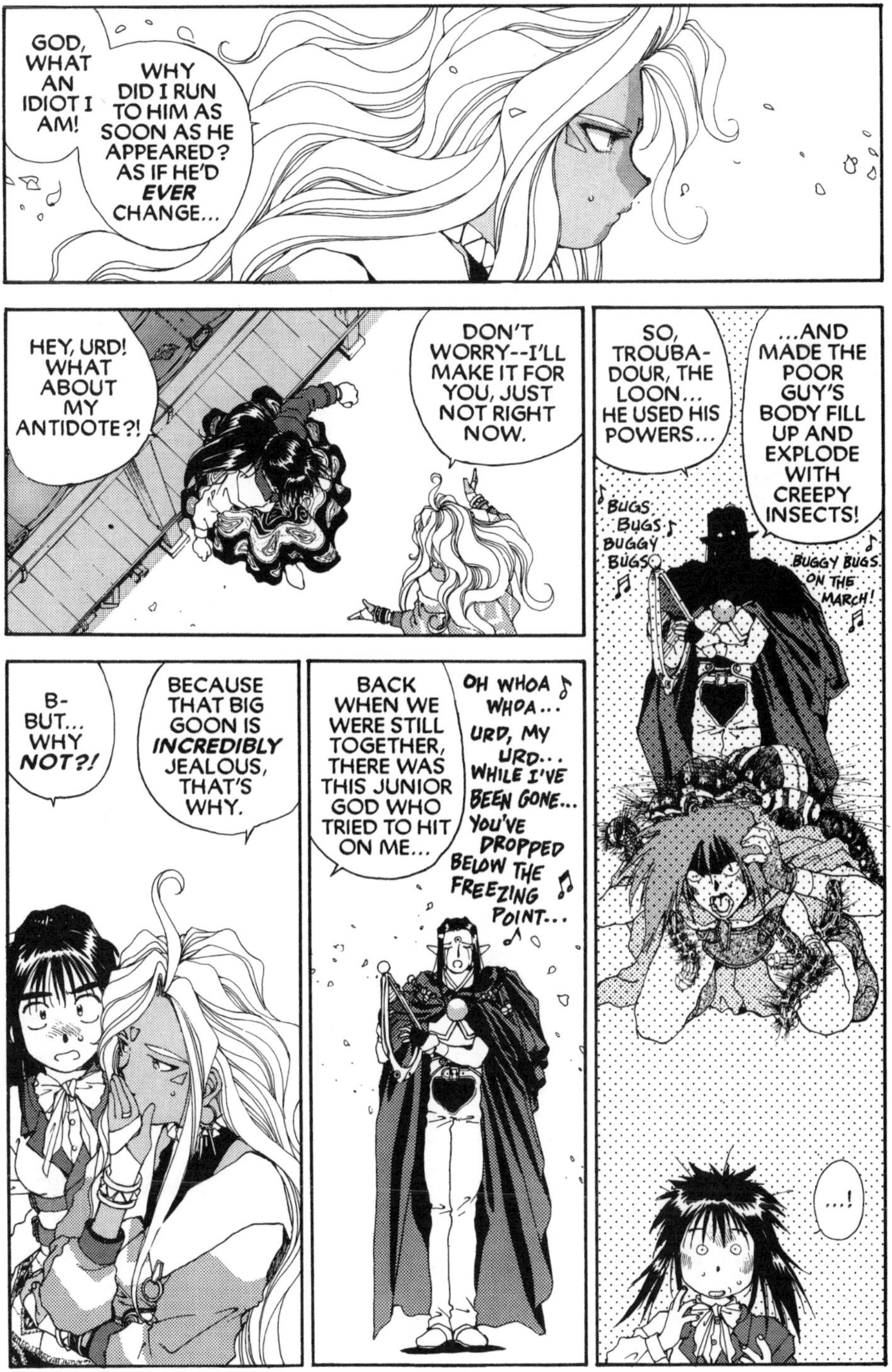
GOD, WHAT AN IDIOT I AM!
WHY DID I RUN TO HIM AS SOON AS HE APPEARED? AS IF HE'D *EVER* CHANGE...
HEY, URD! WHAT ABOUT MY ANTIDOTE?!
DON'T WORRY--I'LL MAKE IT FOR YOU, JUST NOT RIGHT NOW.
B-BUT... WHY *NOT?!*
BECAUSE THAT BIG GOON IS *INCREDIBLY* JEALOUS, THAT'S WHY.
BACK WHEN WE WERE STILL TOGETHER, THERE WAS THIS JUNIOR GOD WHO TRIED TO HIT ON ME...
OH WHOA ♪ WHOA... URD, MY URD... WHILE I'VE BEEN GONE... YOU'VE DROPPED BELOW THE FREEZING POINT... ♪
SO, TROUBA-DOUR, THE LOON... HE USED HIS POWERS...
...AND MADE THE POOR GUY'S BODY FILL UP AND EXPLODE WITH CREEPY INSECTS!
♪ BUGS BUGS ♪ BUGGY BUGS ♪
♪ BUGGY BUGS ON THE MARCH! ♪
...!

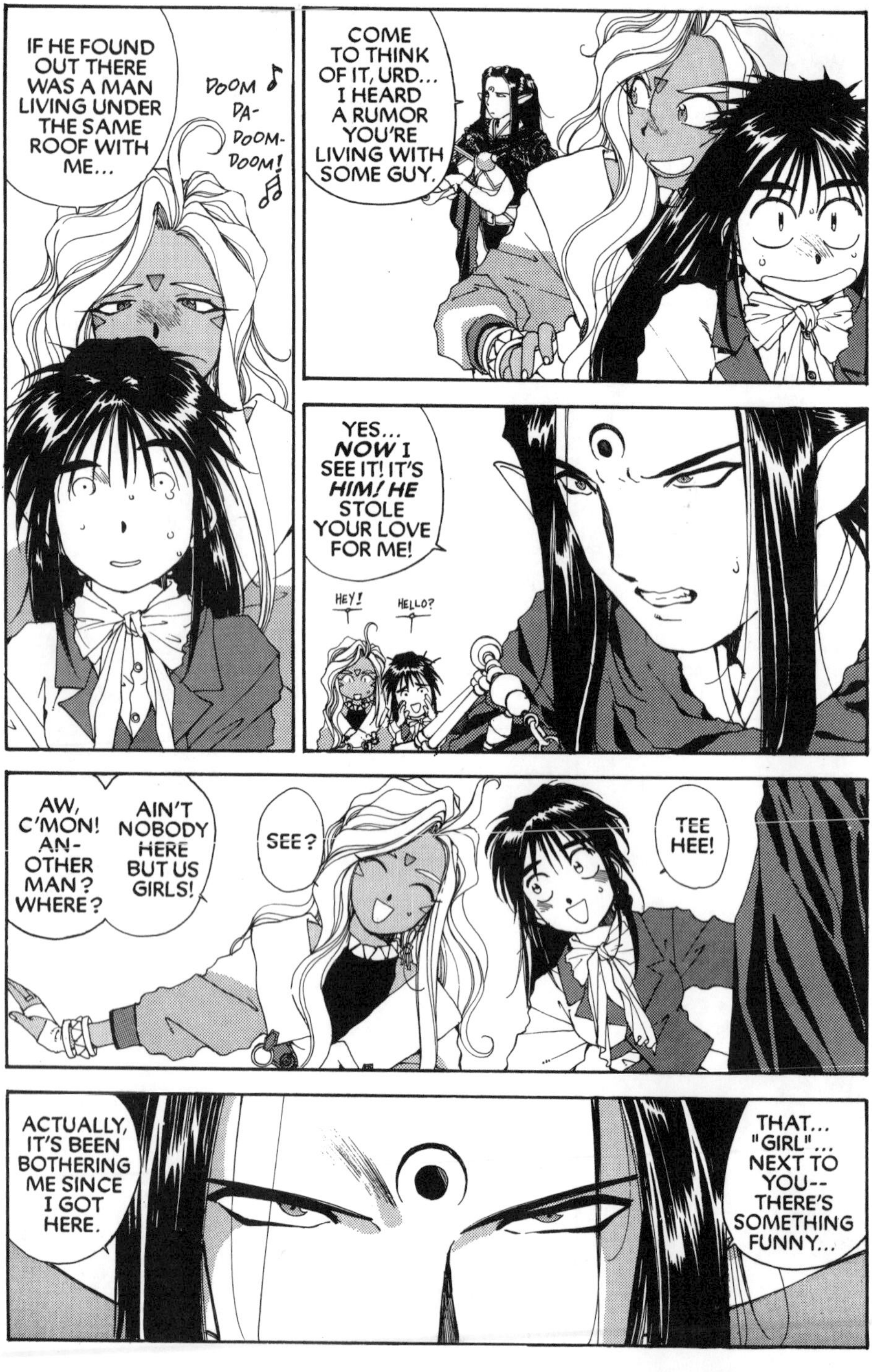
IF HE FOUND OUT THERE WAS A MAN LIVING UNDER THE SAME ROOF WITH ME...
DOOM DA-DOOM-DOOM!
COME TO THINK OF IT, URD... I HEARD A RUMOR YOU'RE LIVING WITH SOME GUY.
YES... *NOW* I SEE IT! IT'S *HIM! HE* STOLE YOUR LOVE FOR ME!
HEY!
HELLO?
AW, C'MON! AN-OTHER MAN? WHERE?
AIN'T NOBODY HERE BUT US GIRLS!
SEE?
TEE HEE!
ACTUALLY, IT'S BEEN BOTHERING ME SINCE I GOT HERE.
THAT... "GIRL"... NEXT TO YOU-- THERE'S SOMETHING FUNNY...

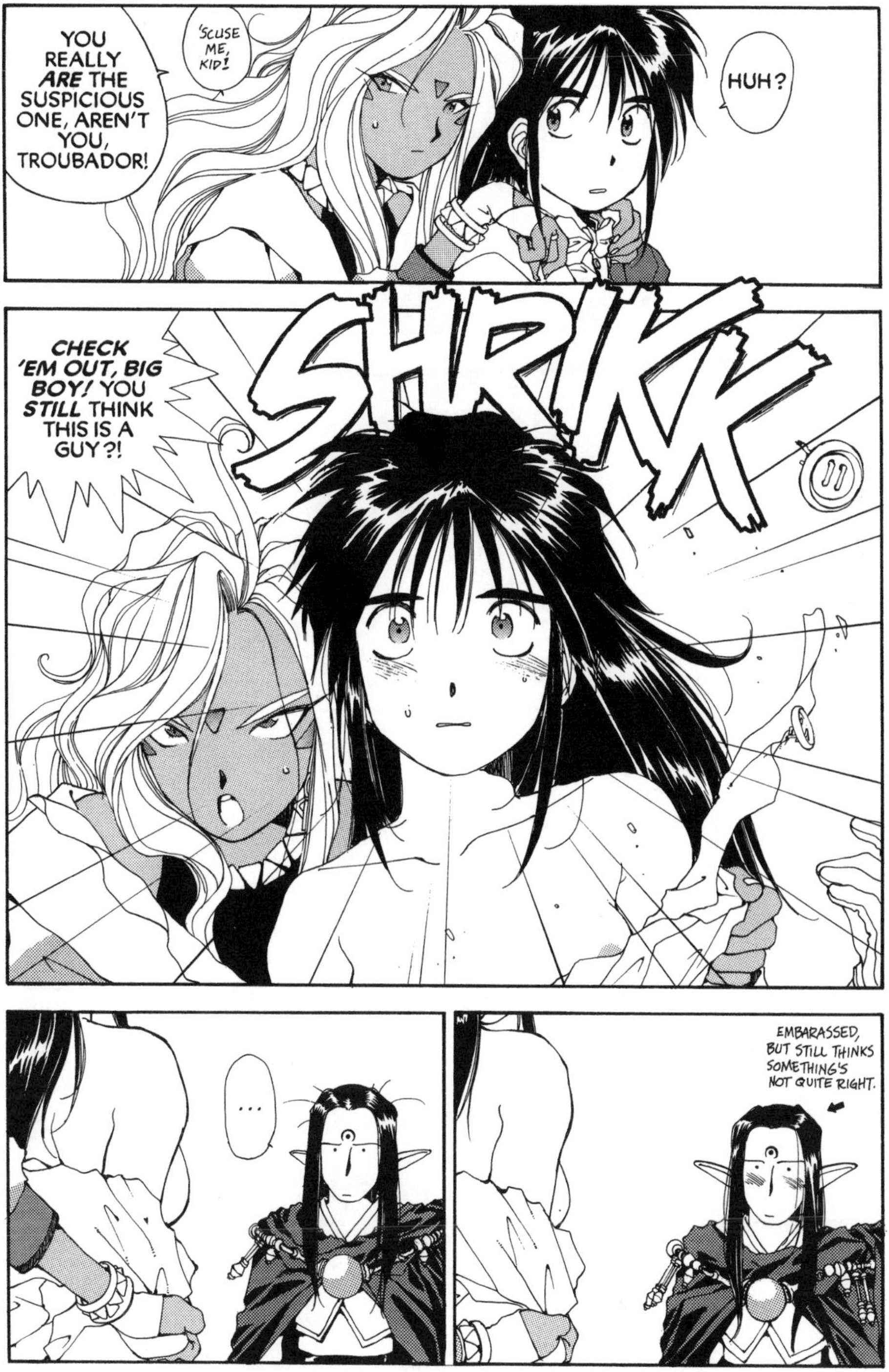
YOU REALLY ARE THE SUSPICIOUS ONE, AREN'T YOU, TROUBADOR!
'SCUSE ME, KID!
HUH?
SHRIKK
CHECK 'EM OUT, BIG BOY! YOU STILL THINK THIS IS A GUY?!
...
EMBARASSED, BUT STILL THINKS SOMETHING'S NOT QUITE RIGHT.

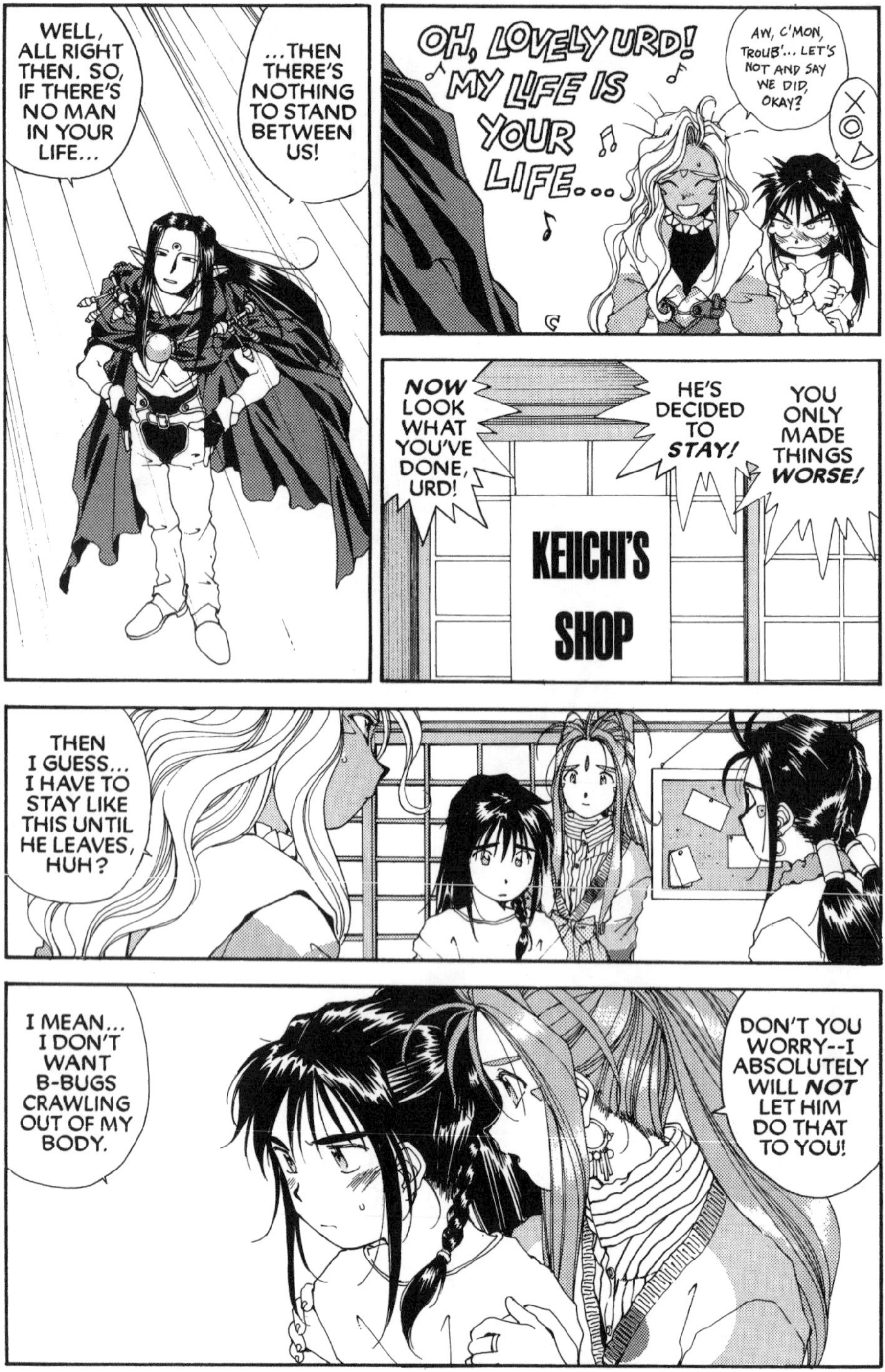
WELL, ALL RIGHT THEN. SO, IF THERE'S NO MAN IN YOUR LIFE...
...THEN THERE'S NOTHING TO STAND BETWEEN US!
OH, LOVELY URD! MY LIFE IS YOUR LIFE...
AW, C'MON, TROUB'... LET'S NOT AND SAY WE DID, OKAY?
NOW LOOK WHAT YOU'VE DONE, URD!
HE'S DECIDED TO STAY!
YOU ONLY MADE THINGS WORSE!
KEIICHI'S SHOP
THEN I GUESS... I HAVE TO STAY LIKE THIS UNTIL HE LEAVES, HUH?
I MEAN... I DON'T WANT B-BUGS CRAWLING OUT OF MY BODY.
DON'T YOU WORRY--I ABSOLUTELY WILL NOT LET HIM DO THAT TO YOU!

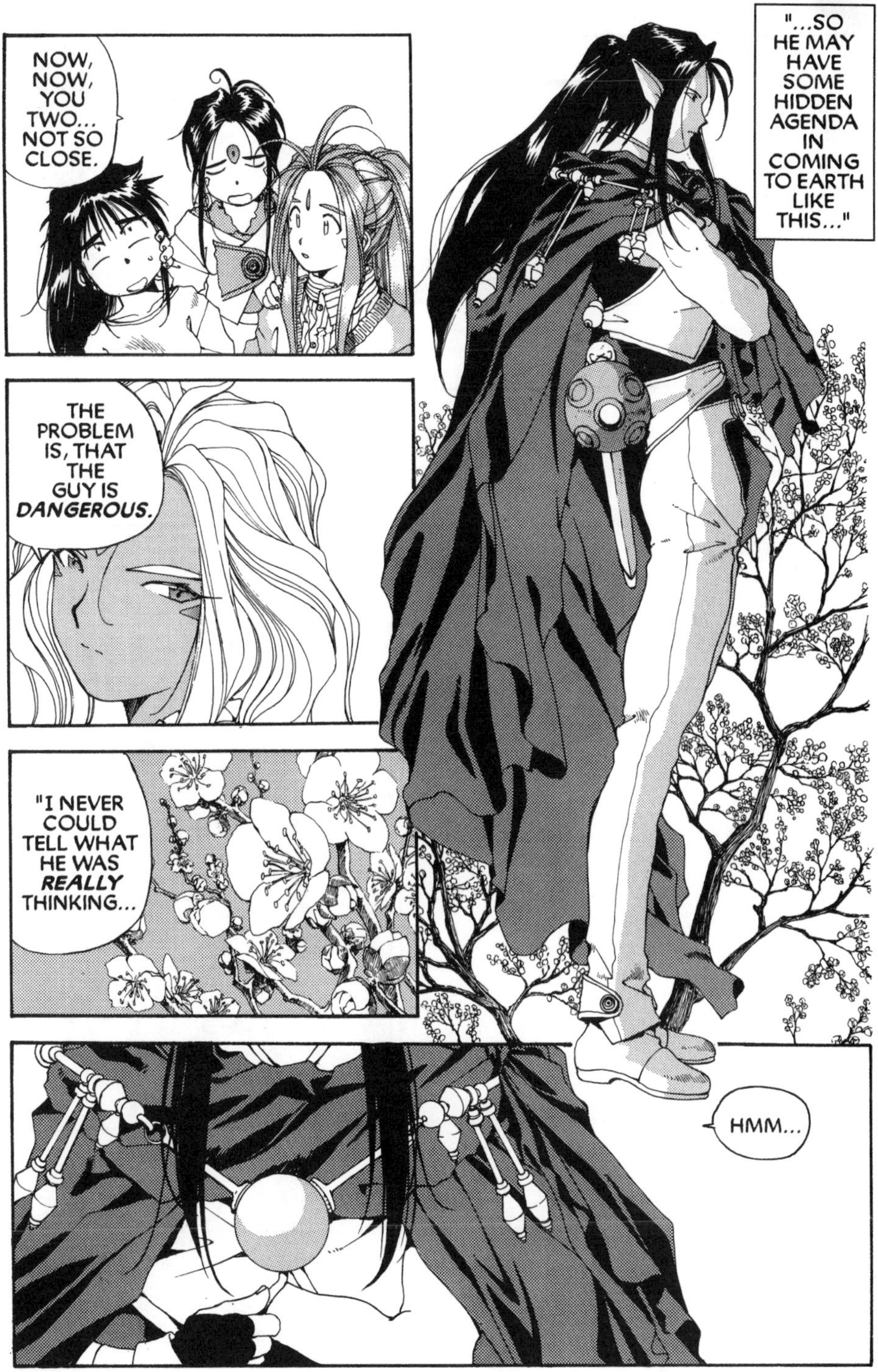
NOW, NOW, YOU TWO... NOT SO CLOSE.
THE PROBLEM IS, THAT THE GUY IS *DANGEROUS.*
"I NEVER COULD TELL WHAT HE WAS *REALLY* THINKING...
"...SO HE MAY HAVE SOME HIDDEN AGENDA IN COMING TO EARTH LIKE THIS..."
HMM...

THE SONG TO SUMMON THE MELODIOUS NIGHTINGALE! THE SCROLL OF GOLDEN VERSE!

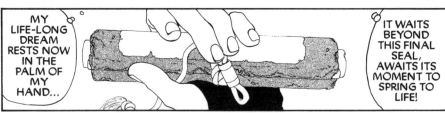

MY LIFE-LONG DREAM RESTS NOW IN THE PALM OF MY HAND...

IT WAITS BEYOND THIS FINAL SEAL, AWAITS ITS MOMENT TO SPRING TO LIFE!

WAITING TO AWAKE...

...WHEN TOUCHED BY *A GODDESS'S TEARS OF LOVE!*

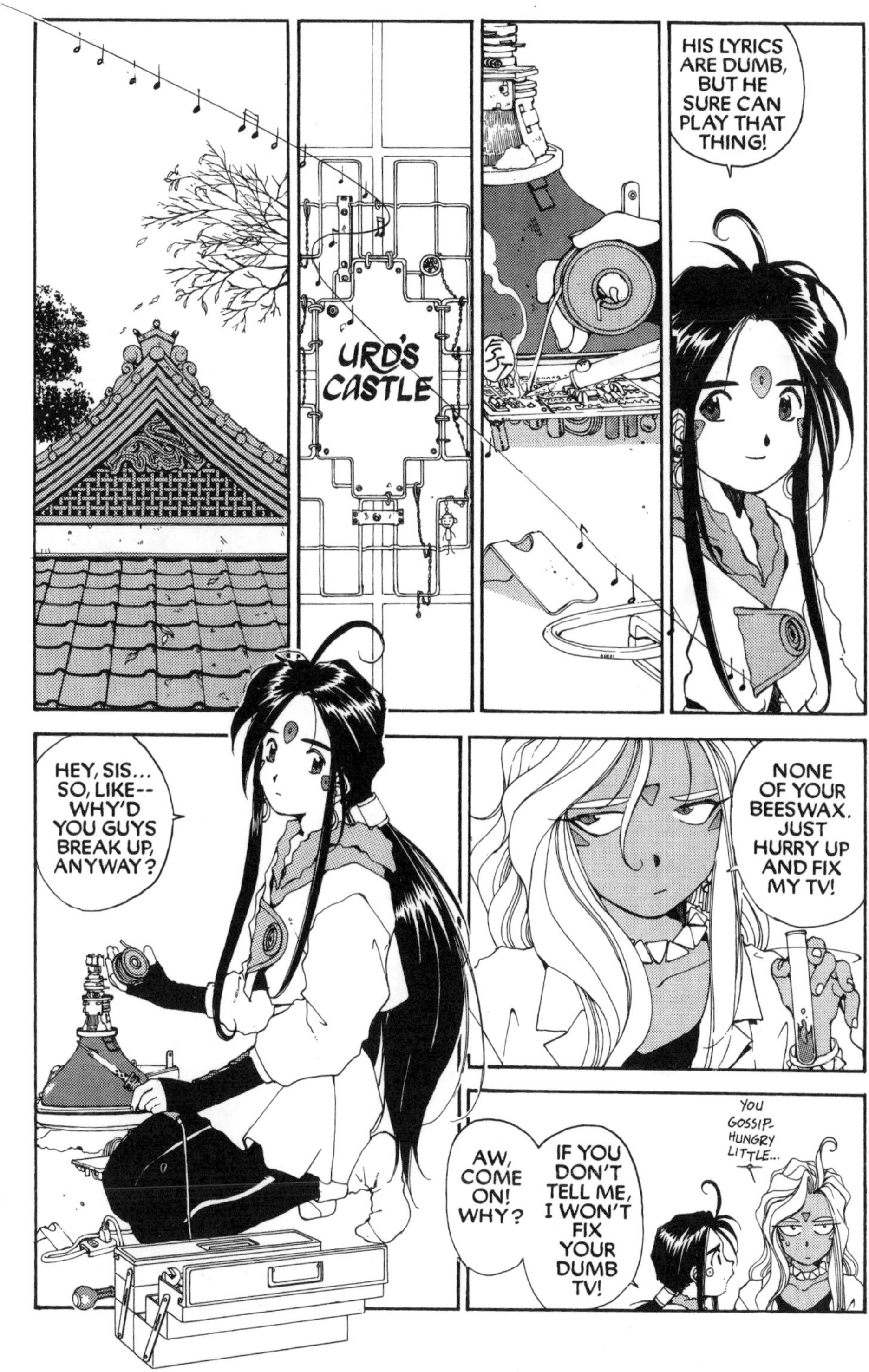
URD'S CASTLE
HIS LYRICS ARE DUMB, BUT HE SURE CAN PLAY THAT THING!
HEY, SIS... SO, LIKE-- WHY'D YOU GUYS BREAK UP, ANYWAY?
NONE OF YOUR BEESWAX. JUST HURRY UP AND FIX MY TV!
AW, COME ON! WHY?
IF YOU DON'T TELL ME, I WON'T FIX YOUR DUMB TV!
YOU GOSSIP-HUNGRY LITTLE...

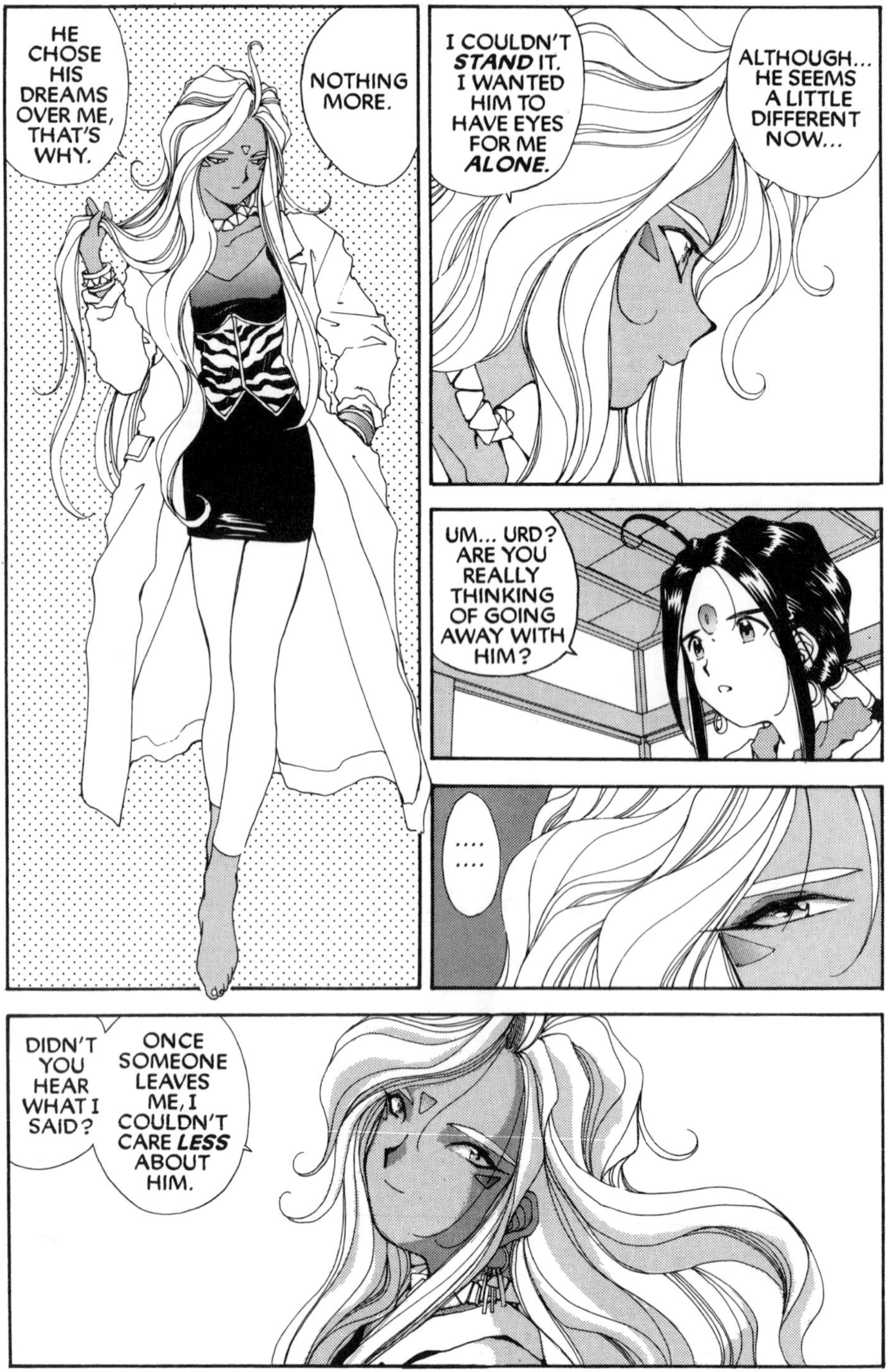
HE CHOSE HIS DREAMS OVER ME, THAT'S WHY.
NOTHING MORE.
I COULDN'T *STAND* IT. I WANTED HIM TO HAVE EYES FOR ME *ALONE*.
ALTHOUGH... HE SEEMS A LITTLE DIFFERENT NOW...
UM... URD? ARE YOU REALLY THINKING OF GOING AWAY WITH HIM?
....
....
DIDN'T YOU HEAR WHAT I SAID?
ONCE SOMEONE LEAVES ME, I COULDN'T CARE *LESS* ABOUT HIM.

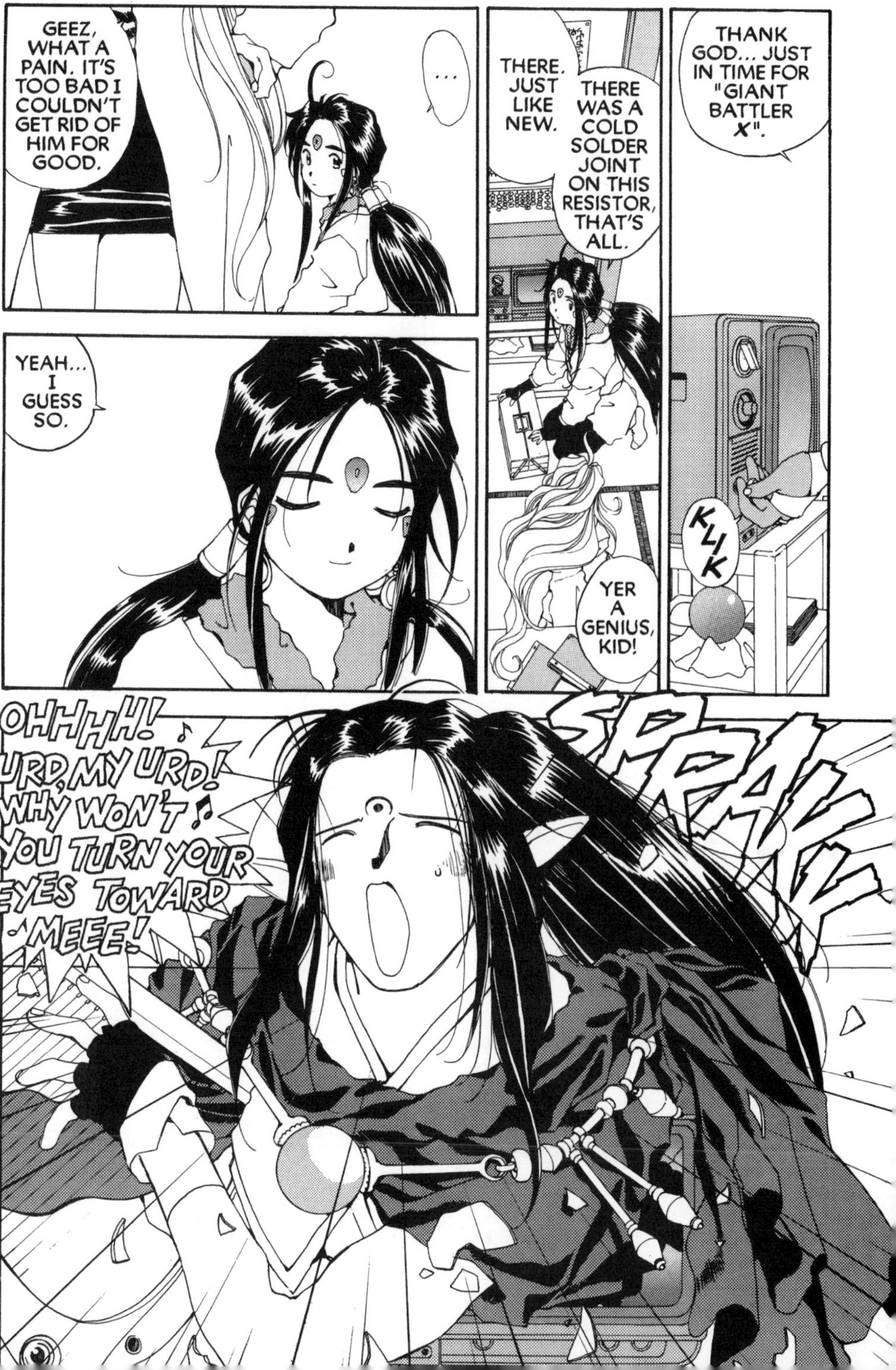
GEEZ, WHAT A PAIN. IT'S TOO BAD I COULDN'T GET RID OF HIM FOR GOOD.
...
YEAH... I GUESS SO.
THERE. JUST LIKE NEW.
THERE WAS A COLD SOLDER JOINT ON THIS RESISTOR, THAT'S ALL.
YER A GENIUS, KID!
THANK GOD... JUST IN TIME FOR "GIANT BATTLER X".
KLIK
OHHHH! URD, MY URD! WHY WON'T YOU TURN YOUR EYES TOWARD MEEE!
SPRAW

TWA NGG

OHHHH!

UH... OH?

HO HO HO. THANK YOU FOR THE LOVELY SONG.

FZZKK

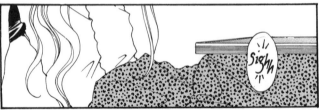

AND I JUST FIXED IT...

NOW I'M GONNA MISS MY FAVORITE TV SHOW!

TWA NGG

FORGIVE ME, FOR LOVE IS MYYYY ONLY CRIME!

DON'T TRY TO SING YOUR WAY OUT OF IT!

SIGHH

WHAT'S WRONG, URD?

NOTHING...

...JUST TROUBADOUR.

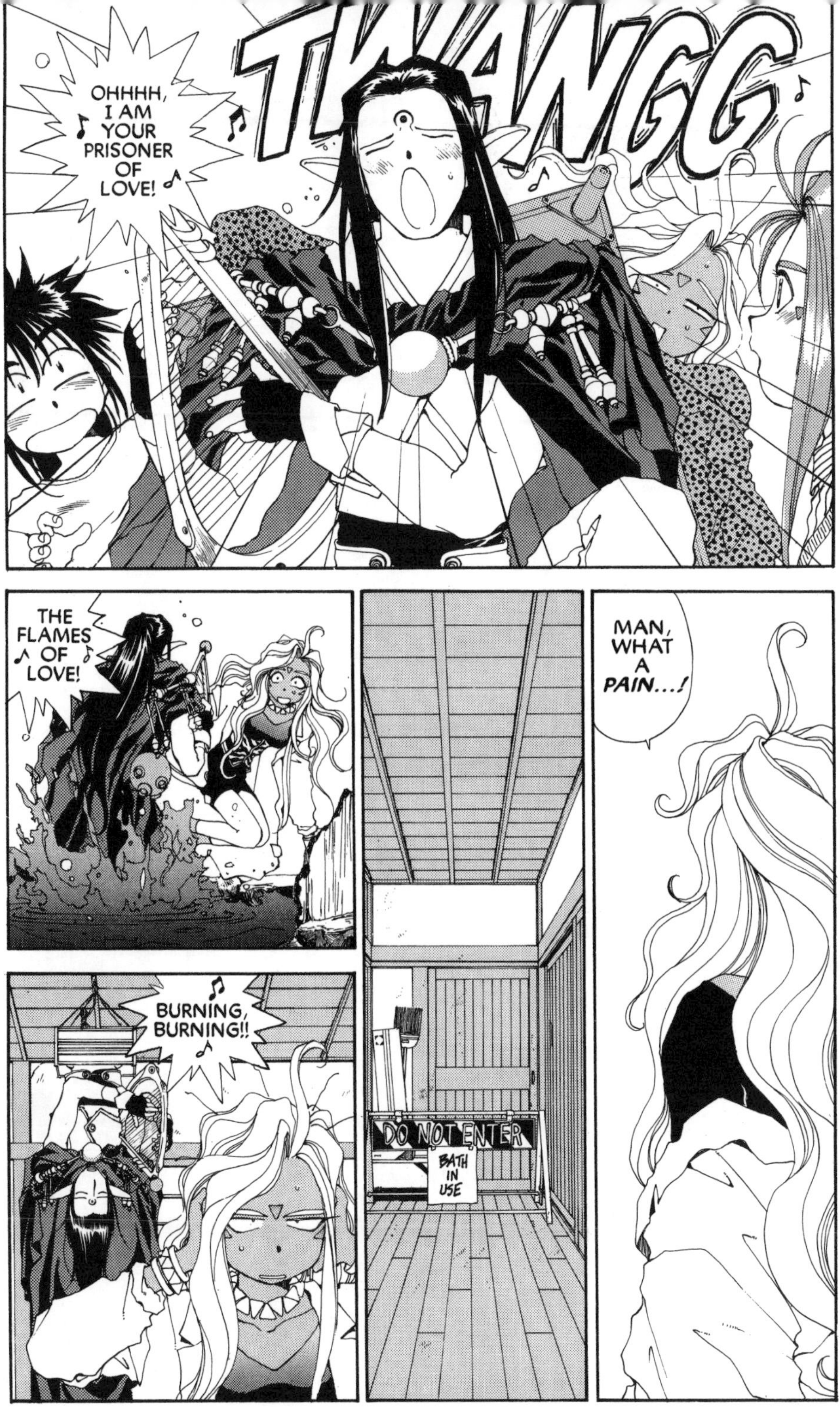
OHHHH, I AM YOUR PRISONER OF LOVE!
TWANGG
THE FLAMES OF LOVE!
BURNING, BURNING!!
DO NOT ENTER
BATH IN USE
MAN, WHAT A *PAIN...!*

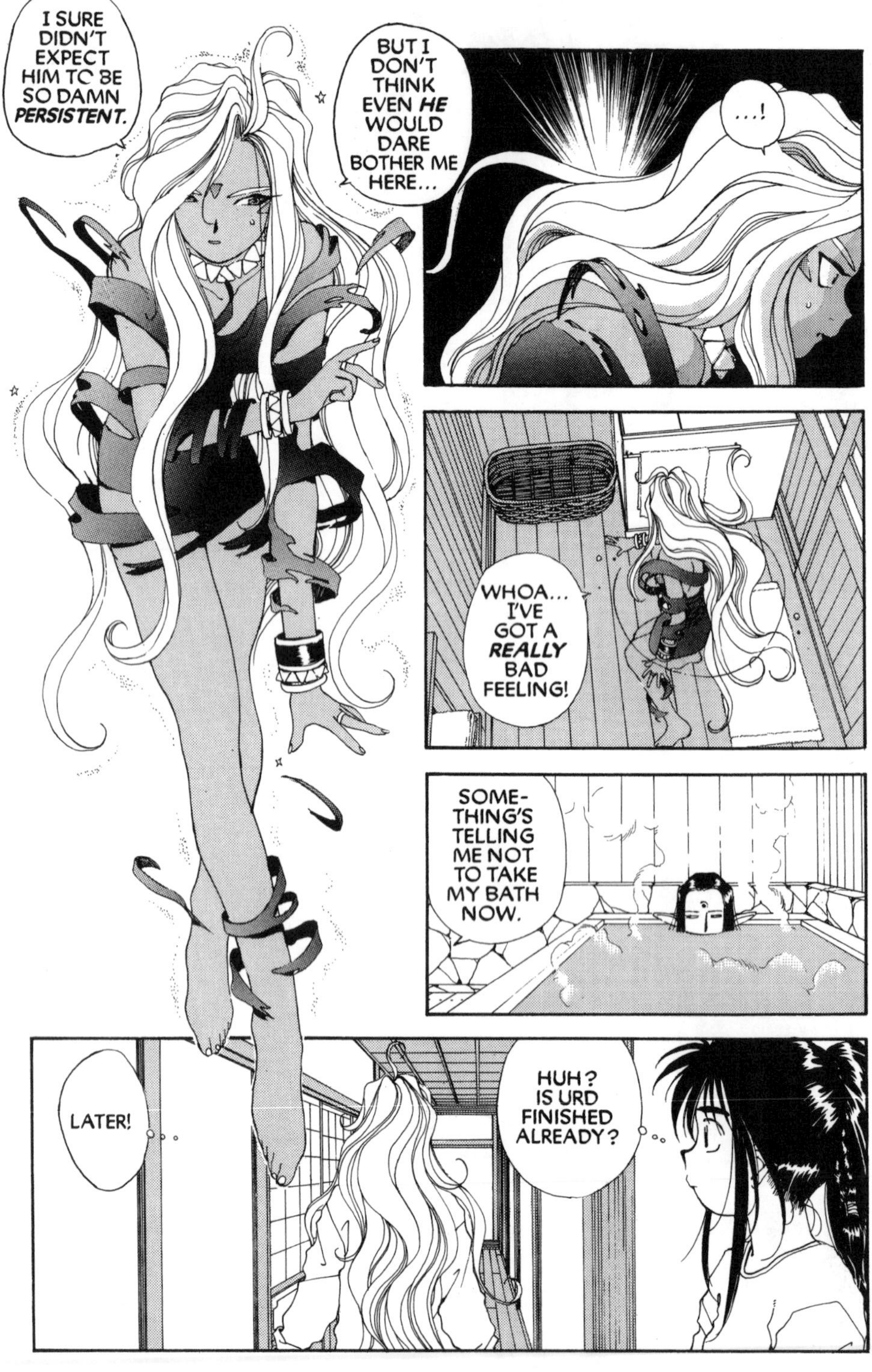
I SURE DIDN'T EXPECT HIM TO BE SO DAMN PERSISTENT.
BUT I DON'T THINK EVEN HE WOULD DARE BOTHER ME HERE...
...!
WHOA... I'VE GOT A REALLY BAD FEELING!
SOME-THING'S TELLING ME NOT TO TAKE MY BATH NOW.
LATER!
HUH? IS URD FINISHED ALREADY?

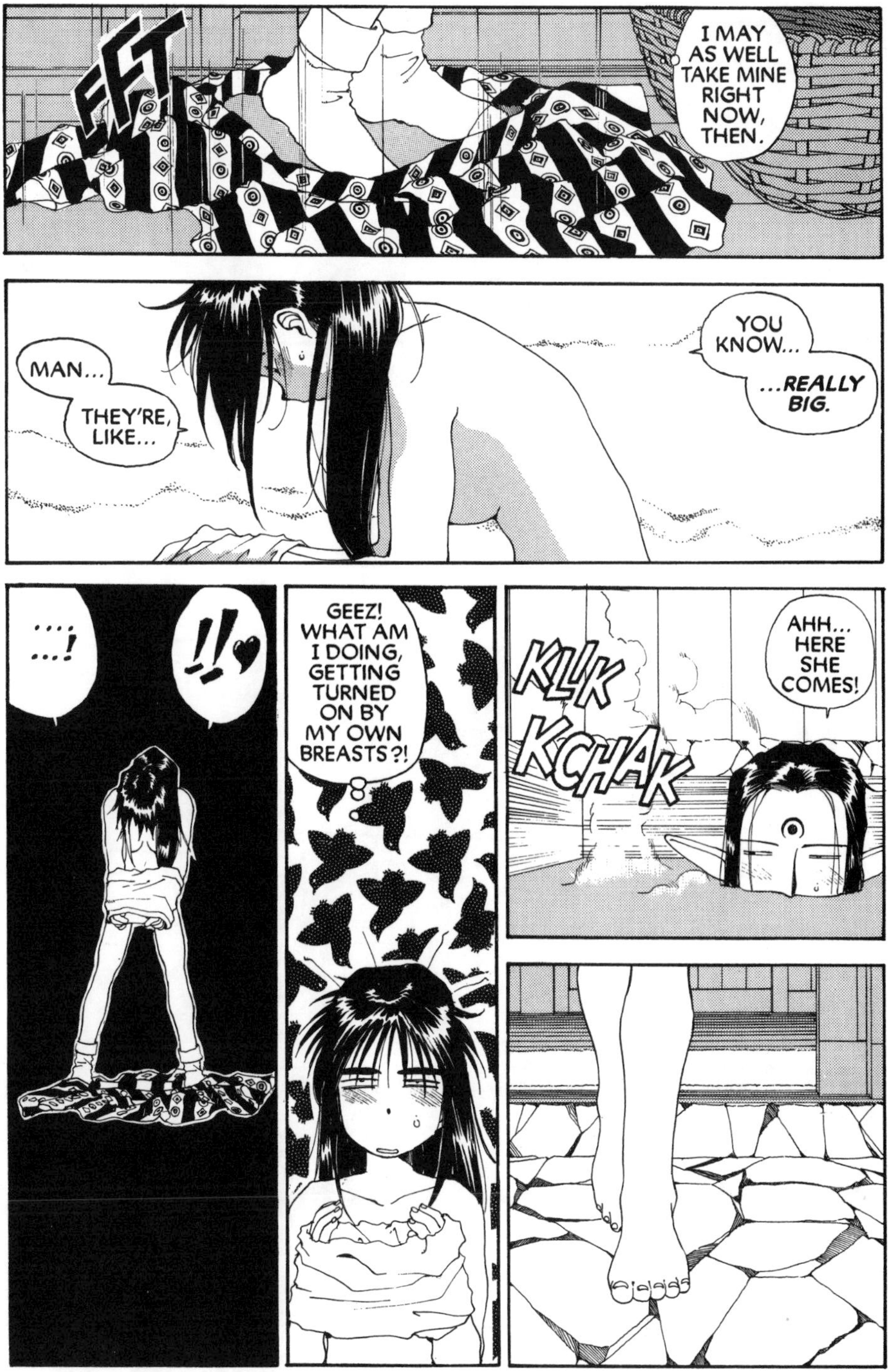
EFFT
I MAY AS WELL TAKE MINE RIGHT NOW, THEN.
MAN...
THEY'RE, LIKE...
YOU KNOW...
...REALLY BIG.
...; ...!
!!♥
GEEZ! WHAT AM I DOING, GETTING TURNED ON BY MY OWN BREASTS?!
KLIK
KCHAK
AHH... HERE SHE COMES!

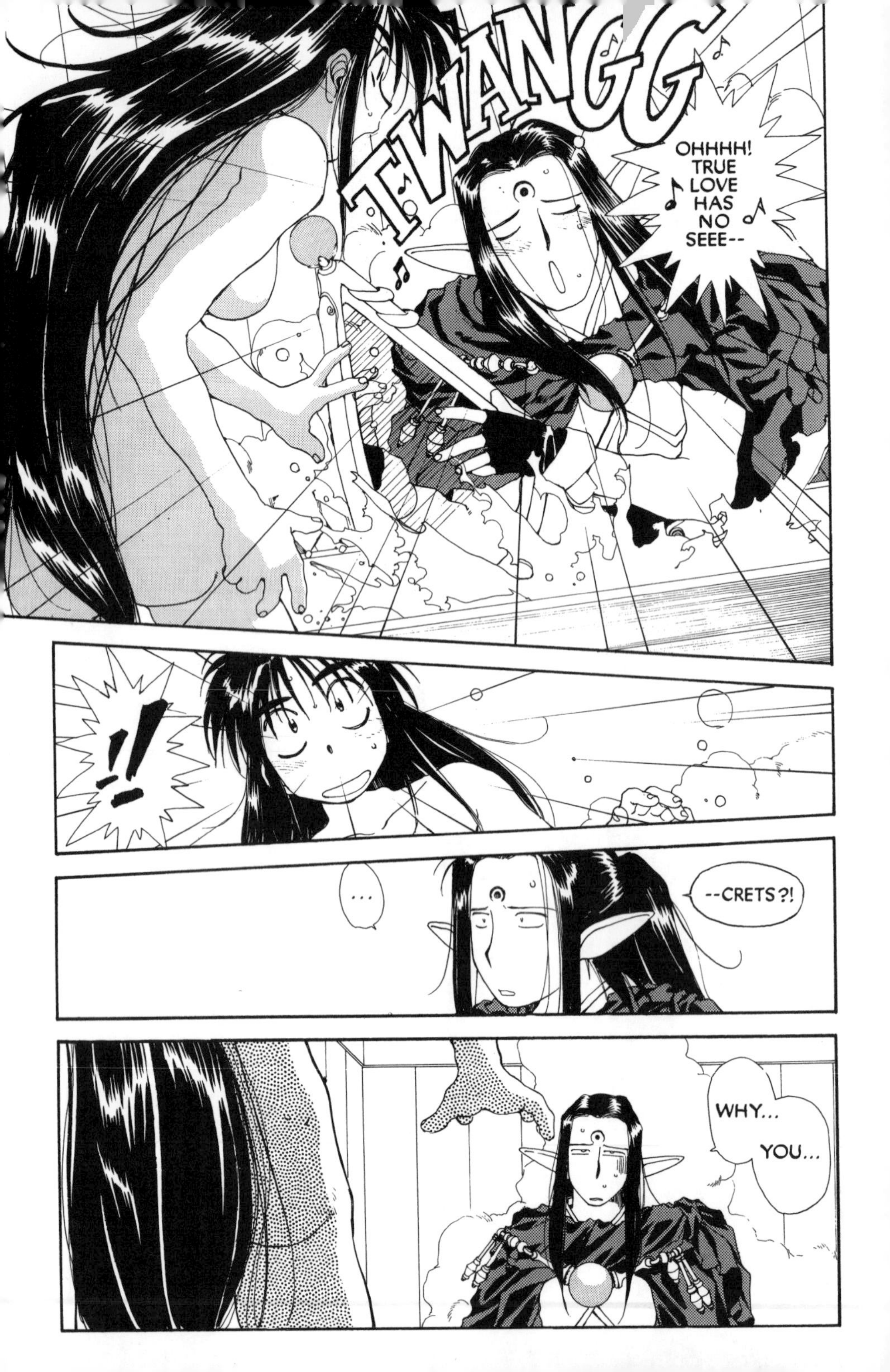
TWANGG
OHHHH! TRUE LOVE HAS NO SEEE--
!!
...
--CRETS?!
WHY... YOU...

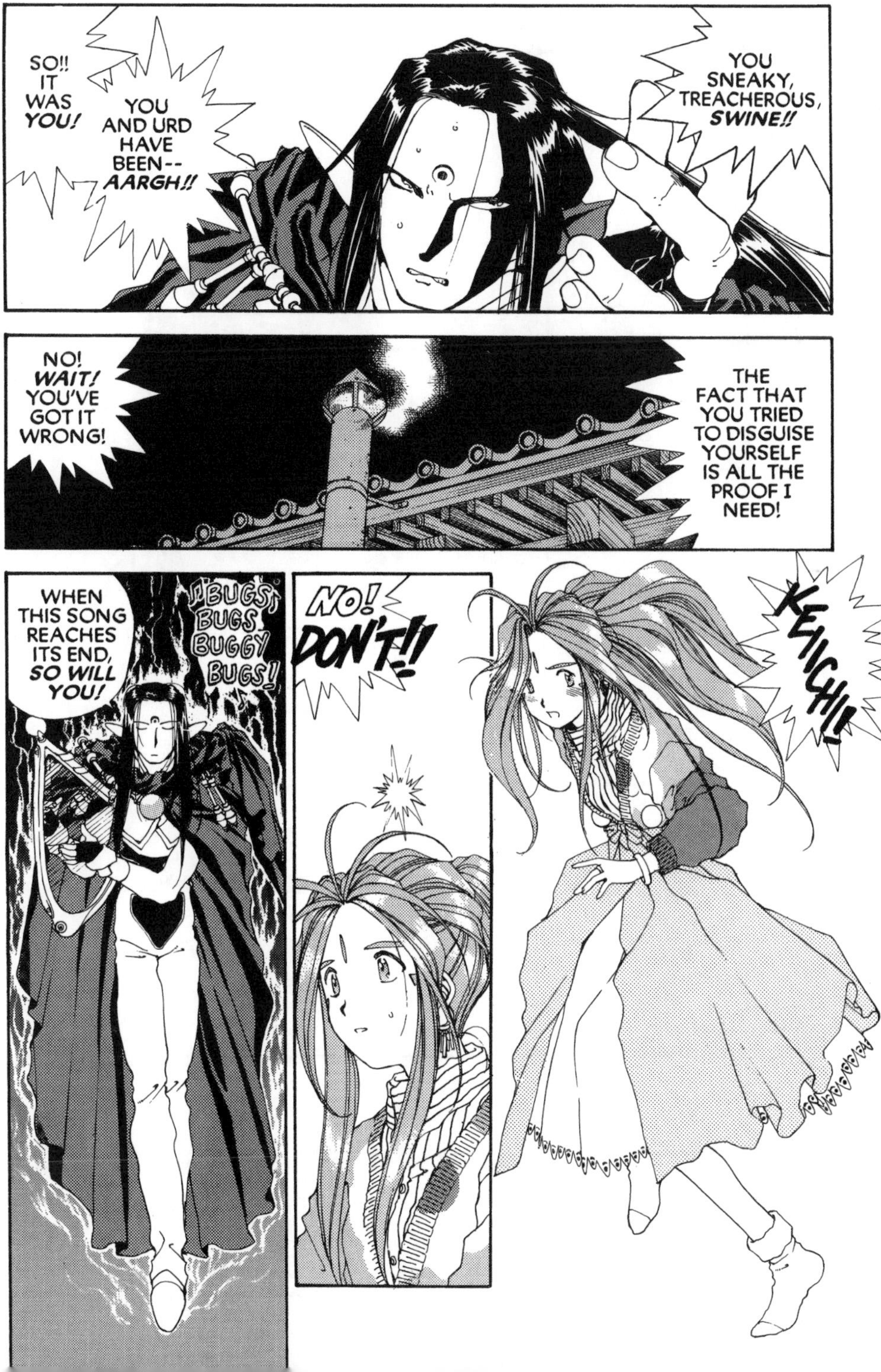
SO!! IT WAS YOU!
YOU AND URD HAVE BEEN-- AARGH!!
YOU SNEAKY, TREACHEROUS, SWINE!!
NO! WAIT! YOU'VE GOT IT WRONG!
THE FACT THAT YOU TRIED TO DISGUISE YOURSELF IS ALL THE PROOF I NEED!
WHEN THIS SONG REACHES ITS END, SO WILL YOU!
BUGS BUGS BUGGY BUGS!
NO! DON'T!!
KEIICHI!!

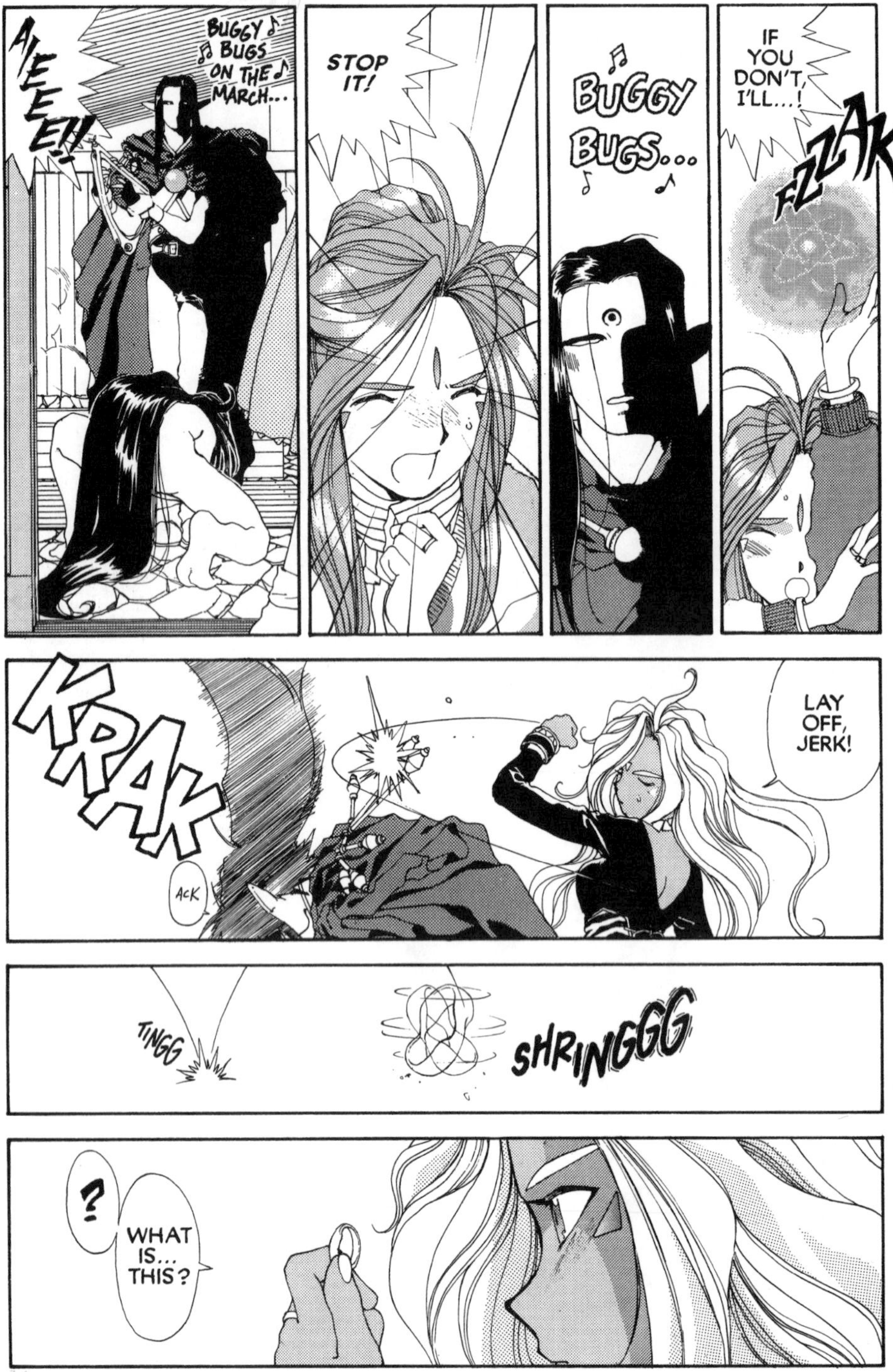
AIEEEE!!
BUGGY ♪ ♫ BUGS ON THE ♪ MARCH...
STOP IT!
♫ BUGGY BUGS... ♪ ♪
IF YOU DON'T, I'LL...!
FZZAK
KRAK
ACK
LAY OFF, JERK!
TINGG
SHRINGGG
?
WHAT IS... THIS?

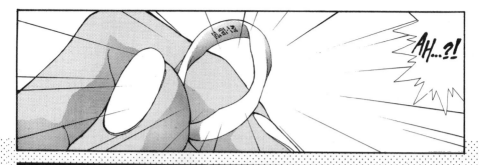

AH...?!

"BACK WHEN WE FIRST STARTED DATING...

"THE TWO OF US...

"...EXCHANGED GIFTS."

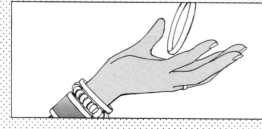

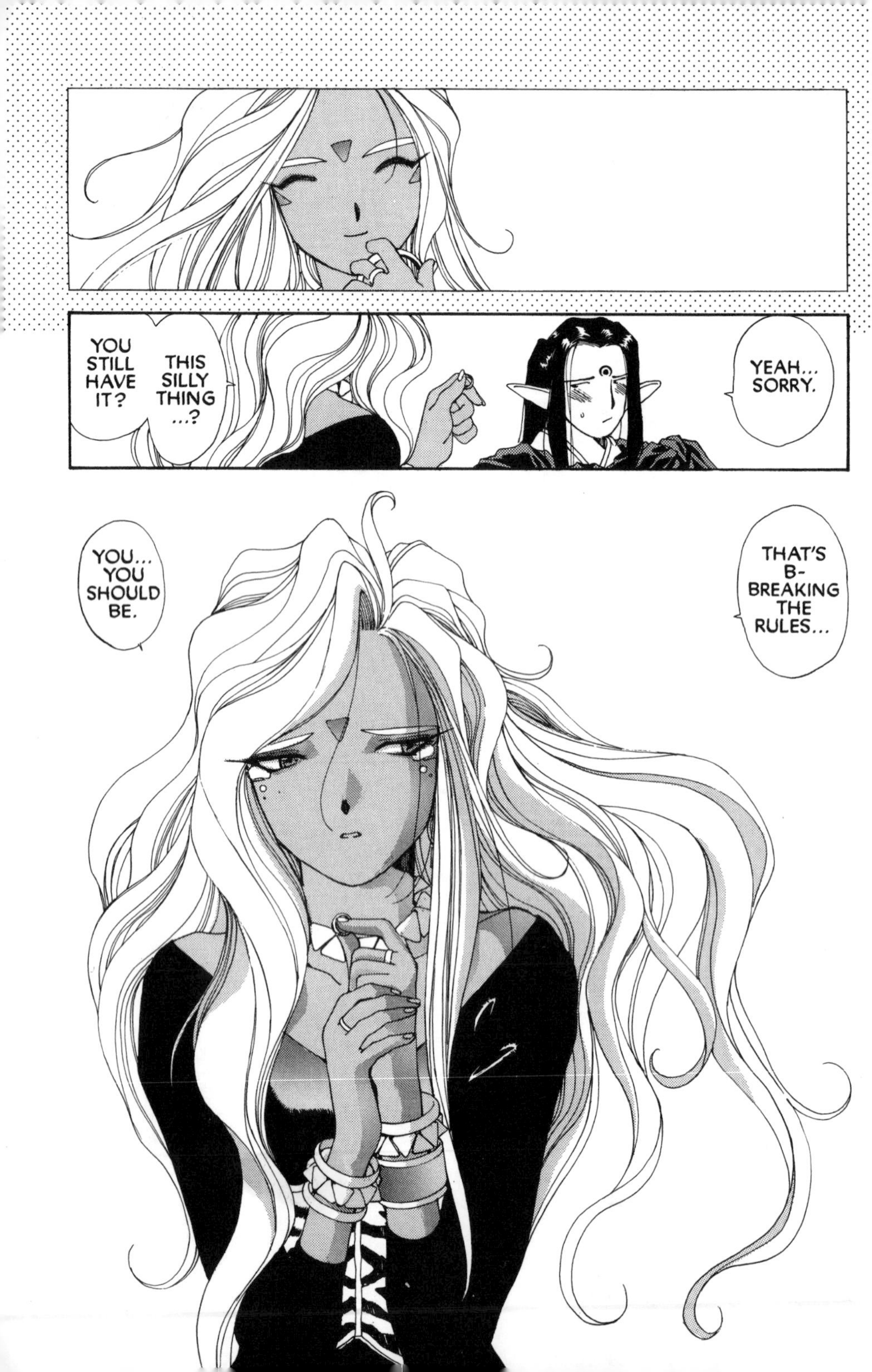
YOU STILL HAVE IT?
THIS SILLY THING ...?
YEAH... SORRY.
YOU... YOU SHOULD BE.
THAT'S B-BREAKING THE RULES...

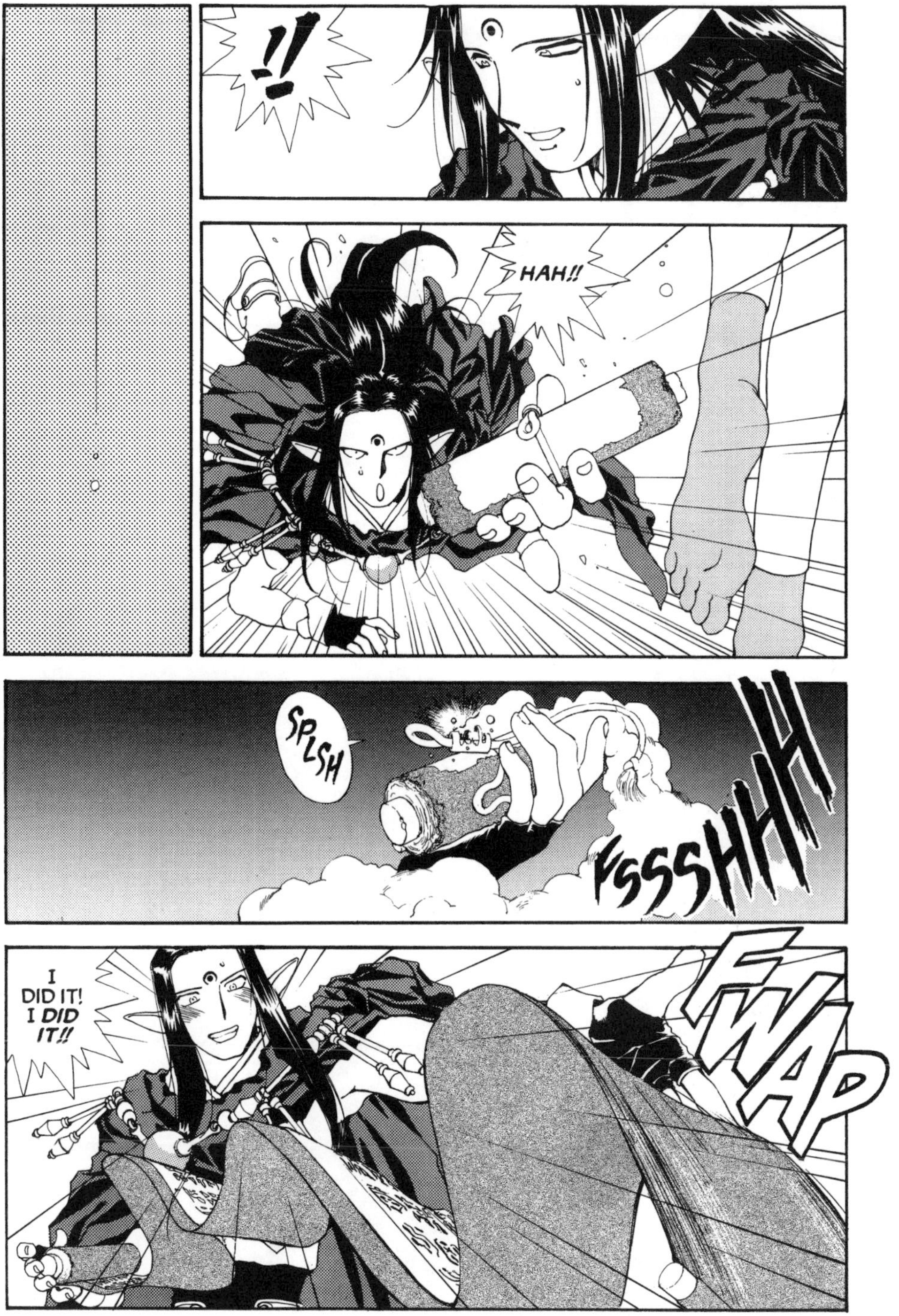
!!
HAH!!
SPLSH
FSSSHHH
I DID IT! I *DID* IT!!
FWAP

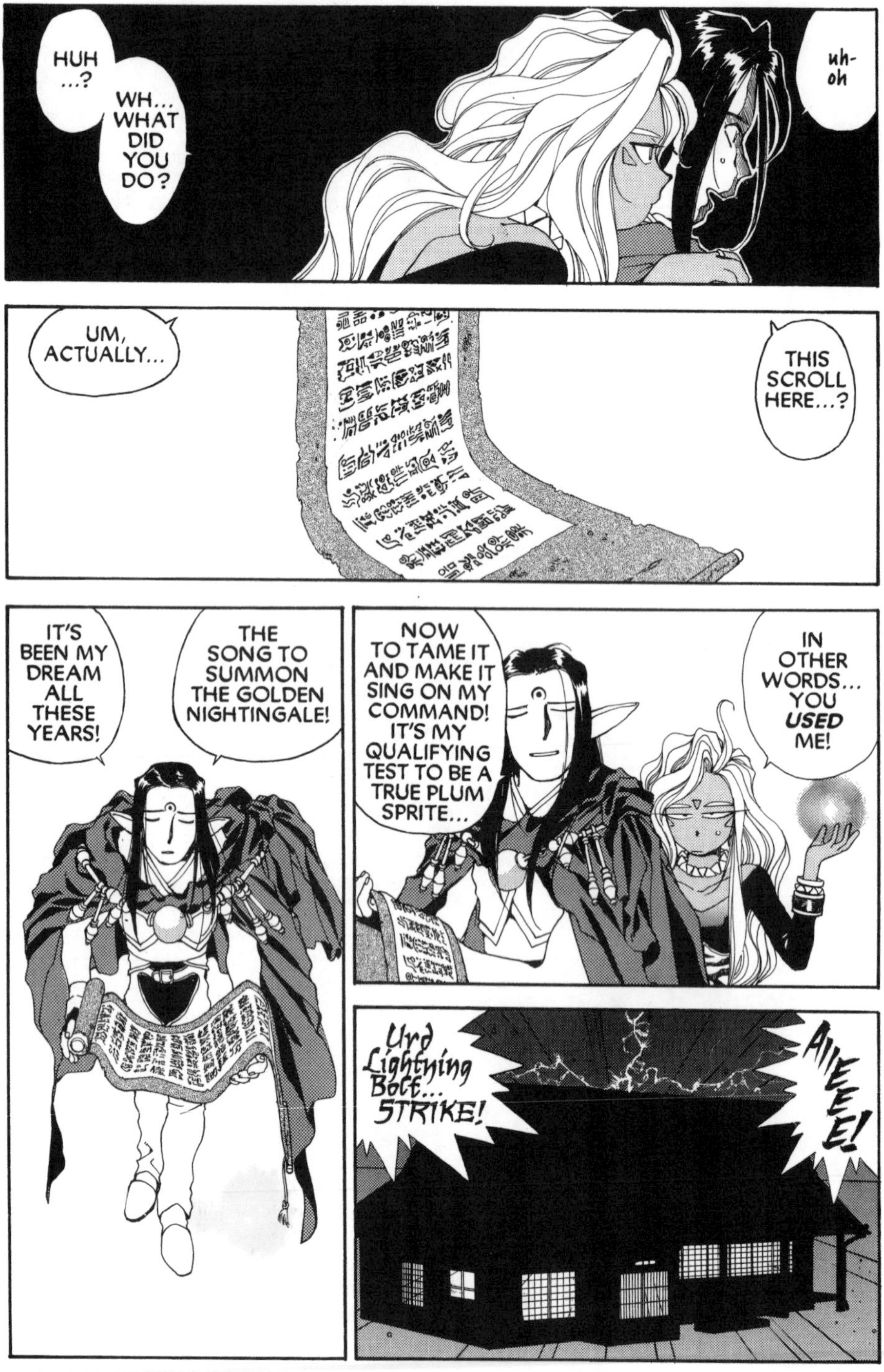
HUH ...?
WH... WHAT DID YOU DO?
uh-oh
UM, ACTUALLY...
THIS SCROLL HERE...?
IT'S BEEN MY DREAM ALL THESE YEARS!
THE SONG TO SUMMON THE GOLDEN NIGHTINGALE!
NOW TO TAME IT AND MAKE IT SING ON MY COMMAND! IT'S MY QUALIFYING TEST TO BE A TRUE PLUM SPRITE...
IN OTHER WORDS... YOU *USED* ME!
Urd Lightning Bolt... STRIKE!
AIEEEE!

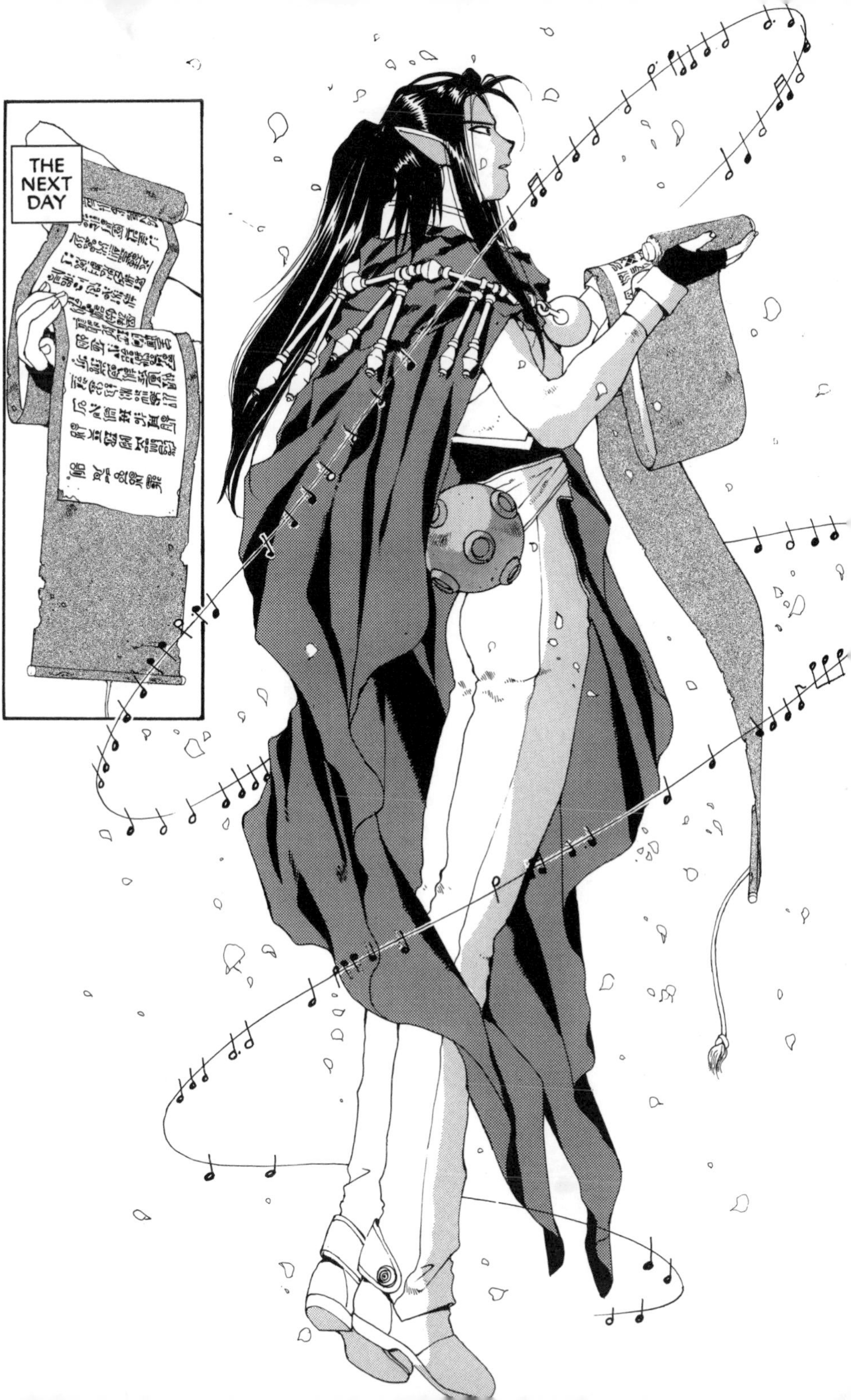
THE NEXT DAY

GOODNESS! SUCH A *BEAUTIFUL* SONG!

IT'S TRUE.

I GUESS WHEN YOU'RE PURSUING YOUR *TRUE* HEART'S DESIRE, YOU CAN COME UP WITH SOMETHING SPECIAL...

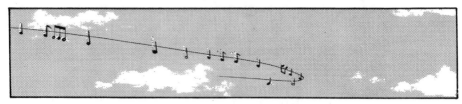

FZZK

FFWHHHSSSHH

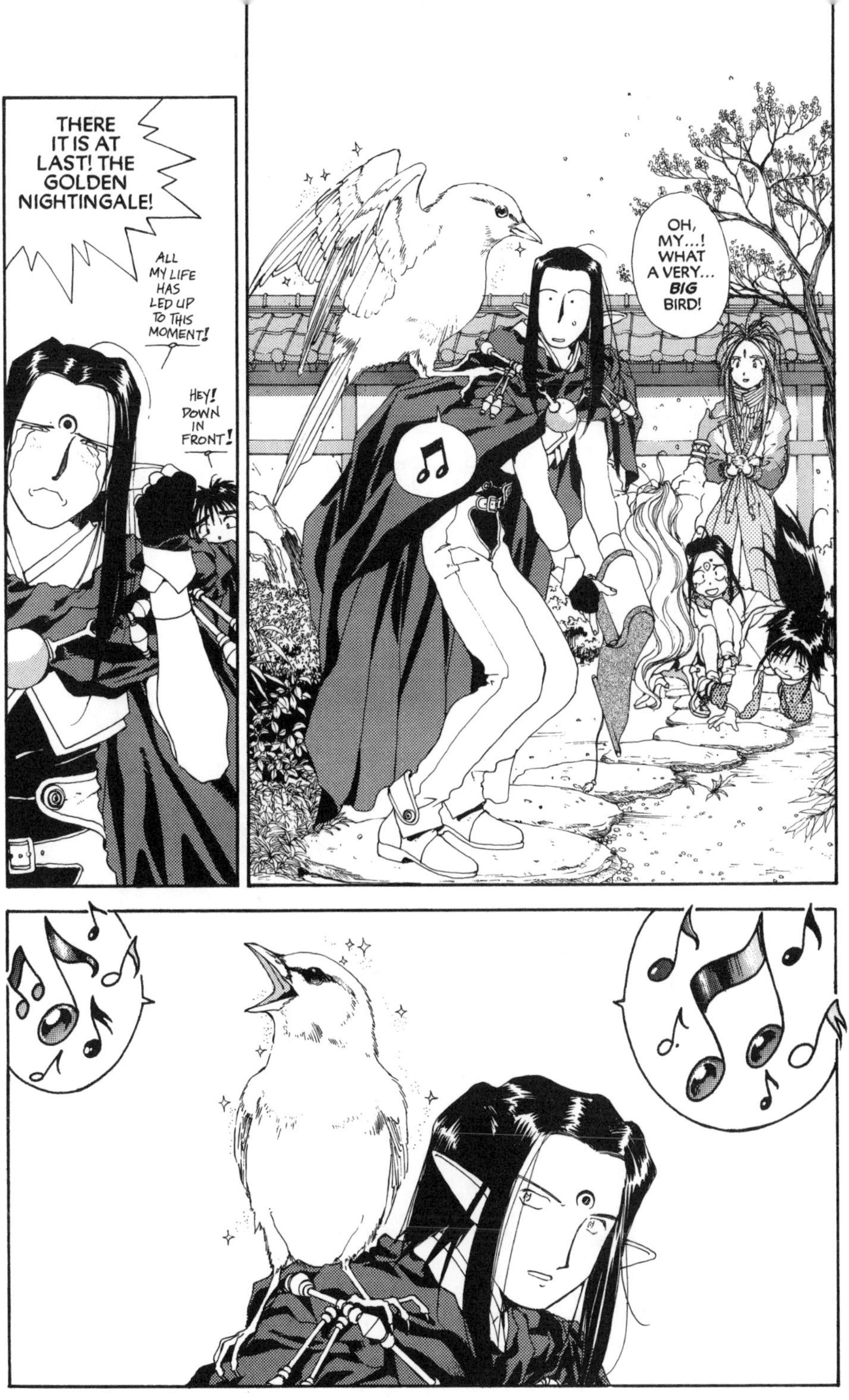
THERE IT IS AT LAST! THE GOLDEN NIGHTINGALE!
ALL MY LIFE HAS LED UP TO THIS MOMENT!
HEY! DOWN IN FRONT!
OH, MY...! WHAT A VERY... BIG BIRD!

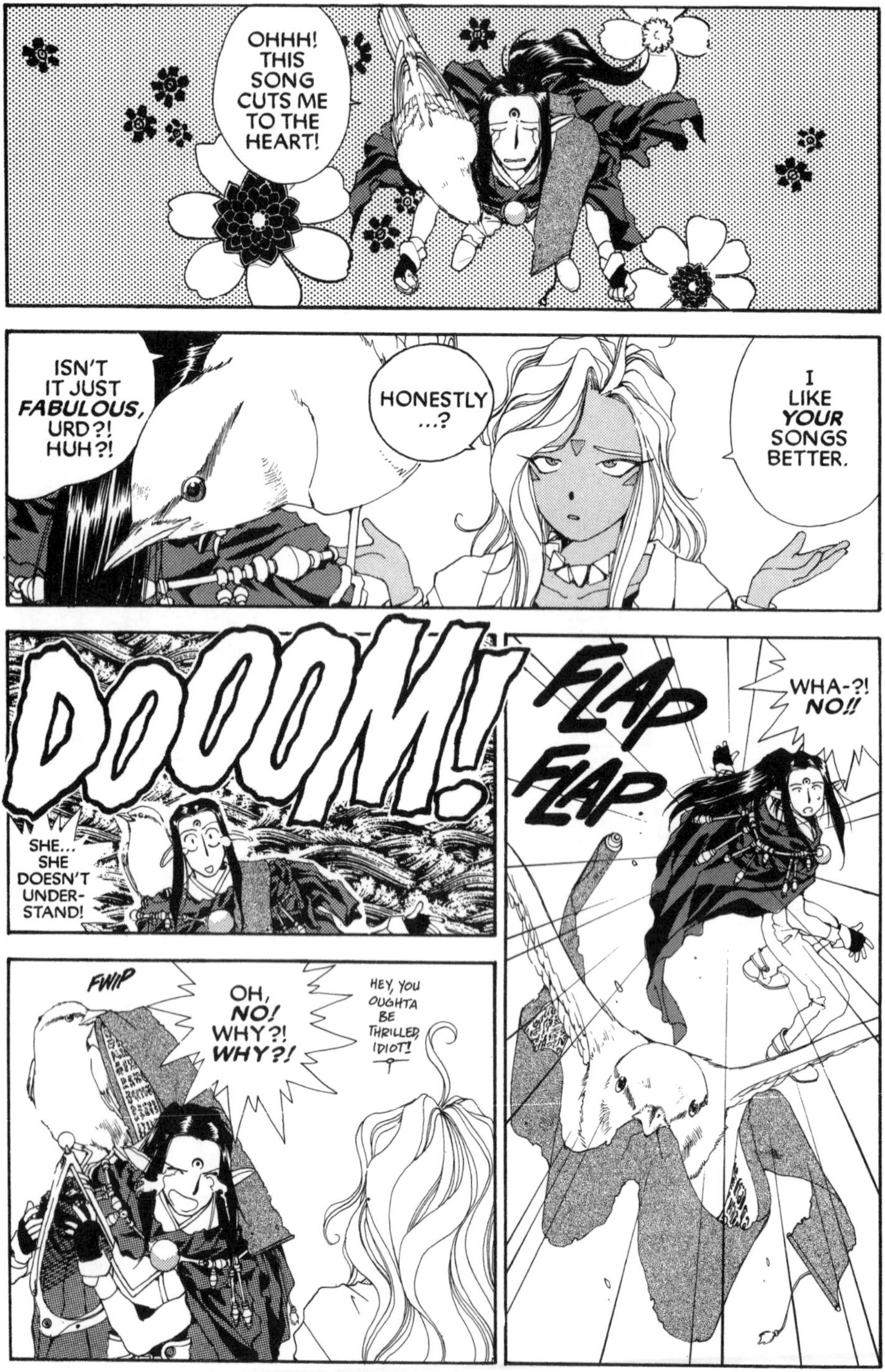
OHHH! THIS SONG CUTS ME TO THE HEART!
ISN'T IT JUST FABULOUS, URD?! HUH?!
HONESTLY ...?
I LIKE YOUR SONGS BETTER.
DOOOM!
SHE... SHE DOESN'T UNDER-STAND!
FWIP
OH, NO! WHY?! WHY?!
HEY, YOU OUGHTA BE THRILLED, IDIOT!
FLAP FLAP
WHA-?! NO!!

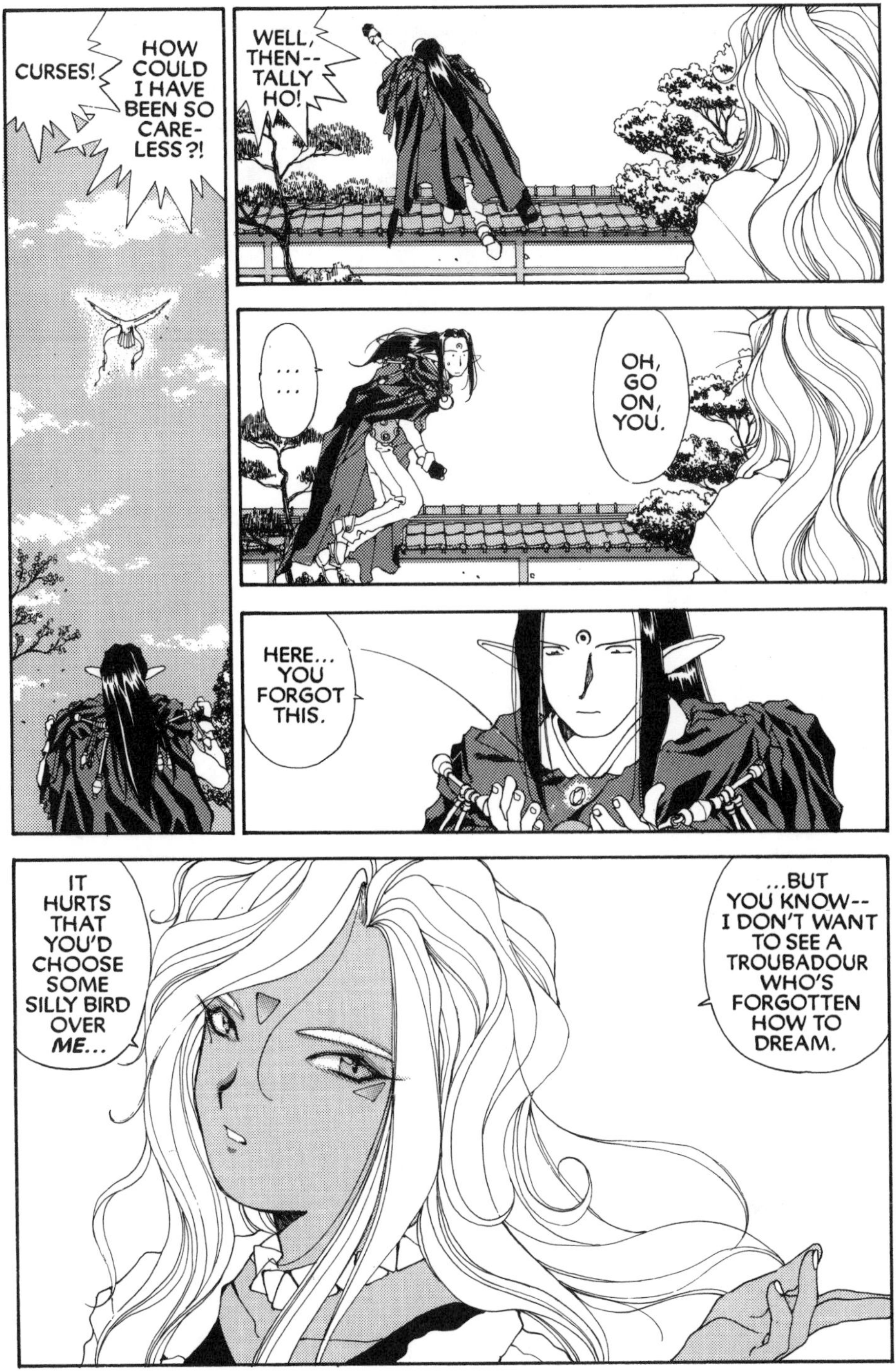
CURSES!
HOW COULD I HAVE BEEN SO CARE-LESS?!
WELL, THEN-- TALLY HO!
....
OH, GO ON, YOU.
HERE... YOU FORGOT THIS.
IT HURTS THAT YOU'D CHOOSE SOME SILLY BIRD OVER *ME*...
...BUT YOU KNOW-- I DON'T WANT TO SEE A TROUBADOUR WHO'S FORGOTTEN HOW TO DREAM.

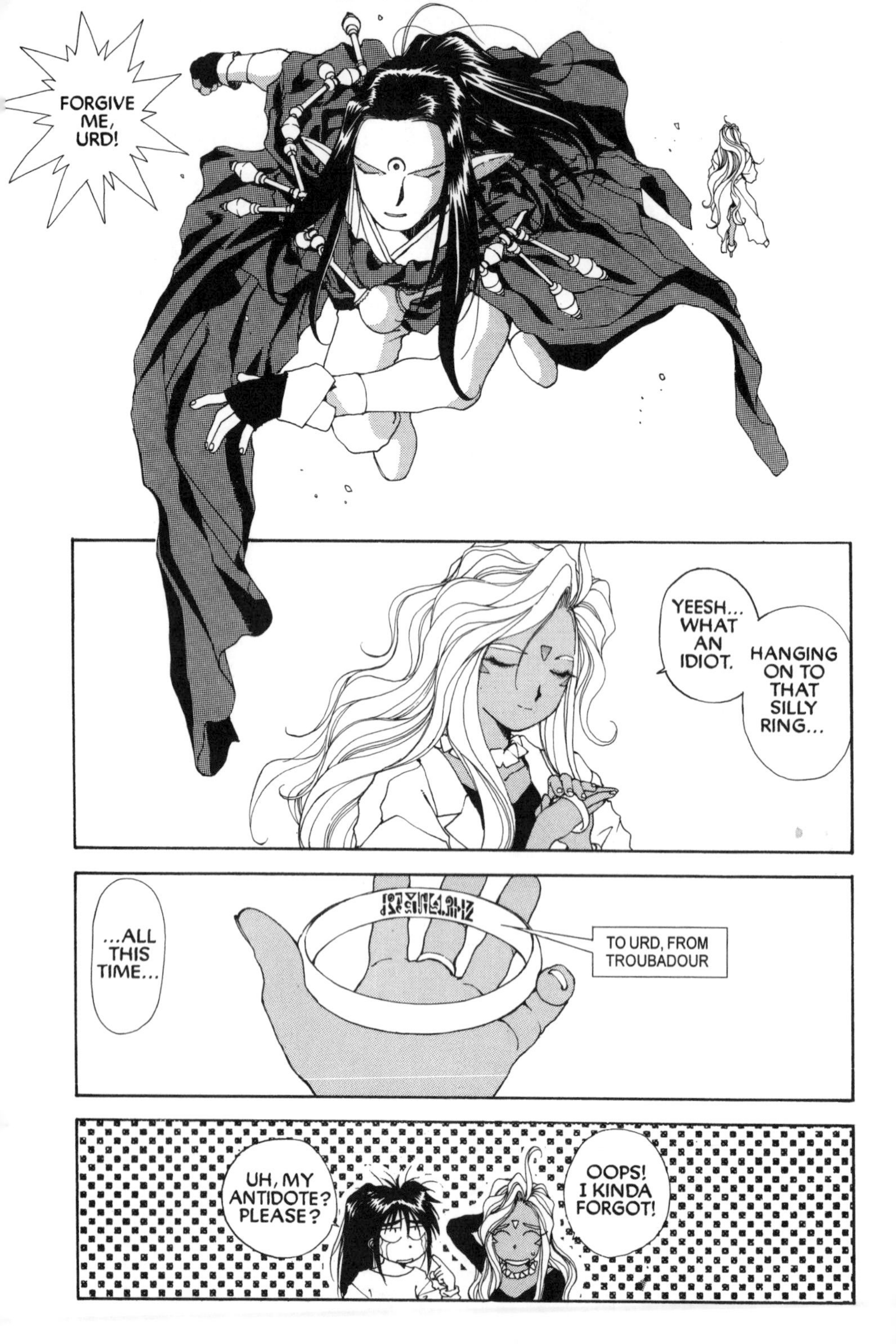
FORGIVE ME, URD!
YEESH... WHAT AN IDIOT.
HANGING ON TO THAT SILLY RING...
...ALL THIS TIME...
TO URD, FROM TROUBADOUR
UH, MY ANTIDOTE? PLEASE?
OOPS! I KINDA FORGOT!

It's Lonely at the Top

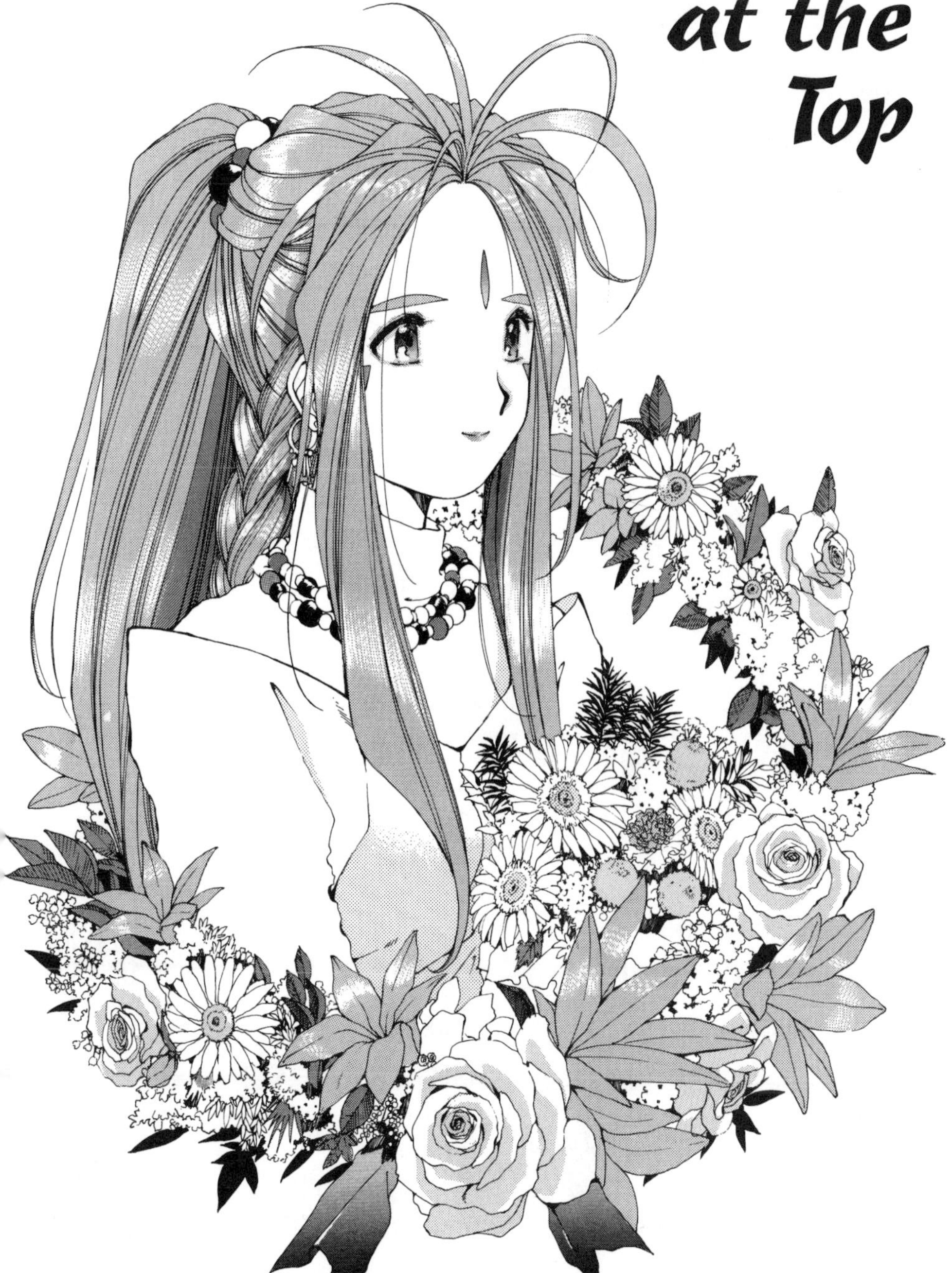

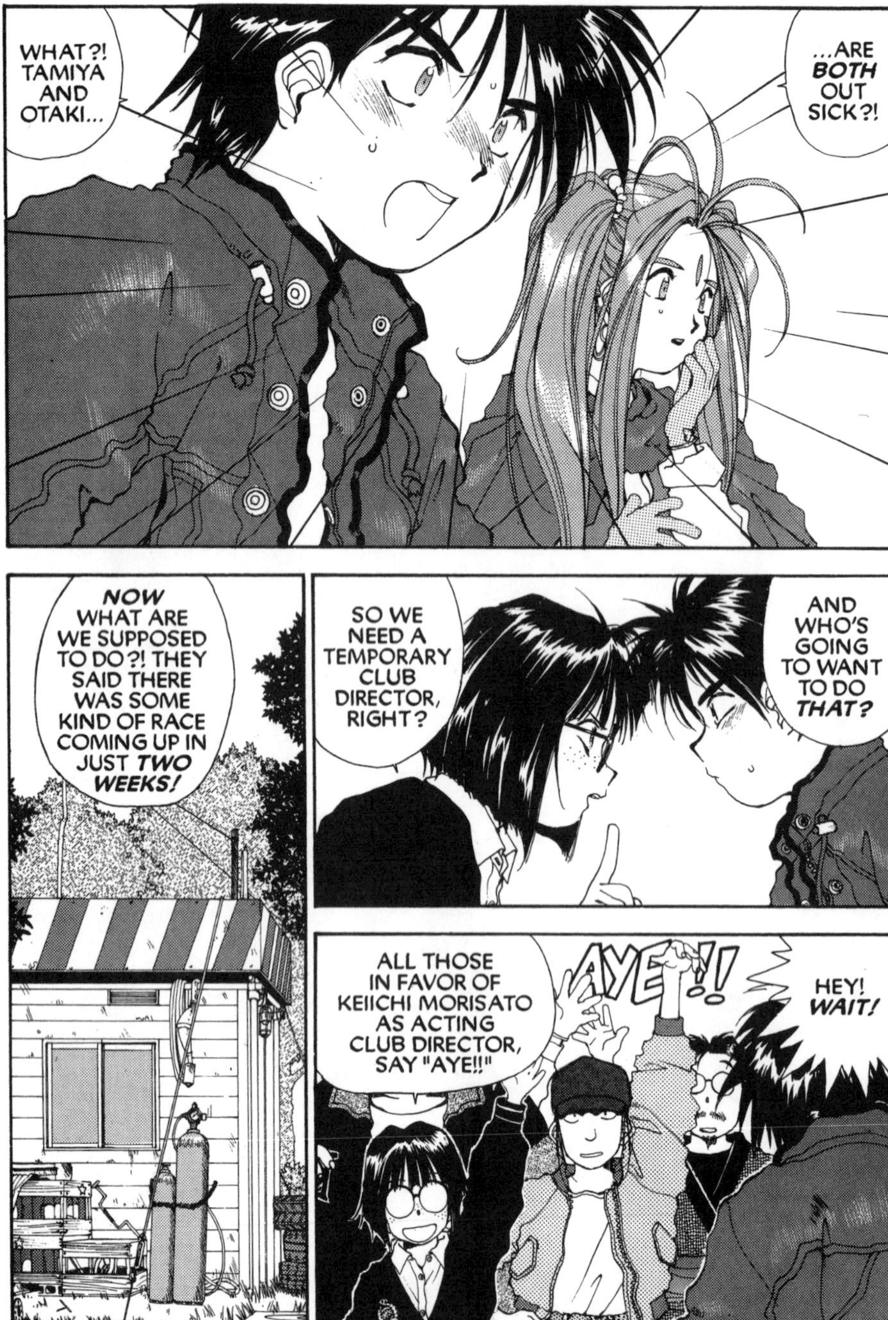
WHAT?! TAMIYA AND OTAKI...
...ARE BOTH OUT SICK?!
NOW WHAT ARE WE SUPPOSED TO DO?! THEY SAID THERE WAS SOME KIND OF RACE COMING UP IN JUST TWO WEEKS!
SO WE NEED A TEMPORARY CLUB DIRECTOR, RIGHT?
AND WHO'S GOING TO WANT TO DO THAT?
ALL THOSE IN FAVOR OF KEIICHI MORISATO AS ACTING CLUB DIRECTOR, SAY "AYE!!"
AYE!!
HEY! WAIT!

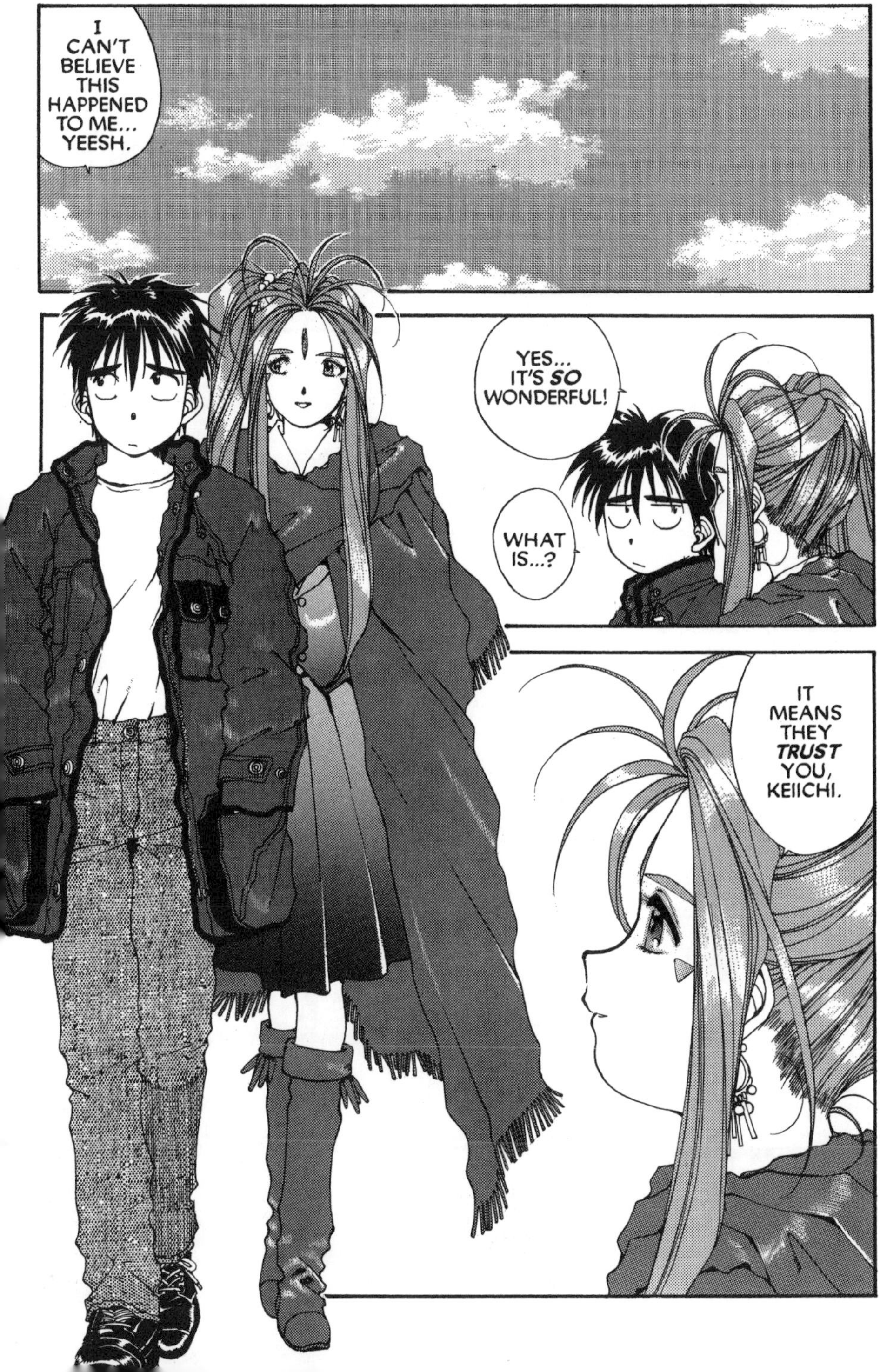
I CAN'T BELIEVE THIS HAPPENED TO ME... YEESH.
YES... IT'S ***SO*** WONDERFUL!
WHAT IS...?
IT MEANS THEY ***TRUST*** YOU, KEIICHI.

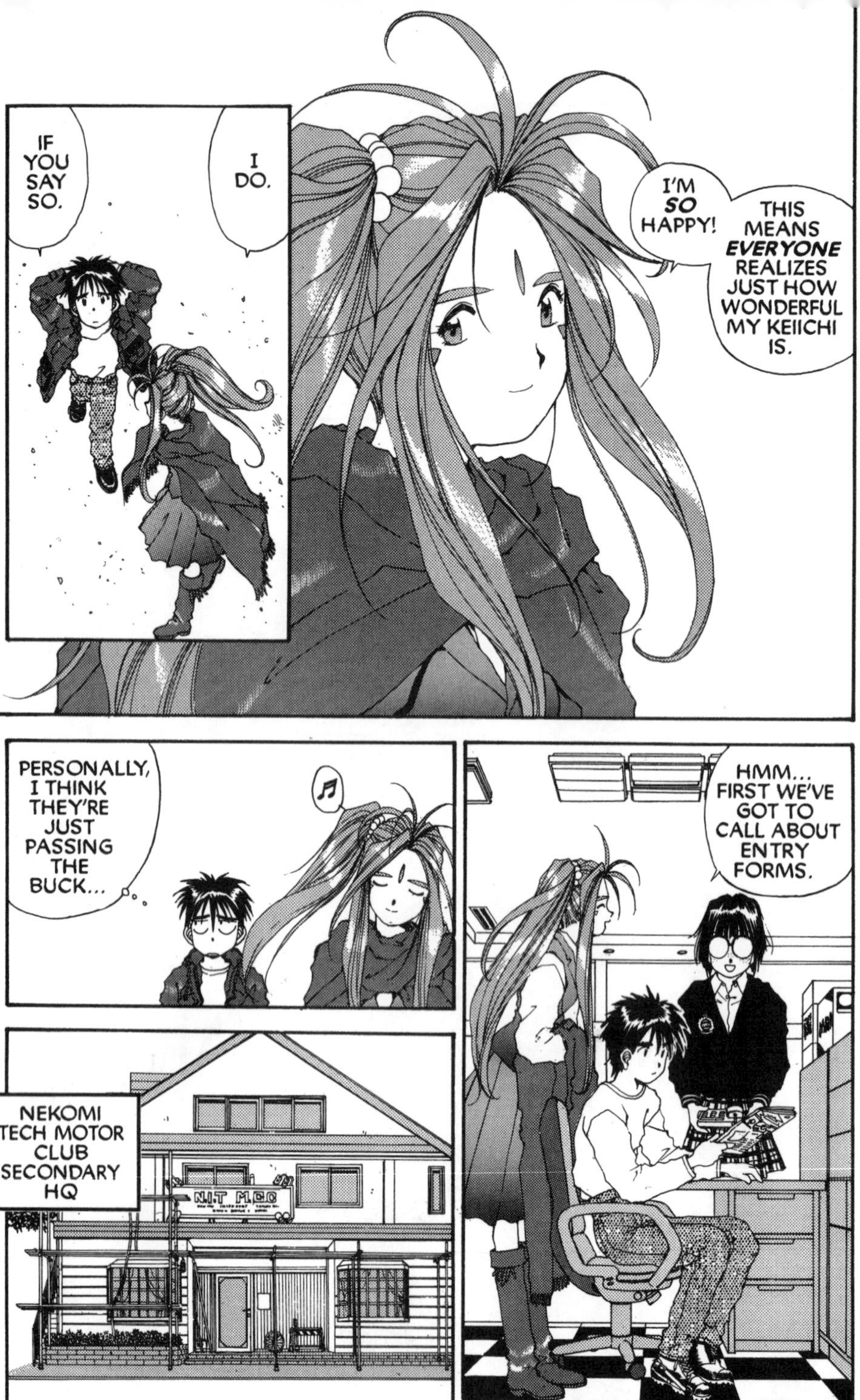
IF YOU SAY SO.
I DO.
I'M *SO* HAPPY!
THIS MEANS ***EVERYONE*** REALIZES JUST HOW WONDERFUL MY KEIICHI IS.
PERSONALLY, I THINK THEY'RE JUST PASSING THE BUCK...
♪
NEKOMI TECH MOTOR CLUB SECONDARY HQ
HMM... FIRST WE'VE GOT TO CALL ABOUT ENTRY FORMS.

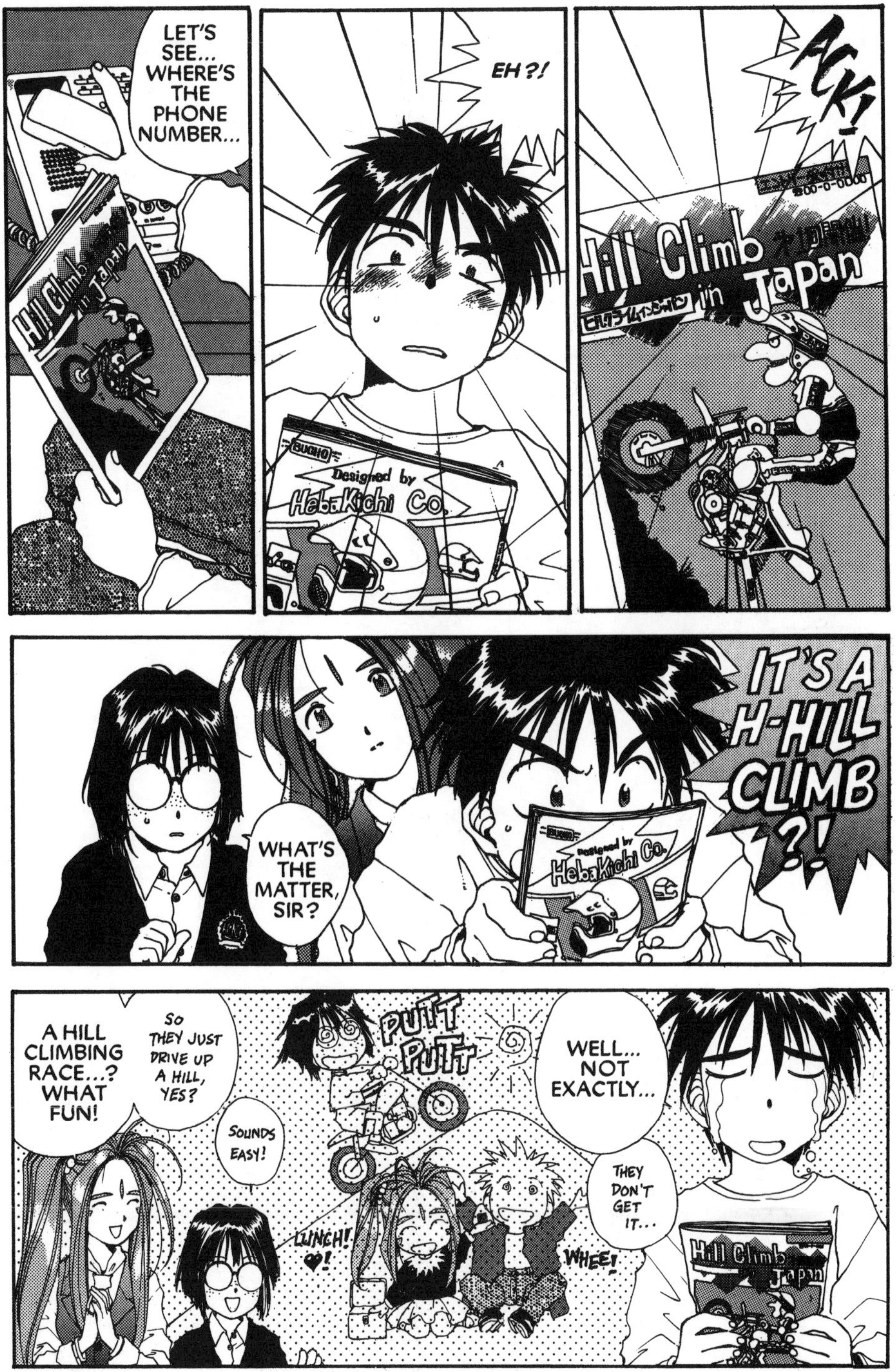
LET'S SEE... WHERE'S THE PHONE NUMBER...
Hill Climb in Japan
EH?!
Designed by HebaKichi Co.
ACK!
Hill Climb in Japan
WHAT'S THE MATTER, SIR?
Designed by HebaKichi Co.
IT'S A H-HILL CLIMB ?!
A HILL CLIMBING RACE...? WHAT FUN!
SO THEY JUST DRIVE UP A HILL, YES?
SOUNDS EASY!
PUTT PUTT
LUNCH! ♥!
WHEE!
WELL... NOT EXACTLY...
THEY DON'T GET IT...
Hill Climb Japan

A HILL CLIMB MEANS TACKLING A GRADE AS STEEP AS SEVENTY OR EVEN *EIGHTY* DEGREES...

...AND YOU GO AT IT IN ONE WILD CHARGE! IT'S *INSANE!*

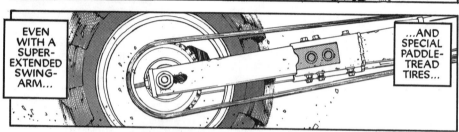

EVEN WITH A SUPER-EXTENDED SWING-ARM...

...AND SPECIAL PADDLE-TREAD TIRES...

...LOTS OF PEOPLE NEVER MAKE IT AND FLIP THEIR BIKES OVER!

CARTWHEELING BACKWARDS DOWN AN EIGHTY DEGREE SLOPE HUNDREDS OF FEET TO THE BOTTOM!

WOW! THAT SOUNDS TOTALLY *AWESOME!*

WELL... THAT'S ONE WAY TO LOOK AT IT.

EE *EEK!!*

BONK

THUD

TEA TIME!

WHEE!

WELL, THEM'S THE BREAKS. BETTER CALL, ANYWAY...

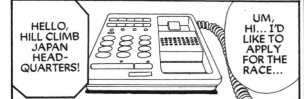

HELLO, HILL CLIMB JAPAN HEAD-QUARTERS!

UM, HI... I'D LIKE TO APPLY FOR THE RACE...

WHAT?!

IT'S CLOSED TO NEW ENTRIES?!

OH, *NO!!* THE DEADLINE WAS *YESTERDAY!!*

TAMIYA... OTAKI... YOU *IDIOTS!!*

≥hahh≤ CALM DOWN...!

AS LONG AS I'M THE HEAD OF THE CLUB... IT'S *MY* RESPONSIBILITY TO DO SOMETHING ABOUT IT.

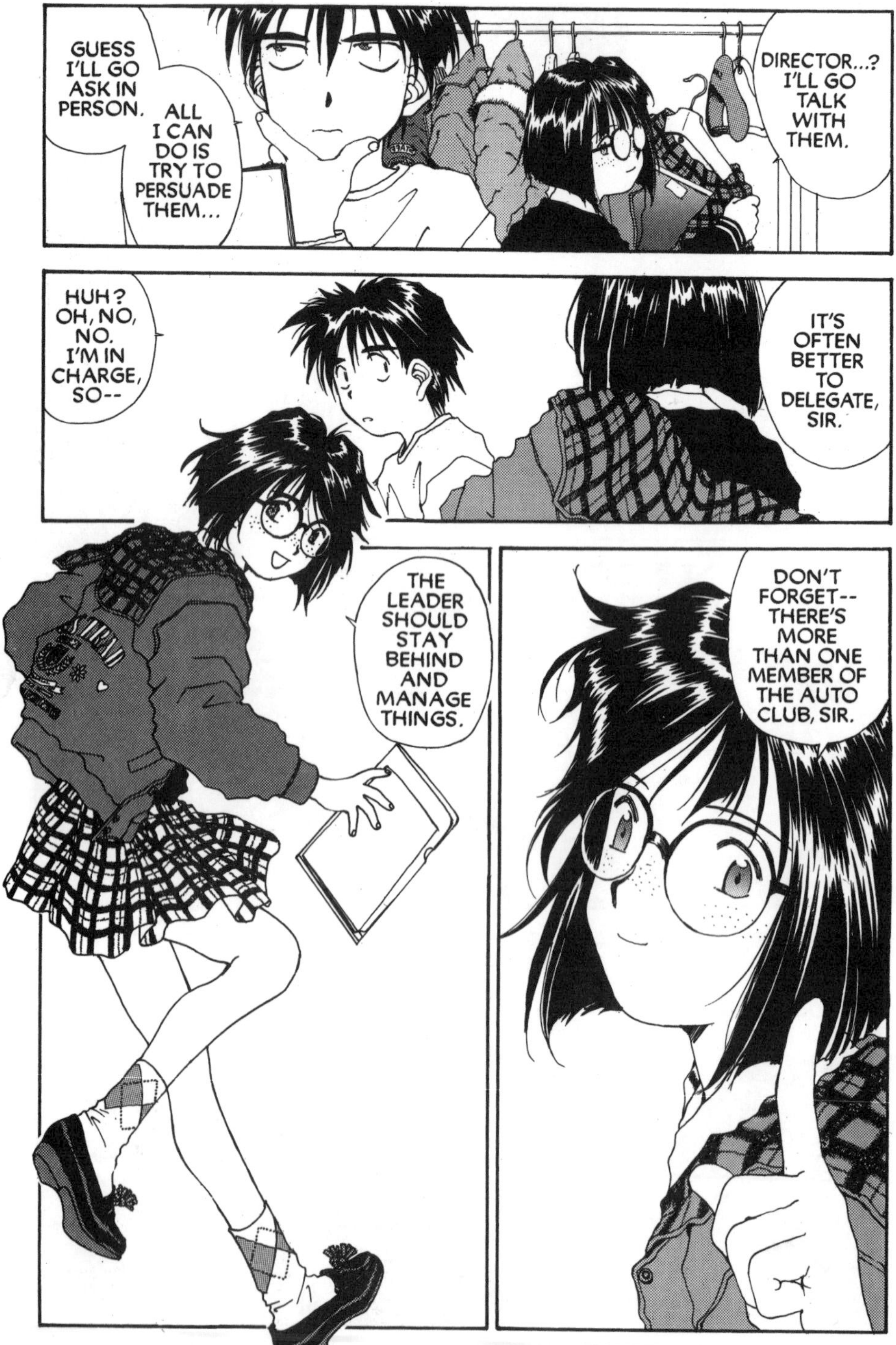
GUESS I'LL GO ASK IN PERSON.
ALL I CAN DO IS TRY TO PERSUADE THEM...
DIRECTOR...? I'LL GO TALK WITH THEM.
HUH? OH, NO, NO. I'M IN CHARGE, SO--
IT'S OFTEN BETTER TO DELEGATE, SIR.
THE LEADER SHOULD STAY BEHIND AND MANAGE THINGS.
DON'T FORGET-- THERE'S MORE THAN ONE MEMBER OF THE AUTO CLUB, SIR.

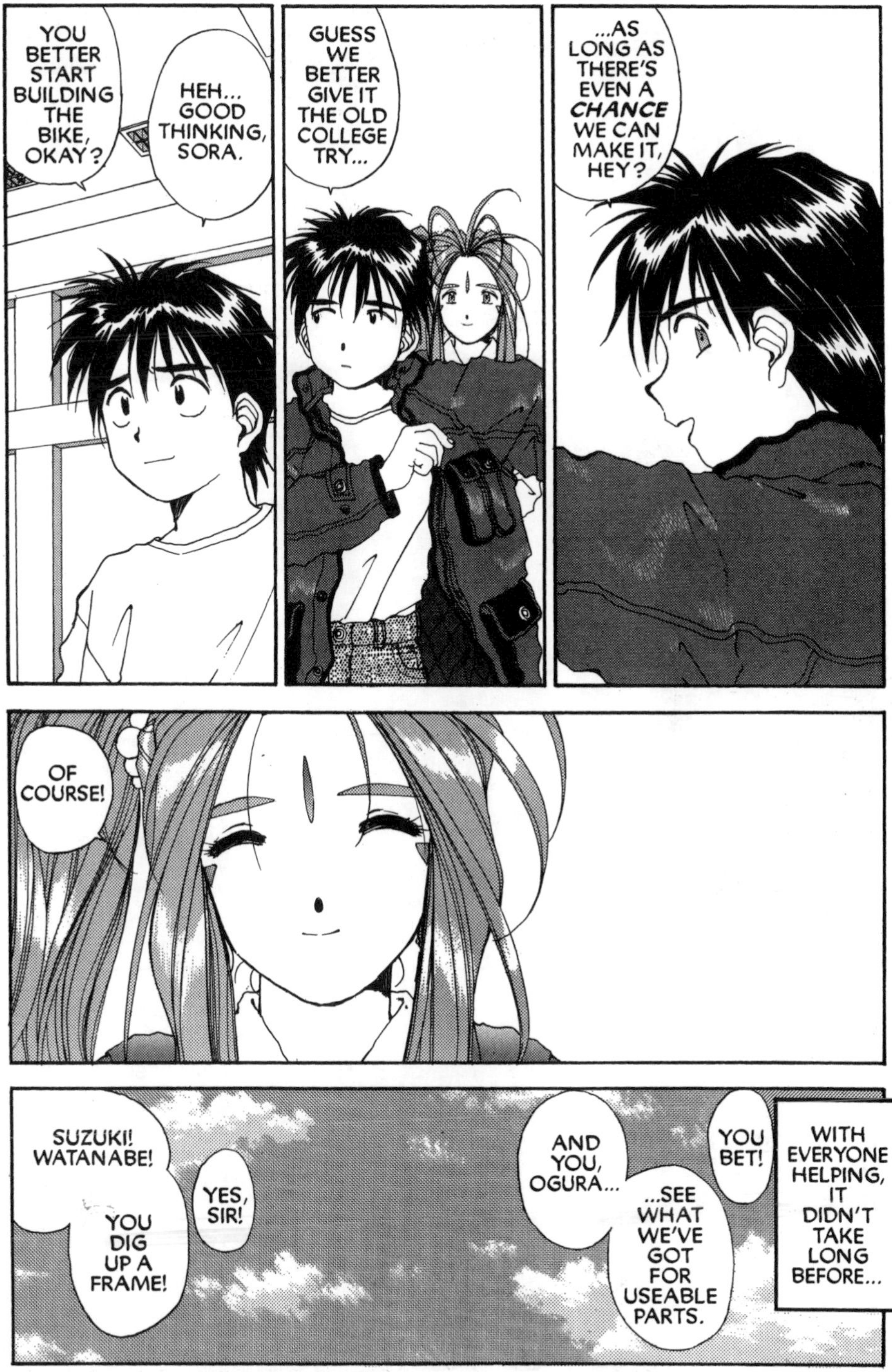
YOU BETTER START BUILDING THE BIKE, OKAY?
HEH... GOOD THINKING, SORA.
GUESS WE BETTER GIVE IT THE OLD COLLEGE TRY...
...AS LONG AS THERE'S EVEN A CHANCE WE CAN MAKE IT, HEY?
OF COURSE!
SUZUKI! WATANABE!
YOU DIG UP A FRAME!
YES, SIR!
AND YOU, OGURA...
...SEE WHAT WE'VE GOT FOR USEABLE PARTS.
YOU BET!
WITH EVERYONE HELPING, IT DIDN'T TAKE LONG BEFORE...

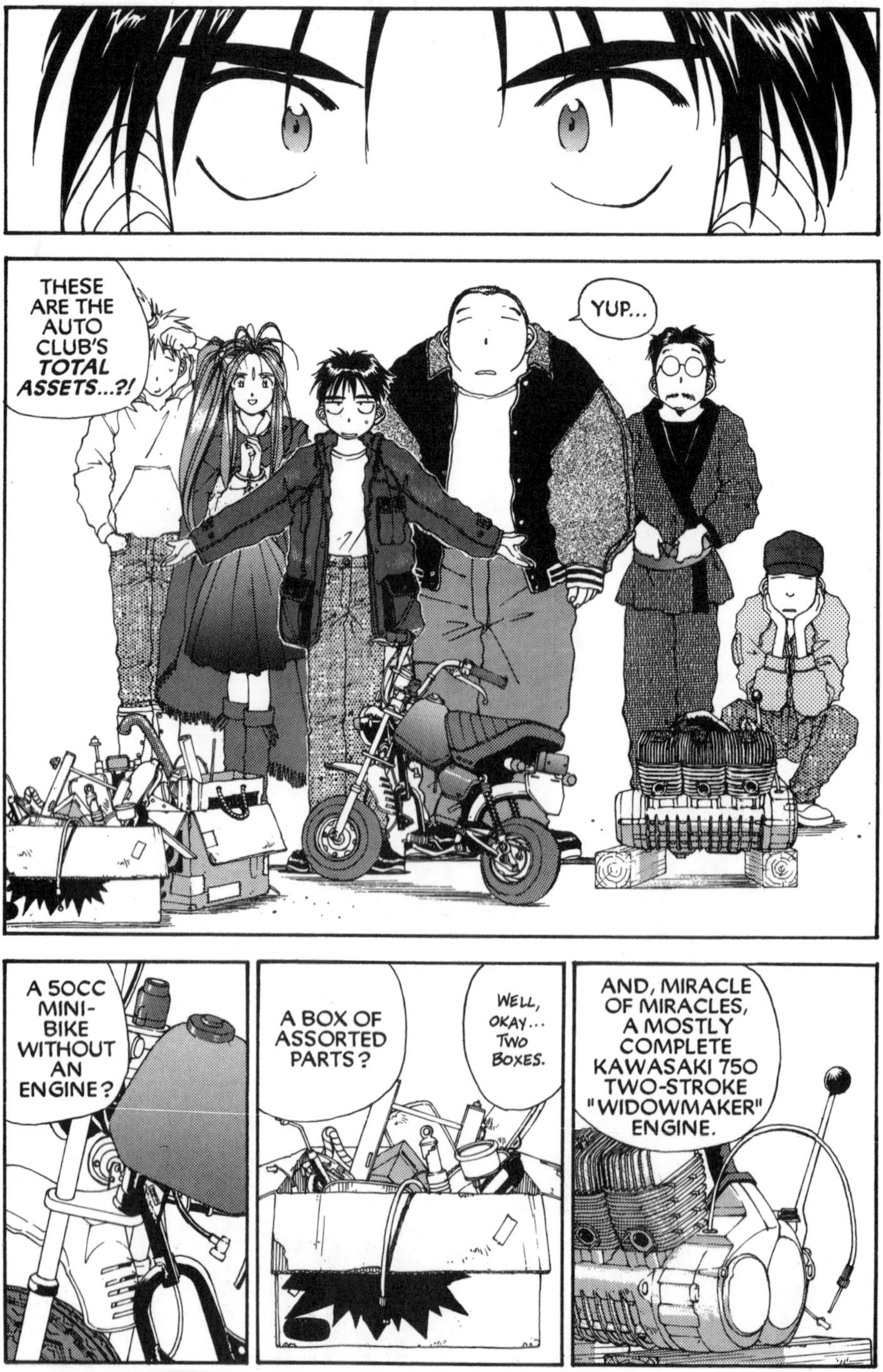
THESE ARE THE AUTO CLUB'S *TOTAL ASSETS...?!*
YUP...
A 50CC MINI-BIKE WITHOUT AN ENGINE?
A BOX OF ASSORTED PARTS?
WELL, OKAY... TWO BOXES.
AND, MIRACLE OF MIRACLES, A MOSTLY COMPLETE KAWASAKI 750 TWO-STROKE "WIDOWMAKER" ENGINE.

WH... WHAT...

...ARE WE SUPPOSED TO DO WITH *THIS* PILE OF JUNK, HUH?!

SIR! THERE IS ONE MORE MACHINE, SIR!

OH, YEAH?! WHAT?! *WHERE?!*

OUR NITRO-FUELED *GSX* DRAG RACER, SIR!

WE CAN'T USE *THAT*, YOU LUMMOX!

IT COST US A FORTUNE!

WELL, OKAY... IF THIS IS WHAT WE'VE GOT, WE'LL MOUNT THE ENGINE INTO A HYPER-REINFORCED MINI-BIKE FRAME...

THEN, AS PART OF THE FRAME MODS...

WE SLAP ON AN EXTENDED BOX-FRAME SWINGARM... HMM...

THAT'S IT, SIR-- YOU'RE STARTING TO THINK LIKE TAMIYA AND OTAKI!

DON'T SAY THAT!

SO... ANY OF YOU GOT ANY EXTRA PARTS HIDDEN SOME-WHERE...?

...

...

...

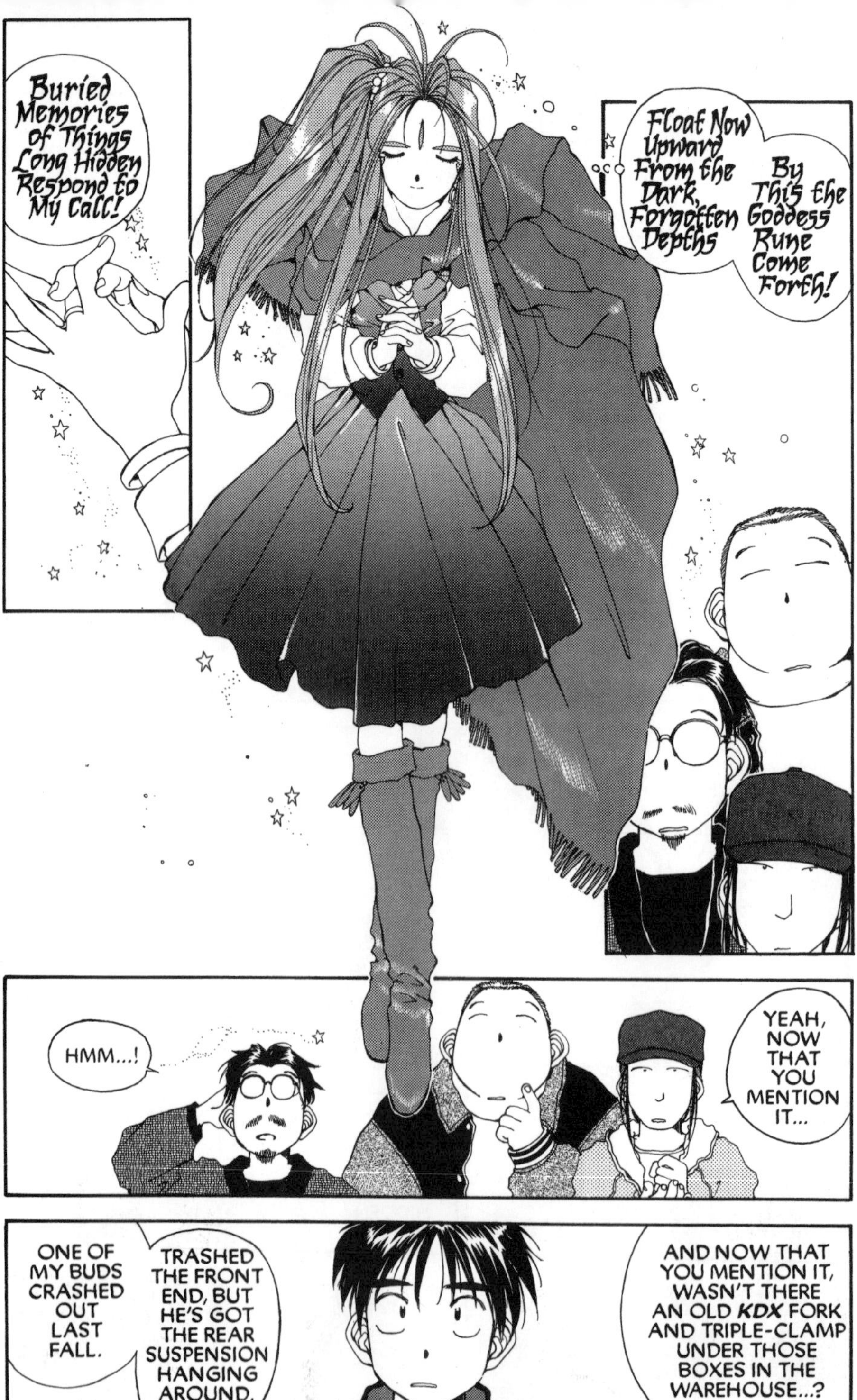
Buried Memories of Things Long Hidden Respond to My Call!
Float Now Upward From the Dark, Forgotten Depths
By This the Goddess Rune Come Forth!
HMM...!
YEAH, NOW THAT YOU MENTION IT...
ONE OF MY BUDS CRASHED OUT LAST FALL.
TRASHED THE FRONT END, BUT HE'S GOT THE REAR SUSPENSION HANGING AROUND.
AND NOW THAT YOU MENTION IT, WASN'T THERE AN OLD KDX FORK AND TRIPLE-CLAMP UNDER THOSE BOXES IN THE WAREHOUSE...?

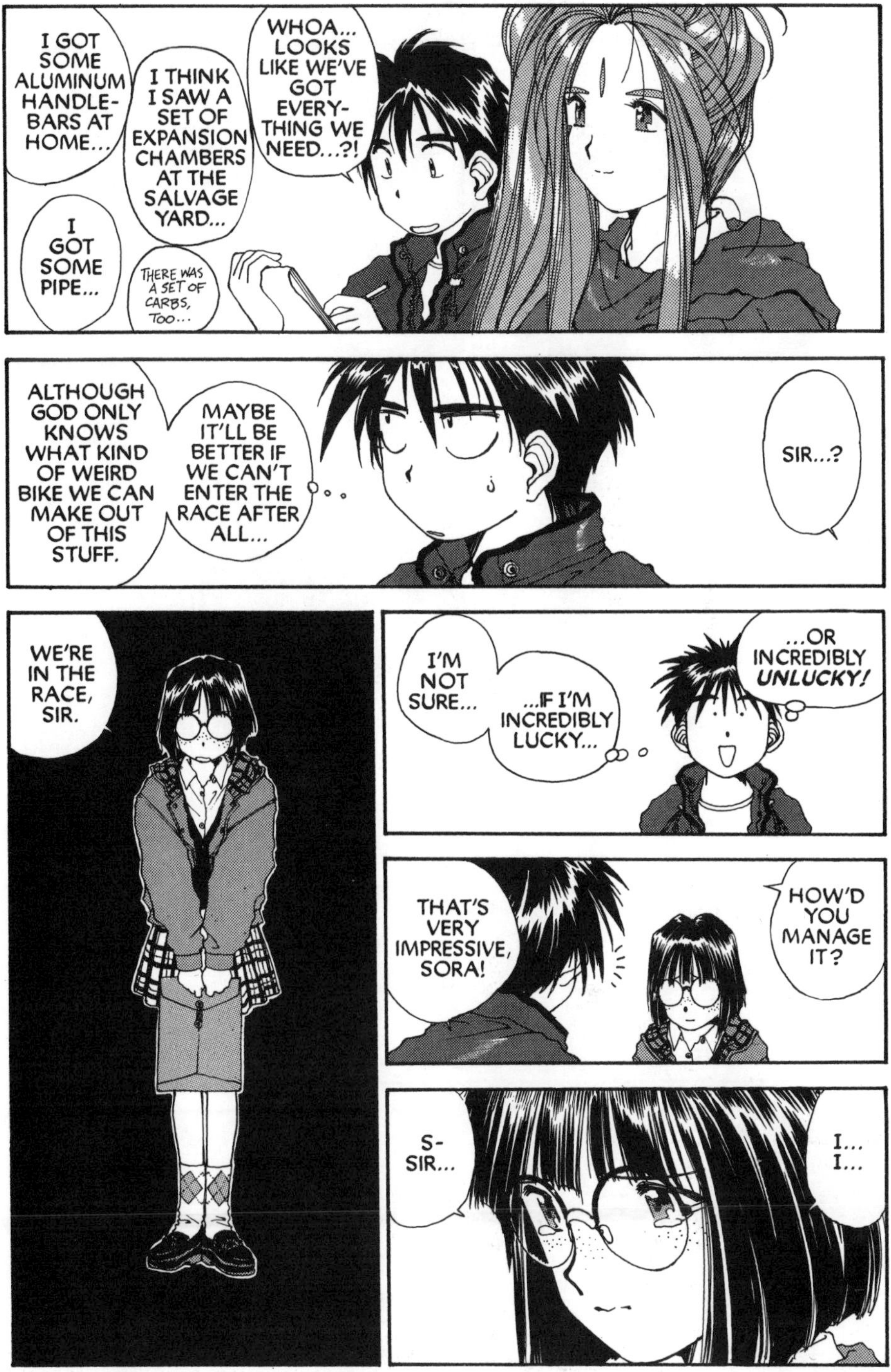
I GOT SOME ALUMINUM HANDLE-BARS AT HOME...
I GOT SOME PIPE...
I THINK I SAW A SET OF EXPANSION CHAMBERS AT THE SALVAGE YARD...
THERE WAS A SET OF CARBS, TOO...
WHOA... LOOKS LIKE WE'VE GOT EVERY-THING WE NEED...?!
ALTHOUGH GOD ONLY KNOWS WHAT KIND OF WEIRD BIKE WE CAN MAKE OUT OF THIS STUFF.
MAYBE IT'LL BE BETTER IF WE CAN'T ENTER THE RACE AFTER ALL...
SIR...?
WE'RE IN THE RACE, SIR.
I'M NOT SURE...
...IF I'M INCREDIBLY LUCKY...
...OR INCREDIBLY *UNLUCKY!*
THAT'S VERY IMPRESSIVE, SORA!
HOW'D YOU MANAGE IT?
S-SIR...
I... I...

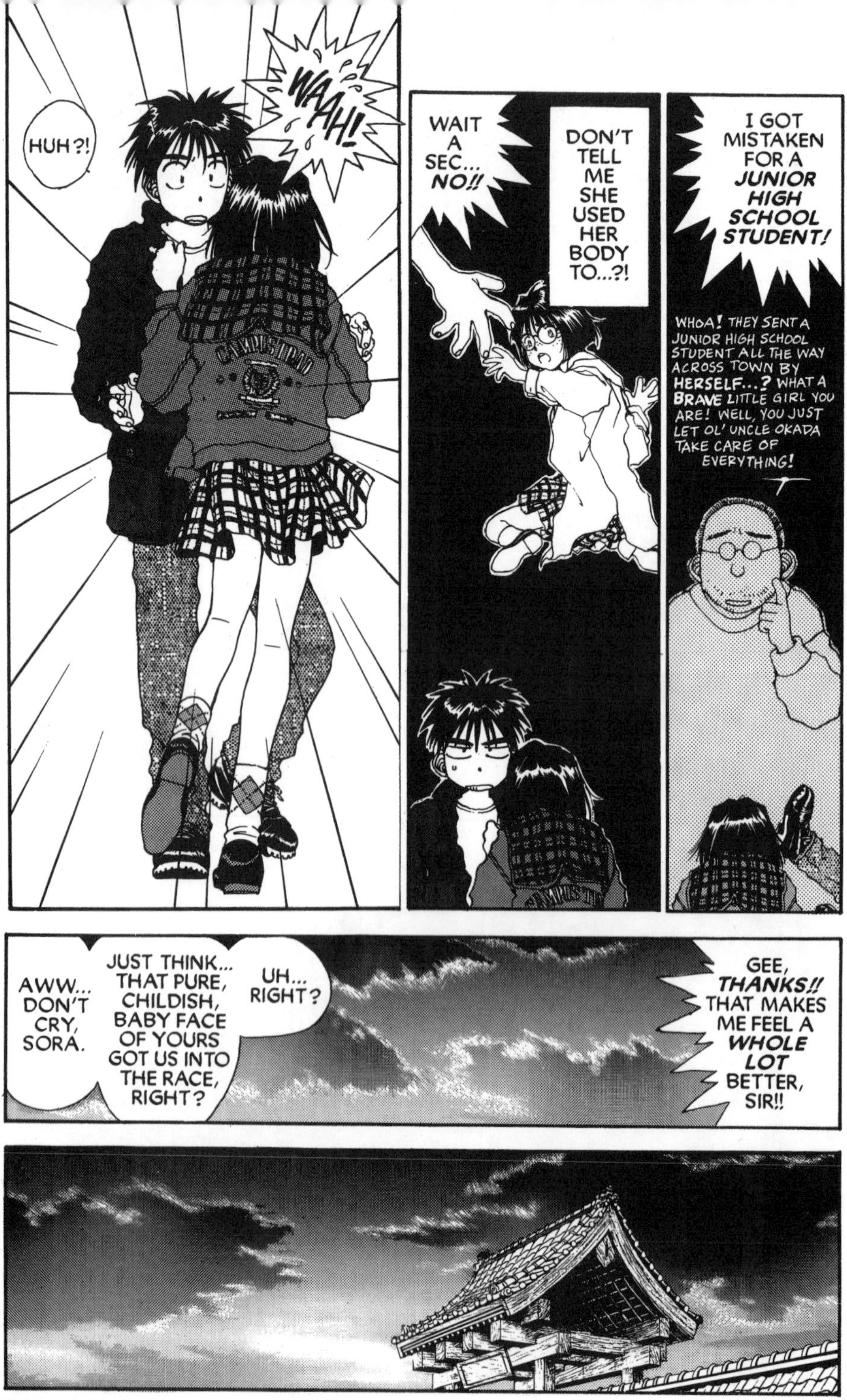

HUH?!
WAAAH!
WAIT A SEC... NO!!
DON'T TELL ME SHE USED HER BODY TO...?!
I GOT MISTAKEN FOR A JUNIOR HIGH SCHOOL STUDENT!
WHOA! THEY SENT A JUNIOR HIGH SCHOOL STUDENT ALL THE WAY ACROSS TOWN BY HERSELF...? WHAT A BRAVE LITTLE GIRL YOU ARE! WELL, YOU JUST LET OL' UNCLE OKADA TAKE CARE OF EVERYTHING!
AWW... DON'T CRY, SORA.
JUST THINK... THAT PURE, CHILDISH, BABY FACE OF YOURS GOT US INTO THE RACE, RIGHT?
UH... RIGHT?
GEE, THANKS!! THAT MAKES ME FEEL A WHOLE LOT BETTER, SIR!!

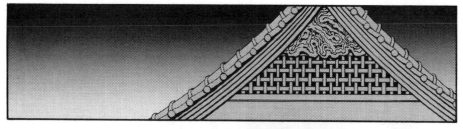

YOU KNOW... IT REALLY WEARS YOU OUT DOING SOMETHING YOU'RE NOT USED TO.

I CAN'T WAIT TO RELAX.

I'LL PUT THE TEA ON...

K-POP!

CONGRAT- ULATIONS KEIICHI!!

SO THEY PUT YOU IN CHARGE OF THE NEXT RACE, EH, LOVER BOY?

ASK ME IF I CARE...

GO KEIICHI!

KEIICHI!

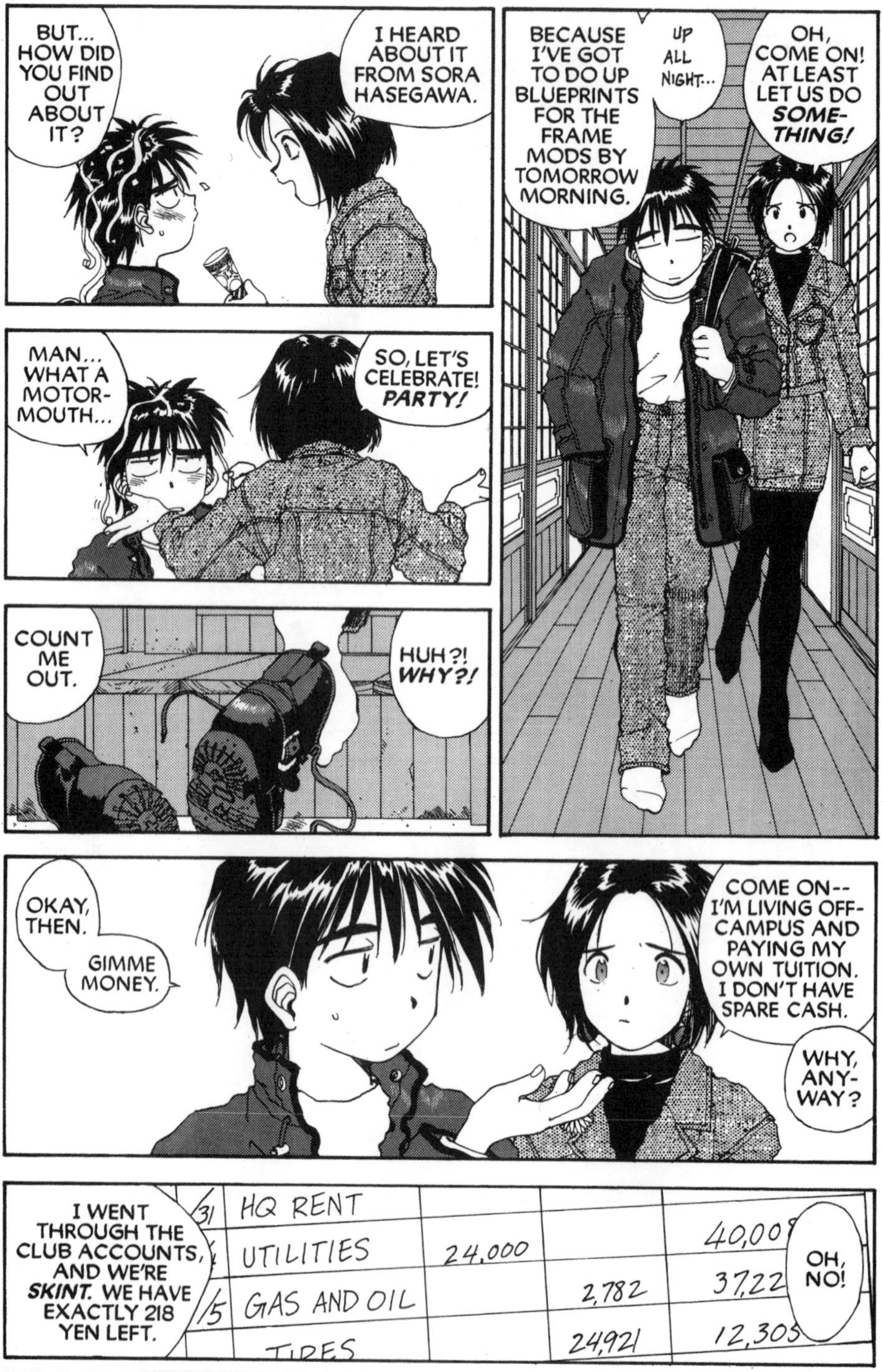
BUT... HOW DID YOU FIND OUT ABOUT IT?
I HEARD ABOUT IT FROM SORA HASEGAWA.
MAN... WHAT A MOTOR-MOUTH...
SO, LET'S CELEBRATE! *PARTY!*
COUNT ME OUT.
HUH?! *WHY?!*
BECAUSE I'VE GOT TO DO UP BLUEPRINTS FOR THE FRAME MODS BY TOMORROW MORNING.
UP ALL NIGHT...
OH, COME ON! AT LEAST LET US DO *SOME-THING!*
OKAY, THEN.
GIMME MONEY.
COME ON-- I'M LIVING OFF-CAMPUS AND PAYING MY OWN TUITION. I DON'T HAVE SPARE CASH.
WHY, ANY-WAY?
I WENT THROUGH THE CLUB ACCOUNTS, AND WE'RE *SKINT.* WE HAVE EXACTLY 218 YEN LEFT.
HQ RENT
UTILITIES 24,000
GAS AND OIL 2,782
24,921
OH, NO!

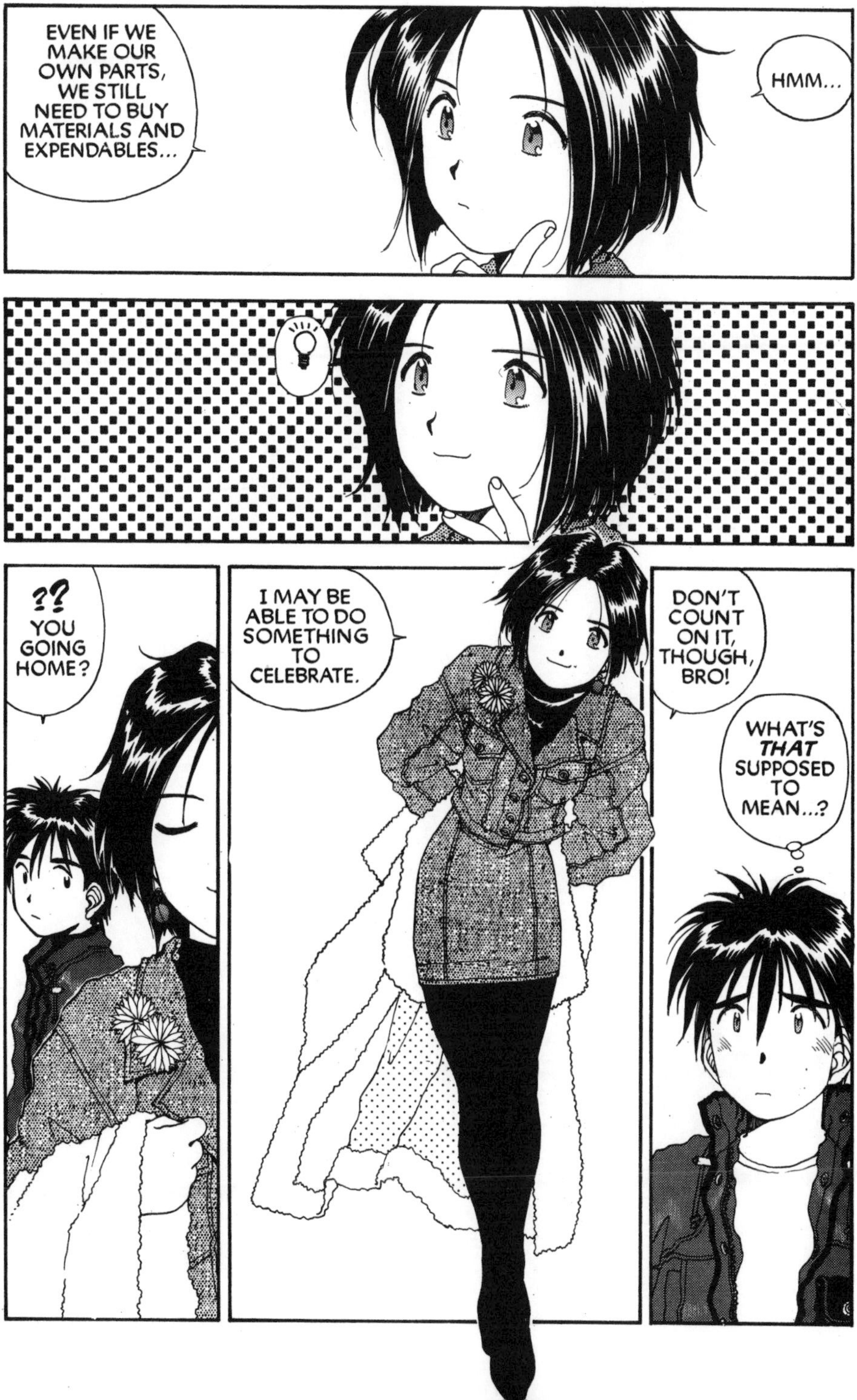

EVEN IF WE MAKE OUR OWN PARTS, WE STILL NEED TO BUY MATERIALS AND EXPENDABLES...
HMM...
?? YOU GOING HOME?
I MAY BE ABLE TO DO SOMETHING TO CELEBRATE.
DON'T COUNT ON IT, THOUGH, BRO!
WHAT'S THAT SUPPOSED TO MEAN...?

KEIICHI'S SHOP

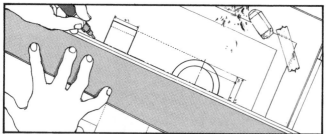

TAK TAK

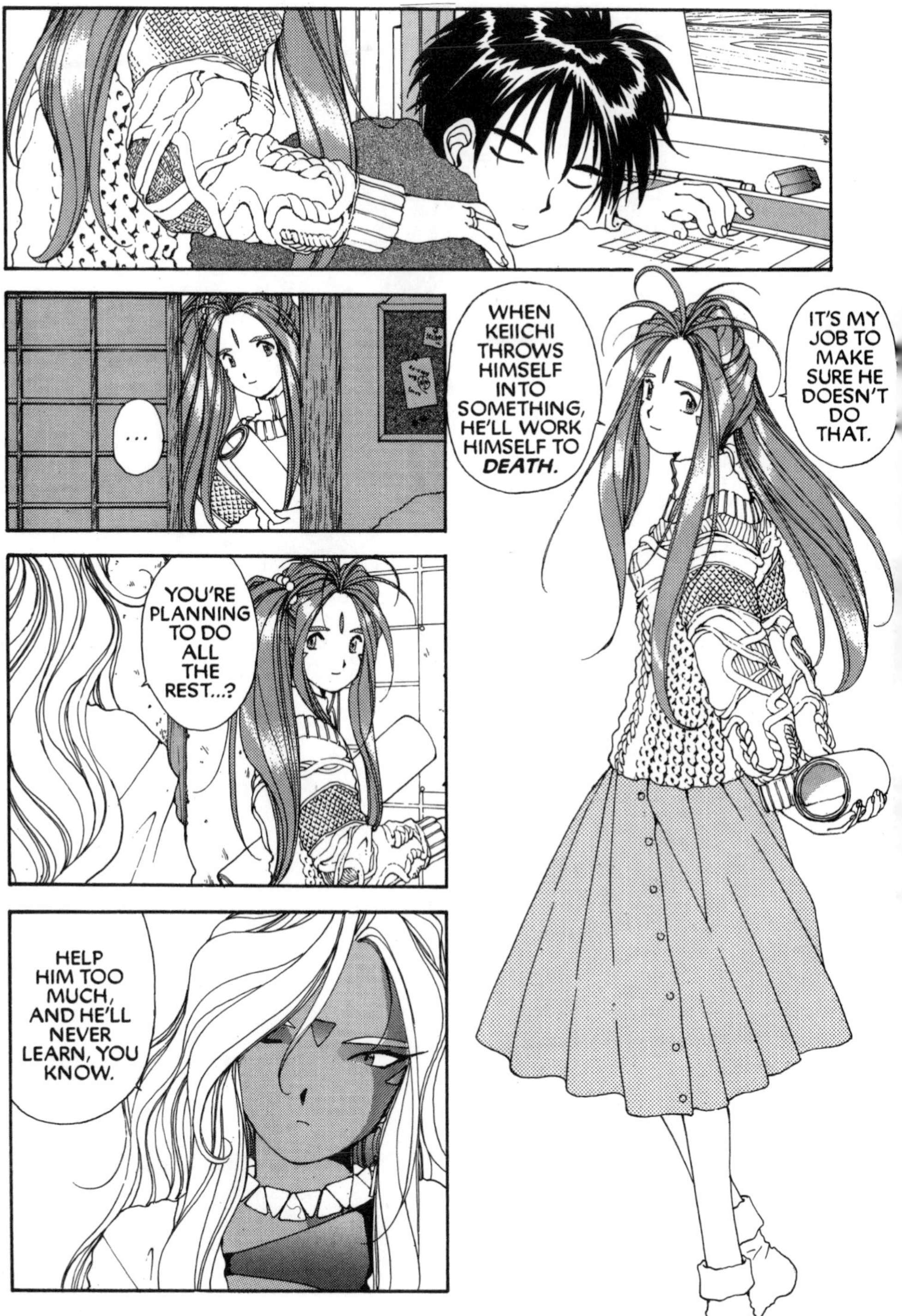
...
YOU'RE PLANNING TO DO ALL THE REST...?
HELP HIM TOO MUCH, AND HE'LL NEVER LEARN, YOU KNOW.
WHEN KEIICHI THROWS HIMSELF INTO SOMETHING, HE'LL WORK HIMSELF TO *DEATH.*
IT'S MY JOB TO MAKE SURE HE DOESN'T DO THAT.

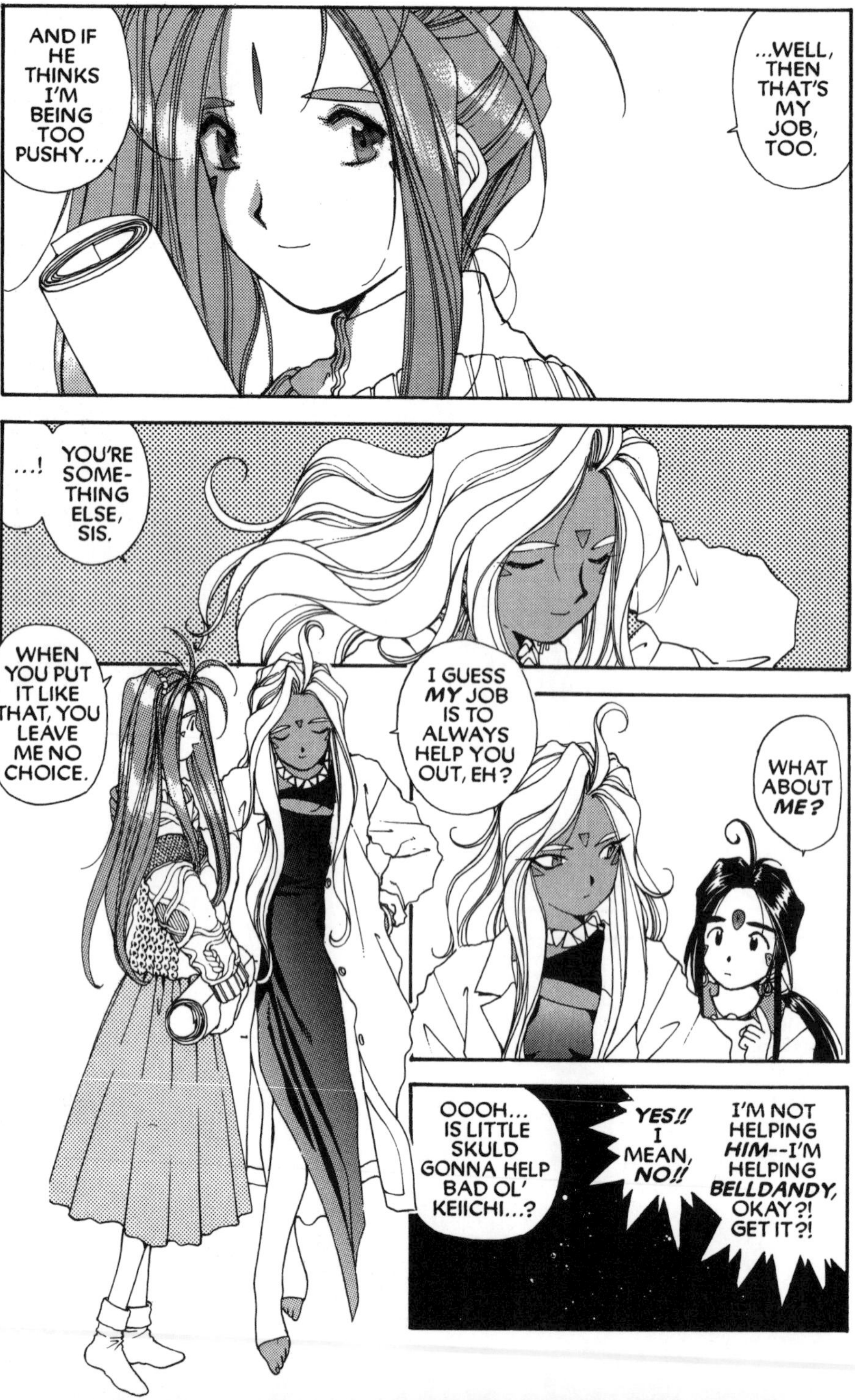
AND IF HE THINKS I'M BEING TOO PUSHY...
...WELL, THEN THAT'S MY JOB, TOO.
...!
YOU'RE SOME-THING ELSE, SIS.
WHEN YOU PUT IT LIKE THAT, YOU LEAVE ME NO CHOICE.
I GUESS *MY* JOB IS TO ALWAYS HELP YOU OUT, EH?
WHAT ABOUT *ME?*
OOOH... IS LITTLE SKULD GONNA HELP BAD OL' KEIICHI...?
YES!! I MEAN, *NO!!*
I'M NOT HELPING *HIM*--I'M HELPING *BELLDANDY,* OKAY?! GET IT?!

AND SO, THE NEXT MORNING...

HUH...?

THE PLANS...? THEY'RE... *FINISHED?!*

WHOA... THE WHOLE BIKE!

WHAT THE HECK...?

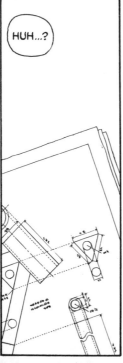

KEIICHI? OH, KEIICHI!

FORGIVE ME! I KNOW I SHOULDN'T HAVE...

...AND YOU'VE GOT EVERY RIGHT TO BE ANGRY.

BUT...

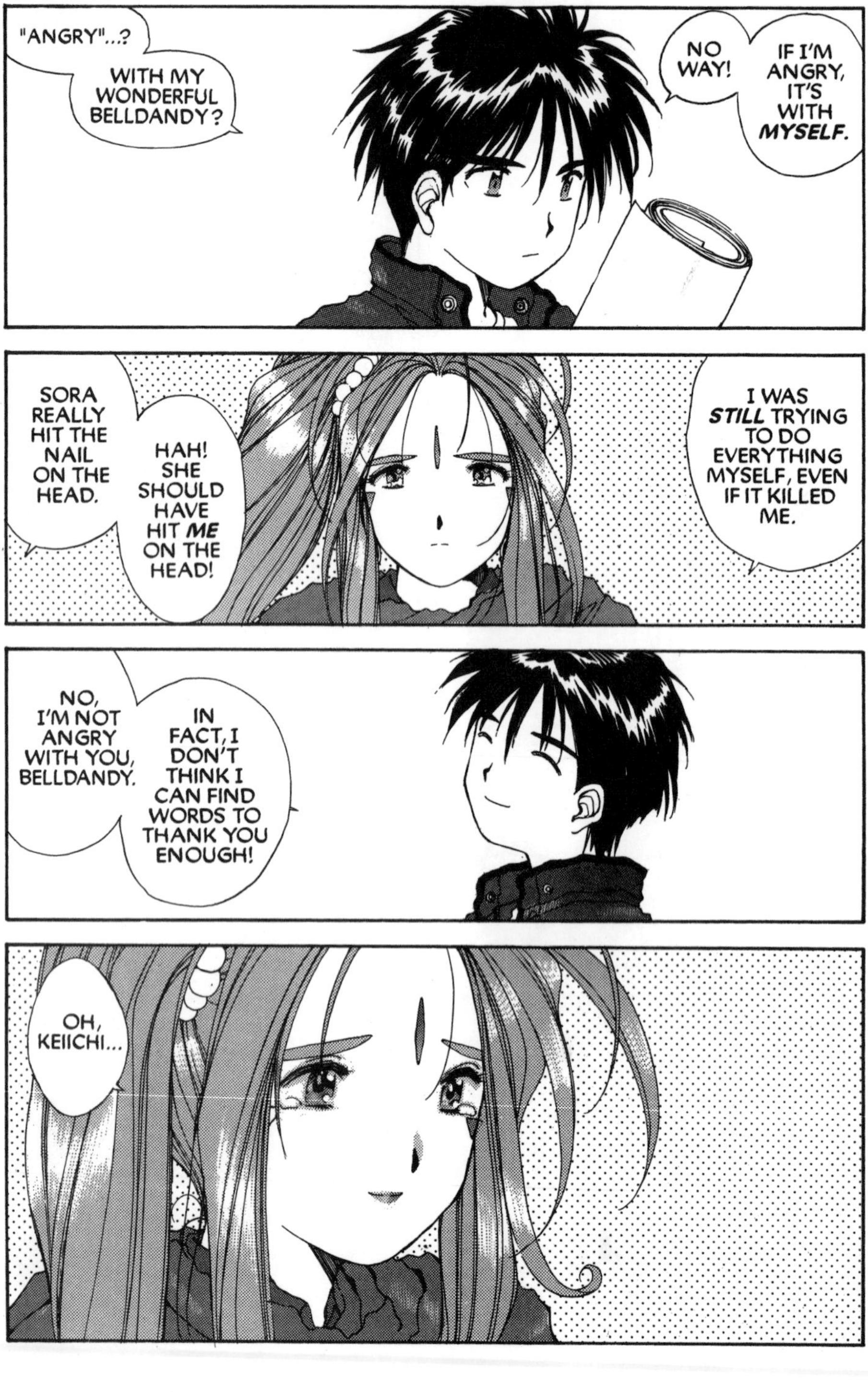
"ANGRY"...?
WITH MY WONDERFUL BELLDANDY?
NO WAY!
IF I'M ANGRY, IT'S WITH *MYSELF*.
SORA REALLY HIT THE NAIL ON THE HEAD.
HAH! SHE SHOULD HAVE HIT *ME* ON THE HEAD!
I WAS *STILL* TRYING TO DO EVERYTHING MYSELF, EVEN IF IT KILLED ME.
NO, I'M NOT ANGRY WITH YOU, BELLDANDY.
IN FACT, I DON'T THINK I CAN FIND WORDS TO THANK YOU ENOUGH!
OH, KEIICHI...

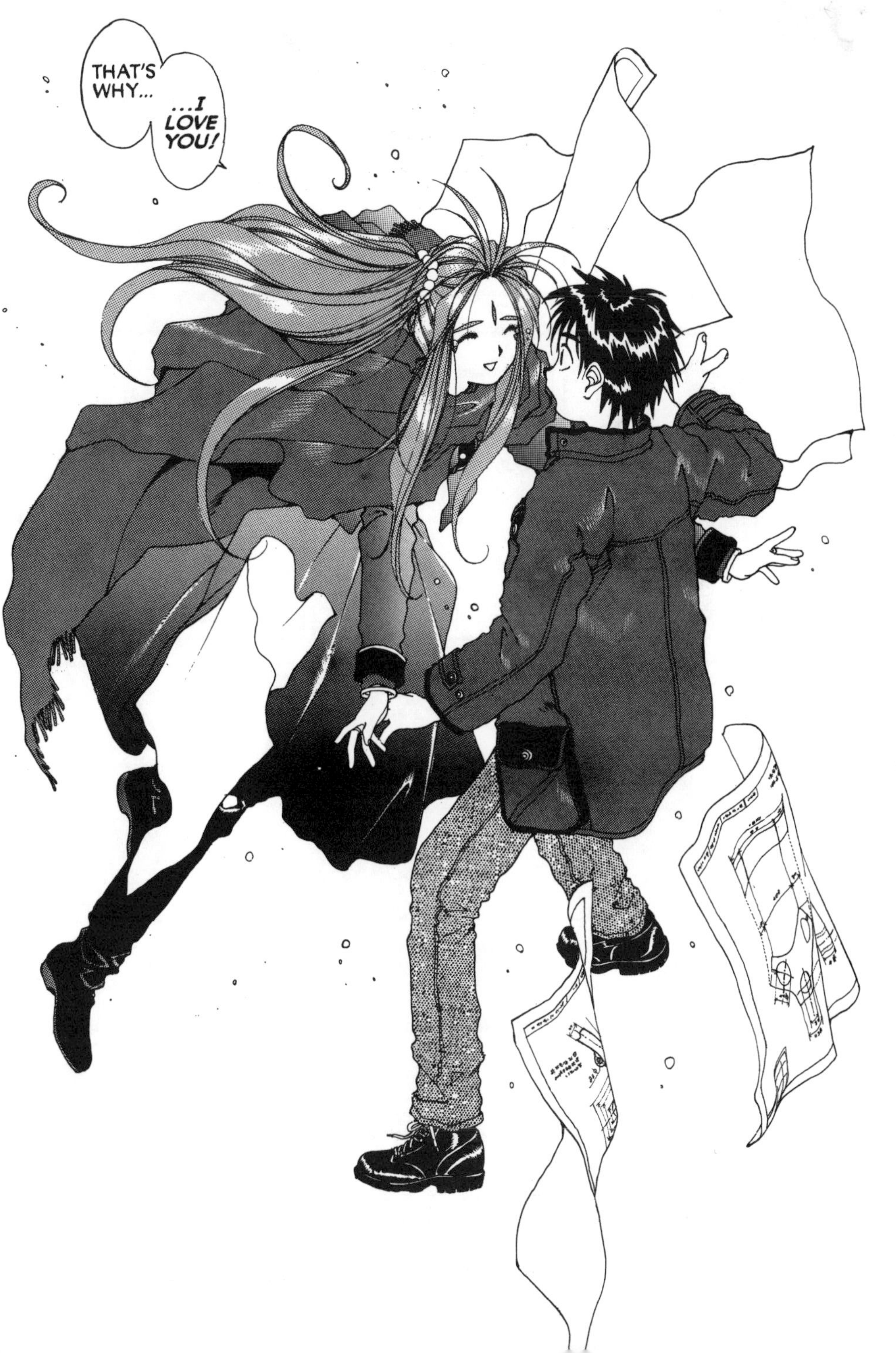
THAT'S WHY...
...I LOVE YOU!

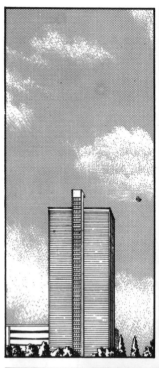

THE PARTS WE MADE FROM THE GODDESS BLUEPRINTS...

...WERE BETTER THAN EVEN THE VERY BEST NEW PARTS.

OH MAN! IT FITS PERFECTLY!

HELLO KEI-ICHI!♪

HUH?

TAA-DAA!

CHECK IT OUT!

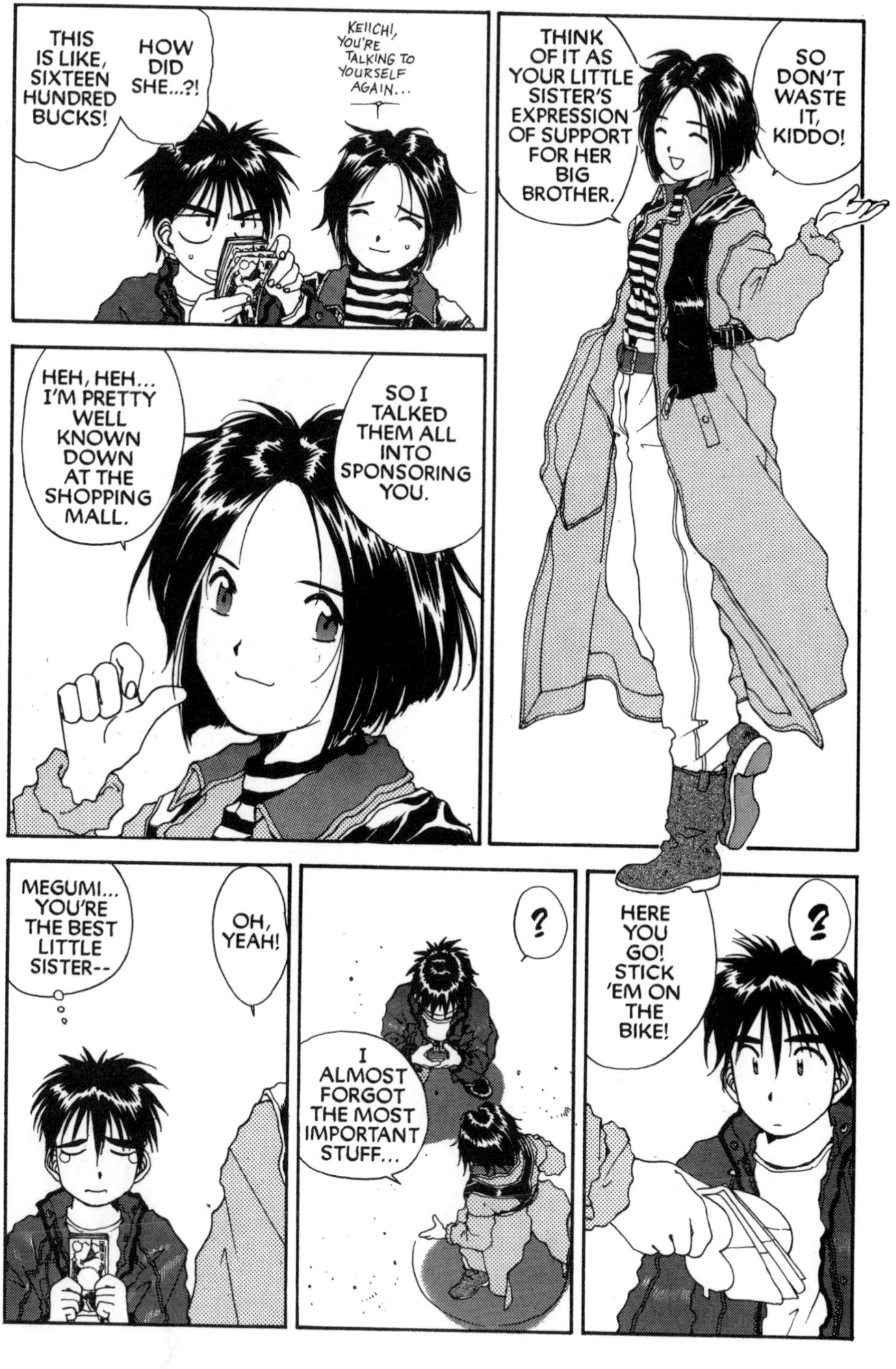
THIS IS LIKE, SIXTEEN HUNDRED BUCKS!
HOW DID SHE...?!
KEIICHI, YOU'RE TALKING TO YOURSELF AGAIN...
HEH, HEH... I'M PRETTY WELL KNOWN DOWN AT THE SHOPPING MALL.
SO I TALKED THEM ALL INTO SPONSORING YOU.
THINK OF IT AS YOUR LITTLE SISTER'S EXPRESSION OF SUPPORT FOR HER BIG BROTHER.
SO DON'T WASTE IT, KIDDO!
MEGUMI... YOU'RE THE BEST LITTLE SISTER--
OH, YEAH!
?
I ALMOST FORGOT THE MOST IMPORTANT STUFF...
HERE YOU GO! STICK 'EM ON THE BIKE!
?

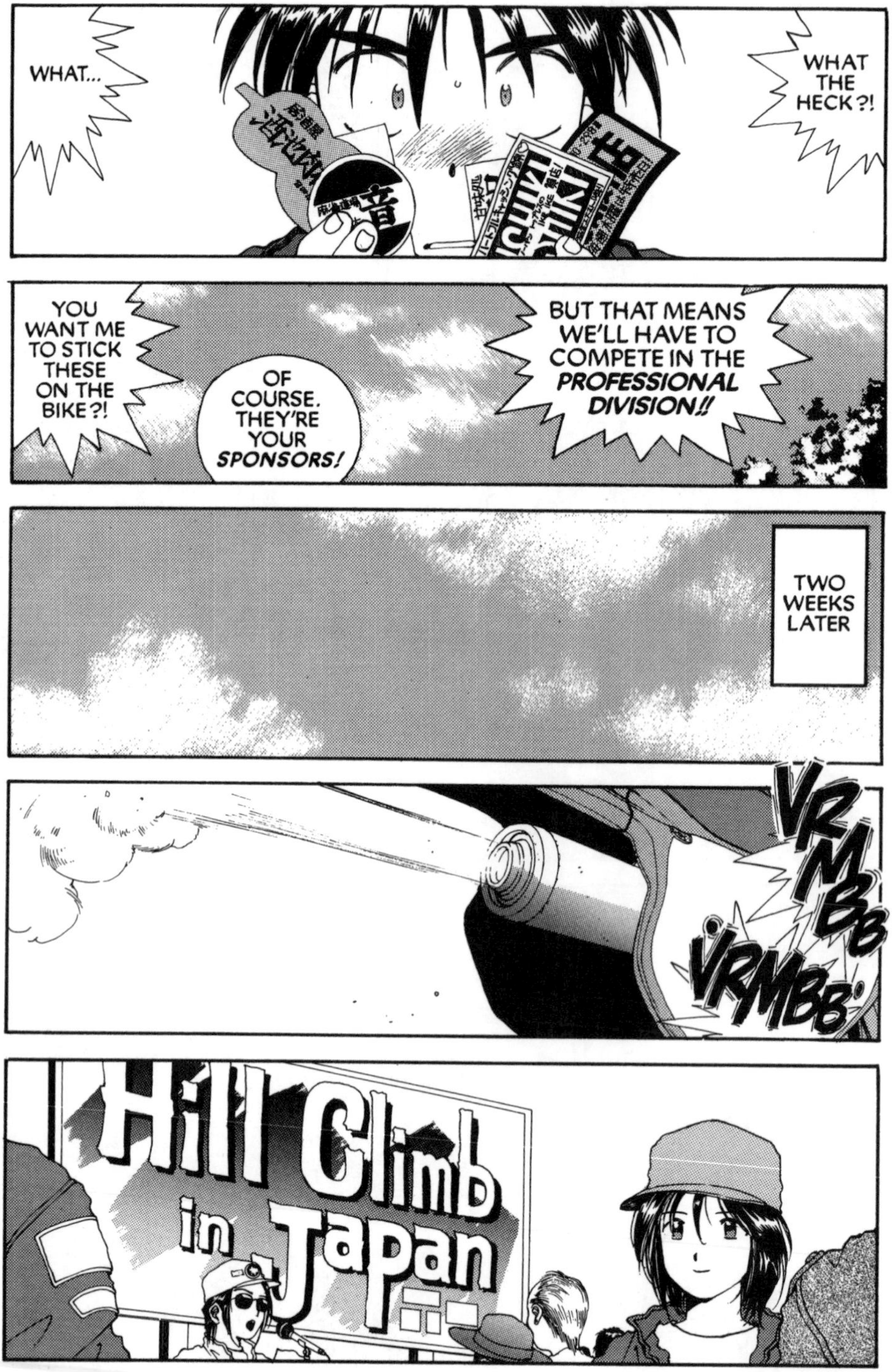
WHAT...
WHAT THE HECK?!
YOU WANT ME TO STICK THESE ON THE BIKE?!
OF COURSE. THEY'RE YOUR *SPONSORS!*
BUT THAT MEANS WE'LL HAVE TO COMPETE IN THE ***PROFESSIONAL DIVISION!!***
TWO WEEKS LATER
VRMBB
VRMBB
Hill Climb in Japan

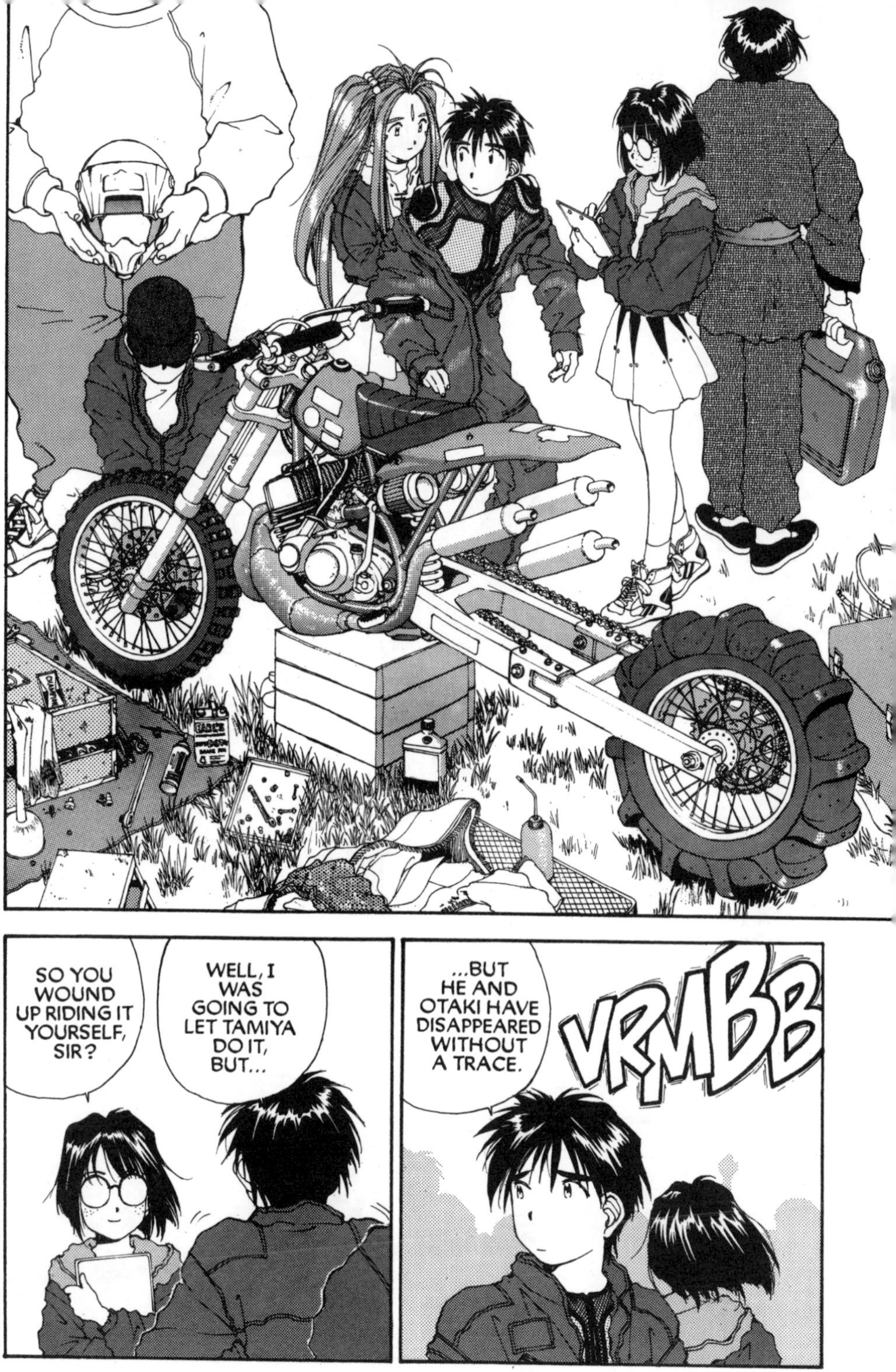
SO YOU WOUND UP RIDING IT YOURSELF, SIR?
WELL, I WAS GOING TO LET TAMIYA DO IT, BUT...
...BUT HE AND OTAKI HAVE DISAPPEARED WITHOUT A TRACE.
VRMBB

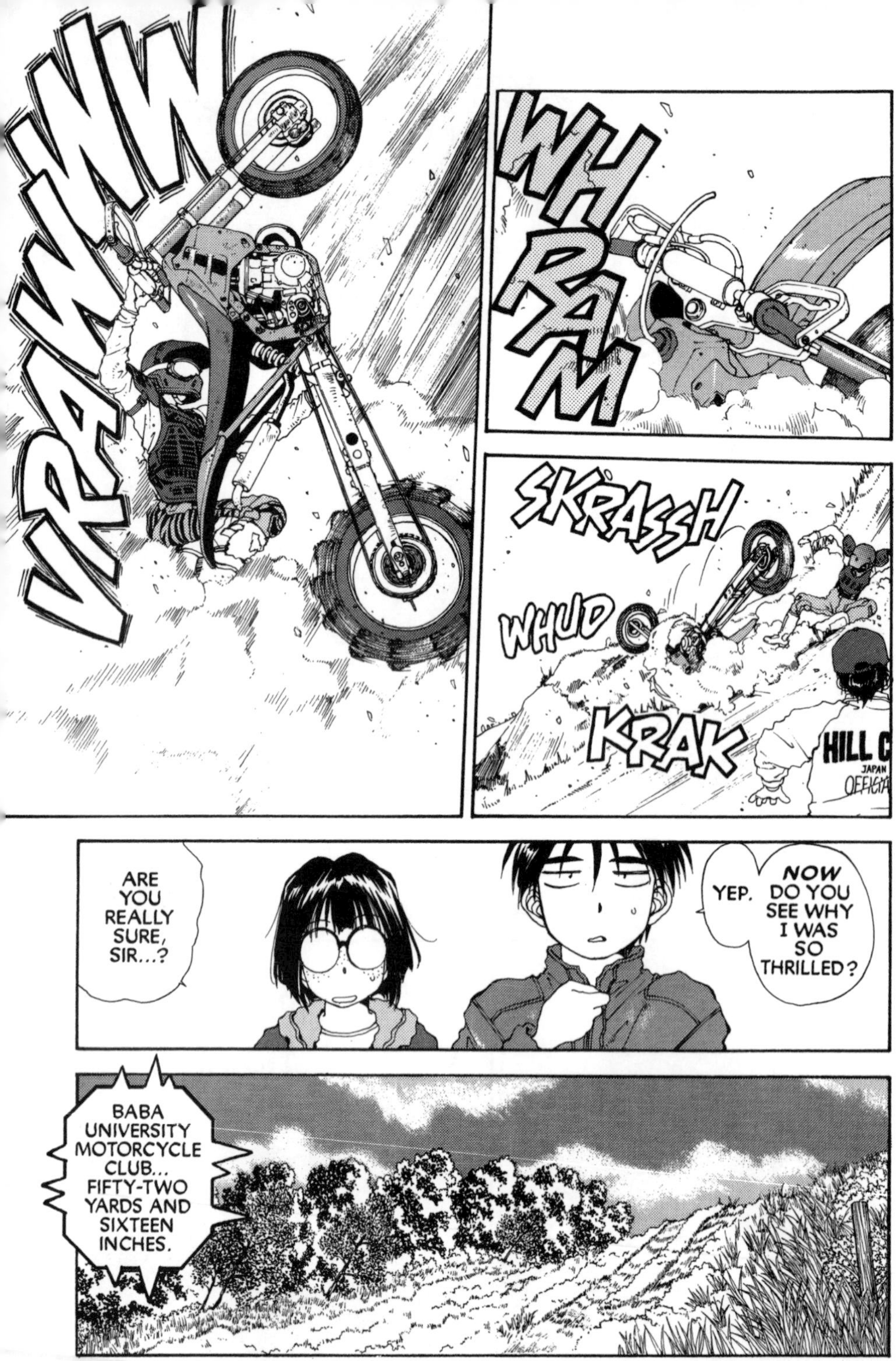
VRAWWW
WHRAM
SKRASSH
WHUD
KRAK
JAPAN
ARE YOU REALLY SURE, SIR...?
YEP.
NOW DO YOU SEE WHY I WAS SO THRILLED?
BABA UNIVERSITY MOTORCYCLE CLUB... FIFTY-TWO YARDS AND SIXTEEN INCHES.

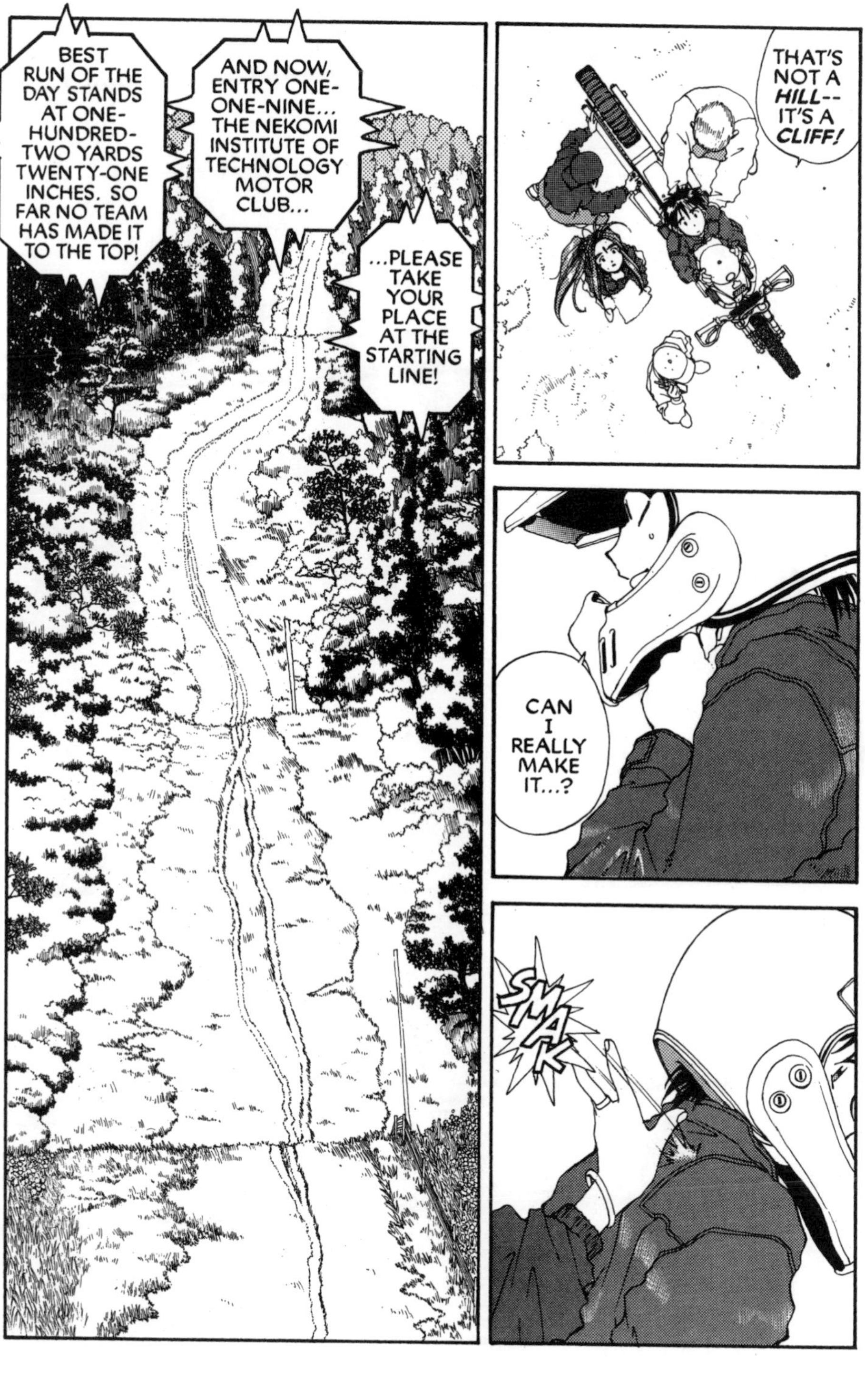
BEST RUN OF THE DAY STANDS AT ONE-HUNDRED-TWO YARDS TWENTY-ONE INCHES. SO FAR NO TEAM HAS MADE IT TO THE TOP!
AND NOW, ENTRY ONE-ONE-NINE... THE NEKOMI INSTITUTE OF TECHNOLOGY MOTOR CLUB...
...PLEASE TAKE YOUR PLACE AT THE STARTING LINE!
THAT'S NOT A HILL-- IT'S A CLIFF!
CAN I REALLY MAKE IT...?
SMAK

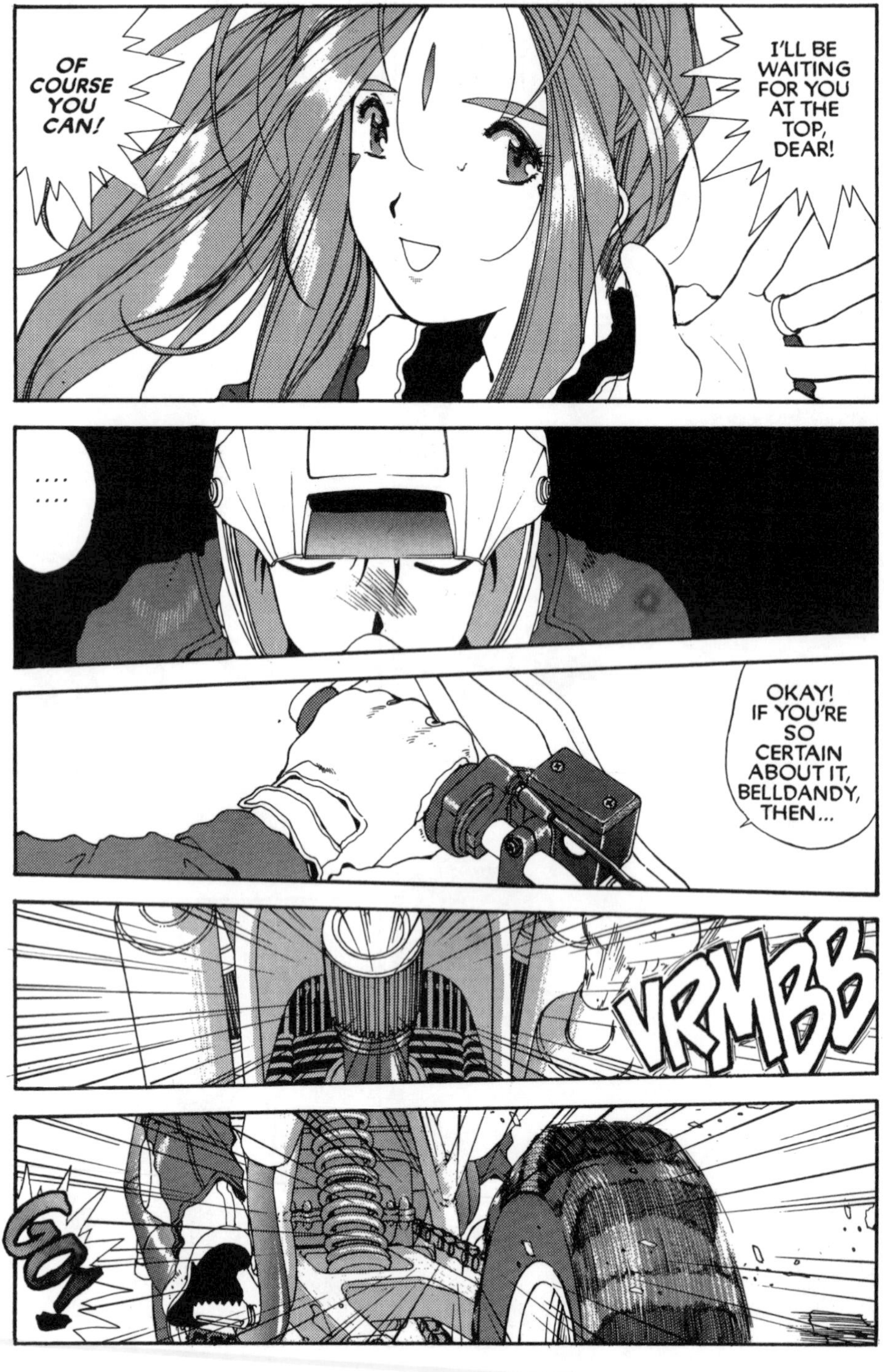
I'LL BE WAITING FOR YOU AT THE TOP, DEAR!
OF COURSE YOU CAN!
....
....
OKAY! IF YOU'RE SO CERTAIN ABOUT IT, BELLDANDY, THEN...
VRMBB
GO!

GO MAN *GO!!*

VRRRAWWW

YOU'VE GOT A *GODDESS* ON YOUR SIDE!

THE FIRST JUMP!

IF I CATCH TOO MUCH AIR I'LL LOSE ACCELERATION...

...GOTTA KEEP THAT REAR TIRE SUCKING DIRT!

VRAAAA

KEEP HER LOW!

HE'S REALLY RIPPING UP THE HILL, THAT BOY!

YUP!

HUH? YOU GUYS?!

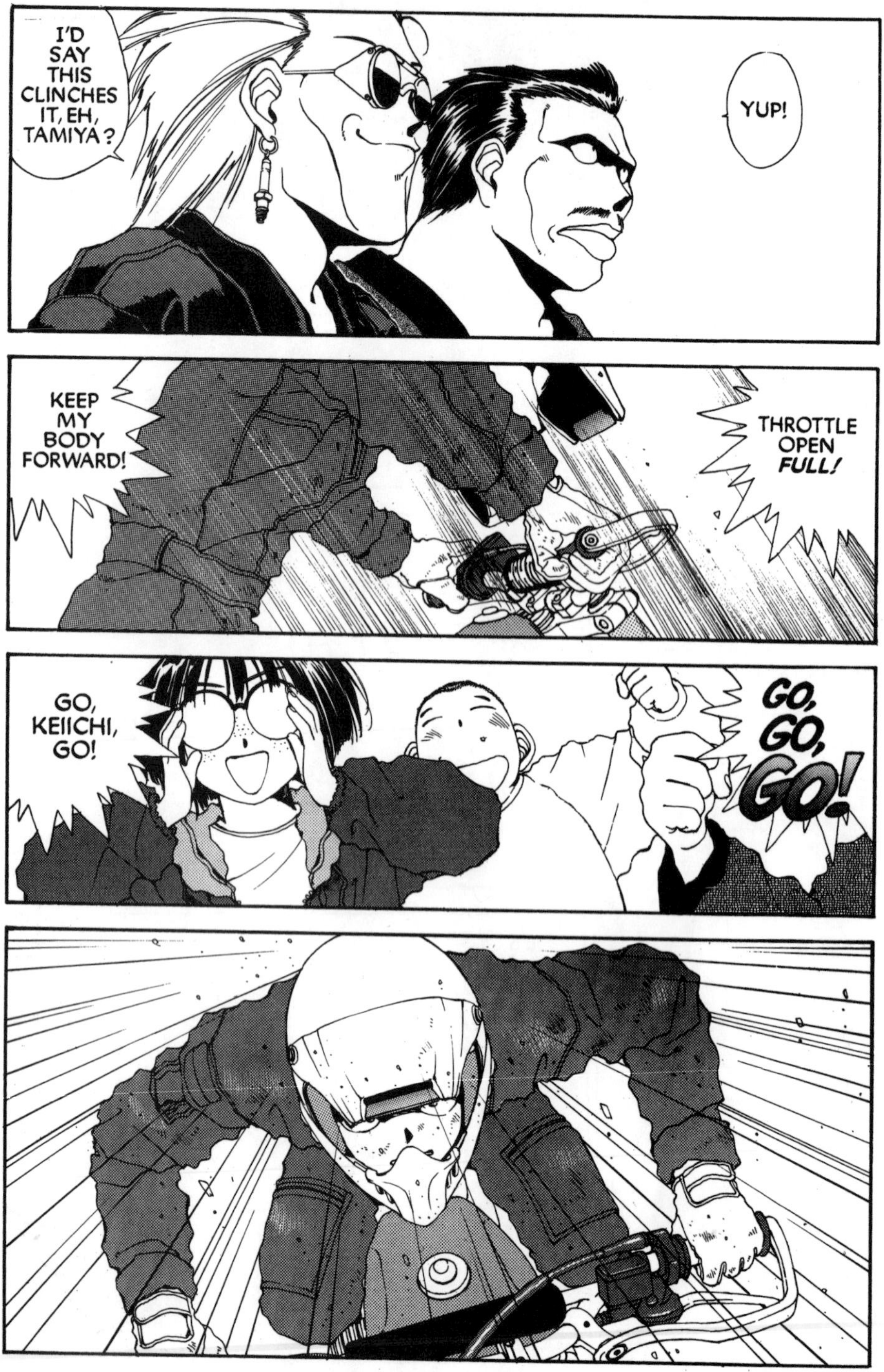
I'D SAY THIS CLINCHES IT, EH, TAMIYA?
YUP!
KEEP MY BODY FORWARD!
THROTTLE OPEN *FULL!*
GO, KEIICHI, GO!
GO, GO, GO!

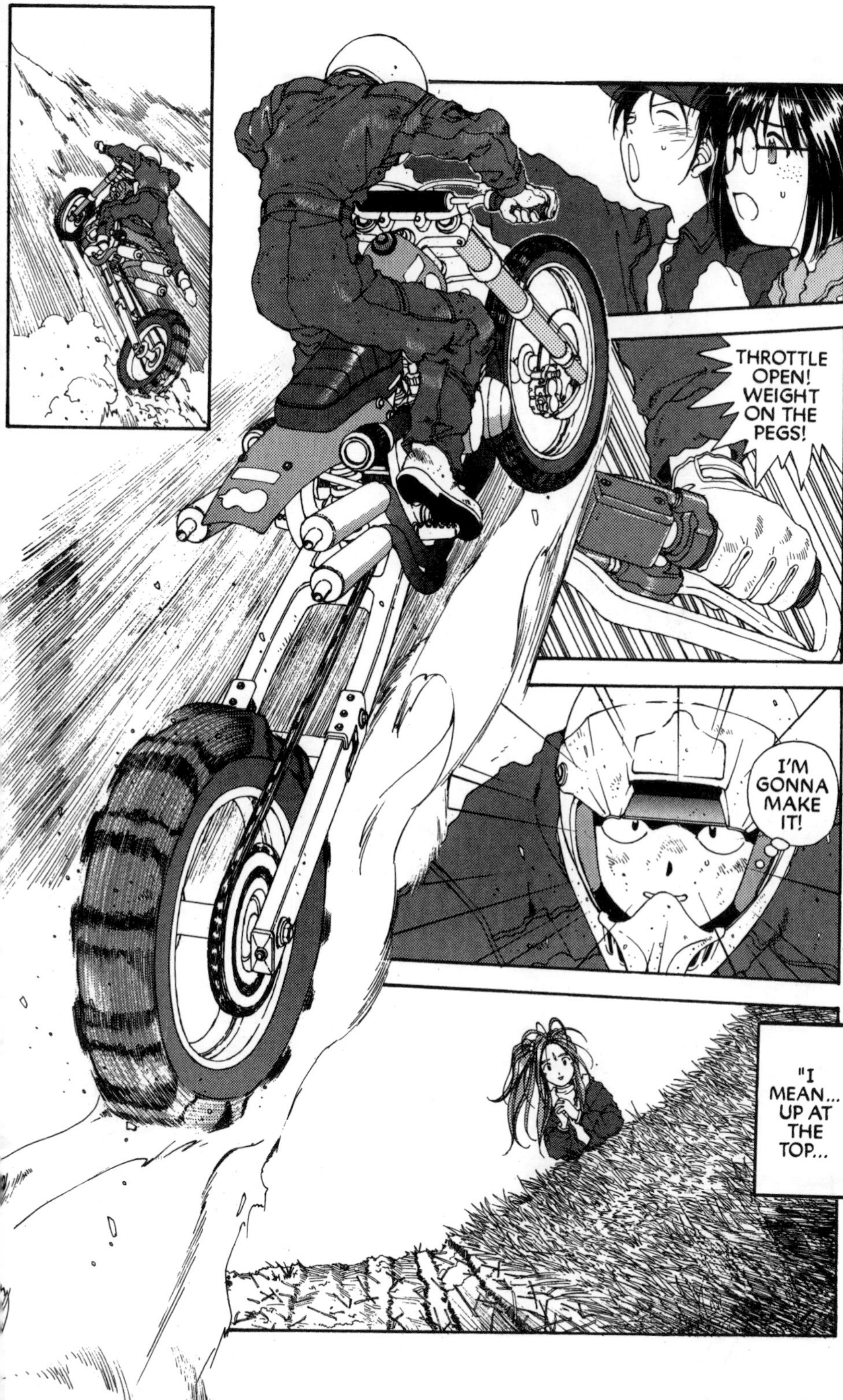
THROTTLE OPEN! WEIGHT ON THE PEGS!
I'M GONNA MAKE IT!
"I MEAN... UP AT THE TOP...

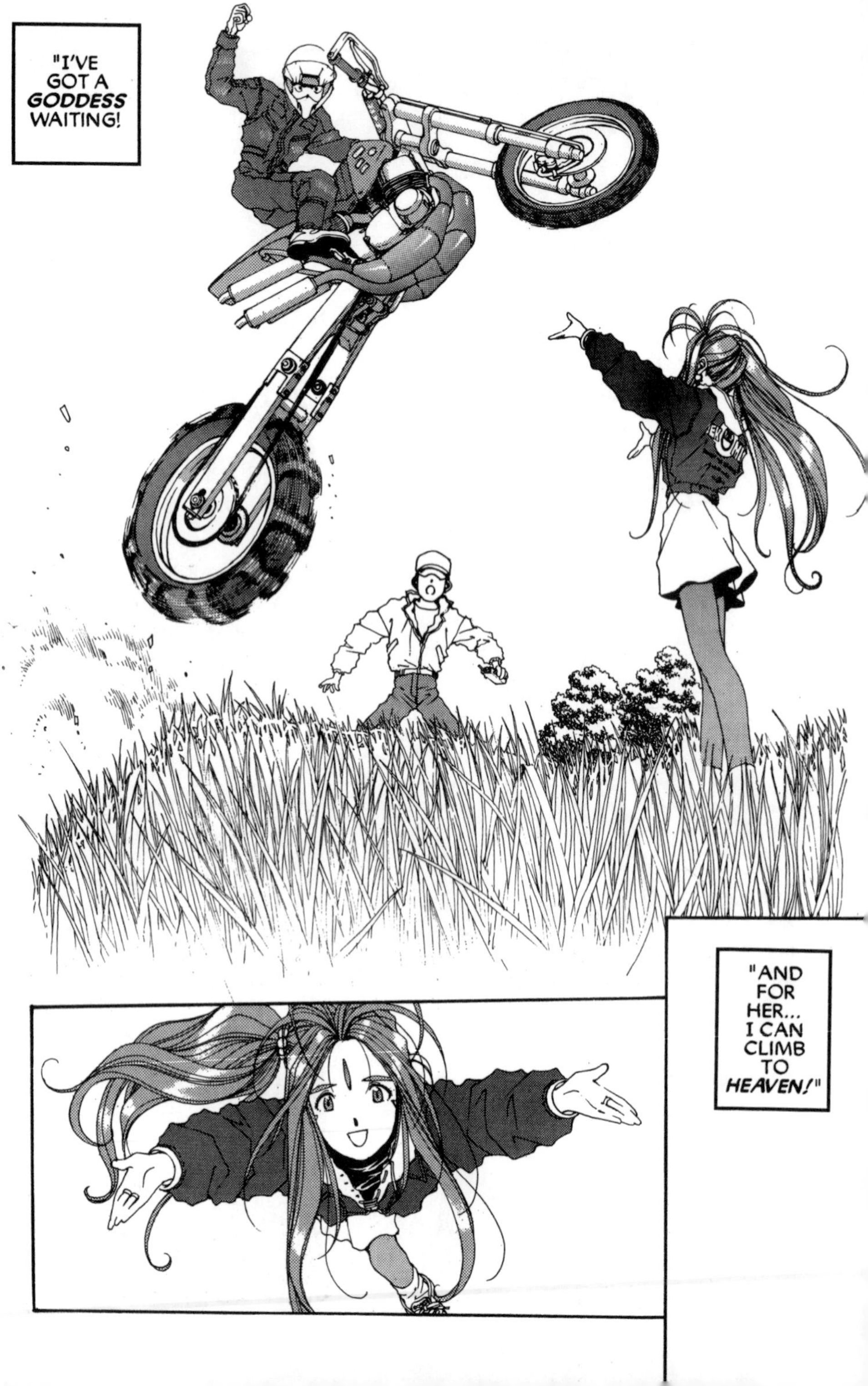
"I'VE GOT A *GODDESS* WAITING!
"AND FOR HER... I CAN CLIMB TO *HEAVEN!*"

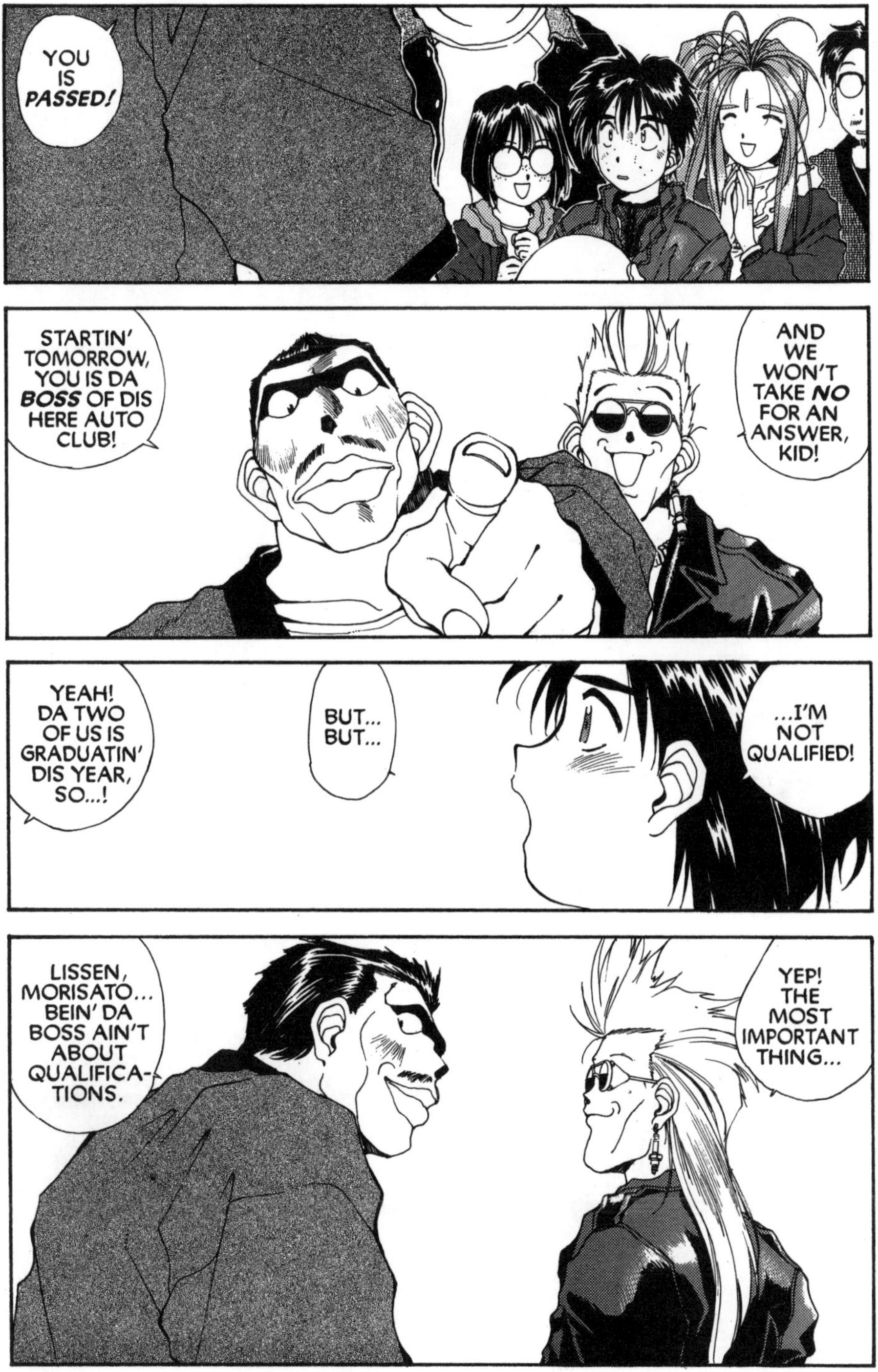
YOU IS PASSED!
STARTIN' TOMORROW, YOU IS DA BOSS OF DIS HERE AUTO CLUB!
AND WE WON'T TAKE NO FOR AN ANSWER, KID!
YEAH! DA TWO OF US IS GRADUATIN' DIS YEAR, SO...!
BUT... BUT...
...I'M NOT QUALIFIED!
LISSEN, MORISATO... BEIN' DA BOSS AIN'T ABOUT QUALIFICA-TIONS.
YEP! THE MOST IMPORTANT THING...

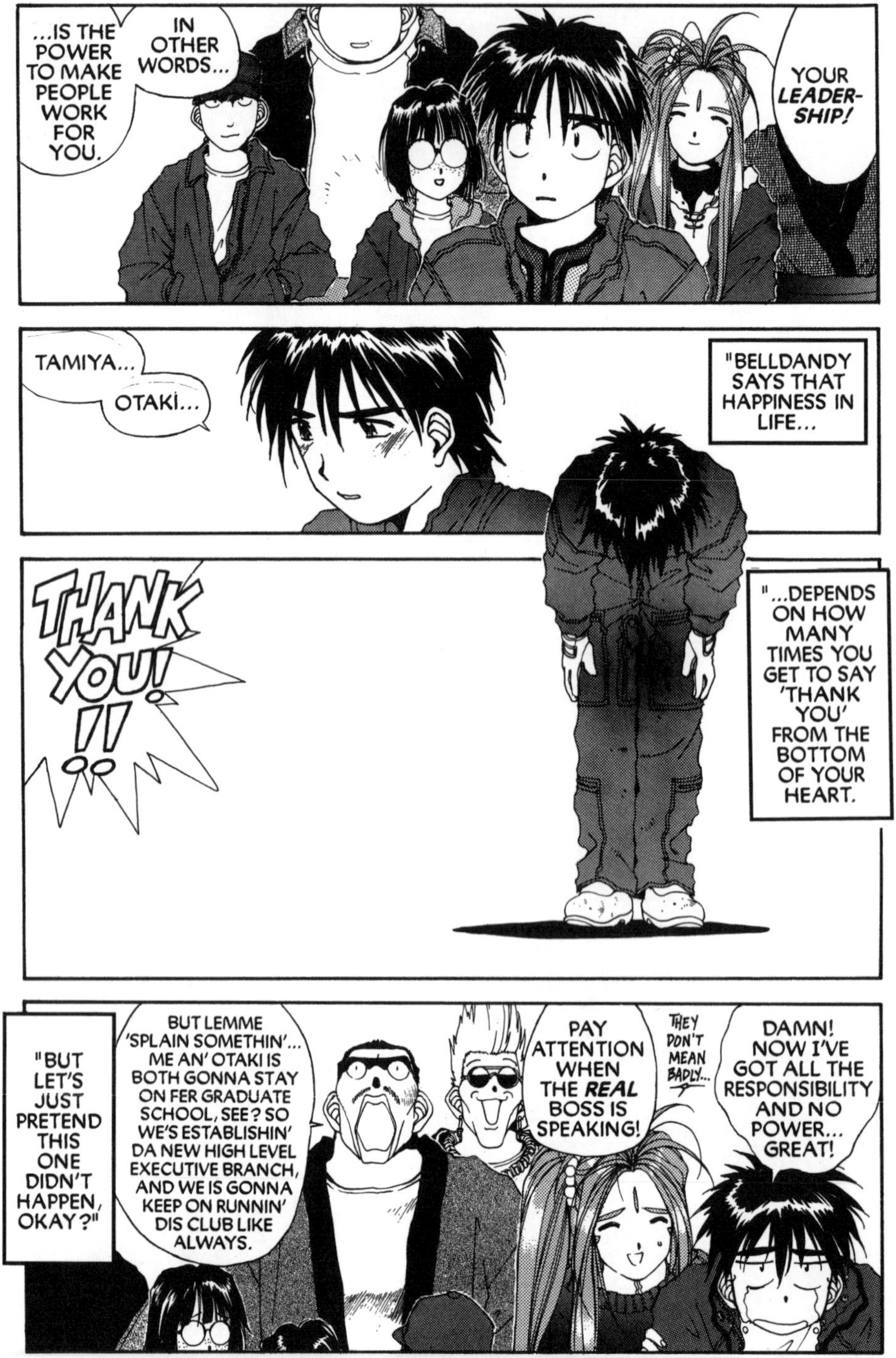
...IS THE POWER TO MAKE PEOPLE WORK FOR YOU.
IN OTHER WORDS...
YOUR *LEADERSHIP!*
TAMIYA...
OTAKI...
"BELLDANDY SAYS THAT HAPPINESS IN LIFE...
THANK YOU!!
"...DEPENDS ON HOW MANY TIMES YOU GET TO SAY 'THANK YOU' FROM THE BOTTOM OF YOUR HEART.
"BUT LET'S JUST PRETEND THIS ONE DIDN'T HAPPEN, OKAY?"
BUT LEMME 'SPLAIN SOMETHIN'... ME AN' OTAKI IS BOTH GONNA STAY ON FER GRADUATE SCHOOL, SEE? SO WE'S ESTABLISHIN' DA NEW HIGH LEVEL EXECUTIVE BRANCH, AND WE IS GONNA KEEP ON RUNNIN' DIS CLUB LIKE ALWAYS.
PAY ATTENTION WHEN THE *REAL* BOSS IS SPEAKING!
THEY DON'T MEAN BADLY...
DAMN! NOW I'VE GOT ALL THE RESPONSIBILITY AND NO POWER... GREAT!

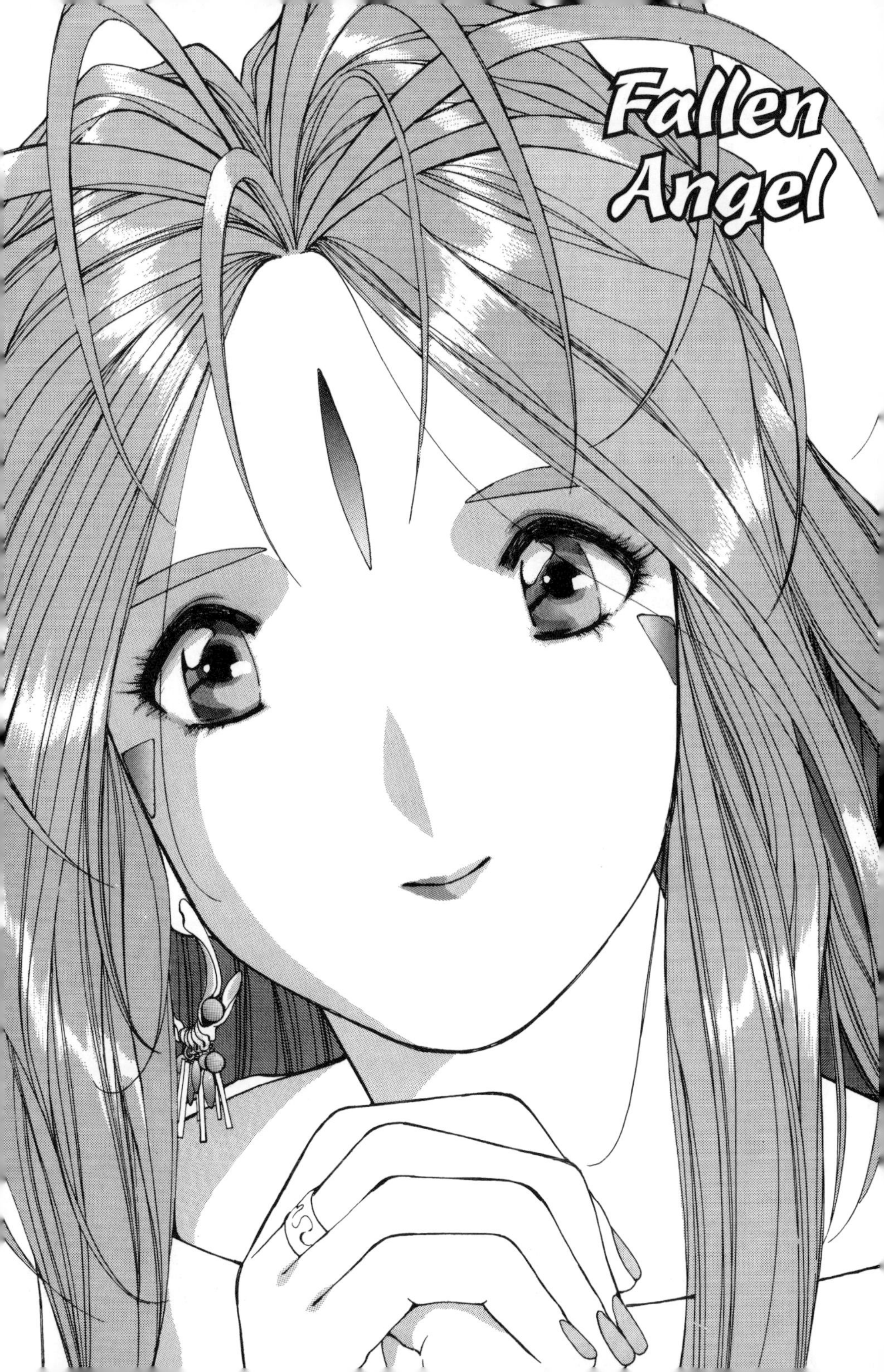
Fallen Angel

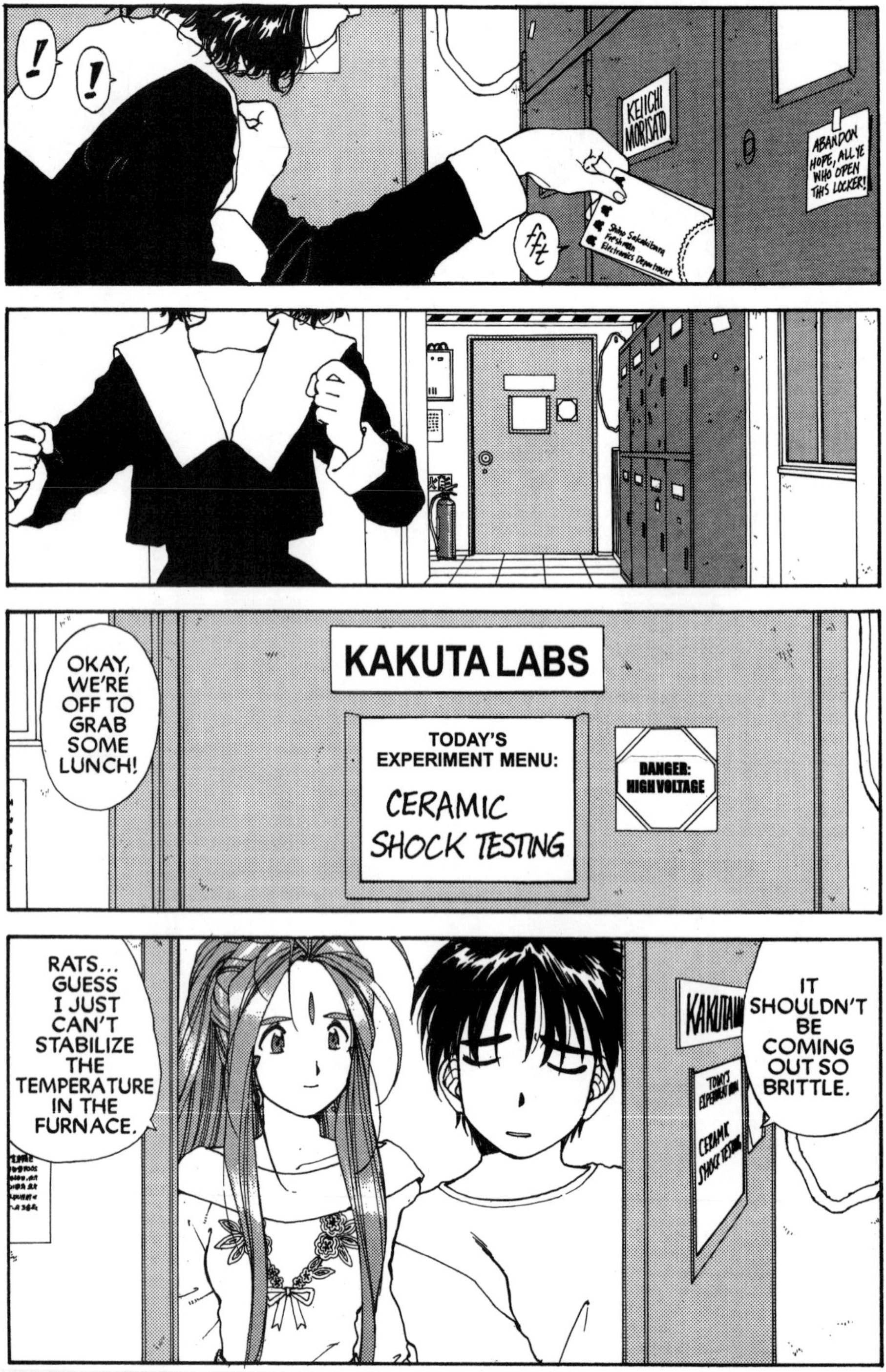
!
!
KEIICHI MORISATO
ABANDON HOPE, ALL YE WHO OPEN THIS LOCKER!
Shiho Sakakibara Freshman Electronics Department
fft
OKAY, WE'RE OFF TO GRAB SOME LUNCH!
KAKUTA LABS
TODAY'S EXPERIMENT MENU:
CERAMIC SHOCK TESTING
DANGER: HIGH VOLTAGE
RATS... GUESS I JUST CAN'T STABILIZE THE TEMPERATURE IN THE FURNACE.
IT SHOULDN'T BE COMING OUT SO BRITTLE.

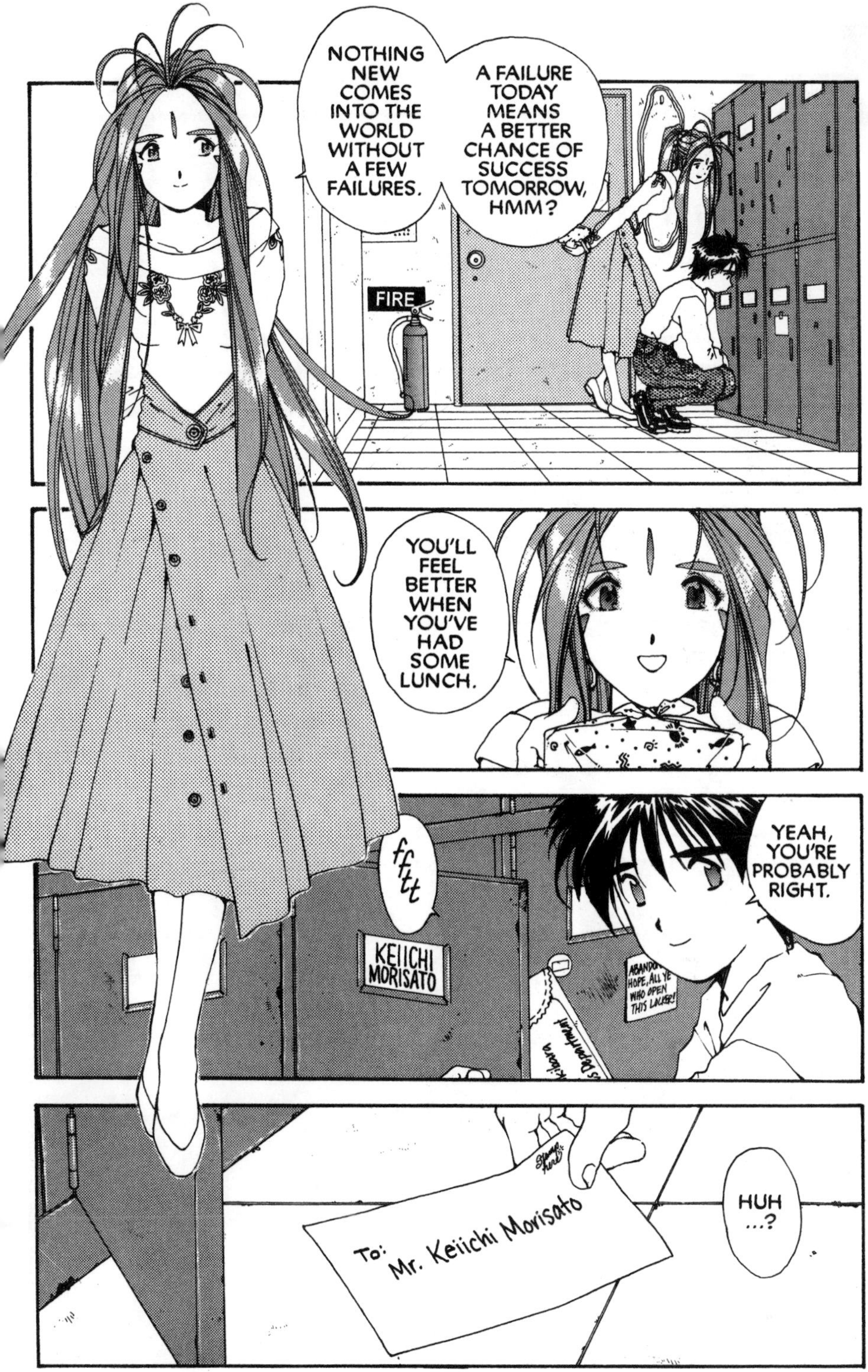

NOTHING NEW COMES INTO THE WORLD WITHOUT A FEW FAILURES.
A FAILURE TODAY MEANS A BETTER CHANCE OF SUCCESS TOMORROW, HMM?
FIRE
YOU'LL FEEL BETTER WHEN YOU'VE HAD SOME LUNCH.
fftt
KEIICHI MORISATO
ABANDO HOPE, ALL YE WHO OPEN THIS LOCKER!
YEAH, YOU'RE PROBABLY RIGHT.
To: Mr. Keiichi Morisato
HUH ...?

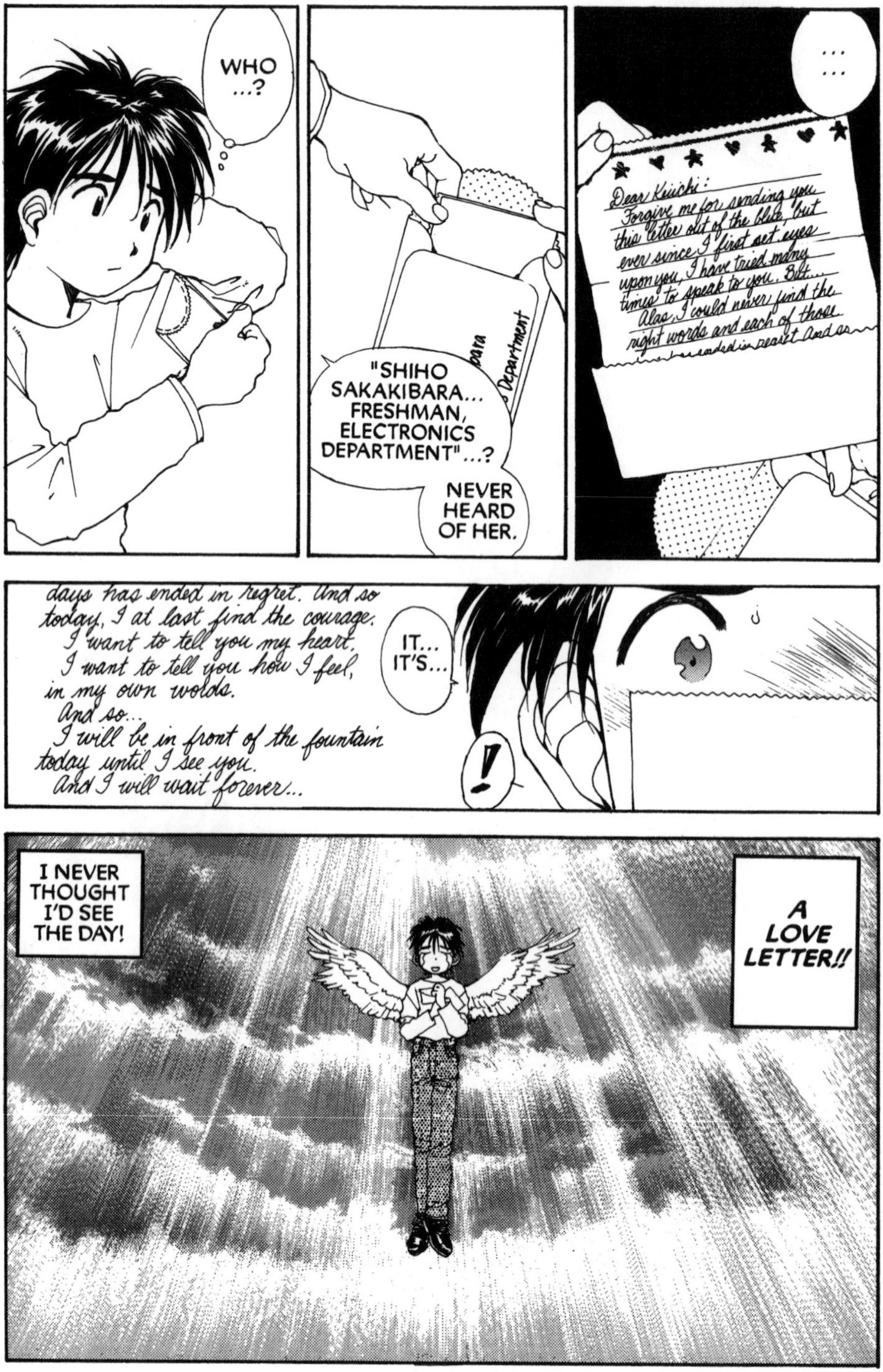
WHO ...?
"SHIHO SAKAKIBARA... FRESHMAN, ELECTRONICS DEPARTMENT"...?
NEVER HEARD OF HER.
... ...
Dear Keiichi:
Forgive me for sending you this letter out of the blue, but ever since I first set eyes upon you, I have tried many times to speak to you. But...
Alas, I could never find the right words and each of those
days has ended in regret. And so today, I at last find the courage.
I want to tell you my heart.
I want to tell you how I feel, in my own words.
And so...
I will be in front of the fountain today until I see you.
And I will wait forever...
IT... IT'S...
!
I NEVER THOUGHT I'D SEE THE DAY!
A LOVE LETTER!!

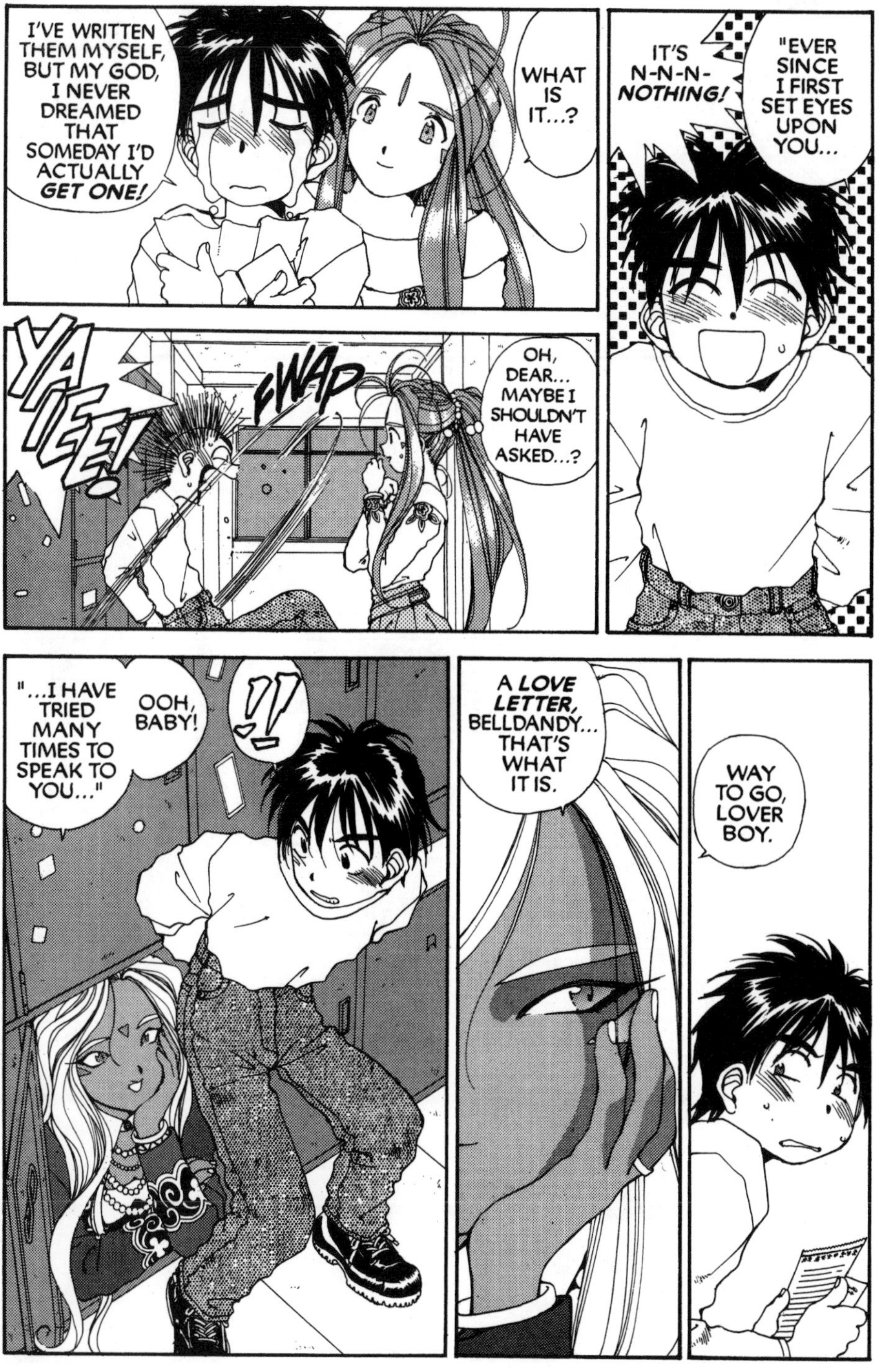
I'VE WRITTEN THEM MYSELF, BUT MY GOD, I NEVER DREAMED THAT SOMEDAY I'D ACTUALLY *GET ONE!*
WHAT IS IT...?
YAIEEE!
FWAP
OH, DEAR... MAYBE I SHOULDN'T HAVE ASKED...?
IT'S N-N-N-*NOTHING!*
"EVER SINCE I FIRST SET EYES UPON YOU...
"...I HAVE TRIED MANY TIMES TO SPEAK TO YOU..."
OOH, BABY!
!?
A *LOVE LETTER,* BELLDANDY... THAT'S WHAT IT IS.
WAY TO GO, LOVER BOY.

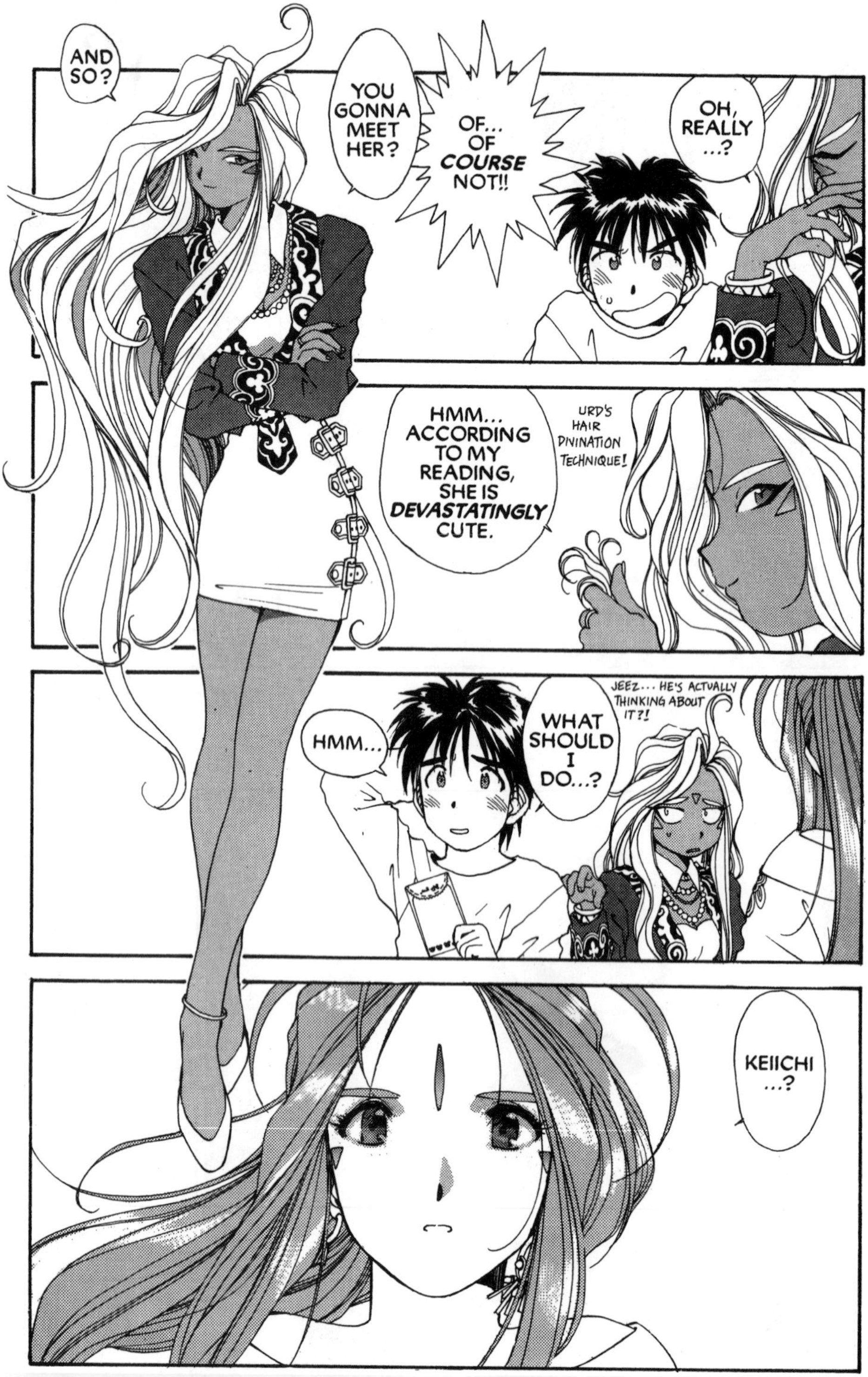
AND SO?
YOU GONNA MEET HER?
OF... OF COURSE NOT!!
OH, REALLY ...?
HMM... ACCORDING TO MY READING, SHE IS DEVASTATINGLY CUTE.
URD'S HAIR DIVINATION TECHNIQUE!
HMM...
WHAT SHOULD I DO...?
JEEZ... HE'S ACTUALLY THINKING ABOUT IT?!
KEIICHI ...?

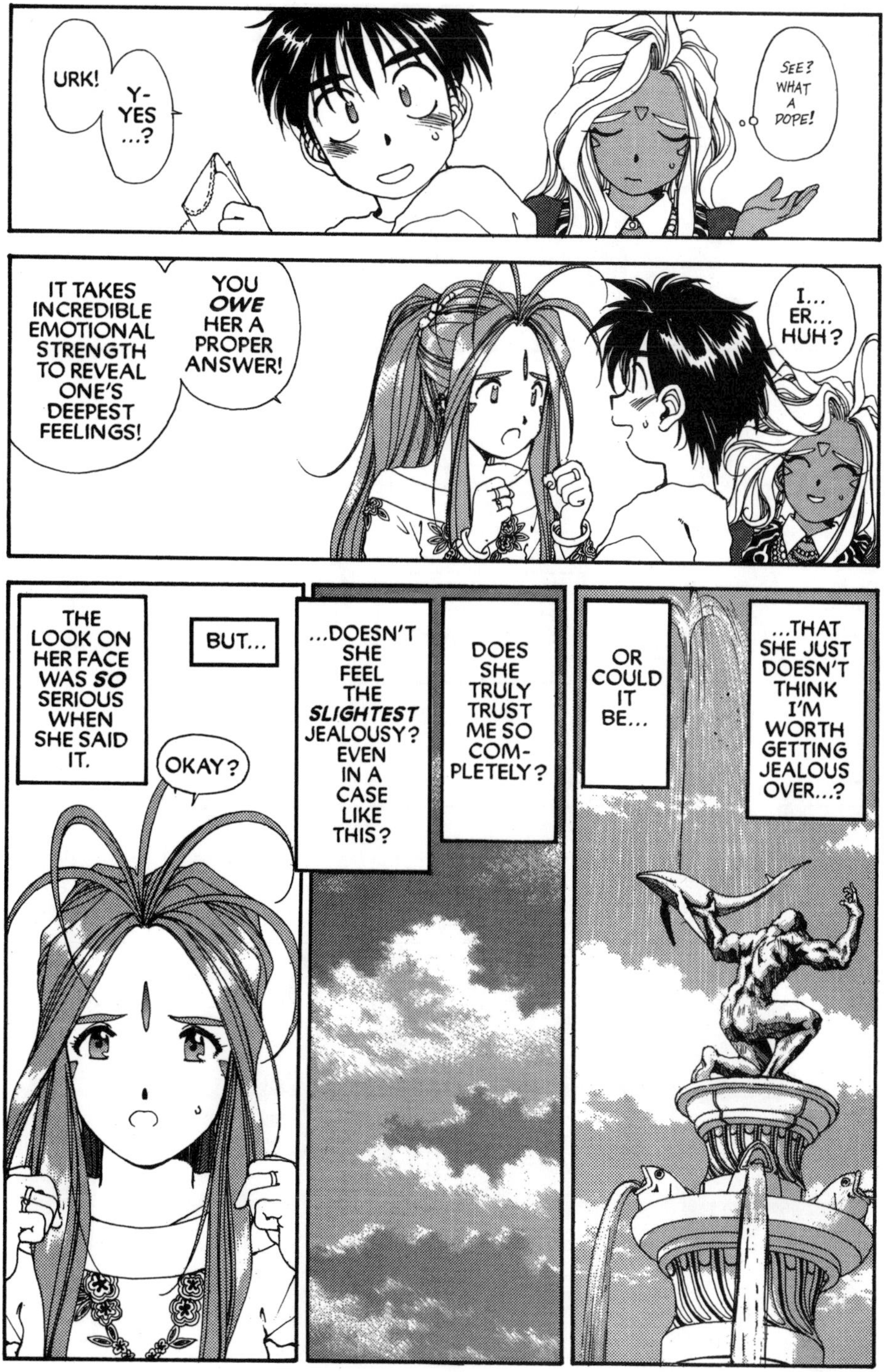
URK!
Y-YES...?
SEE? WHAT A DOPE!
IT TAKES INCREDIBLE EMOTIONAL STRENGTH TO REVEAL ONE'S DEEPEST FEELINGS!
YOU *OWE* HER A PROPER ANSWER!
I... ER... HUH?
THE LOOK ON HER FACE WAS *SO* SERIOUS WHEN SHE SAID IT.
BUT...
OKAY?
...DOESN'T SHE FEEL THE *SLIGHTEST* JEALOUSY? EVEN IN A CASE LIKE THIS?
DOES SHE TRULY TRUST ME SO COMPLETELY?
OR COULD IT BE...
...THAT SHE JUST DOESN'T THINK I'M WORTH GETTING JEALOUS OVER...?

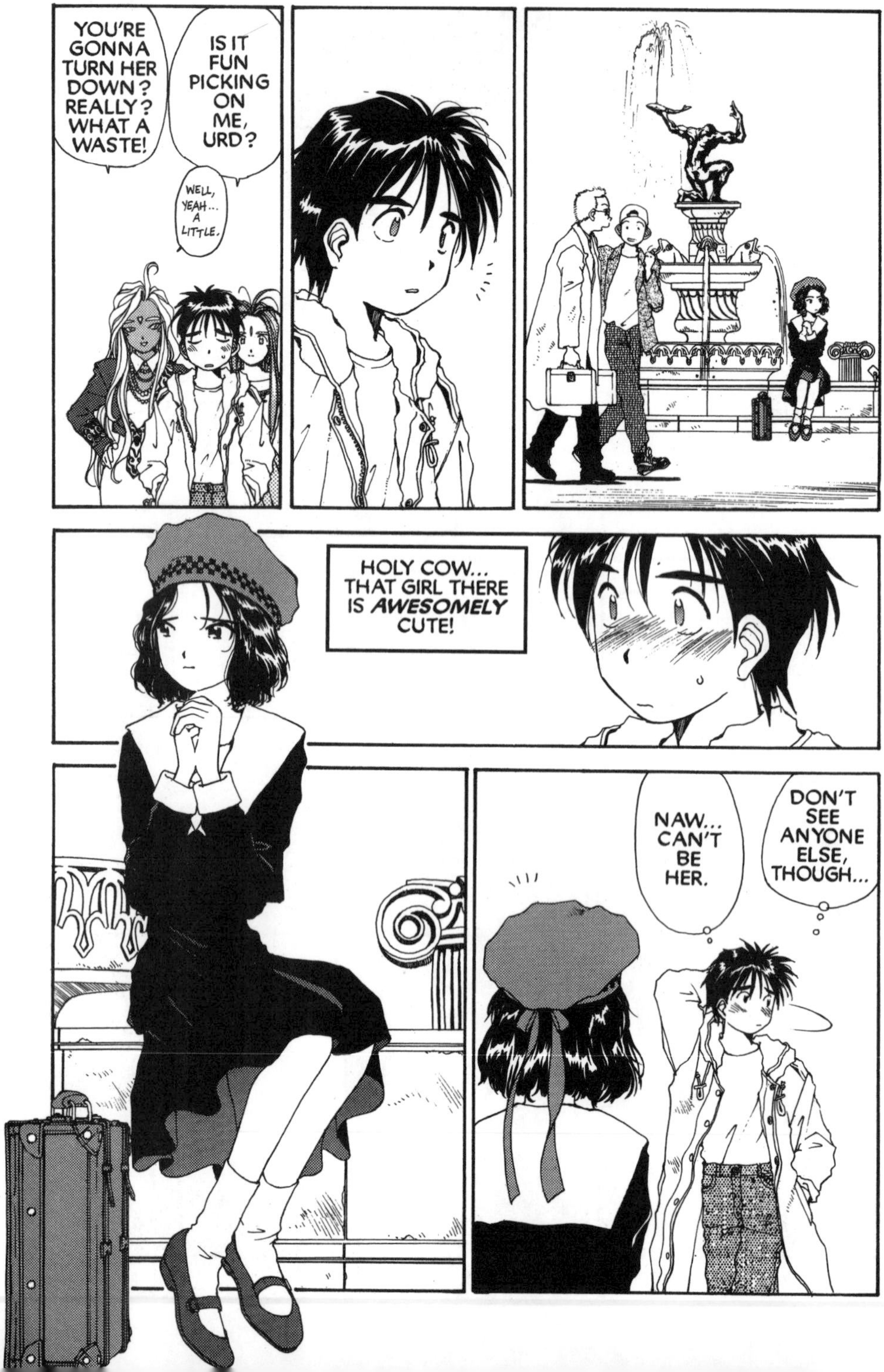
YOU'RE GONNA TURN HER DOWN? REALLY? WHAT A WASTE!
IS IT FUN PICKING ON ME, URD?
WELL, YEAH... A LITTLE.
HOLY COW... THAT GIRL THERE IS *AWESOMELY* CUTE!
NAW... CAN'T BE HER.
DON'T SEE ANYONE ELSE, THOUGH...

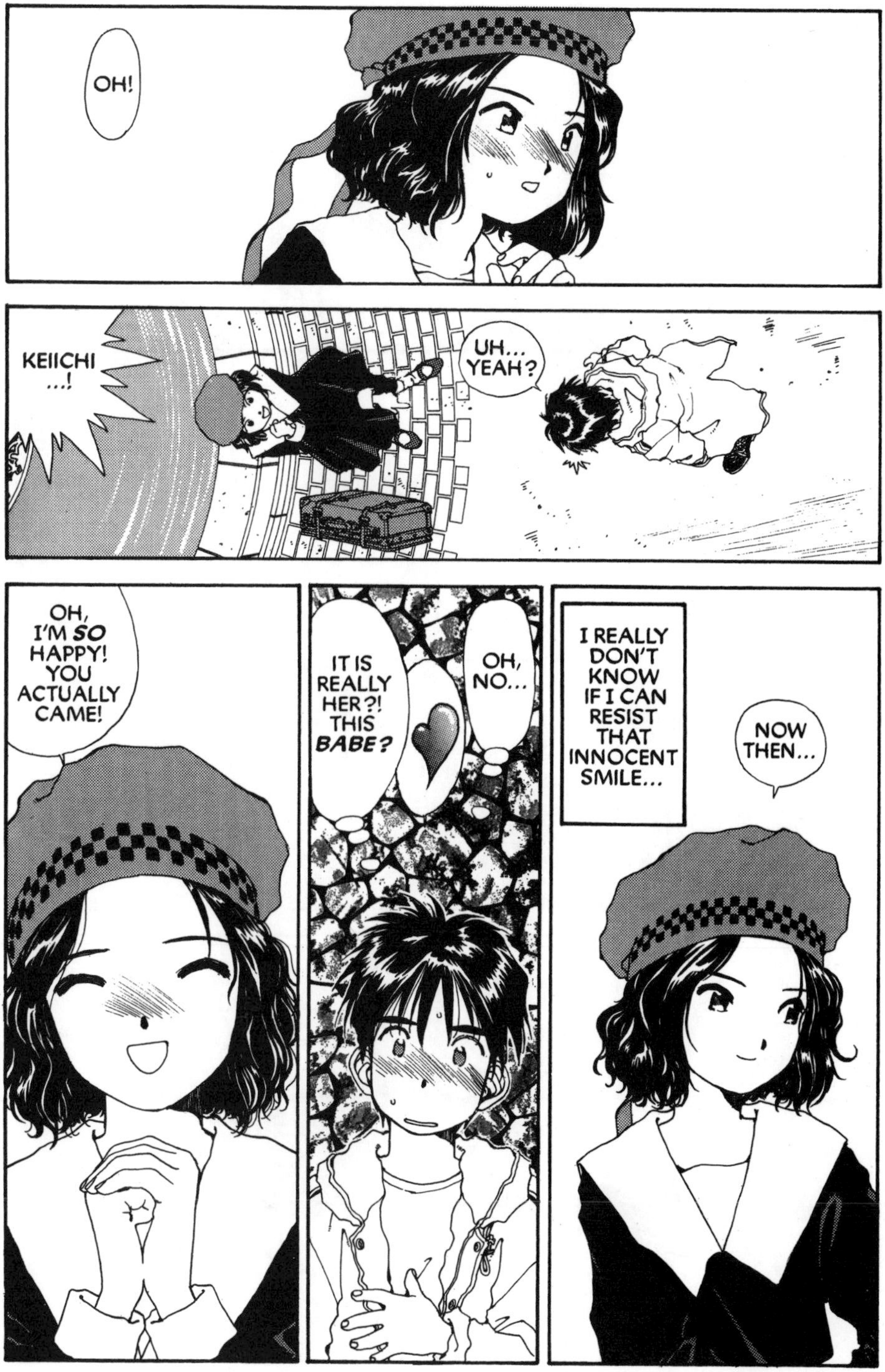
OH!
KEIICHI ...!
UH... YEAH?
OH, I'M SO HAPPY! YOU ACTUALLY CAME!
IT IS REALLY HER?! THIS BABE?
OH, NO...
I REALLY DON'T KNOW IF I CAN RESIST THAT INNOCENT SMILE...
NOW THEN...

I KNOW... I'VE GOT IT... *THERE!*

I'M SORRY!

BUT I JUST--

HUH?

DON'T MOVE!

UH ...?

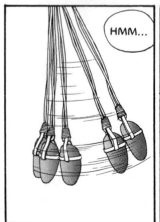

HMM...

AH *HAH!*

I WAS *RIGHT!*

YOU WERE?

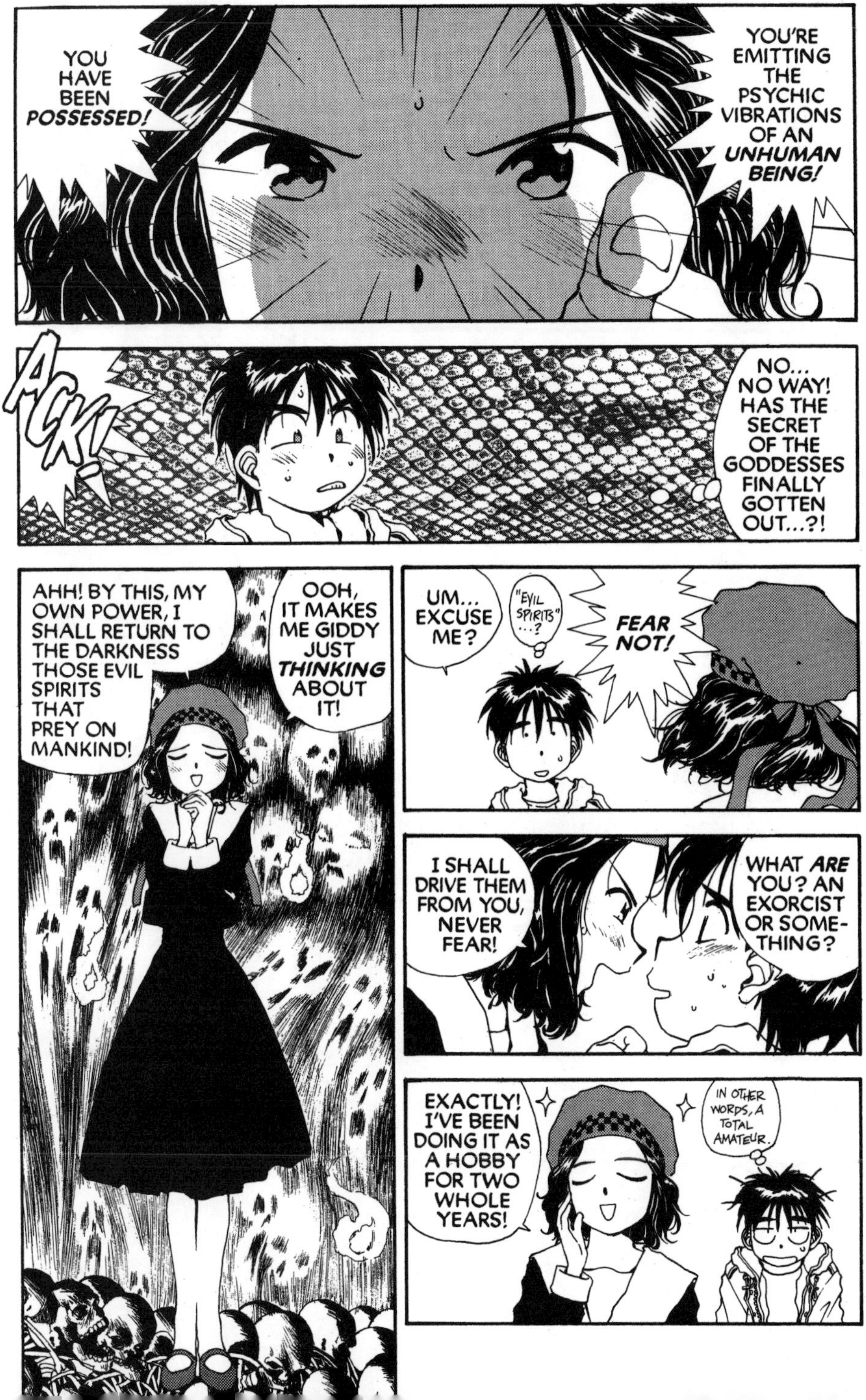
YOU HAVE BEEN *POSSESSED!*
YOU'RE EMITTING THE PSYCHIC VIBRATIONS OF AN *UNHUMAN BEING!*
ACK!
NO... NO WAY! HAS THE SECRET OF THE GODDESSES FINALLY GOTTEN OUT...?!
AHH! BY THIS, MY OWN POWER, I SHALL RETURN TO THE DARKNESS THOSE EVIL SPIRITS THAT PREY ON MANKIND!
OOH, IT MAKES ME GIDDY JUST *THINKING* ABOUT IT!
UM... EXCUSE ME?
"EVIL SPIRITS"...?
FEAR NOT!
I SHALL DRIVE THEM FROM YOU, NEVER FEAR!
WHAT *ARE* YOU? AN EXORCIST OR SOME-THING?
EXACTLY! I'VE BEEN DOING IT AS A HOBBY FOR TWO WHOLE YEARS!
IN OTHER WORDS, A TOTAL AMATEUR.

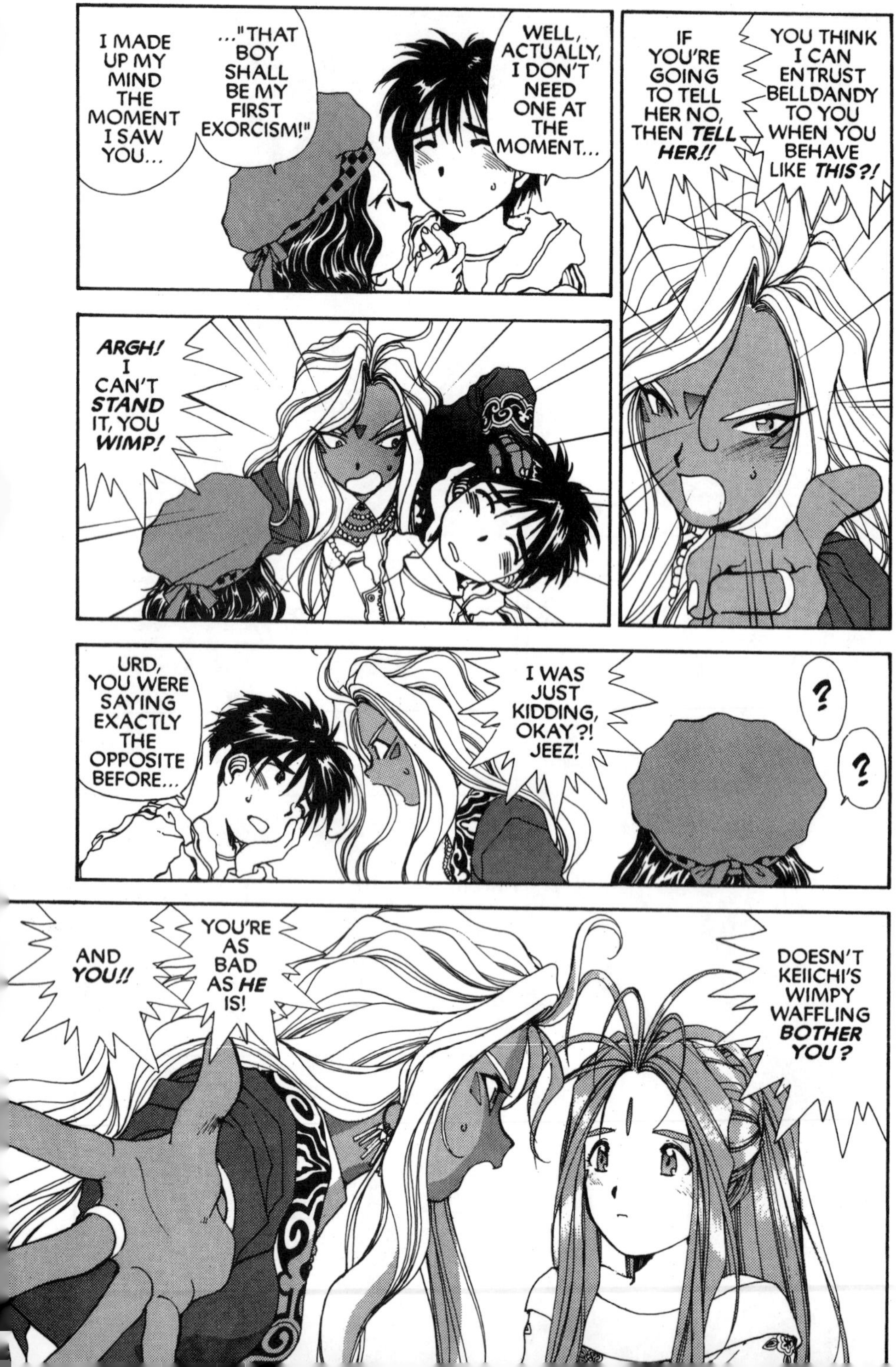

I MADE UP MY MIND THE MOMENT I SAW YOU...
..."THAT BOY SHALL BE MY FIRST EXORCISM!"
WELL, ACTUALLY, I DON'T NEED ONE AT THE MOMENT...
ARGH! I CAN'T STAND IT, YOU WIMP!
IF YOU'RE GOING TO TELL HER NO, THEN TELL HER!!
YOU THINK I CAN ENTRUST BELLDANDY TO YOU WHEN YOU BEHAVE LIKE THIS?!
URD, YOU WERE SAYING EXACTLY THE OPPOSITE BEFORE...
I WAS JUST KIDDING, OKAY?! JEEZ!
?
?
AND YOU!!
YOU'RE AS BAD AS HE IS!
DOESN'T KEIICHI'S WIMPY WAFFLING BOTHER YOU?

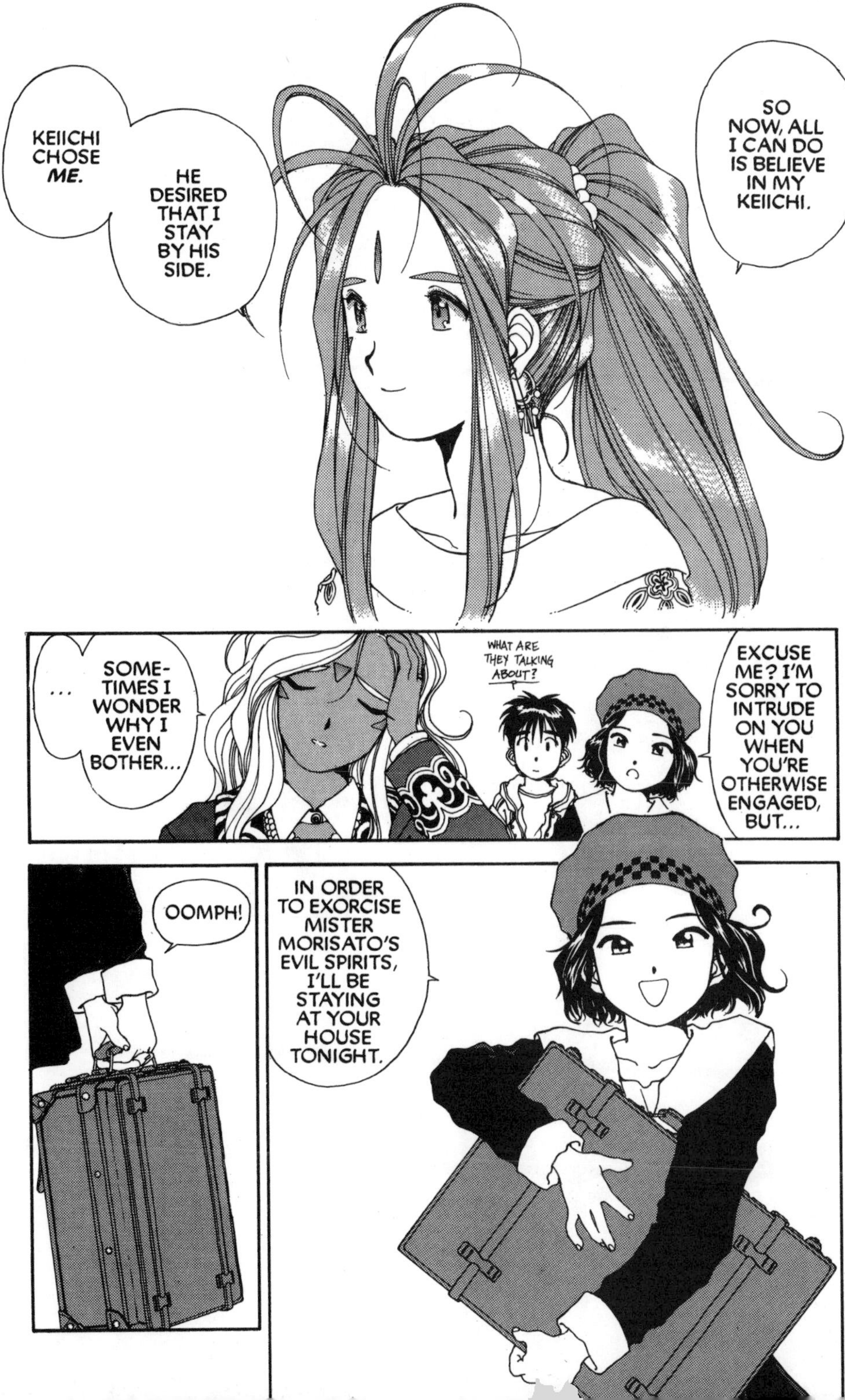
KEIICHI CHOSE *ME.*
HE DESIRED THAT I STAY BY HIS SIDE.
SO NOW, ALL I CAN DO IS BELIEVE IN MY KEIICHI.
... SOMETIMES I WONDER WHY I EVEN BOTHER...
WHAT ARE THEY TALKING ABOUT?
EXCUSE ME? I'M SORRY TO INTRUDE ON YOU WHEN YOU'RE OTHERWISE ENGAGED, BUT...
OOMPH!
IN ORDER TO EXORCISE MISTER MORISATO'S EVIL SPIRITS, I'LL BE STAYING AT YOUR HOUSE TONIGHT.

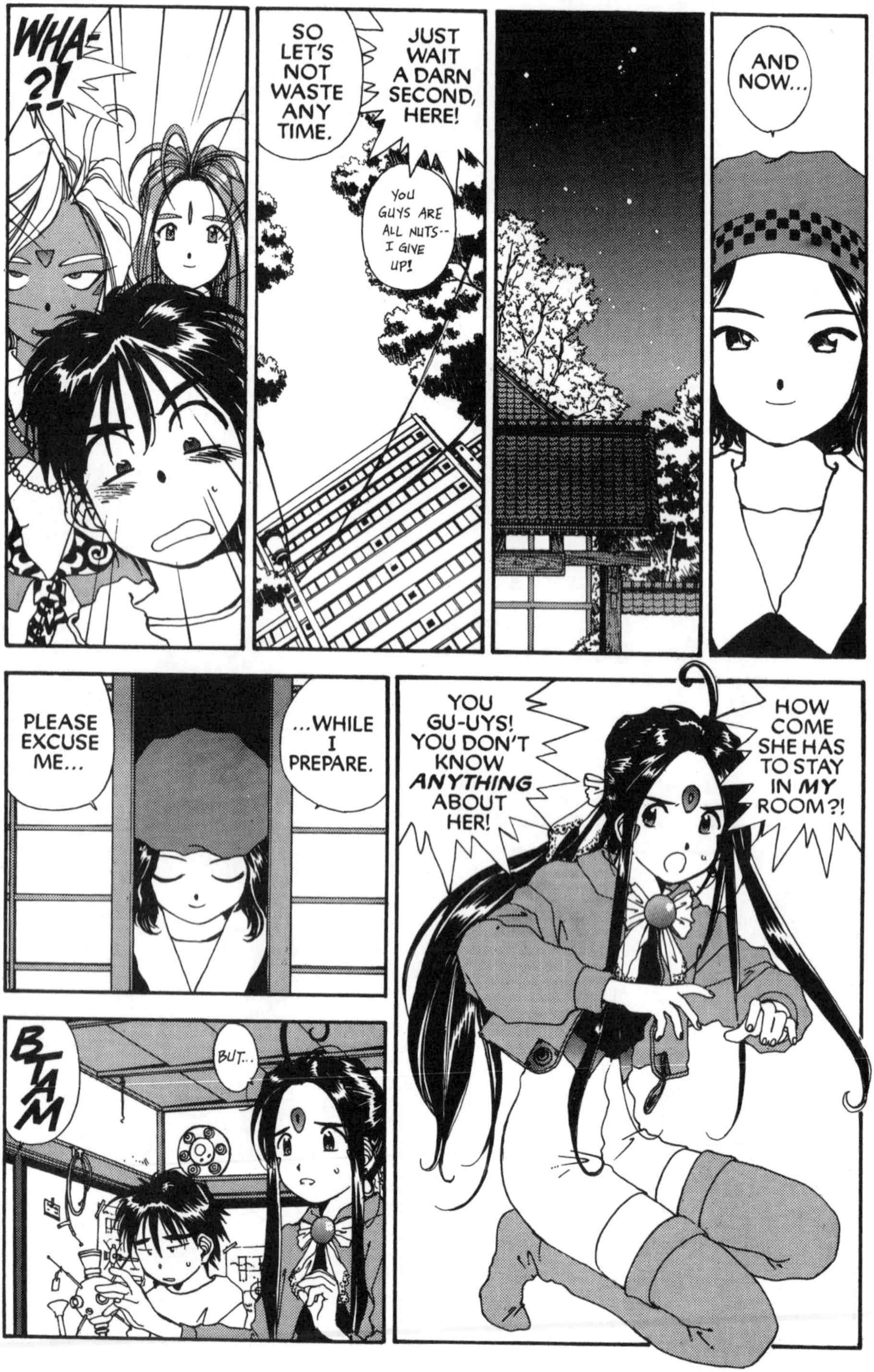
WHA-?!
SO LET'S NOT WASTE ANY TIME.
JUST WAIT A DARN SECOND, HERE!
YOU GUYS ARE ALL NUTS-- I GIVE UP!
AND NOW...
PLEASE EXCUSE ME...
...WHILE I PREPARE.
BTAM
BUT...
YOU GU-UYS! YOU DON'T KNOW ANYTHING ABOUT HER!
HOW COME SHE HAS TO STAY IN MY ROOM?!

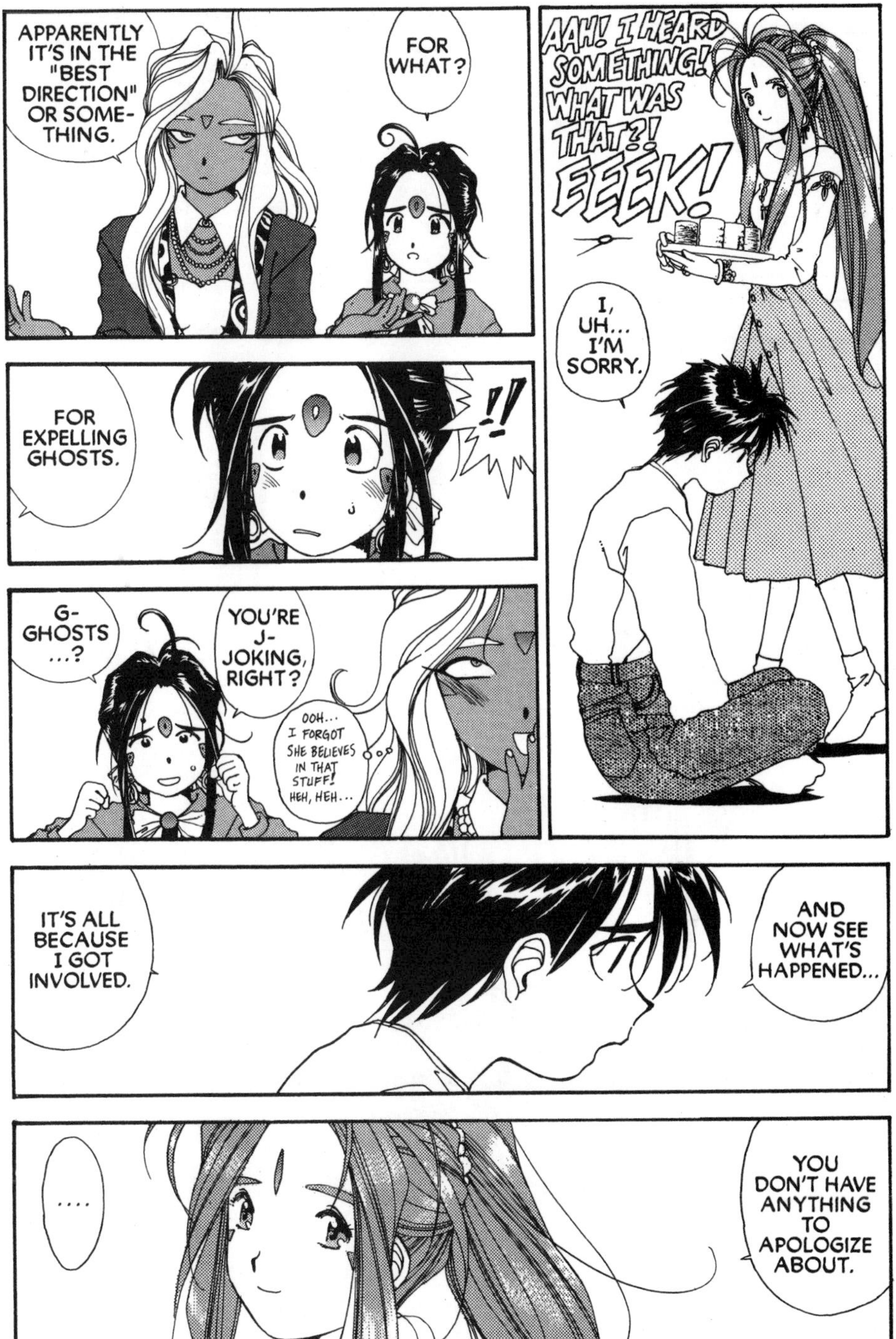
APPARENTLY IT'S IN THE "BEST DIRECTION" OR SOMETHING.
FOR WHAT?
FOR EXPELLING GHOSTS.
!!
G-GHOSTS ...?
YOU'RE J-JOKING, RIGHT?
OOH... I FORGOT SHE BELIEVES IN THAT STUFF! HEH, HEH...
AAH! I HEARD SOMETHING! WHAT WAS THAT?! EEEK!
I, UH... I'M SORRY.
IT'S ALL BECAUSE I GOT INVOLVED.
AND NOW SEE WHAT'S HAPPENED...
....
YOU DON'T HAVE ANYTHING TO APOLOGIZE ABOUT.

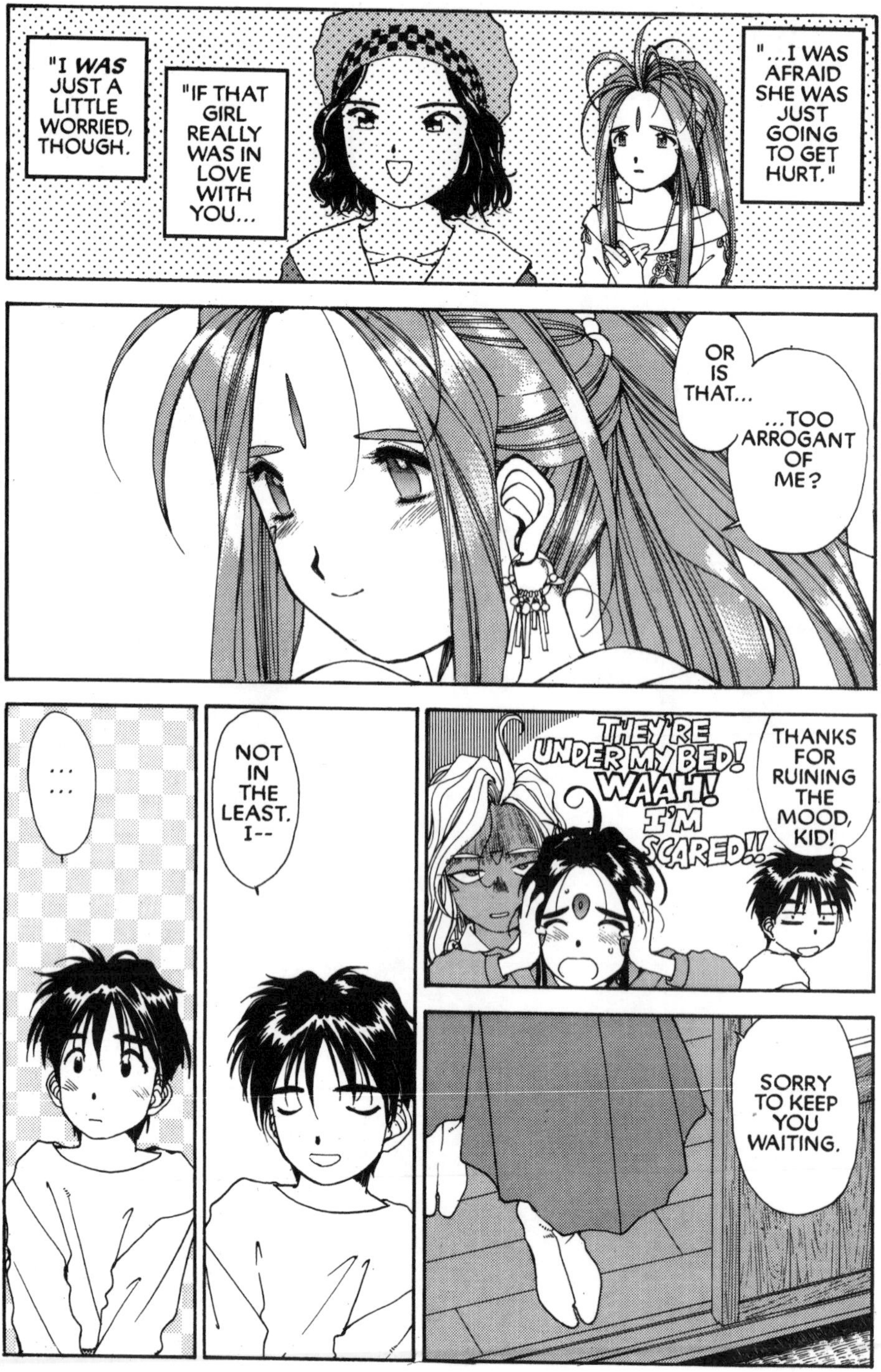
"I *WAS* JUST A LITTLE WORRIED, THOUGH.
"IF THAT GIRL REALLY WAS IN LOVE WITH YOU...
"...I WAS AFRAID SHE WAS JUST GOING TO GET HURT."
OR IS THAT...
...TOO ARROGANT OF ME?
......
NOT IN THE LEAST. I--
THEY'RE UNDER MY BED! WAAH! I'M SCARED!!
THANKS FOR RUINING THE MOOD, KID!
SORRY TO KEEP YOU WAITING.

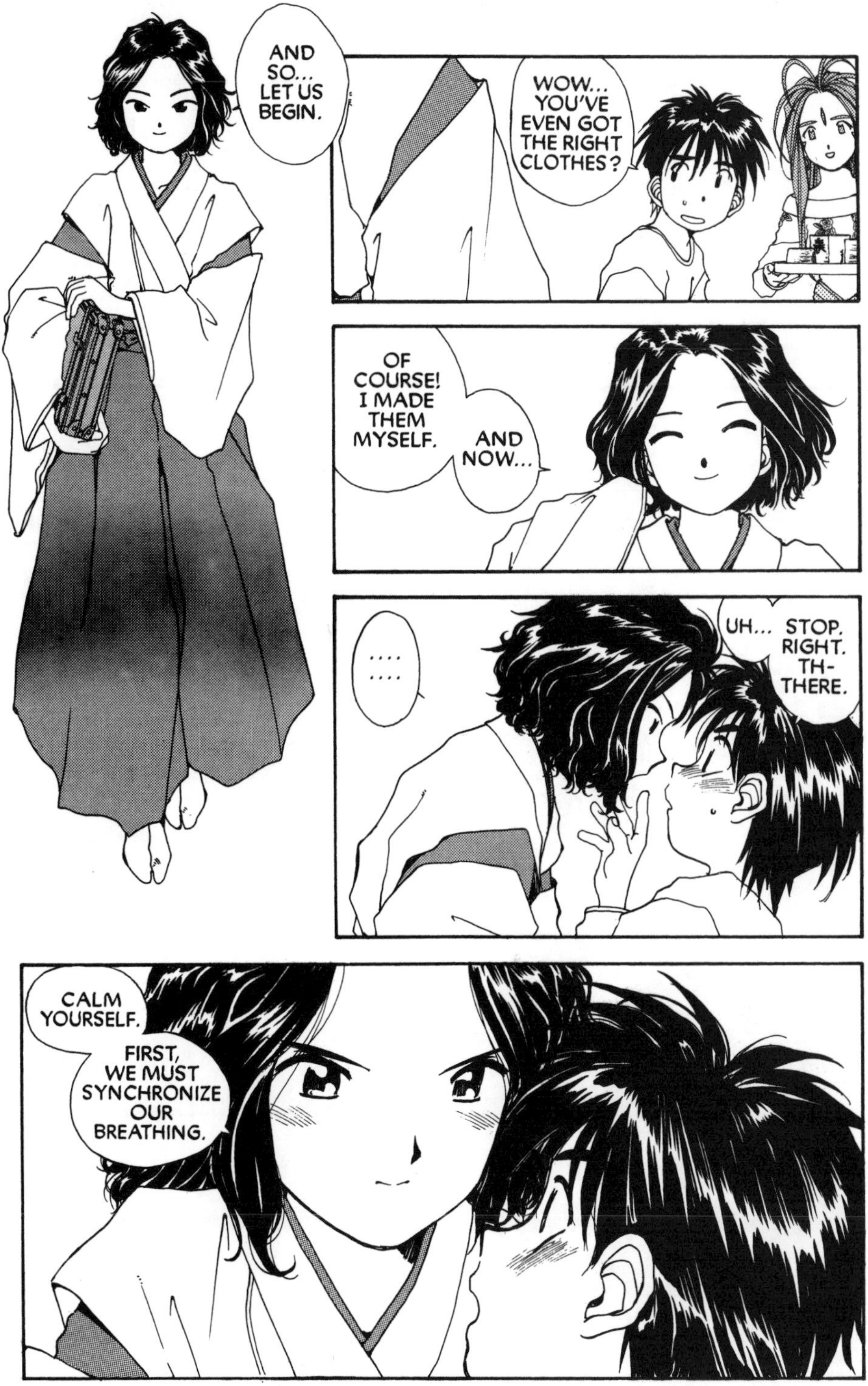
AND SO... LET US BEGIN.
WOW... YOU'VE EVEN GOT THE RIGHT CLOTHES?
OF COURSE! I MADE THEM MYSELF.
AND NOW...
....
UH... STOP. RIGHT. TH- THERE.
CALM YOURSELF.
FIRST, WE MUST SYNCHRONIZE OUR BREATHING.

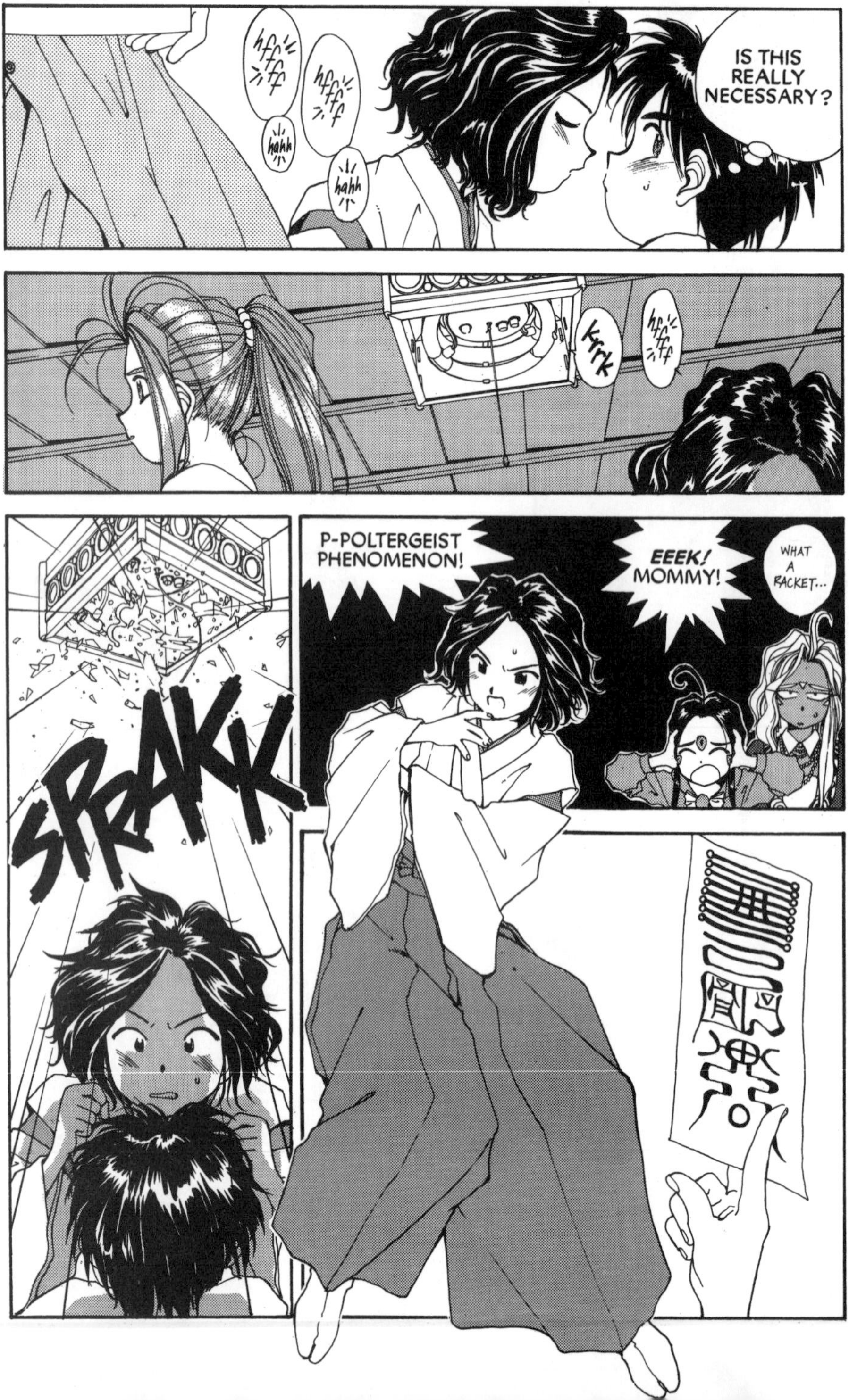
hfff
hahh
hfff
hahh
IS THIS REALLY NECESSARY?
Krrk
hfff
SPRAKK
P-POLTERGEIST PHENOMENON!
EEEK! MOMMY!
WHAT A RACKET...

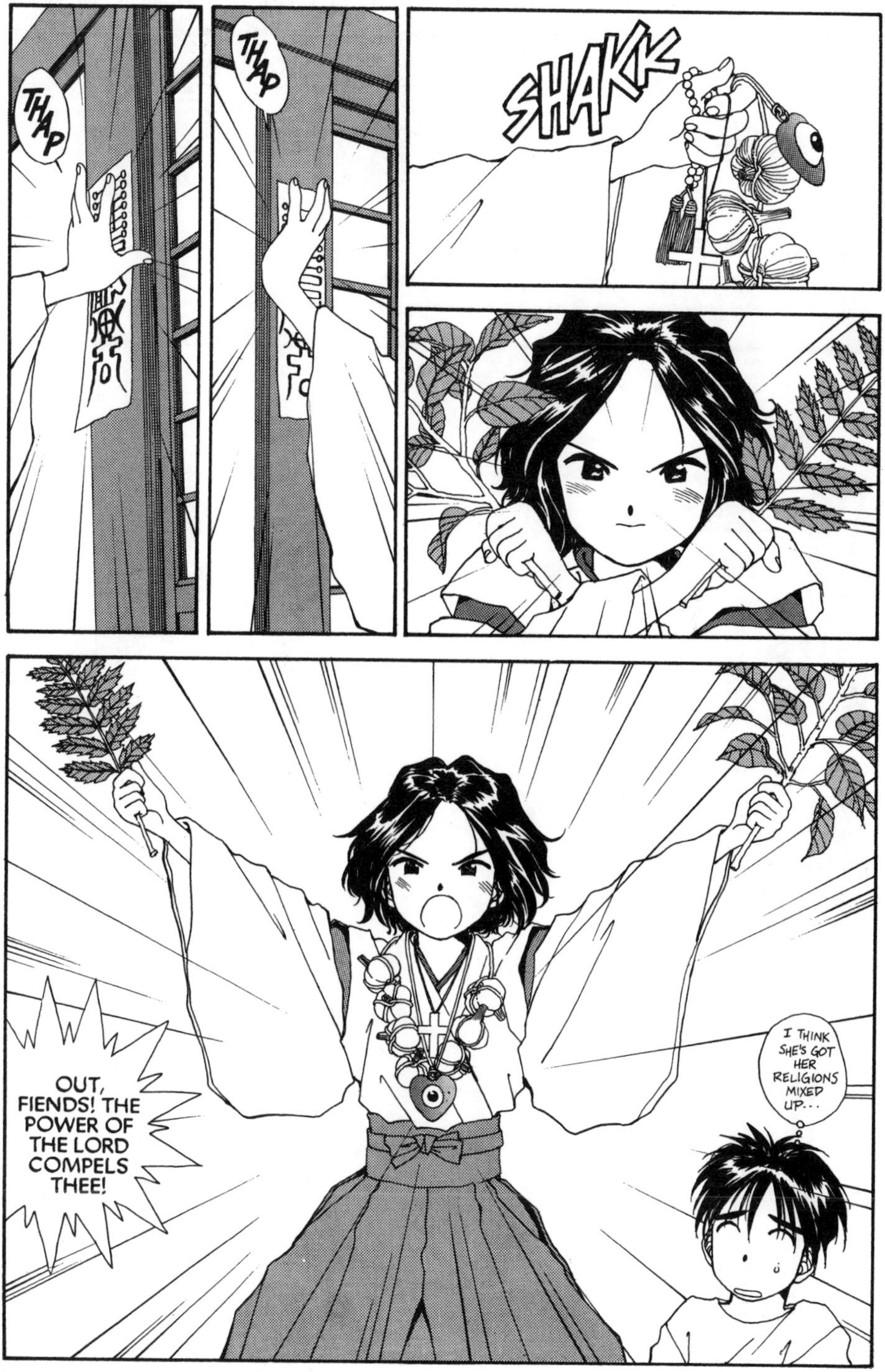
THAP
THAP
SHAKK
OUT, FIENDS! THE POWER OF THE LORD COMPELS THEE!
I THINK SHE'S GOT HER RELIGIONS MIXED UP...

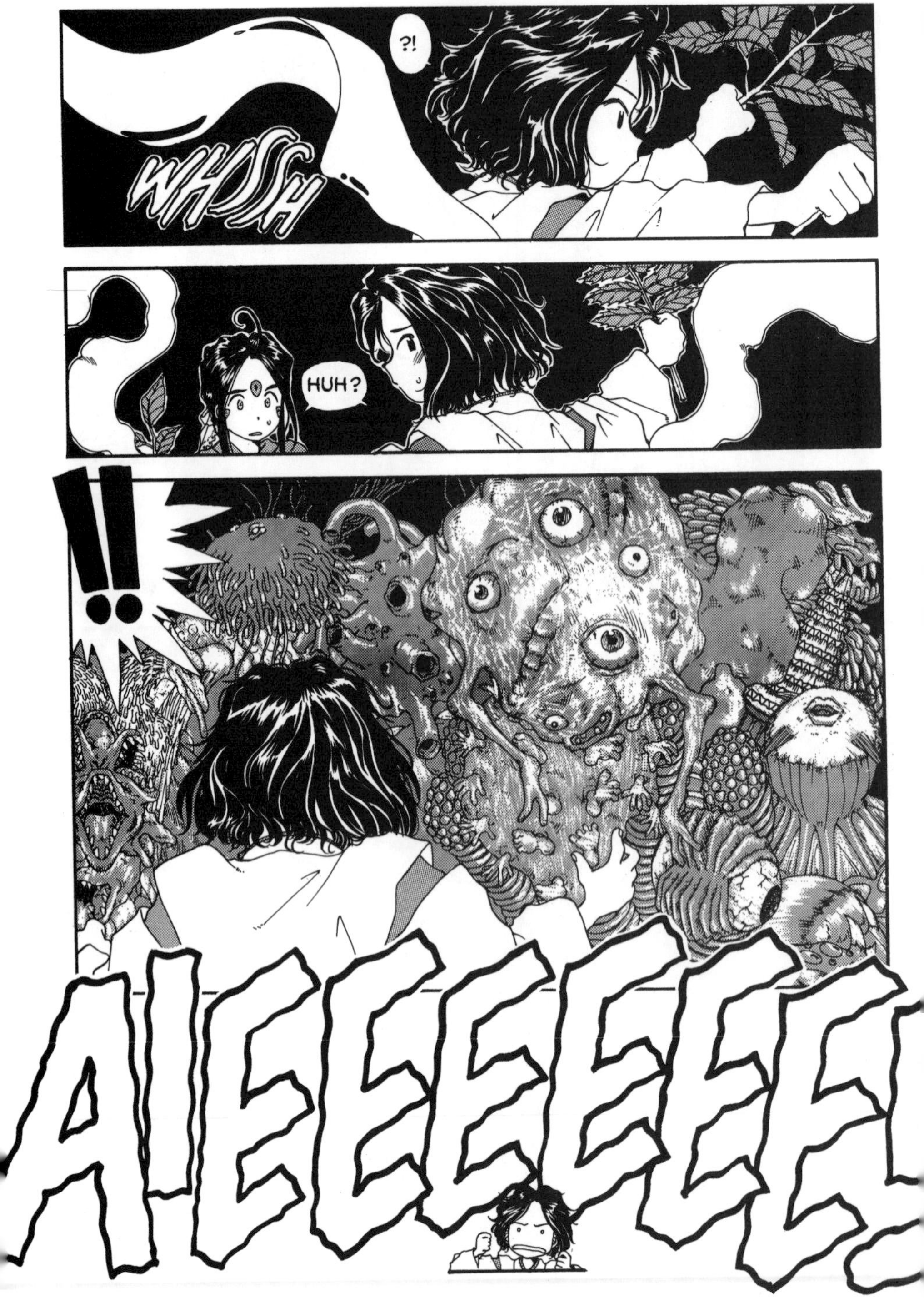

WHISH
?!
HUH?
!!
AIEEEEEEE

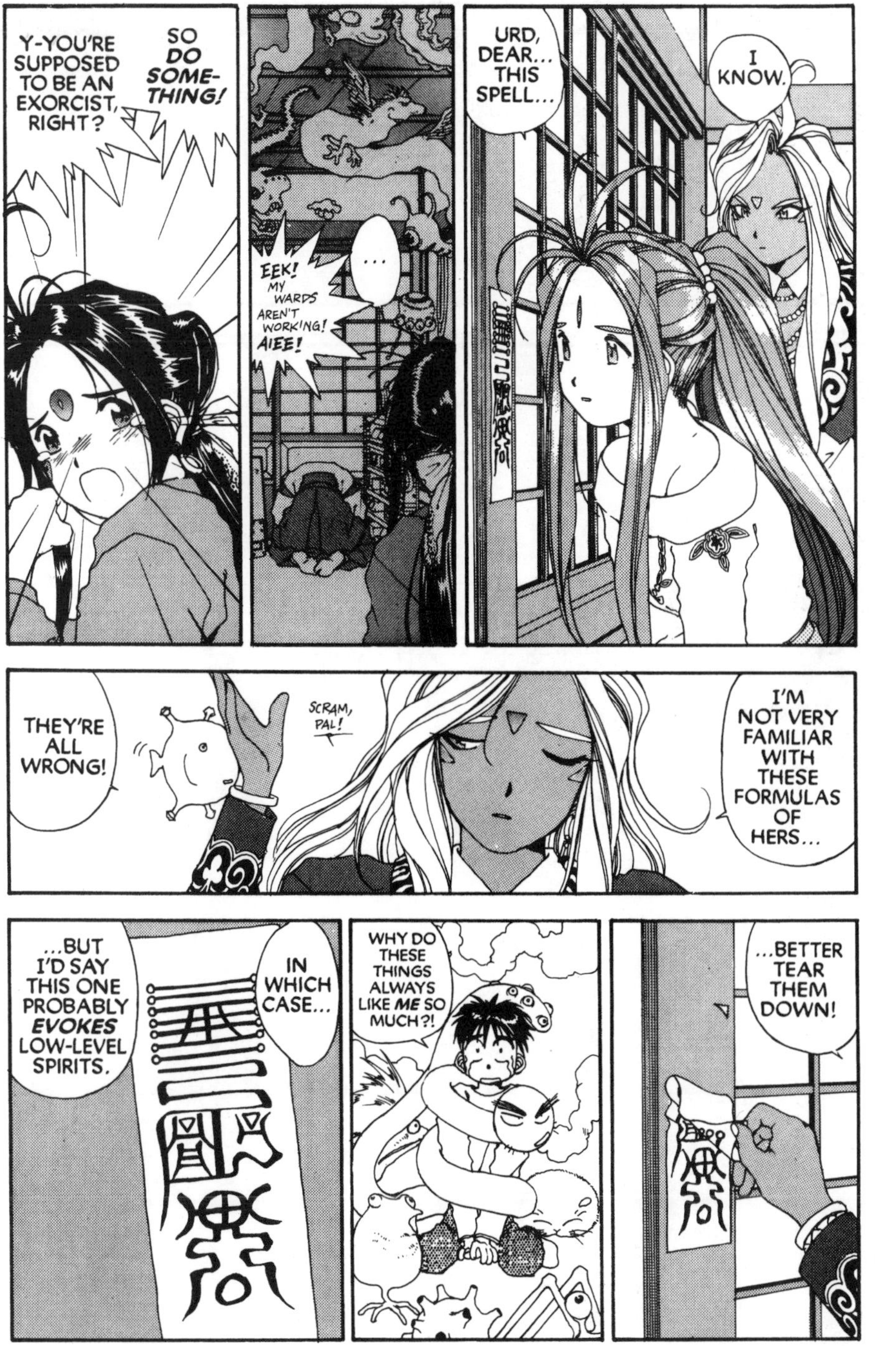

Y-YOU'RE SUPPOSED TO BE AN EXORCIST, RIGHT?
SO DO SOME-THING!
EEK! MY WARDS AREN'T WORKING! AIEE!
...
URD, DEAR... THIS SPELL...
I KNOW.
THEY'RE ALL WRONG!
SCRAM, PAL!
I'M NOT VERY FAMILIAR WITH THESE FORMULAS OF HERS...
...BUT I'D SAY THIS ONE PROBABLY EVOKES LOW-LEVEL SPIRITS.
IN WHICH CASE...
WHY DO THESE THINGS ALWAYS LIKE ME SO MUCH?!
...BETTER TEAR THEM DOWN!

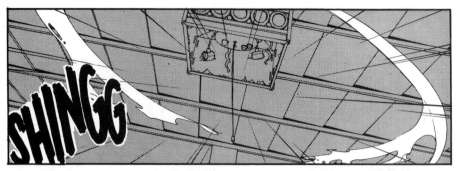

SHINGG

HUH? WHA--?

?

GREAT! MY WARDS WORKED, AFTER ALL!

I... I...

THEY'RE... GONE?

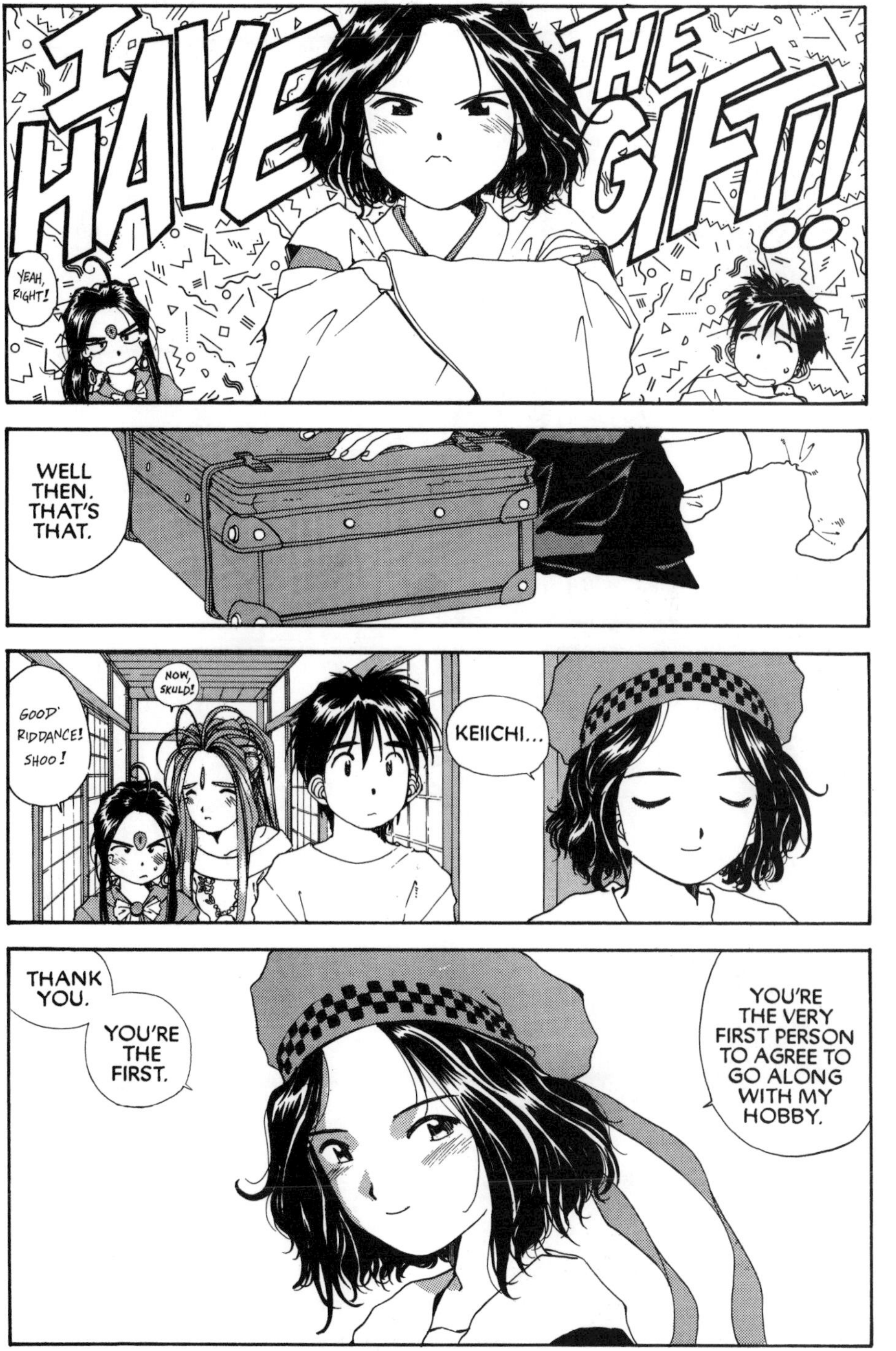
I HAVE THE GIFT!!
YEAH, RIGHT!
WELL THEN. THAT'S THAT.
GOOD RIDDANCE! SHOO!
NOW, SKULD!
KEIICHI...
THANK YOU.
YOU'RE THE FIRST.
YOU'RE THE VERY FIRST PERSON TO AGREE TO GO ALONG WITH MY HOBBY.

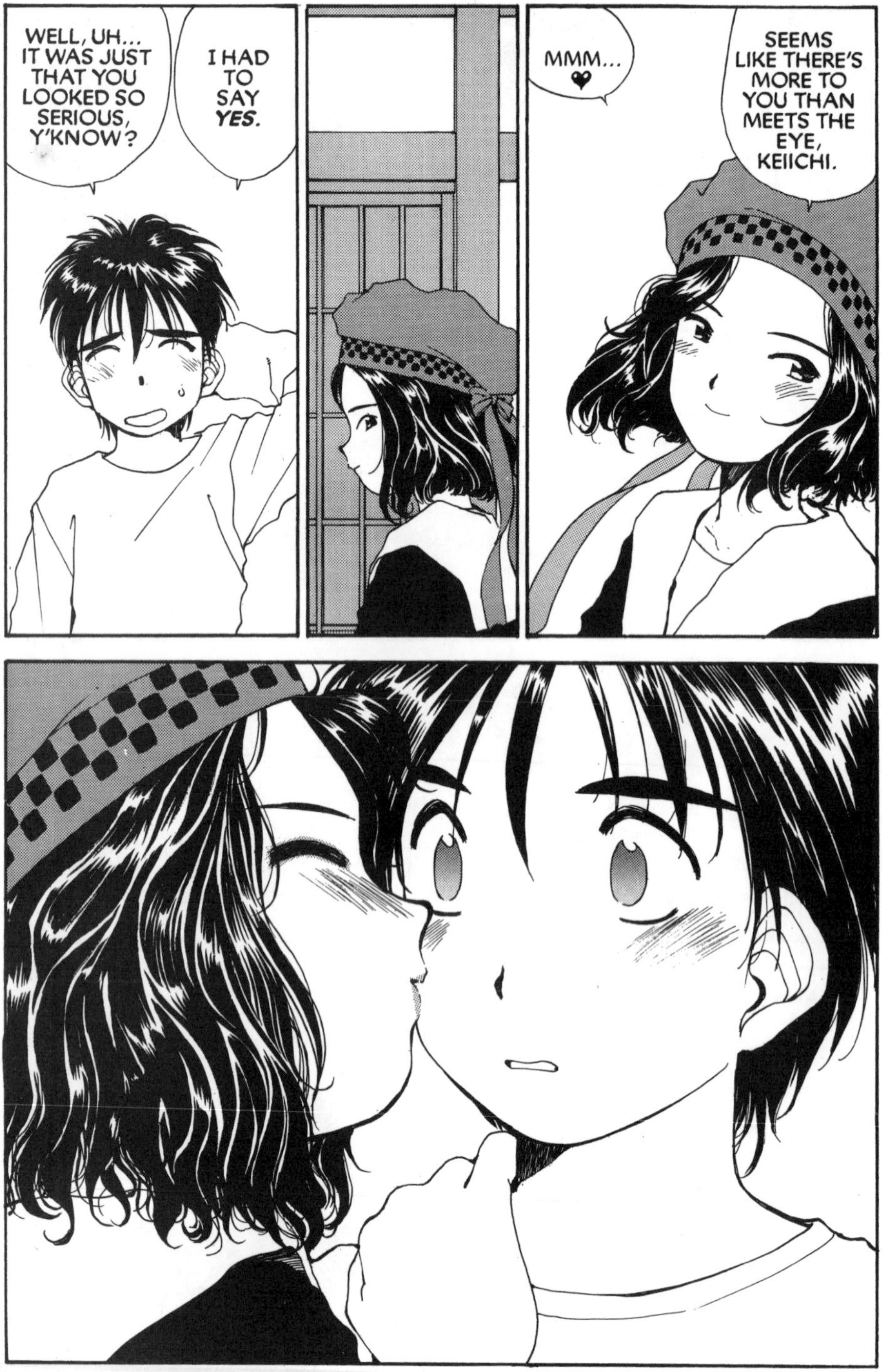
WELL, UH... IT WAS JUST THAT YOU LOOKED SO SERIOUS, Y'KNOW?
I HAD TO SAY ***YES.***
MMM... ❤
SEEMS LIKE THERE'S MORE TO YOU THAN MEETS THE EYE, KEIICHI.

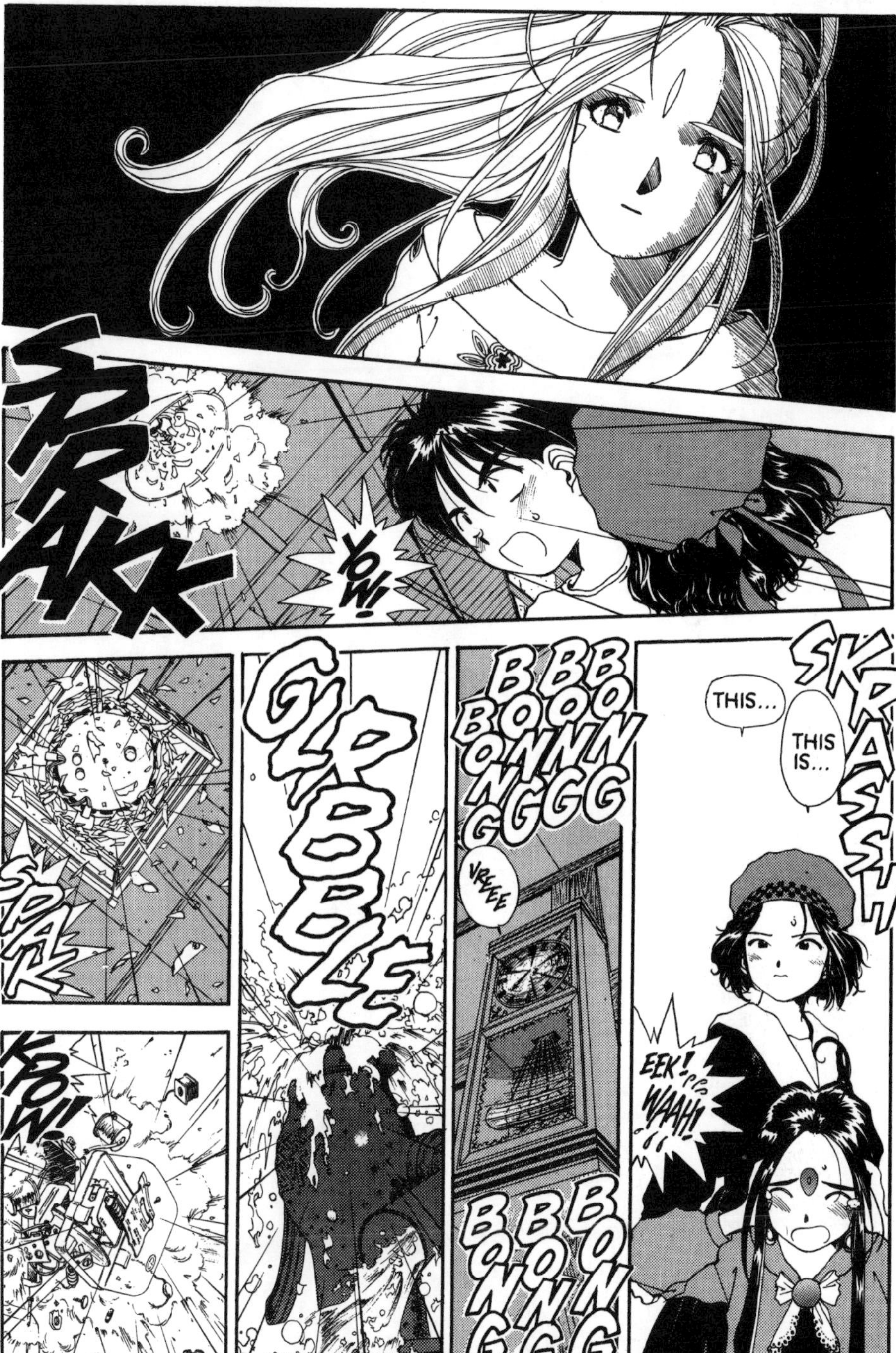
SPAKK
YOW!
SPARK
KPOW!
GLPBBLE
BONG
BONG
BONG
BONG
VREEEE
BONG
BONNG
BONG
THIS...
THIS IS...
SKRASSH
EEK! WAAH!

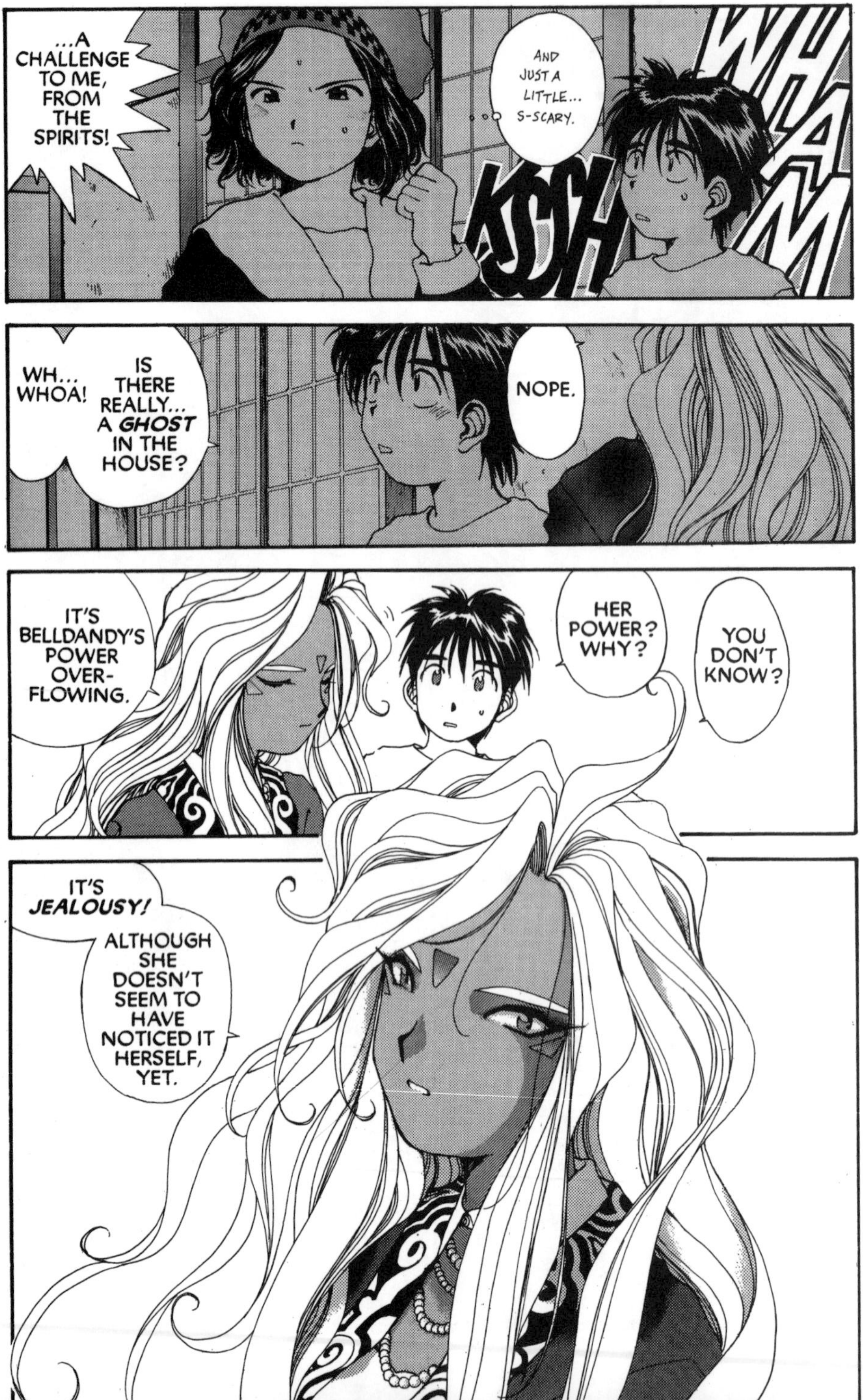
...A CHALLENGE TO ME, FROM THE SPIRITS!
AND JUST A LITTLE... S-SCARY.
KSCH
WHAM
WH... WHOA!
IS THERE REALLY... A GHOST IN THE HOUSE?
NOPE.
IT'S BELLDANDY'S POWER OVER-FLOWING.
HER POWER? WHY?
YOU DON'T KNOW?
IT'S JEALOUSY!
ALTHOUGH SHE DOESN'T SEEM TO HAVE NOTICED IT HERSELF, YET.

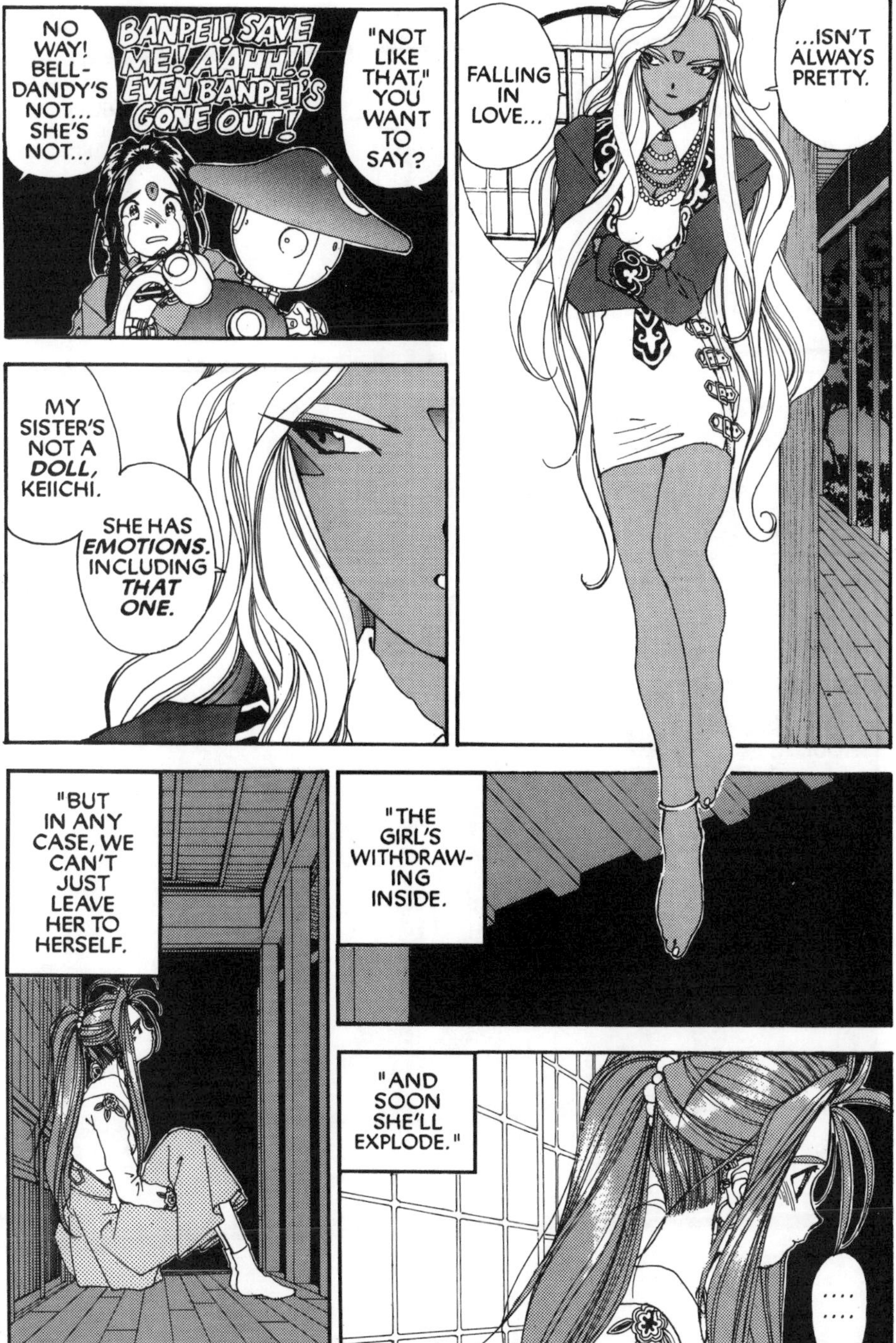
NO WAY! BELL-DANDY'S NOT... SHE'S NOT...
BANPEI! SAVE ME! AAHH!! EVEN BANPEI'S GONE OUT!
"NOT LIKE THAT," YOU WANT TO SAY?
MY SISTER'S NOT A *DOLL,* KEIICHI.
SHE HAS *EMOTIONS.* INCLUDING *THAT ONE.*
FALLING IN LOVE...
...ISN'T ALWAYS PRETTY.
"BUT IN ANY CASE, WE CAN'T JUST LEAVE HER TO HERSELF.
"THE GIRL'S WITHDRAWING INSIDE.
"AND SOON SHE'LL EXPLODE."
....

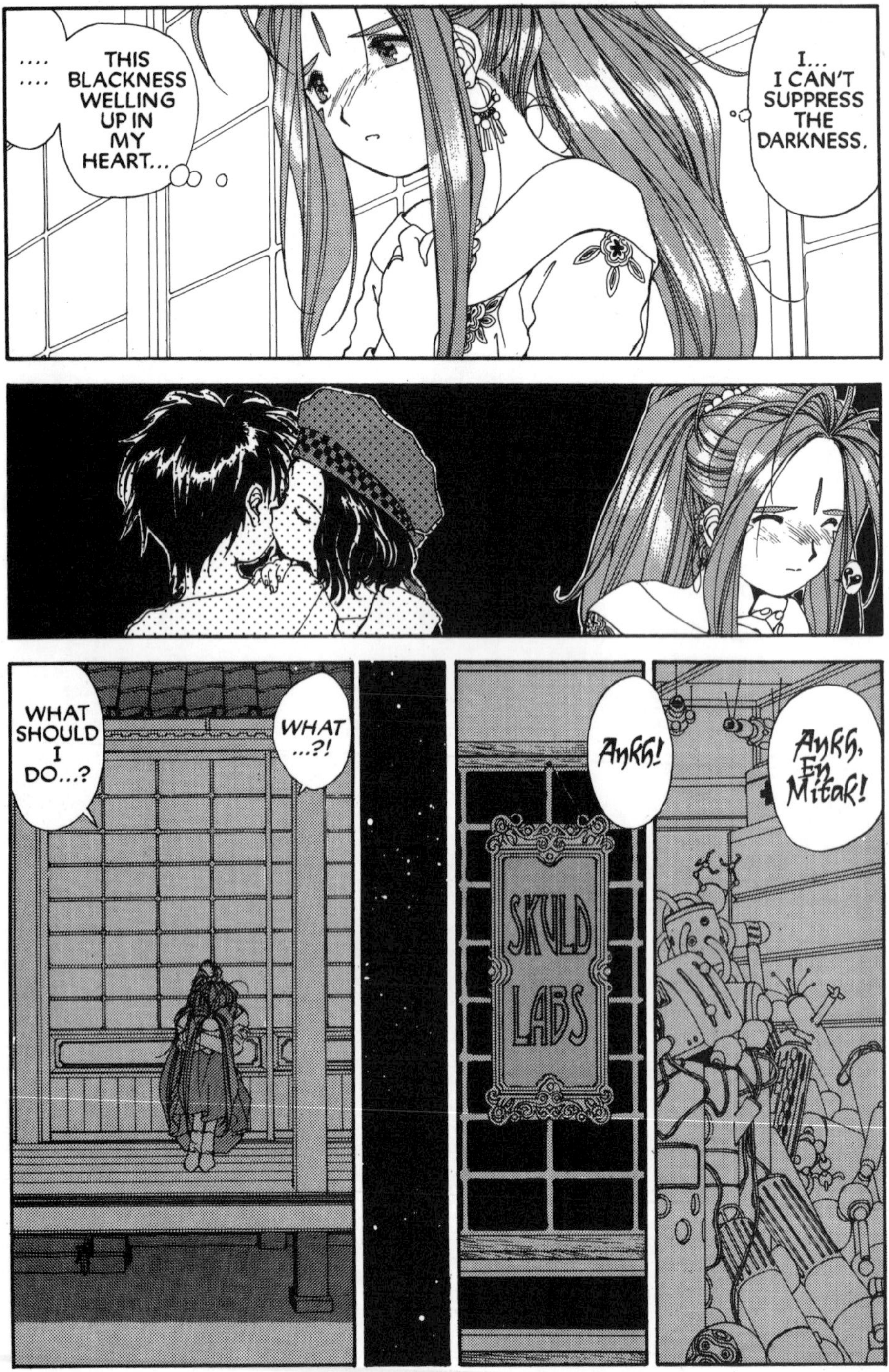
....
....
THIS BLACKNESS WELLING UP IN MY HEART...
I... I CAN'T SUPPRESS THE DARKNESS.
WHAT SHOULD I DO...?
WHAT ...?!
Ankh!
SKULD LABS
Ankh, En Mitak!

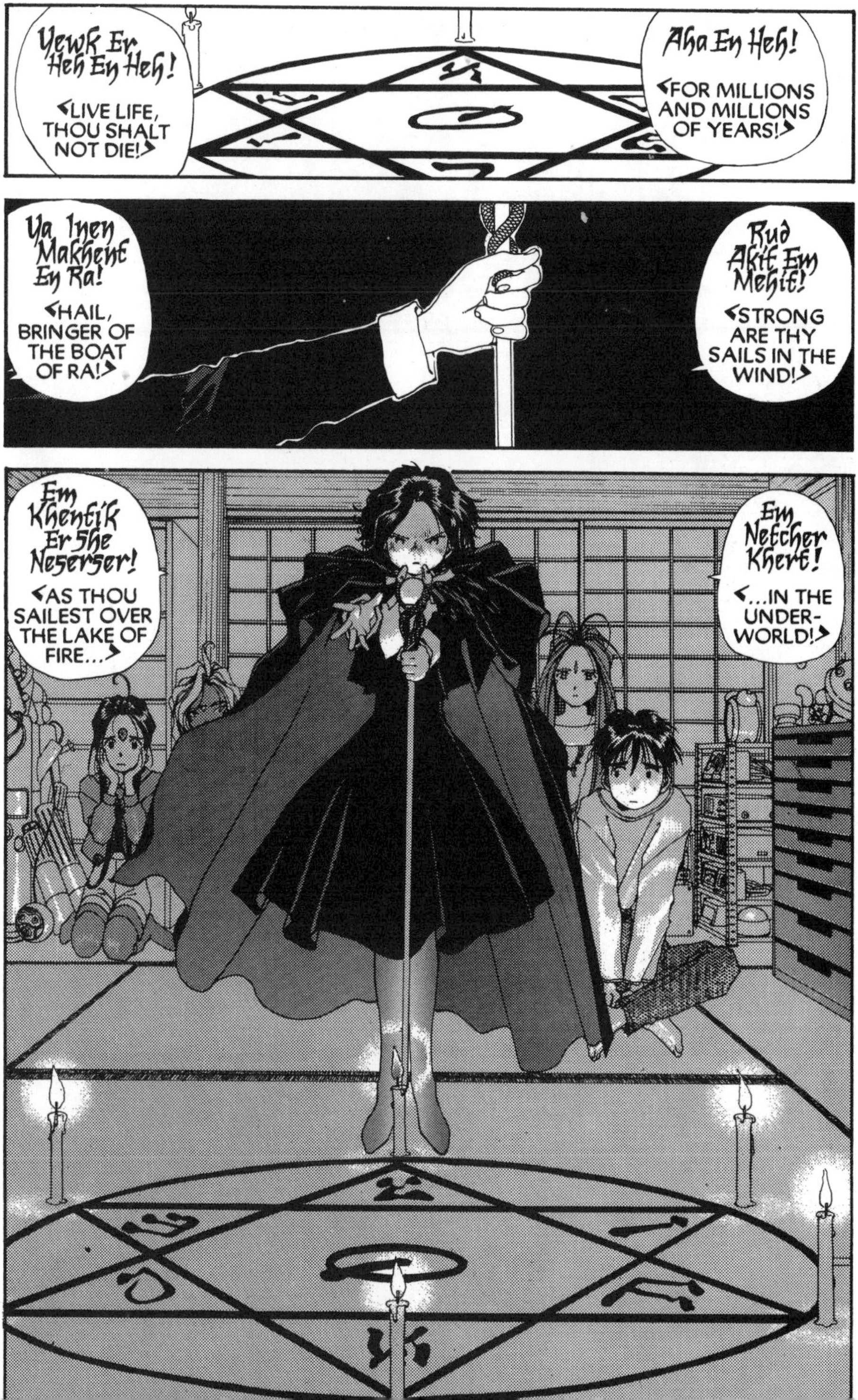

Yewk Er Heh En Heh!
<LIVE LIFE, THOU SHALT NOT DIE!>
Aha En Heh!
<FOR MILLIONS AND MILLIONS OF YEARS!>
Ya Inen Makhent En Ra!
<HAIL, BRINGER OF THE BOAT OF RA!>
Rud Akit Em Mehit!
<STRONG ARE THY SAILS IN THE WIND!>
Em Khentik Er She Neserser!
<AS THOU SAILEST OVER THE LAKE OF FIRE...>
Em Netcher Kheret!
<...IN THE UNDER-WORLD!>

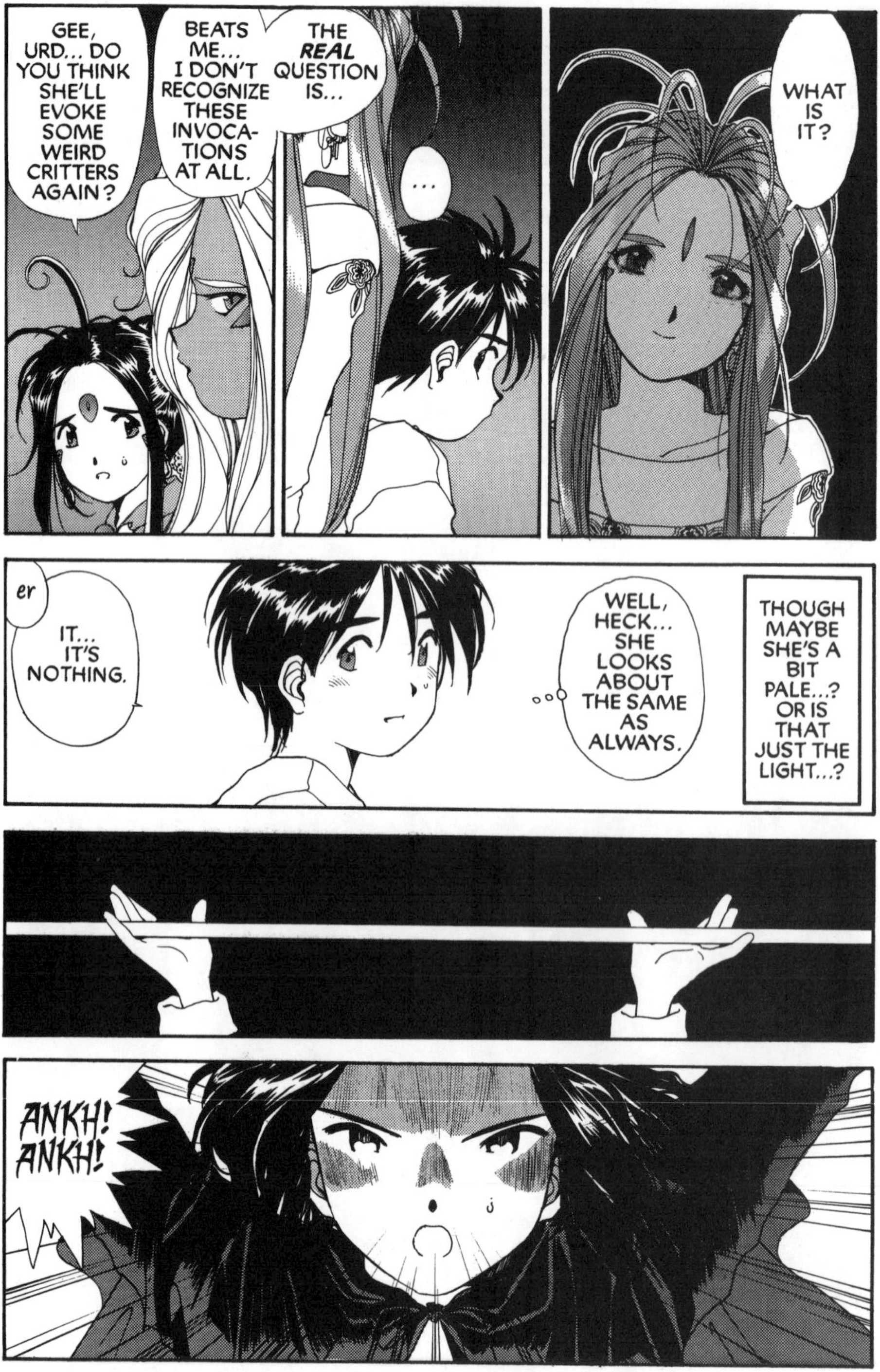
GEE, URD... DO YOU THINK SHE'LL EVOKE SOME WEIRD CRITTERS AGAIN?
BEATS ME... I DON'T RECOGNIZE THESE INVOCATIONS AT ALL.
THE REAL QUESTION IS...
...
WHAT IS IT?
er
IT... IT'S NOTHING.
WELL, HECK... SHE LOOKS ABOUT THE SAME AS ALWAYS.
THOUGH MAYBE SHE'S A BIT PALE...? OR IS THAT JUST THE LIGHT...?
ANKH! ANKH!

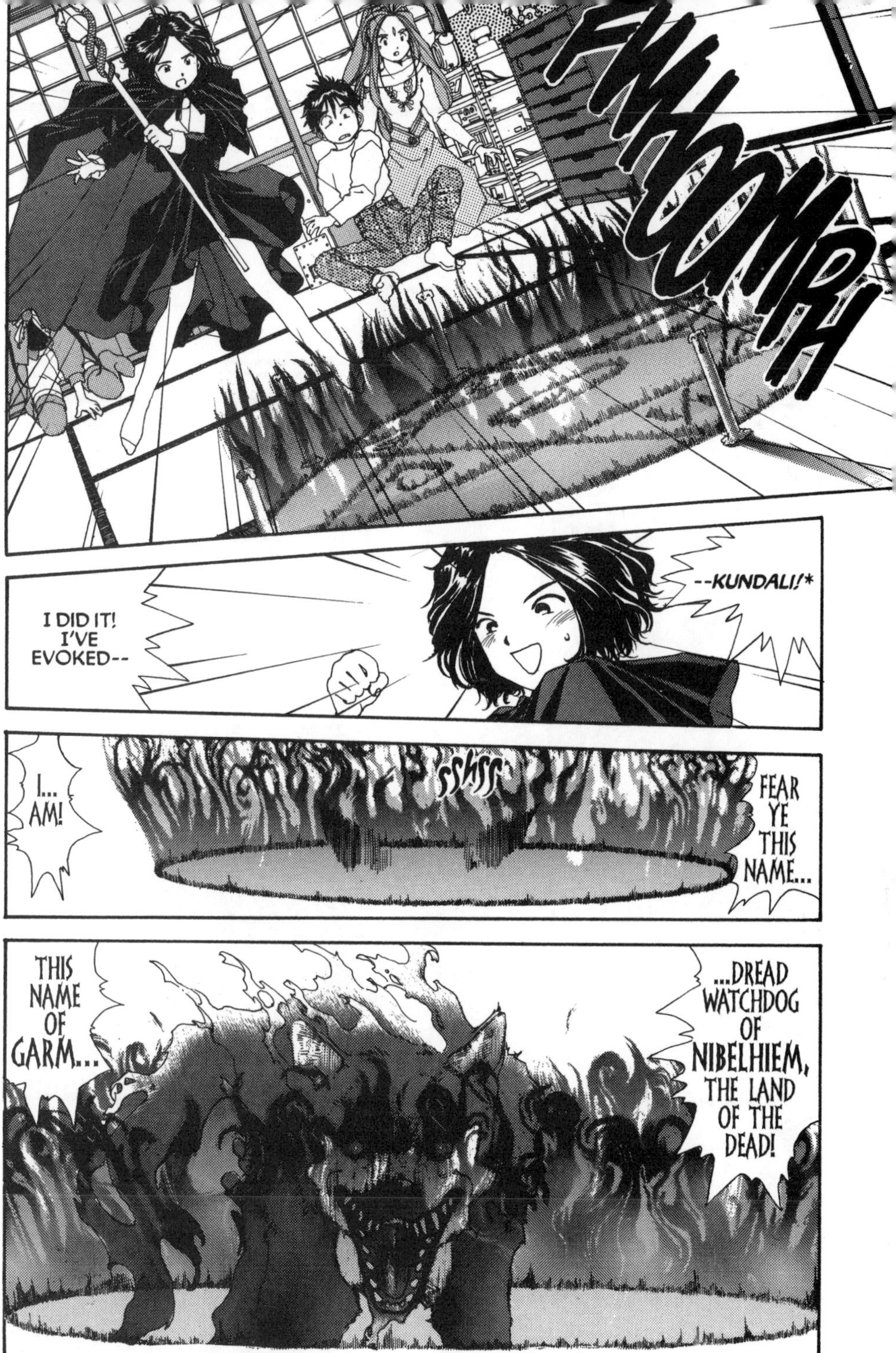
FWOOOMP!
I DID IT! I'VE EVOKED--
--KUNDALI!*
I... AM!
SSHSS
FEAR YE THIS NAME...
THIS NAME OF GARM...
...DREAD WATCHDOG OF NIBELHIEM, THE LAND OF THE DEAD!

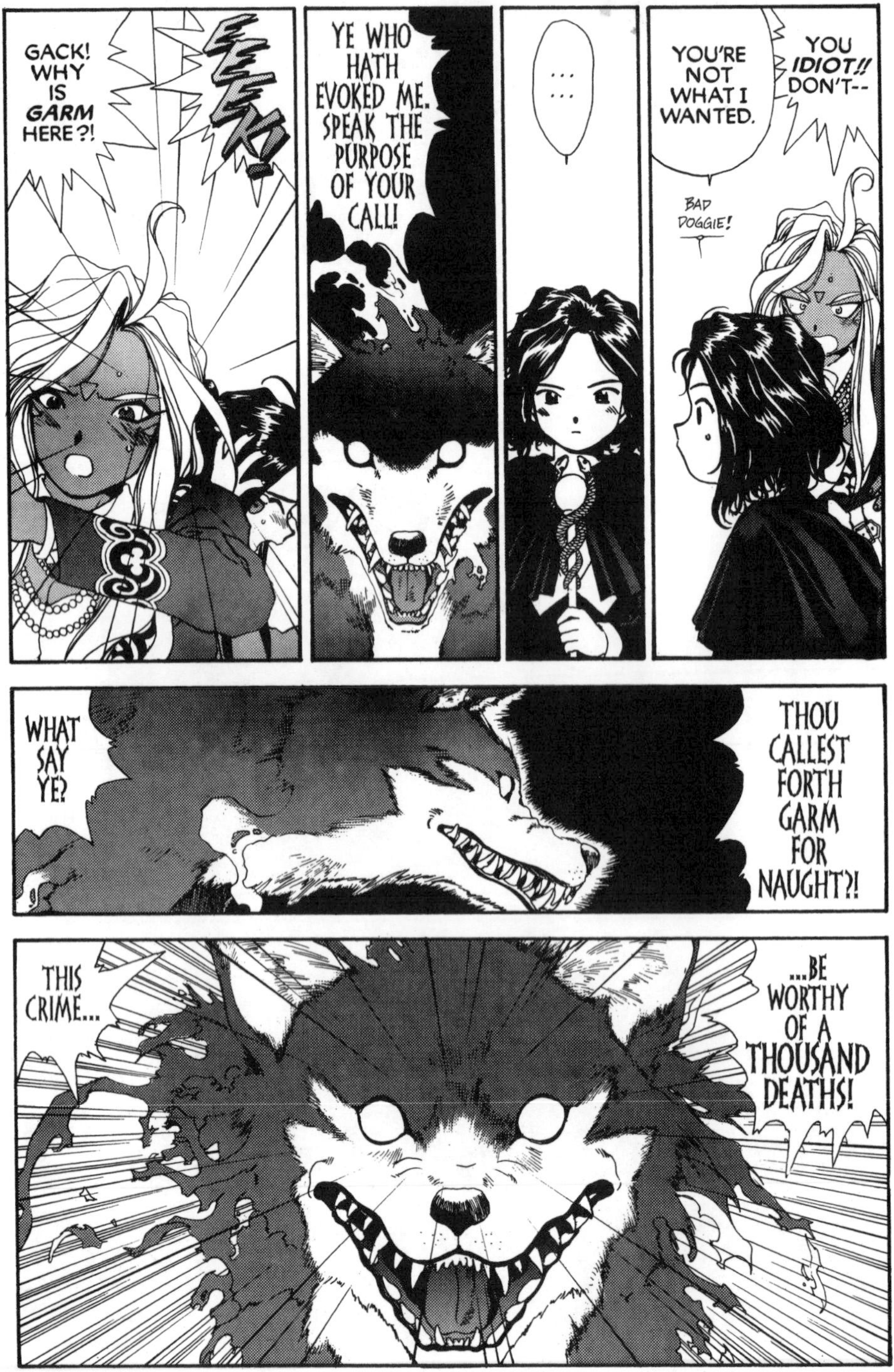
GACK! WHY IS GARM HERE?!
EEEEK!
YE WHO HATH EVOKED ME. SPEAK THE PURPOSE OF YOUR CALL!
... ...
YOU'RE NOT WHAT I WANTED.
YOU IDIOT!! DON'T--
BAD DOGGIE!
WHAT SAY YE?
THOU CALLEST FORTH GARM FOR NAUGHT?!
THIS CRIME...
...BE WORTHY OF A THOUSAND DEATHS!

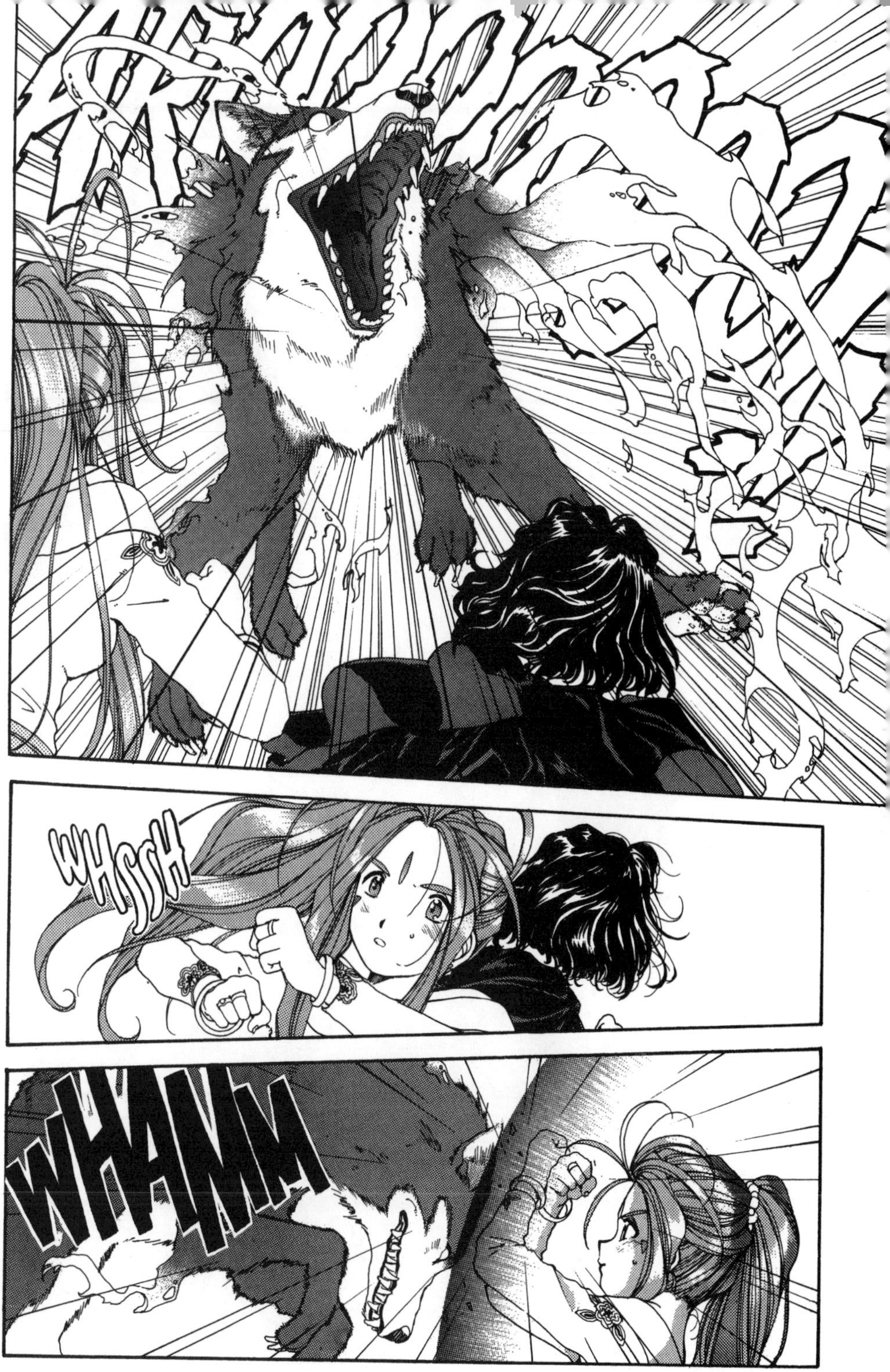
WHSSH
WHAMM

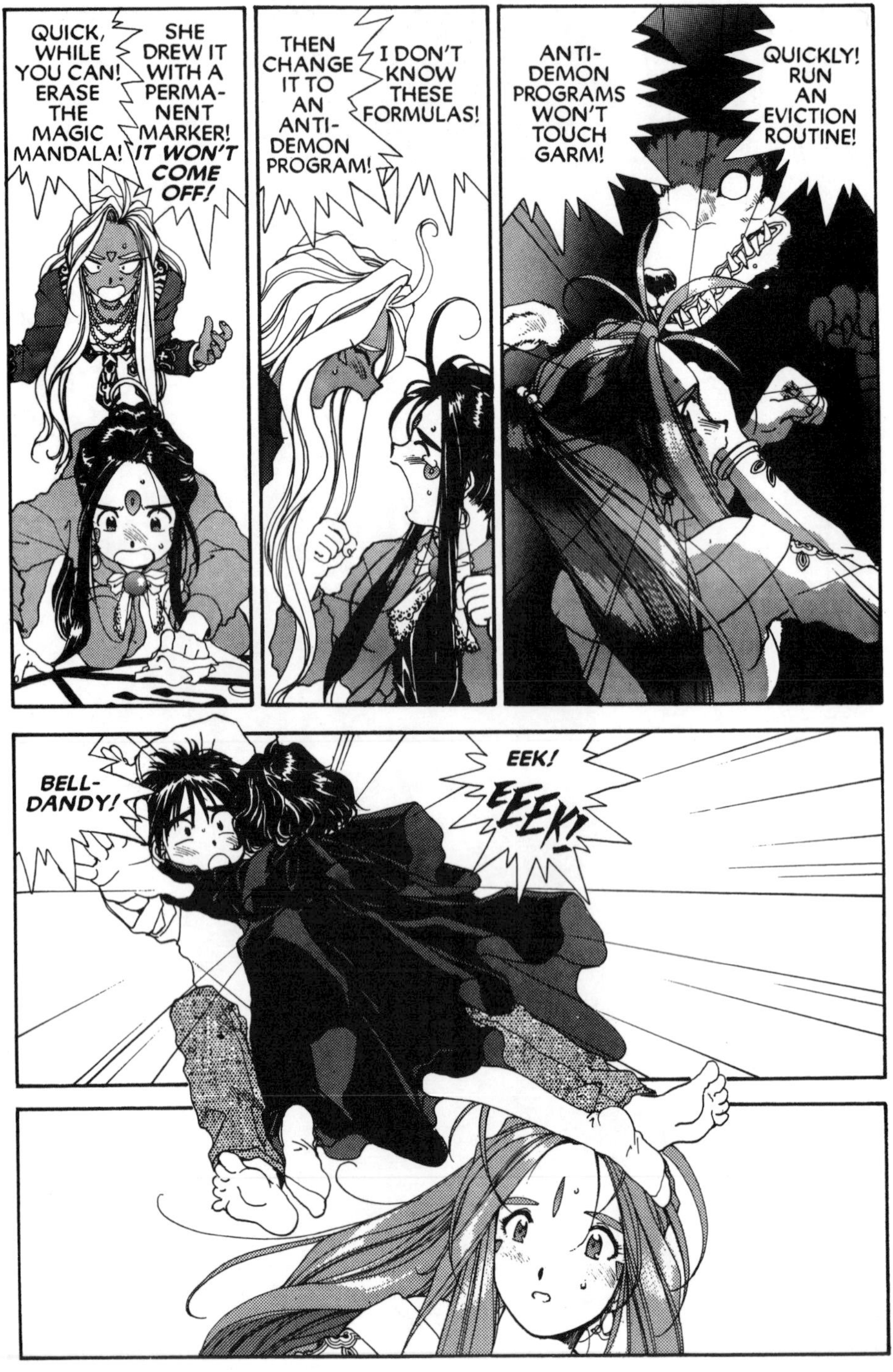
QUICK, WHILE YOU CAN! ERASE THE MAGIC MANDALA!
SHE DREW IT WITH A PERMA-NENT MARKER! *IT WON'T COME OFF!*
THEN CHANGE IT TO AN ANTI-DEMON PROGRAM!
I DON'T KNOW THESE FORMULAS!
ANTI-DEMON PROGRAMS WON'T TOUCH GARM!
QUICKLY! RUN AN EVICTION ROUTINE!
BELL-DANDY!
EEK!
EEEK!

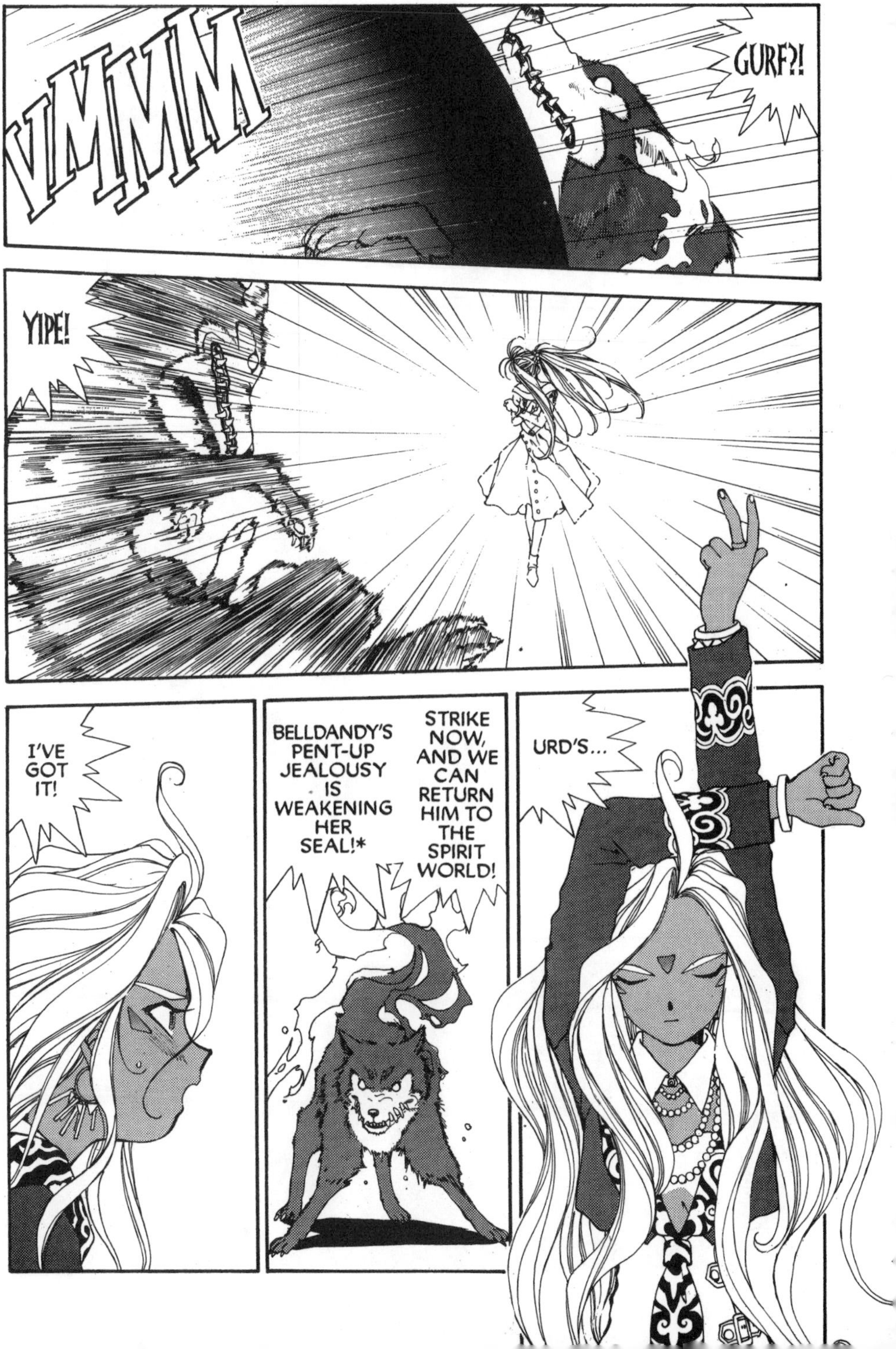
VMMMM
GURF?!
YIPE!
I'VE GOT IT!
BELLDANDY'S PENT-UP JEALOUSY IS WEAKENING HER SEAL!*
STRIKE NOW, AND WE CAN RETURN HIM TO THE SPIRIT WORLD!
URD'S...

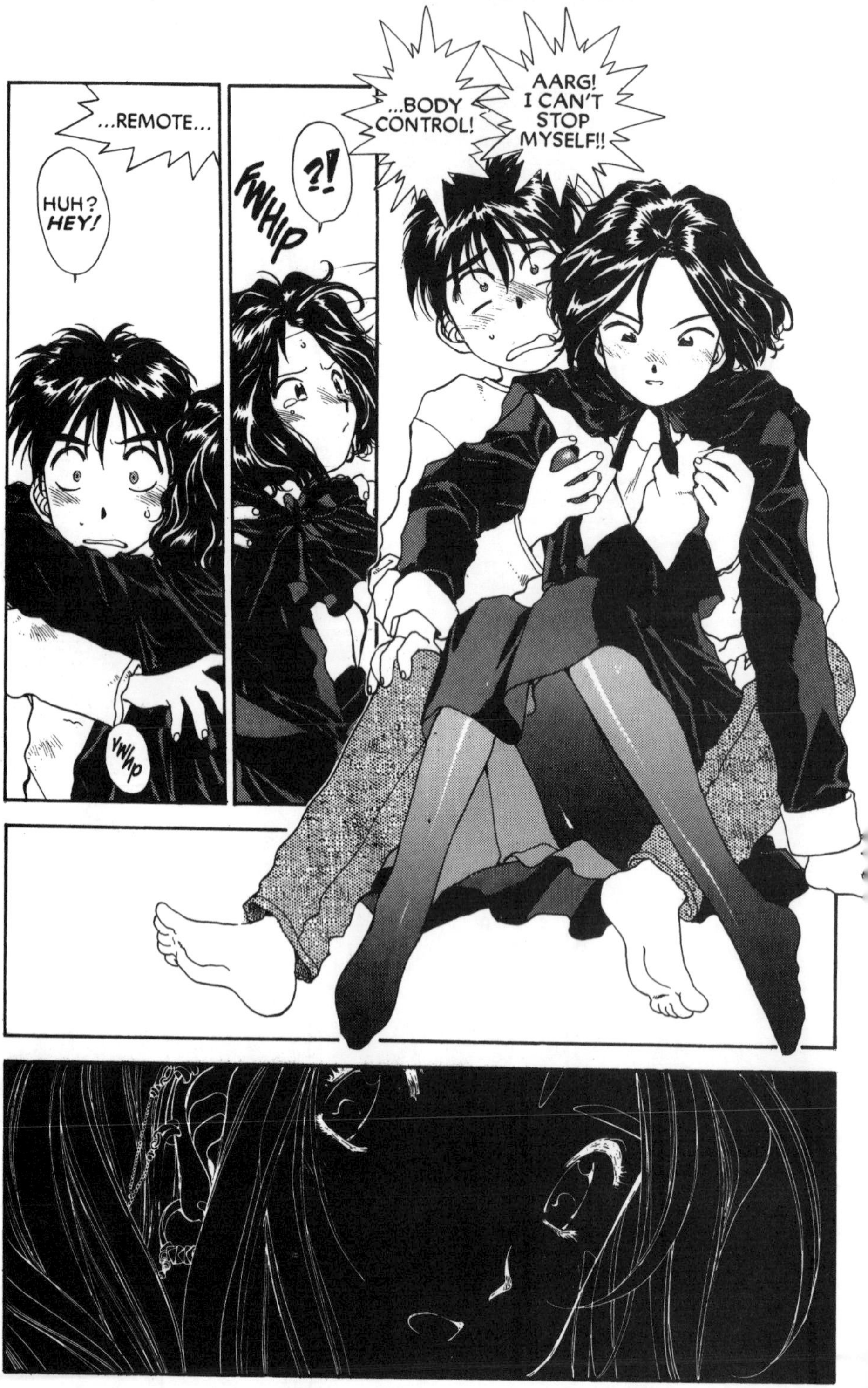
...REMOTE...
HUH? HEY!
vwhip
?!
FWHIP
...BODY CONTROL!
AARG! I CAN'T STOP MYSELF!!

I UNDERSTAND NOW.

I WAS AFRAID.

ME...

AROOO!!

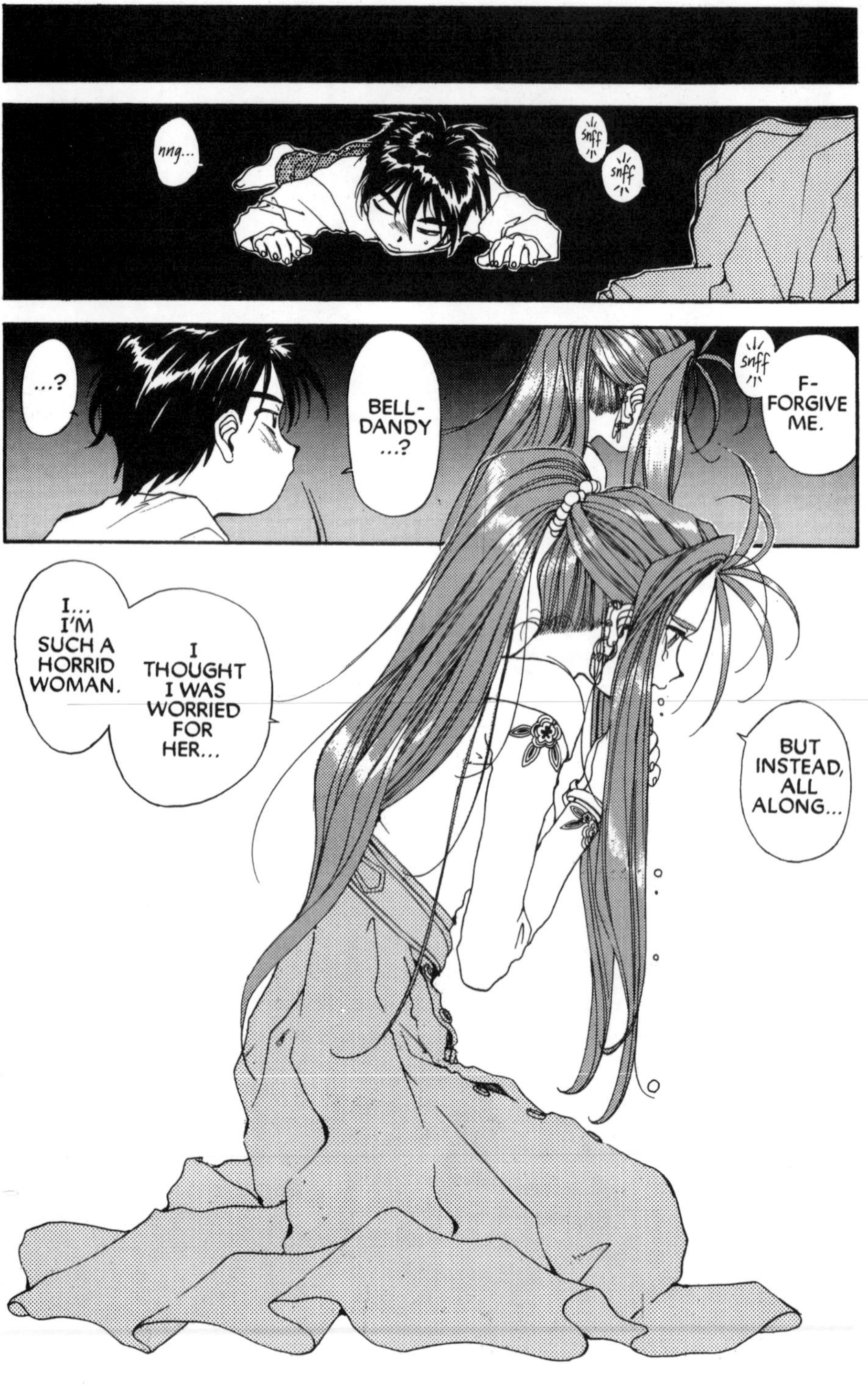
nng...
snff
snff
...?
BELL-DANDY ...?
snff
F-FORGIVE ME.
I... I'M SUCH A HORRID WOMAN.
I THOUGHT I WAS WORRIED FOR HER...
BUT INSTEAD, ALL ALONG...

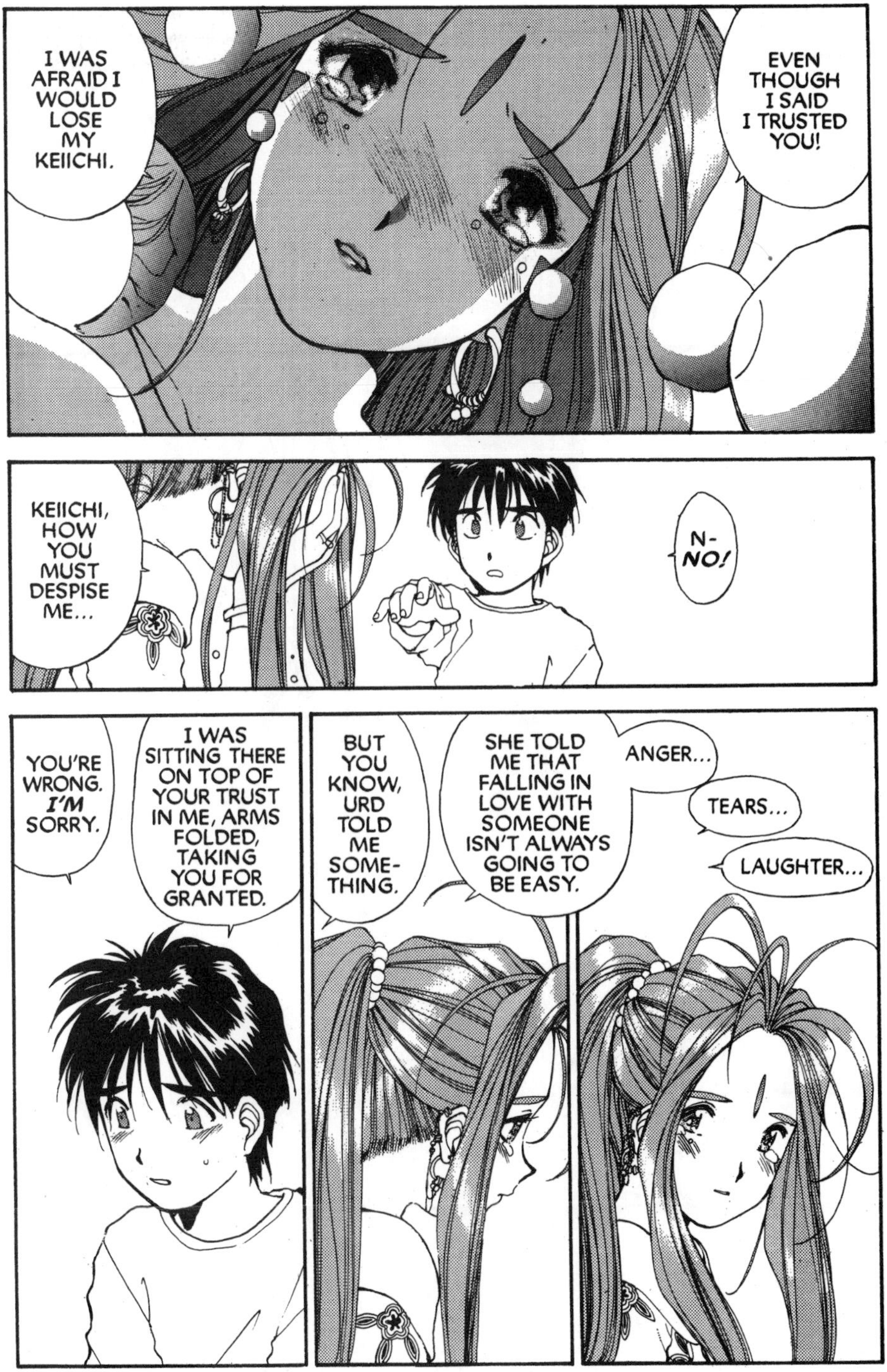
I WAS AFRAID I WOULD LOSE MY KEIICHI.
EVEN THOUGH I SAID I TRUSTED YOU!
KEIICHI, HOW YOU MUST DESPISE ME...
N- *NO!*
YOU'RE WRONG. ***I'M*** SORRY.
I WAS SITTING THERE ON TOP OF YOUR TRUST IN ME, ARMS FOLDED, TAKING YOU FOR GRANTED.
BUT YOU KNOW, URD TOLD ME SOME-THING.
SHE TOLD ME THAT FALLING IN LOVE WITH SOMEONE ISN'T ALWAYS GOING TO BE EASY.
ANGER...
TEARS...
LAUGHTER...

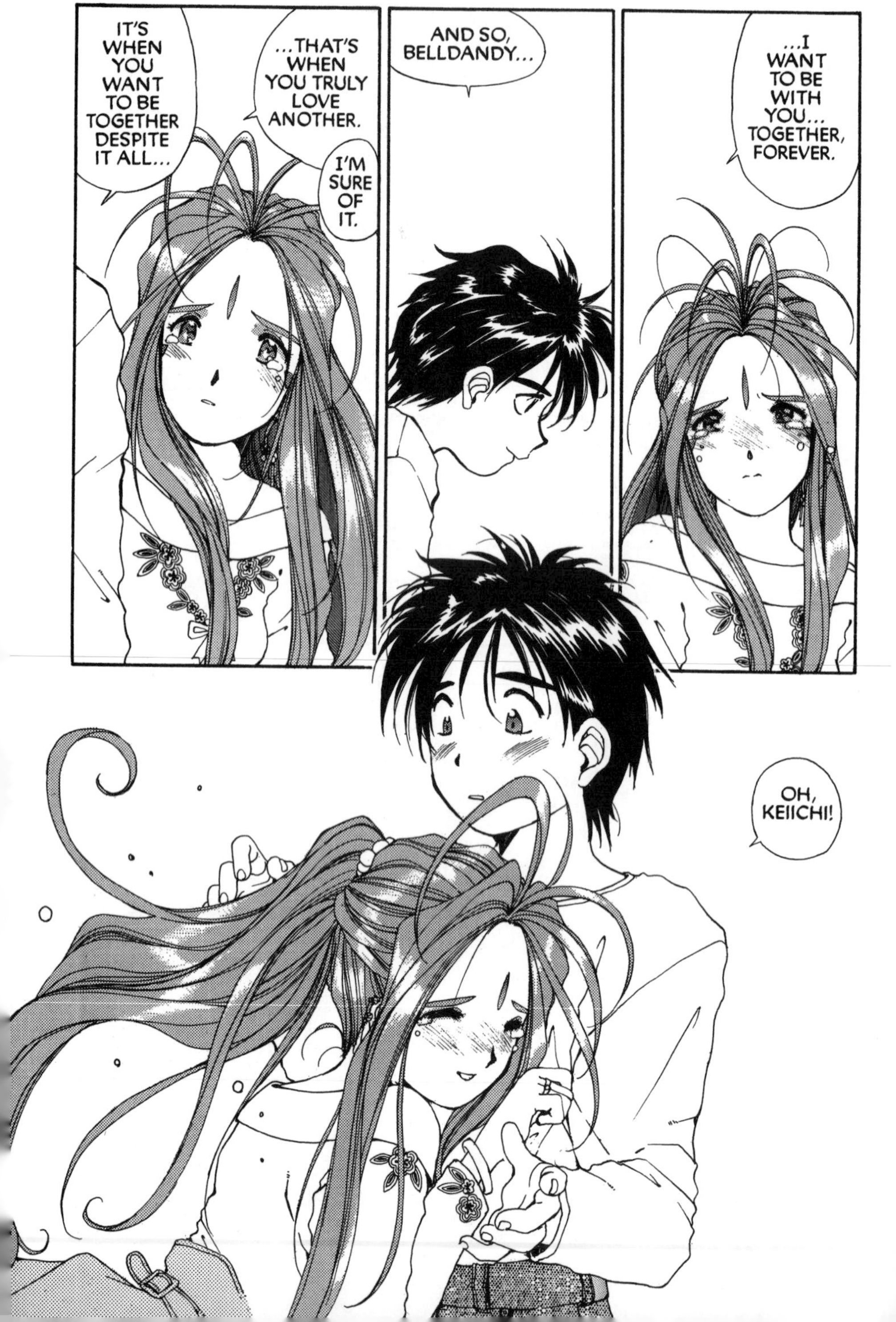
IT'S WHEN YOU WANT TO BE TOGETHER DESPITE IT ALL...
...THAT'S WHEN YOU TRULY LOVE ANOTHER.
I'M SURE OF IT.
AND SO, BELLDANDY...
...I WANT TO BE WITH YOU... TOGETHER, FOREVER.
OH, KEIICHI!

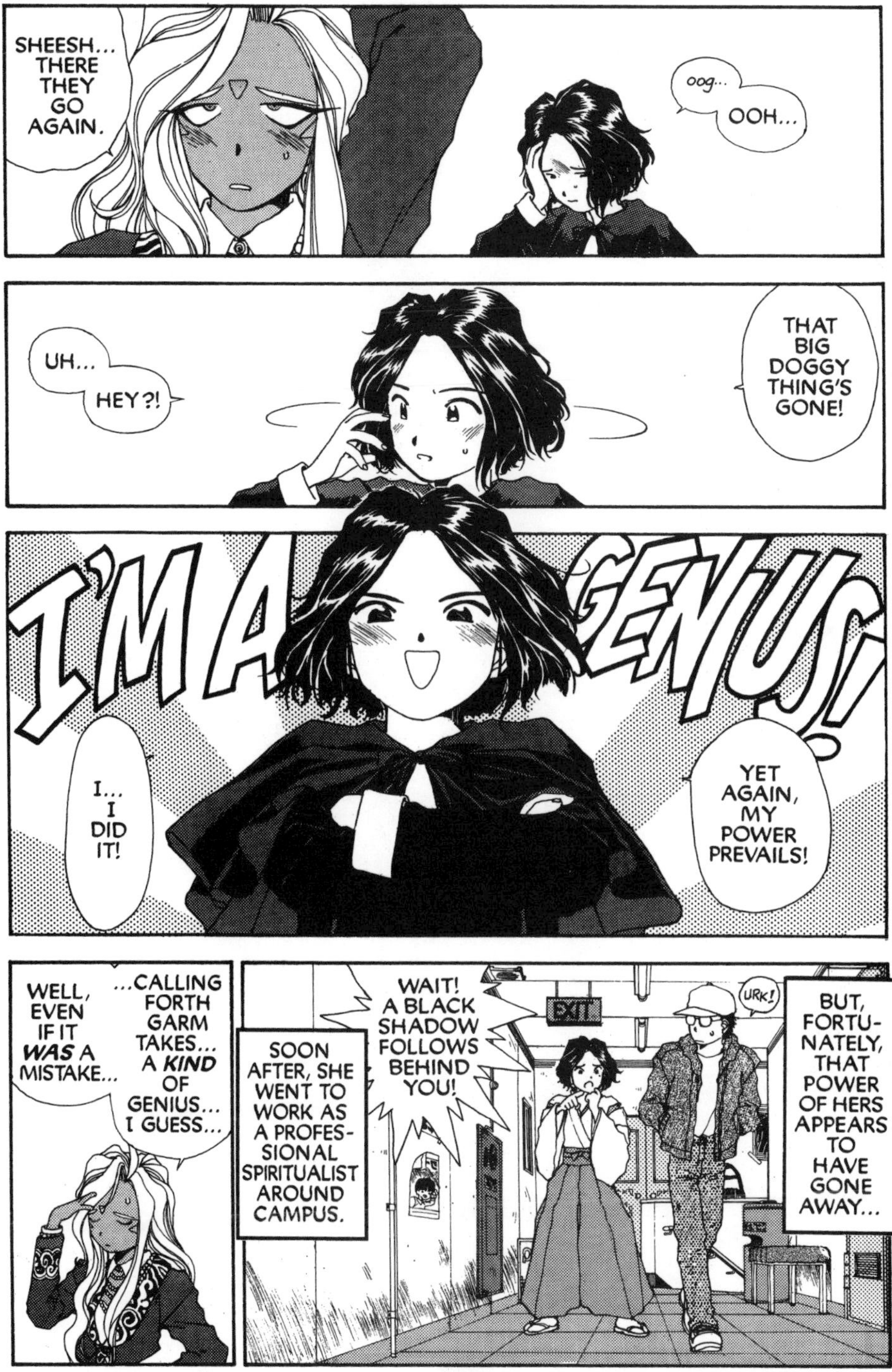
SHEESH... THERE THEY GO AGAIN.
oog... OOH...
UH... HEY?!
THAT BIG DOGGY THING'S GONE!
I'M A GENIUS!
I... I DID IT!
YET AGAIN, MY POWER PREVAILS!
WELL, EVEN IF IT WAS A MISTAKE...
...CALLING FORTH GARM TAKES... A KIND OF GENIUS... I GUESS...
SOON AFTER, SHE WENT TO WORK AS A PROFESSIONAL SPIRITUALIST AROUND CAMPUS.
WAIT! A BLACK SHADOW FOLLOWS BEHIND YOU!
EXIT
URK!
BUT, FORTUNATELY, THAT POWER OF HERS APPEARS TO HAVE GONE AWAY...

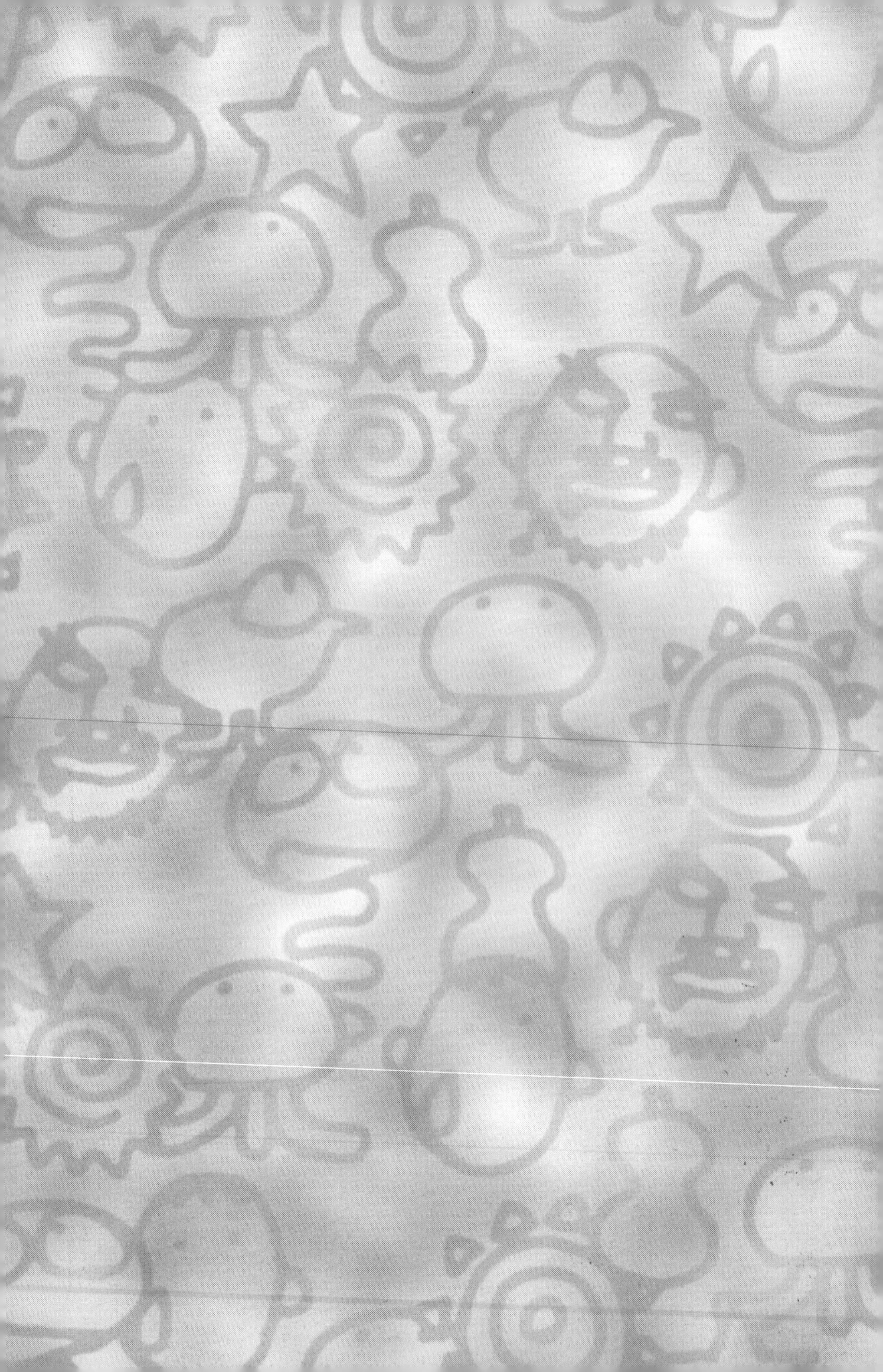

Play the Game

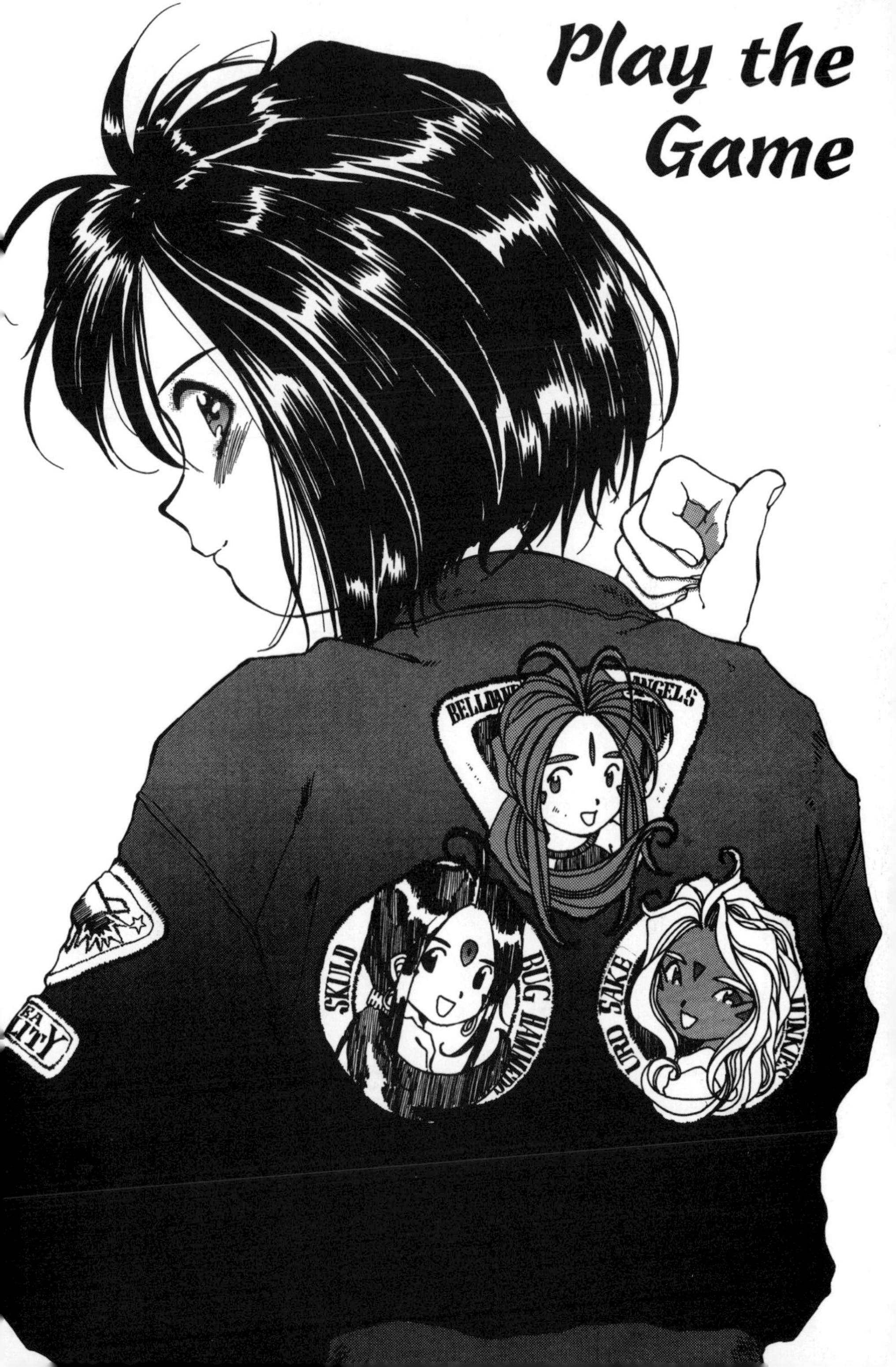
SKULD
BUG HAMMERS
URD SAKE

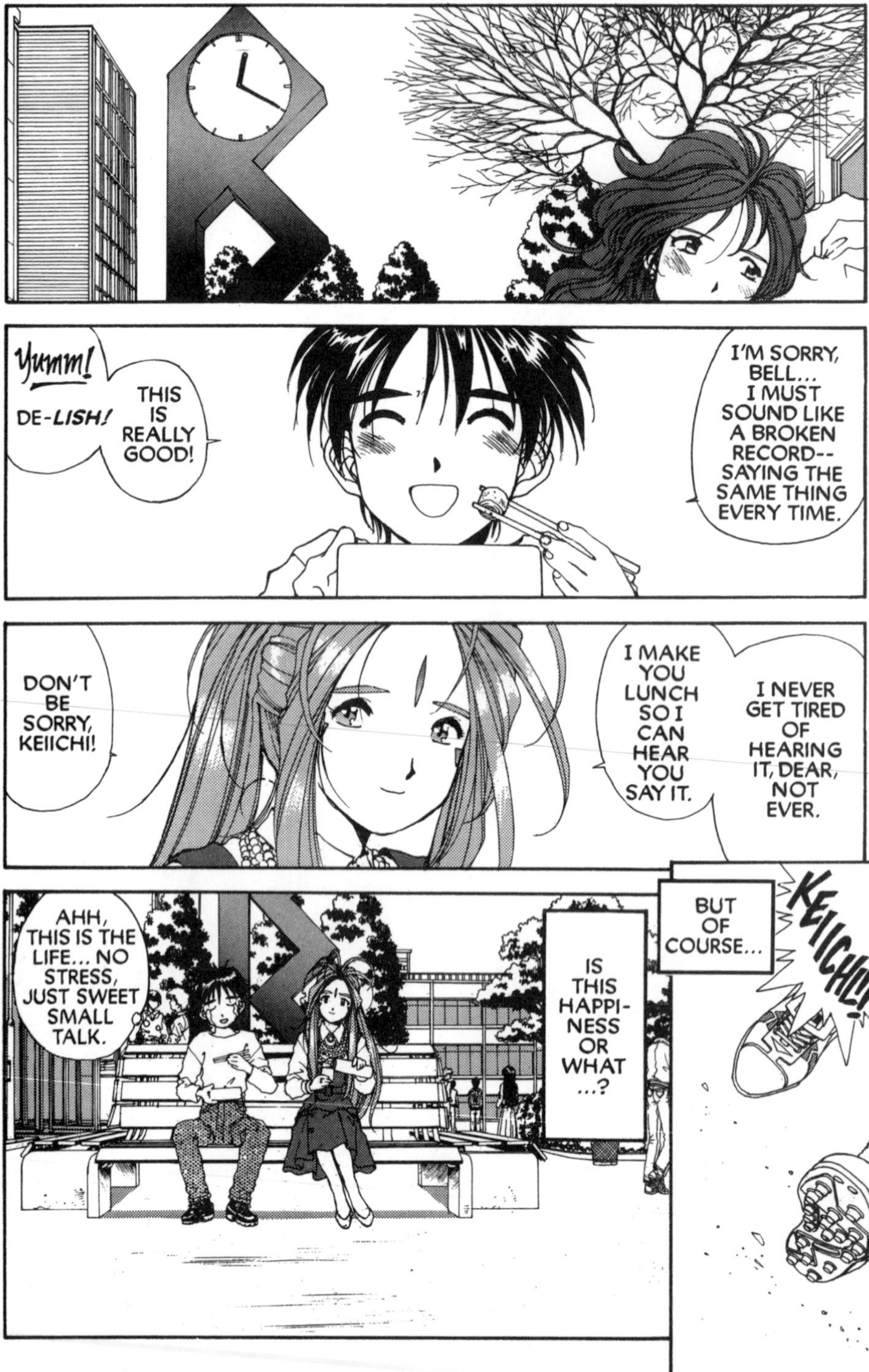

YUMM!
DE-LISH!
THIS IS REALLY GOOD!
I'M SORRY, BELL... I MUST SOUND LIKE A BROKEN RECORD--SAYING THE SAME THING EVERY TIME.
DON'T BE SORRY, KEIICHI!
I MAKE YOU LUNCH SO I CAN HEAR YOU SAY IT.
I NEVER GET TIRED OF HEARING IT, DEAR, NOT EVER.
AHH, THIS IS THE LIFE... NO STRESS, JUST SWEET SMALL TALK.
IS THIS HAPPINESS OR WHAT ...?
BUT OF COURSE...
KEIICHI!!

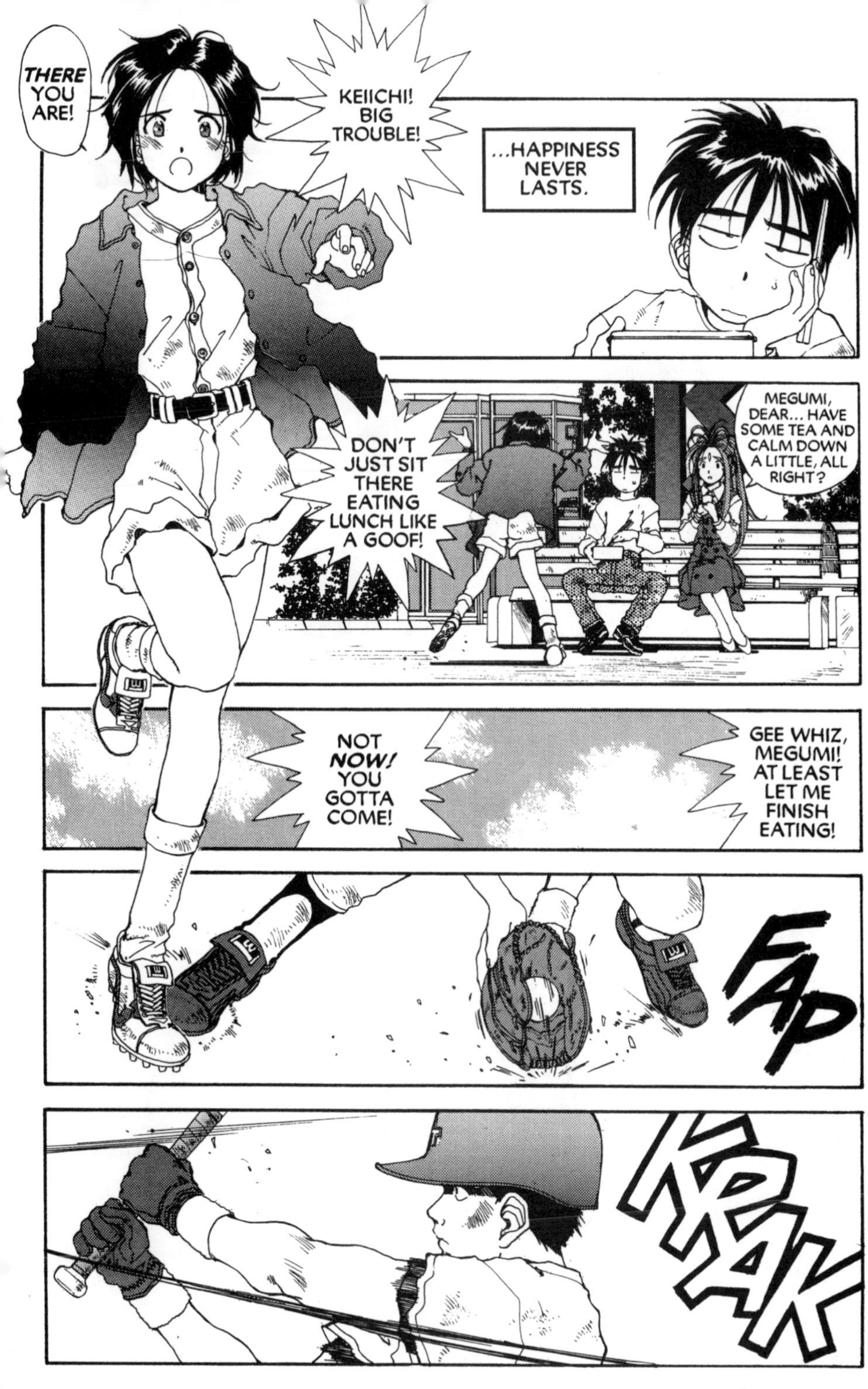
THERE YOU ARE!
KEIICHI! BIG TROUBLE!
...HAPPINESS NEVER LASTS.
DON'T JUST SIT THERE EATING LUNCH LIKE A GOOF!
MEGUMI, DEAR... HAVE SOME TEA AND CALM DOWN A LITTLE, ALL RIGHT?
NOT NOW! YOU GOTTA COME!
GEE WHIZ, MEGUMI! AT LEAST LET ME FINISH EATING!
FAP
KRAK

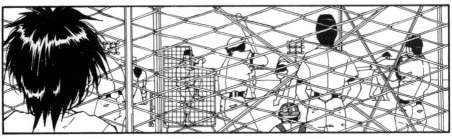

YEAH? SO? IT'S THE BASEBALL CLUB PRACTICING, RIGHT?

BUT ON MONDAY AND FRIDAY IT'S SUPPOSED TO BE *SOFTBALL CLUB PRACTICE!*

JUST BECAUSE THERE AREN'T VERY MANY OF US...

THEY KICKED US OFF THE DIAMOND! THEY'RE TRYING TO KILL OUR CLUB!

WELL, IF THAT HAPPENS, YOU CAN ALWAYS JOIN THE MOTOR CLUB...

FORGET IT!

I DON'T *WANT* TO QUIT. I... I LOVE PLAYING SOFTBALL...

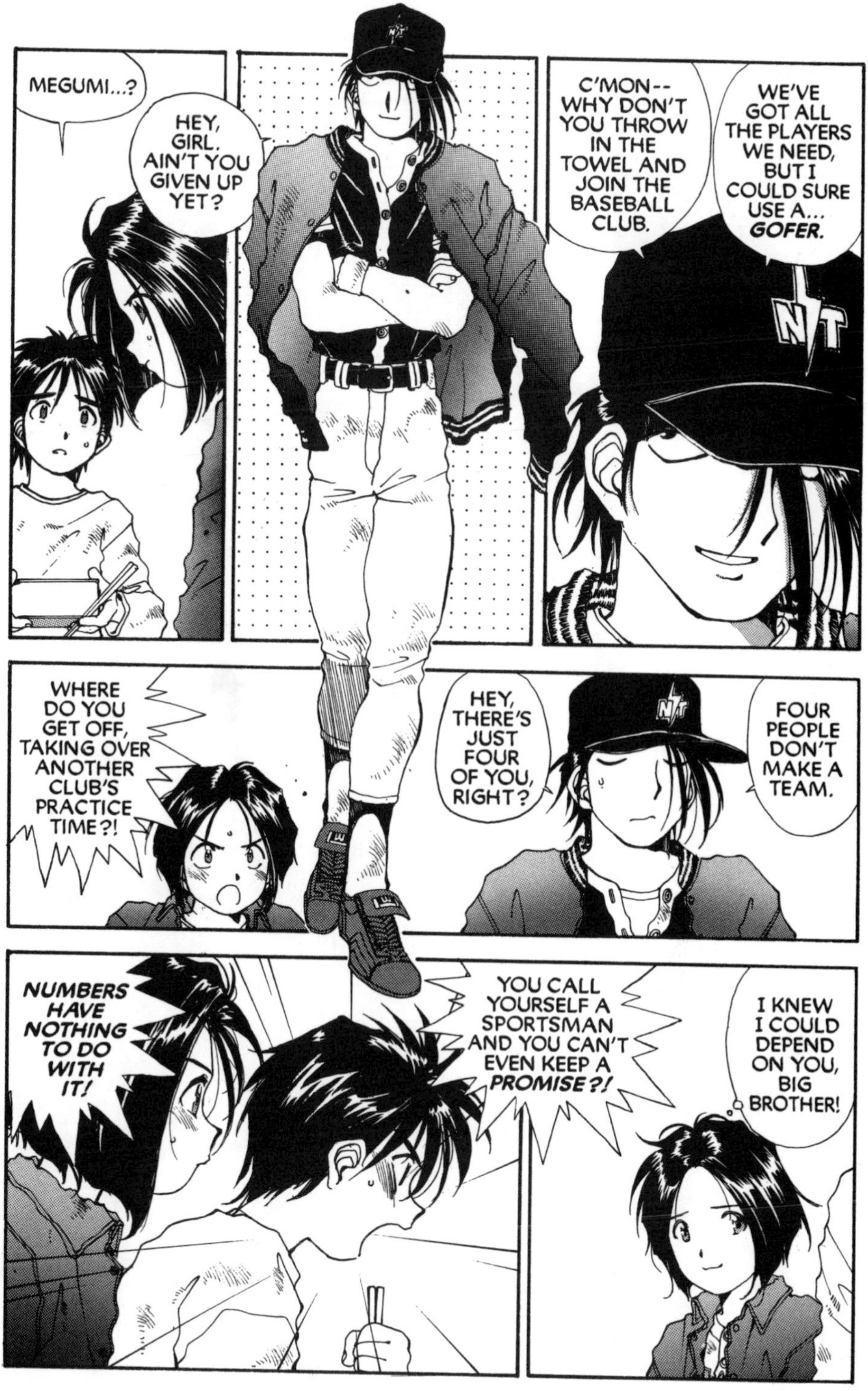
MEGUMI...?
HEY, GIRL. AIN'T YOU GIVEN UP YET?
C'MON-- WHY DON'T YOU THROW IN THE TOWEL AND JOIN THE BASEBALL CLUB.
WE'VE GOT ALL THE PLAYERS WE NEED, BUT I COULD SURE USE A... ***GOFER.***
WHERE DO YOU GET OFF, TAKING OVER ANOTHER CLUB'S PRACTICE TIME?!
HEY, THERE'S JUST FOUR OF YOU, RIGHT?
FOUR PEOPLE DON'T MAKE A TEAM.
NUMBERS HAVE NOTHING TO DO WITH IT!
YOU CALL YOURSELF A SPORTSMAN AND YOU CAN'T EVEN KEEP A ***PROMISE?!***
I KNEW I COULD DEPEND ON YOU, BIG BROTHER!

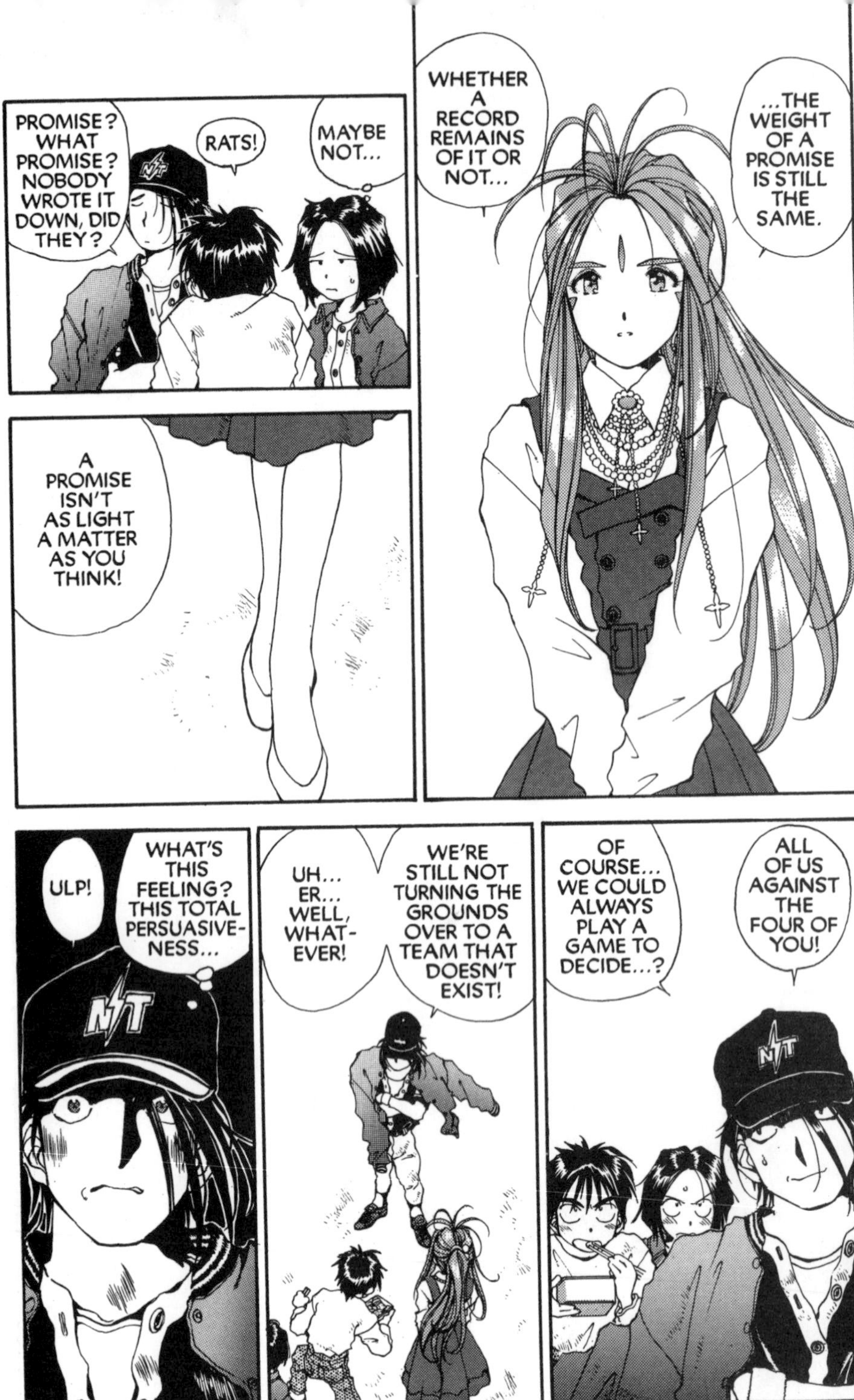
PROMISE? WHAT PROMISE? NOBODY WROTE IT DOWN, DID THEY?
RATS!
MAYBE NOT...
A PROMISE ISN'T AS LIGHT A MATTER AS YOU THINK!
WHETHER A RECORD REMAINS OF IT OR NOT...
...THE WEIGHT OF A PROMISE IS STILL THE SAME.
ULP!
WHAT'S THIS FEELING? THIS TOTAL PERSUASIVE-NESS...
UH... ER... WELL, WHAT-EVER!
WE'RE STILL NOT TURNING THE GROUNDS OVER TO A TEAM THAT DOESN'T EXIST!
OF COURSE... WE COULD ALWAYS PLAY A GAME TO DECIDE...?
ALL OF US AGAINST THE FOUR OF YOU!

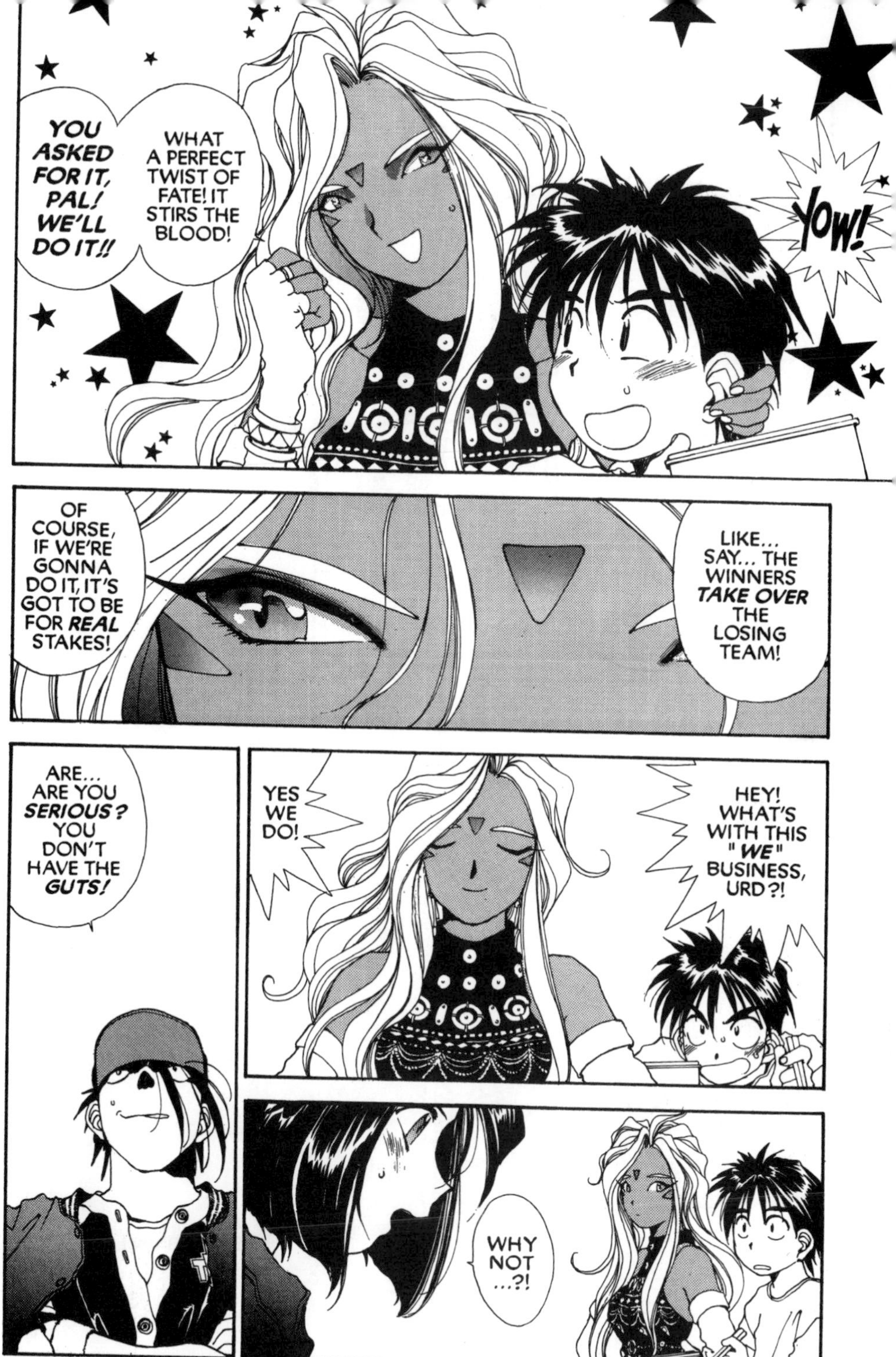
YOU ASKED FOR IT, PAL! WE'LL DO IT!!
WHAT A PERFECT TWIST OF FATE! IT STIRS THE BLOOD!
YOW!
OF COURSE, IF WE'RE GONNA DO IT, IT'S GOT TO BE FOR REAL STAKES!
LIKE... SAY... THE WINNERS TAKE OVER THE LOSING TEAM!
ARE... ARE YOU SERIOUS? YOU DON'T HAVE THE GUTS!
YES WE DO!
HEY! WHAT'S WITH THIS "WE" BUSINESS, URD?!
WHY NOT ...?!

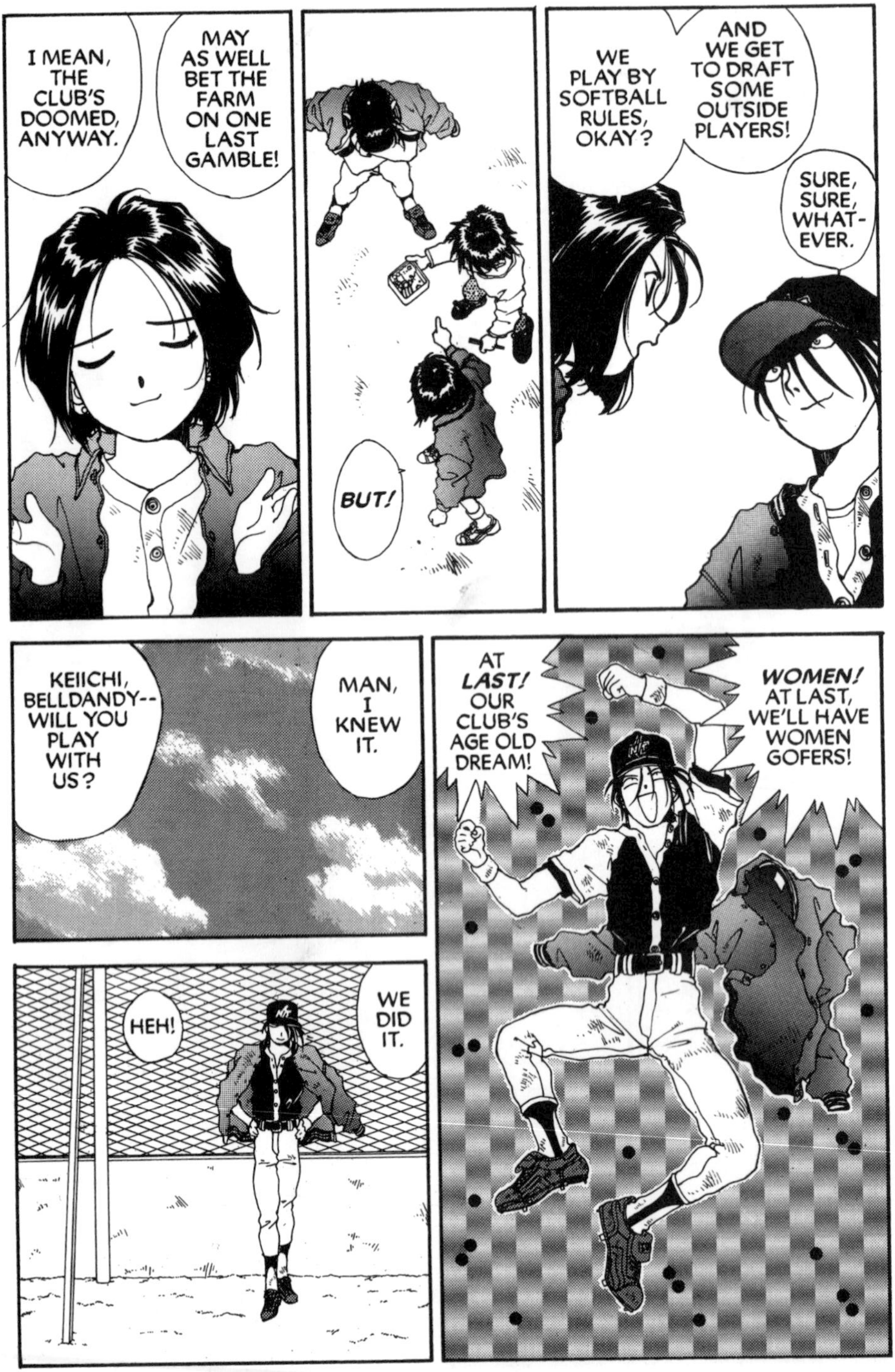
I MEAN, THE CLUB'S DOOMED, ANYWAY.
MAY AS WELL BET THE FARM ON ONE LAST GAMBLE!
BUT!
WE PLAY BY SOFTBALL RULES, OKAY?
AND WE GET TO DRAFT SOME OUTSIDE PLAYERS!
SURE, SURE, WHATEVER.
KEIICHI, BELLDANDY-- WILL YOU PLAY WITH US?
MAN, I KNEW IT.
HEH!
WE DID IT.
AT LAST! OUR CLUB'S AGE OLD DREAM!
WOMEN! AT LAST, WE'LL HAVE WOMEN GOFERS!

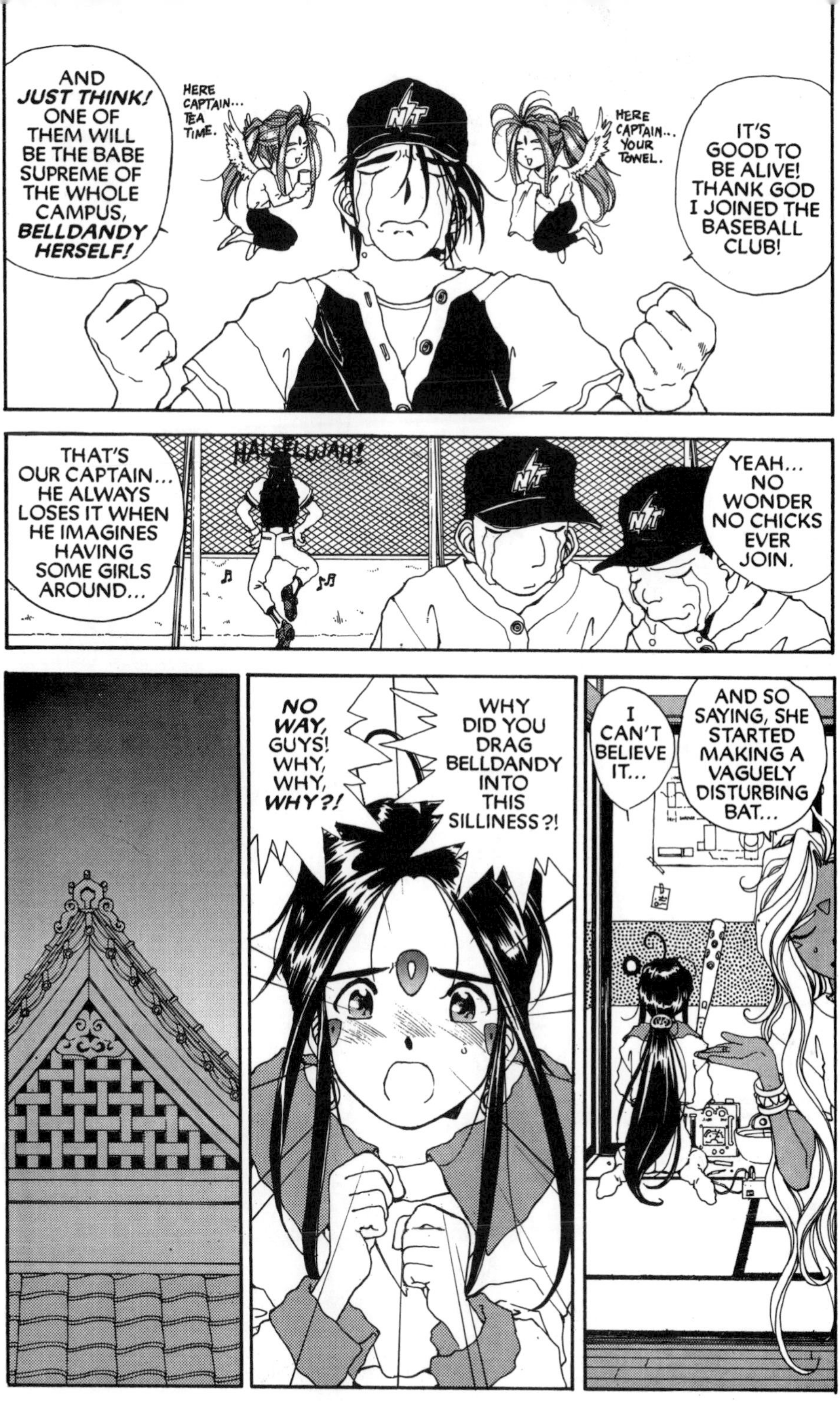
AND JUST THINK! ONE OF THEM WILL BE THE BABE SUPREME OF THE WHOLE CAMPUS, BELLDANDY HERSELF!
HERE CAPTAIN... TEA TIME.
HERE CAPTAIN... YOUR TOWEL.
IT'S GOOD TO BE ALIVE! THANK GOD I JOINED THE BASEBALL CLUB!
THAT'S OUR CAPTAIN... HE ALWAYS LOSES IT WHEN HE IMAGINES HAVING SOME GIRLS AROUND...
HALLELUJAH!
YEAH... NO WONDER NO CHICKS EVER JOIN.
NO WAY, GUYS! WHY, WHY, WHY?!
WHY DID YOU DRAG BELLDANDY INTO THIS SILLINESS?!
I CAN'T BELIEVE IT...
AND SO SAYING, SHE STARTED MAKING A VAGUELY DISTURBING BAT...

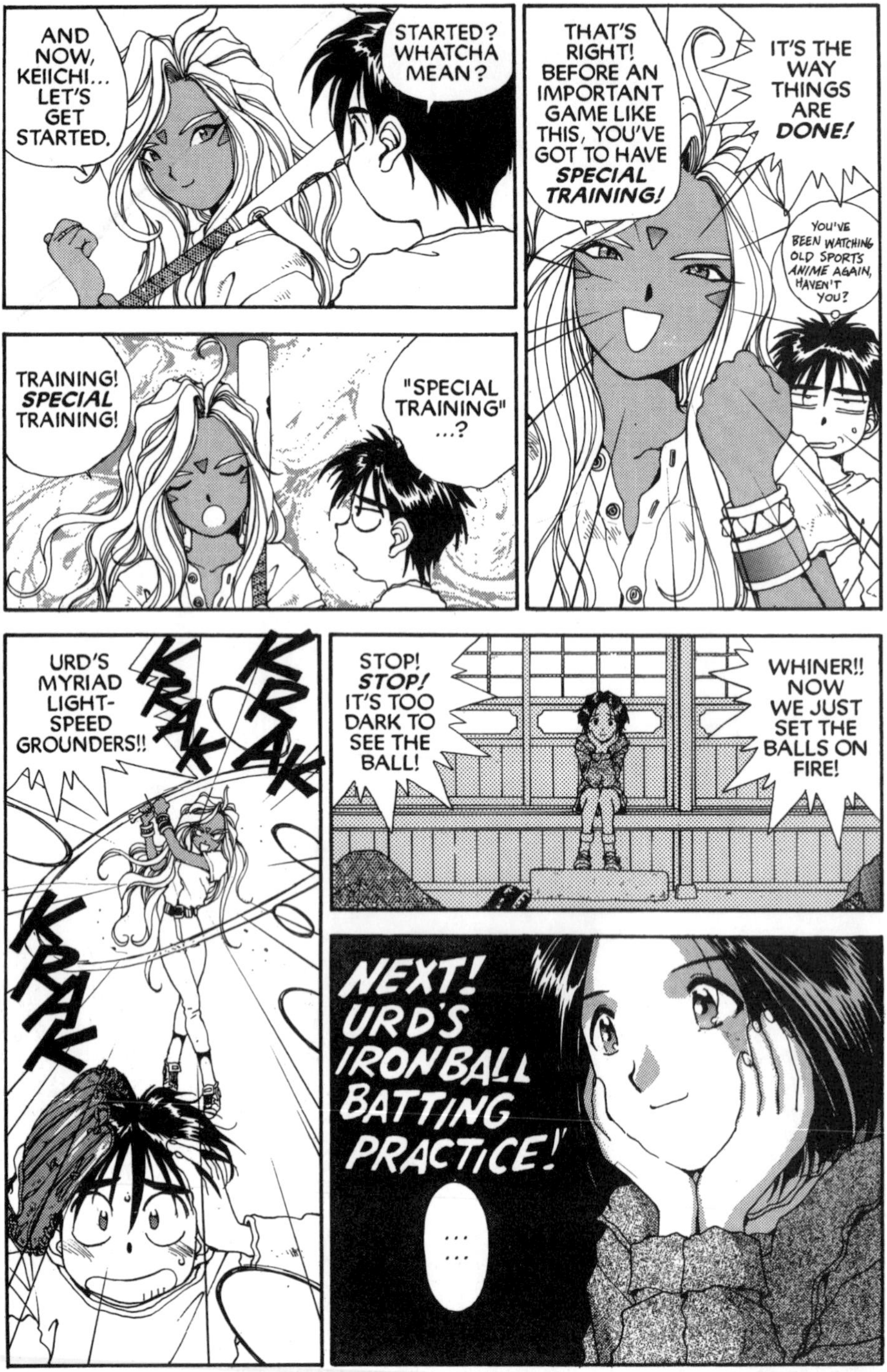
AND NOW, KEIICHI... LET'S GET STARTED.
STARTED? WHATCHA MEAN?
THAT'S RIGHT! BEFORE AN IMPORTANT GAME LIKE THIS, YOU'VE GOT TO HAVE SPECIAL TRAINING!
IT'S THE WAY THINGS ARE DONE!
YOU'VE BEEN WATCHING OLD SPORTS ANIME AGAIN, HAVEN'T YOU?
TRAINING! SPECIAL TRAINING!
"SPECIAL TRAINING" ...?
URD'S MYRIAD LIGHT-SPEED GROUNDERS!!
KRAK KRAK KRAK
STOP! STOP! IT'S TOO DARK TO SEE THE BALL!
WHINER!! NOW WE JUST SET THE BALLS ON FIRE!
NEXT! URD'S IRONBALL BATTING PRACTICE!
... ...

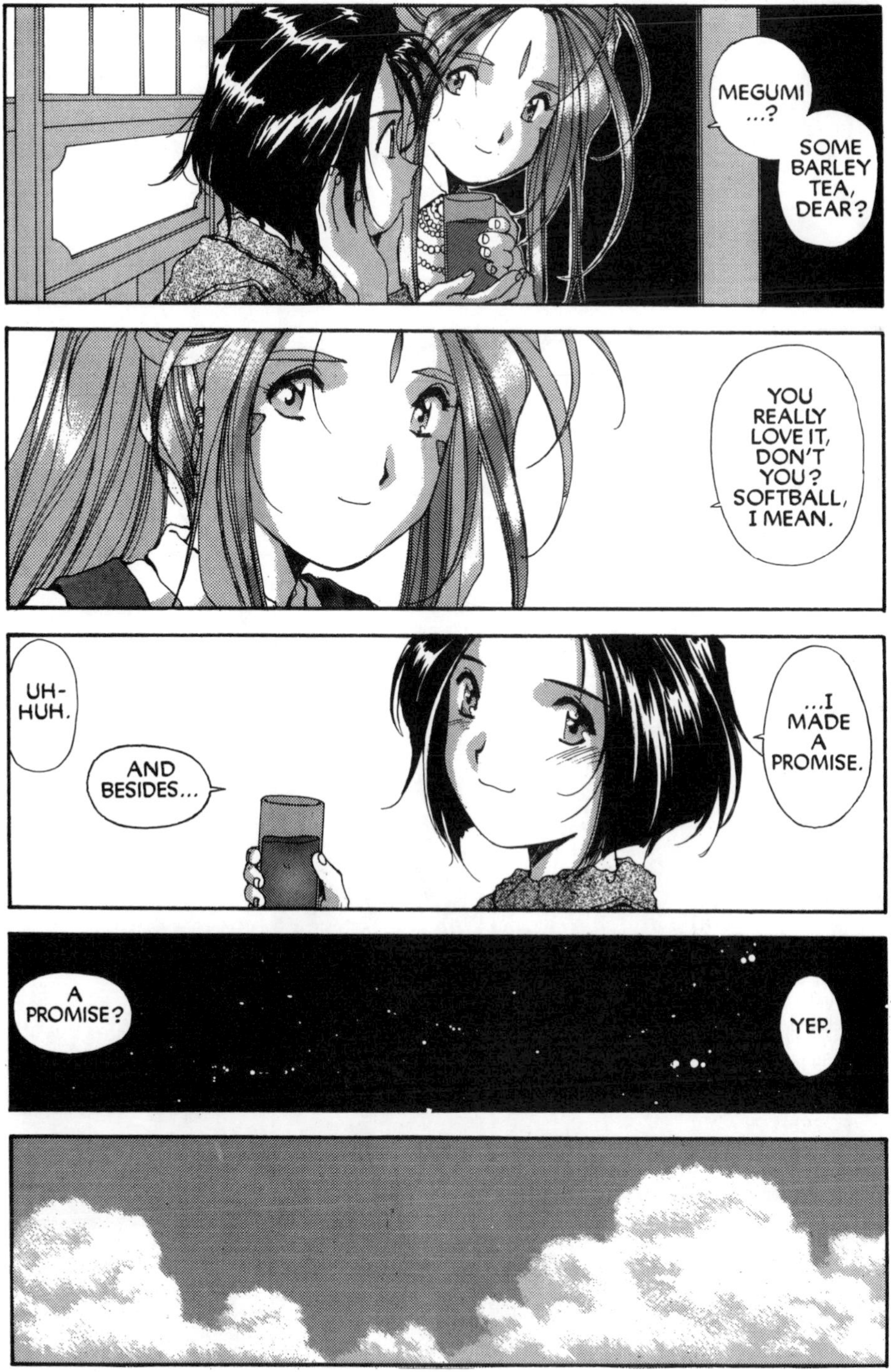
MEGUMI ...?
SOME BARLEY TEA, DEAR?
YOU REALLY LOVE IT, DON'T YOU? SOFTBALL, I MEAN.
UH-HUH.
AND BESIDES...
...I MADE A PROMISE.
A PROMISE?
YEP.

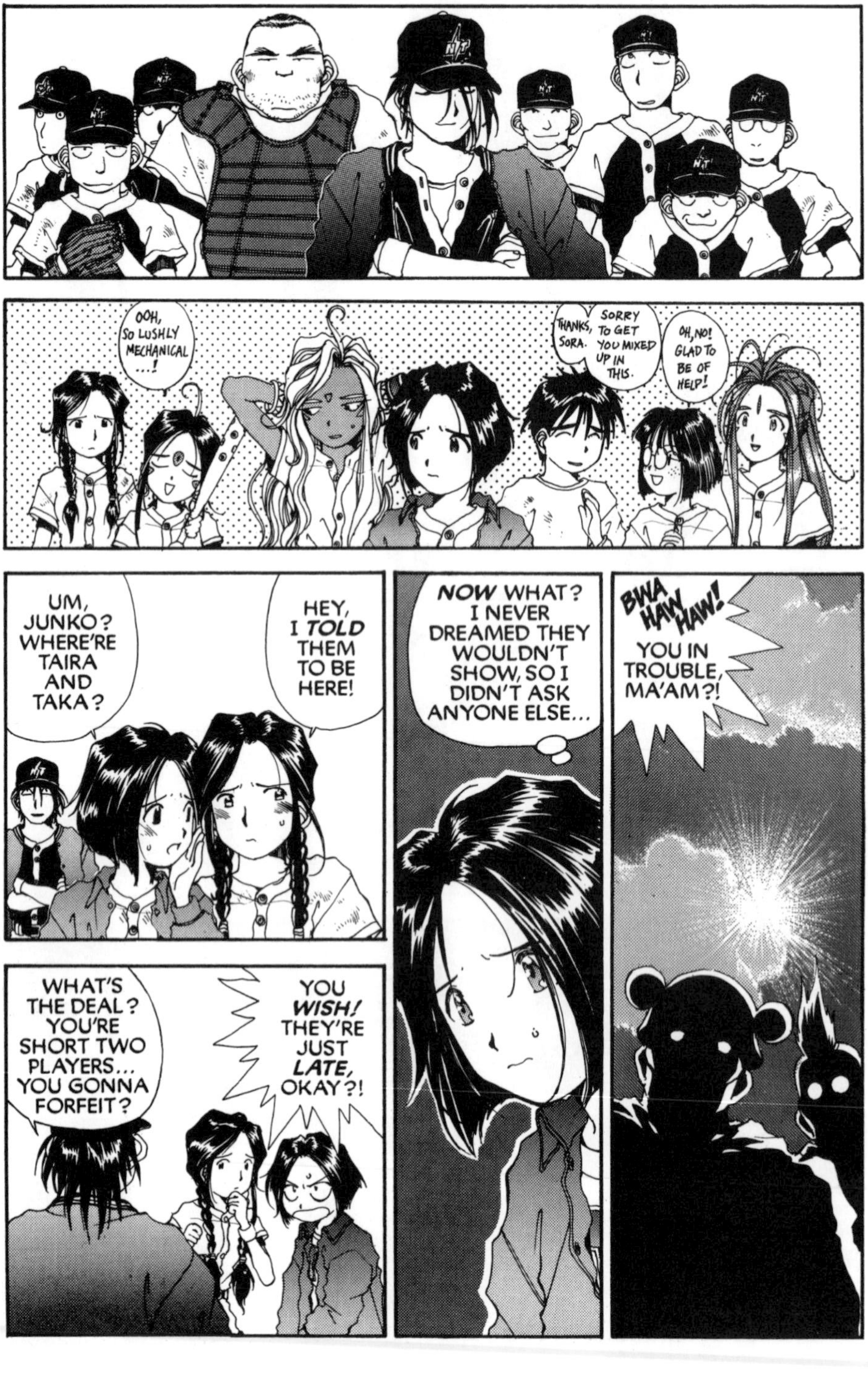
OOH, SO LUSHLY MECHANICAL...!
THANKS, SORA.
SORRY TO GET YOU MIXED UP IN THIS.
OH, NO! GLAD TO BE OF HELP!
UM, JUNKO? WHERE'RE TAIRA AND TAKA?
HEY, I TOLD THEM TO BE HERE!
WHAT'S THE DEAL? YOU'RE SHORT TWO PLAYERS... YOU GONNA FORFEIT?
YOU WISH! THEY'RE JUST LATE, OKAY?!
NOW WHAT? I NEVER DREAMED THEY WOULDN'T SHOW, SO I DIDN'T ASK ANYONE ELSE...
BWA HAW HAW!
YOU IN TROUBLE, MA'AM?!

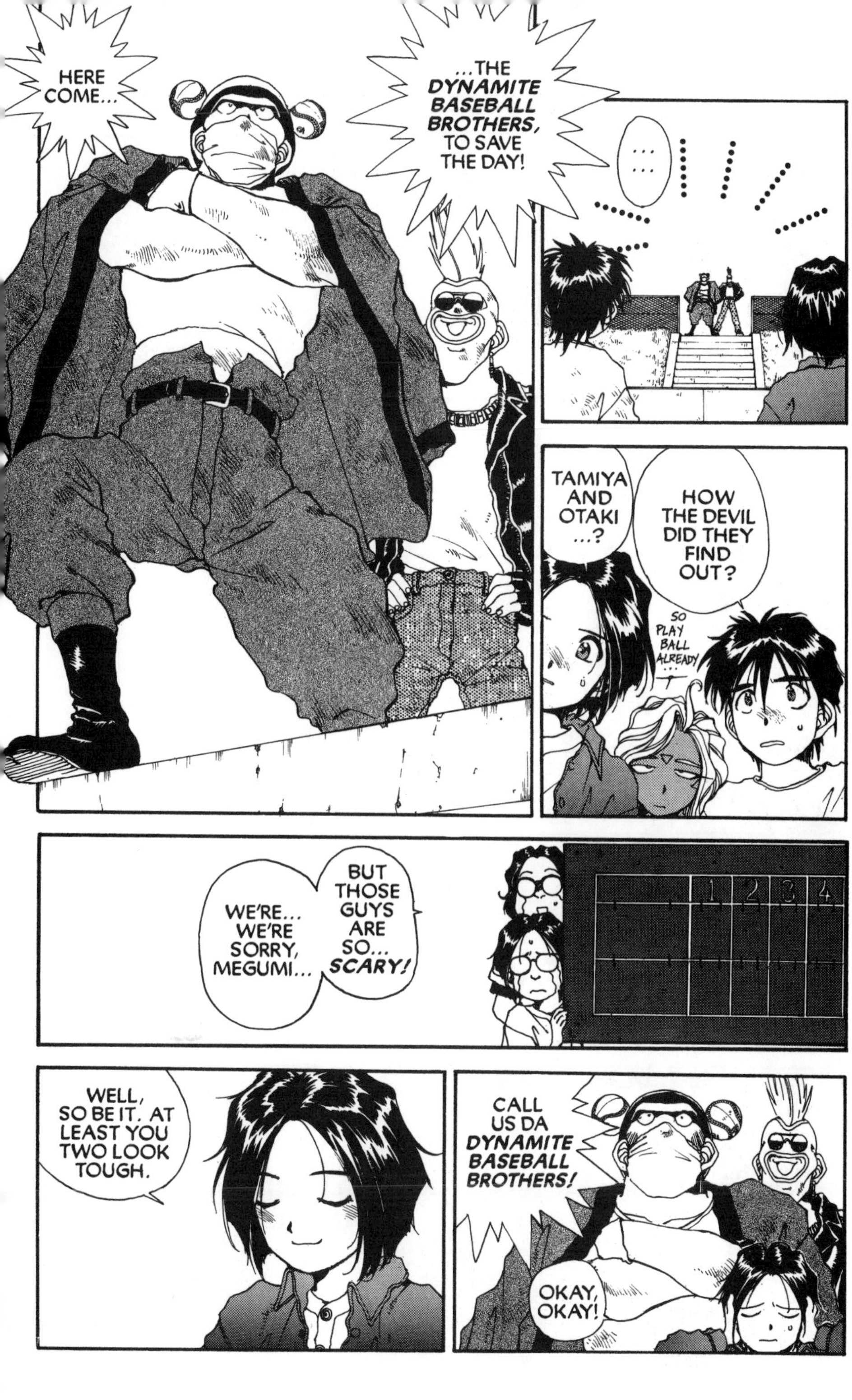
HERE COME...
...THE DYNAMITE BASEBALL BROTHERS, TO SAVE THE DAY!
...
TAMIYA AND OTAKI ...?
HOW THE DEVIL DID THEY FIND OUT?
SO PLAY BALL ALREADY ...
WE'RE... WE'RE SORRY, MEGUMI...
BUT THOSE GUYS ARE SO... SCARY!
1 2 3 4
WELL, SO BE IT. AT LEAST YOU TWO LOOK TOUGH.
CALL US DA DYNAMITE BASEBALL BROTHERS!
OKAY, OKAY!

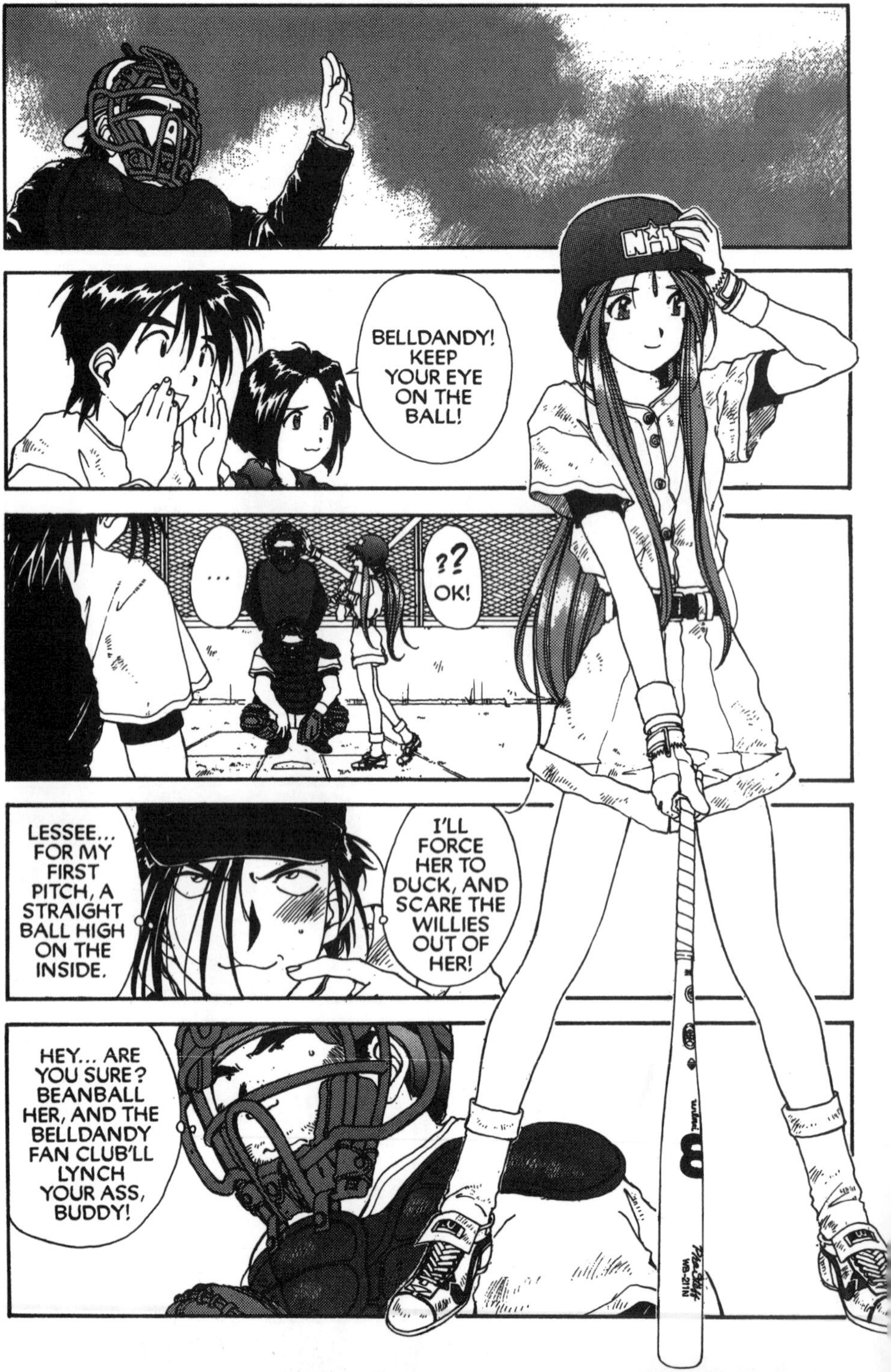
BELLDANDY! KEEP YOUR EYE ON THE BALL!
...
?? OK!
LESSEE... FOR MY FIRST PITCH, A STRAIGHT BALL HIGH ON THE INSIDE.
I'LL FORCE HER TO DUCK, AND SCARE THE WILLIES OUT OF HER!
HEY... ARE YOU SURE? BEANBALL HER, AND THE BELLDANDY FAN CLUB'LL LYNCH YOUR ASS, BUDDY!

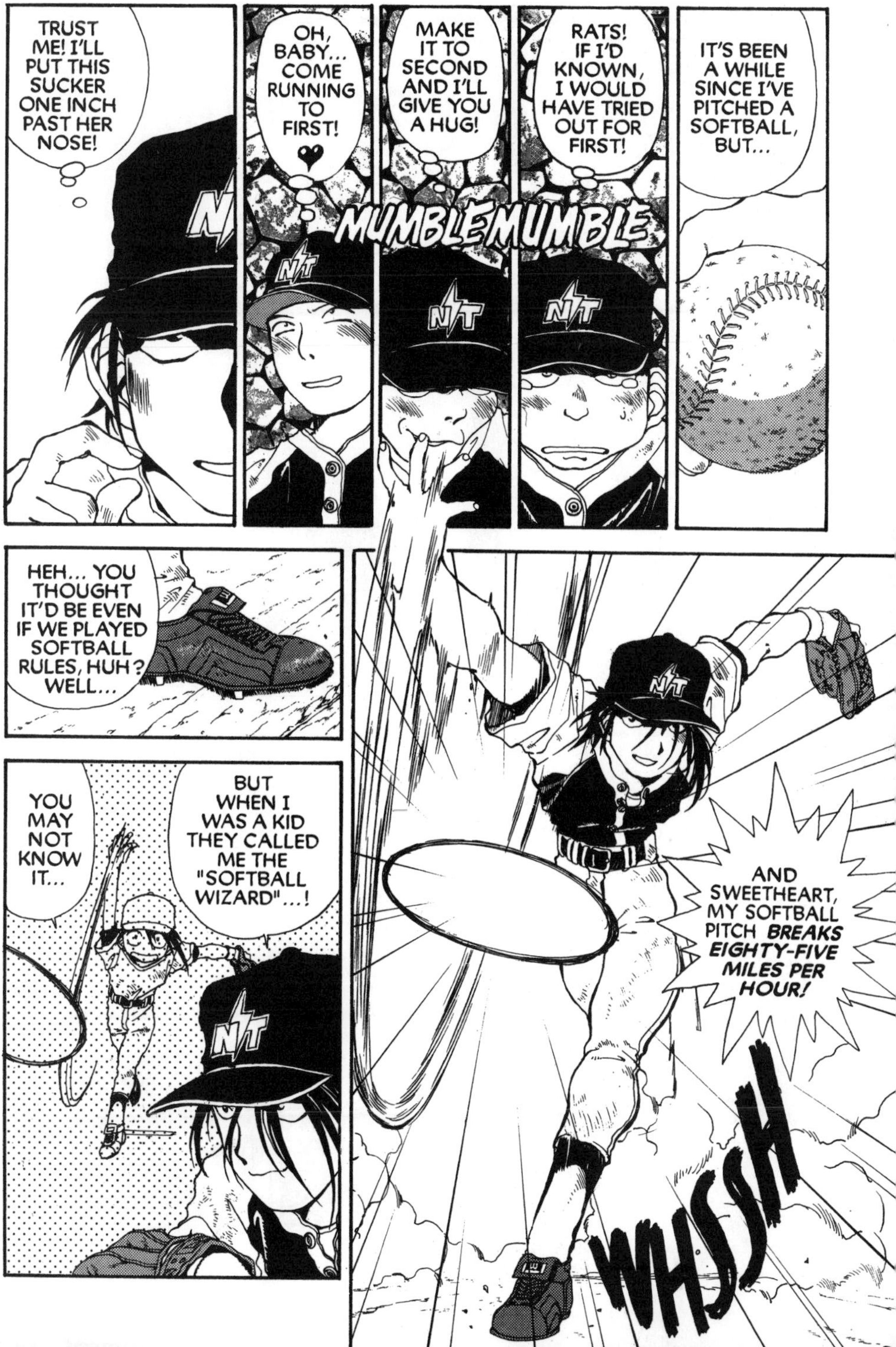

TRUST ME! I'LL PUT THIS SUCKER ONE INCH PAST HER NOSE!
OH, BABY... COME RUNNING TO FIRST! ♥
MAKE IT TO SECOND AND I'LL GIVE YOU A HUG!
RATS! IF I'D KNOWN, I WOULD HAVE TRIED OUT FOR FIRST!
MUMBLE MUMBLE
IT'S BEEN A WHILE SINCE I'VE PITCHED A SOFTBALL, BUT...
HEH... YOU THOUGHT IT'D BE EVEN IF WE PLAYED SOFTBALL RULES, HUH? WELL...
YOU MAY NOT KNOW IT...
BUT WHEN I WAS A KID THEY CALLED ME THE "SOFTBALL WIZARD"...!
AND SWEETHEART, MY SOFTBALL PITCH ***BREAKS EIGHTY-FIVE MILES PER HOUR!***
WHSSH

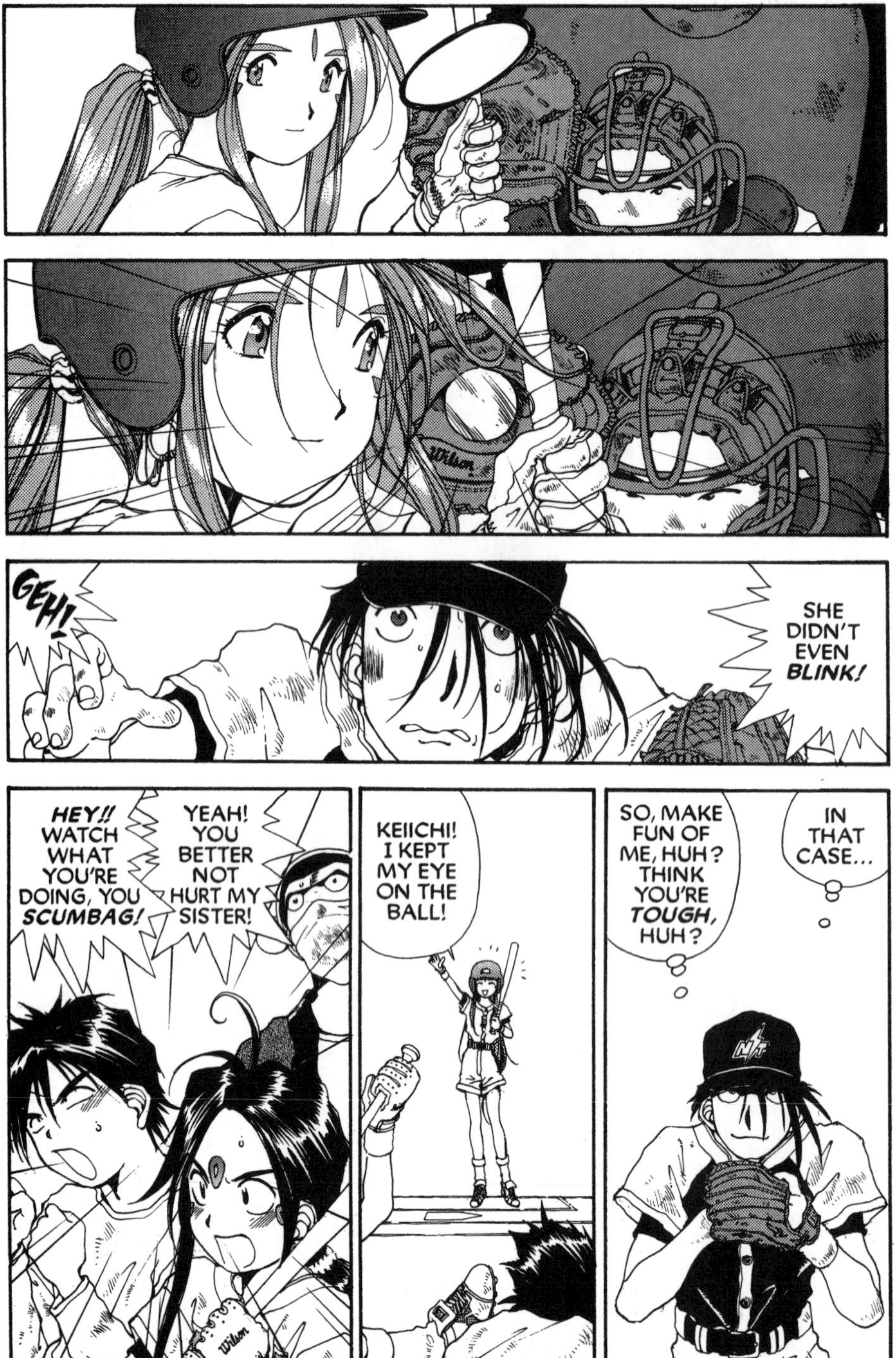
GEH!
SHE DIDN'T EVEN BLINK!
HEY!! WATCH WHAT YOU'RE DOING, YOU SCUMBAG!
YEAH! YOU BETTER NOT HURT MY SISTER!
KEIICHI! I KEPT MY EYE ON THE BALL!
SO, MAKE FUN OF ME, HUH? THINK YOU'RE TOUGH, HUH?
IN THAT CASE...

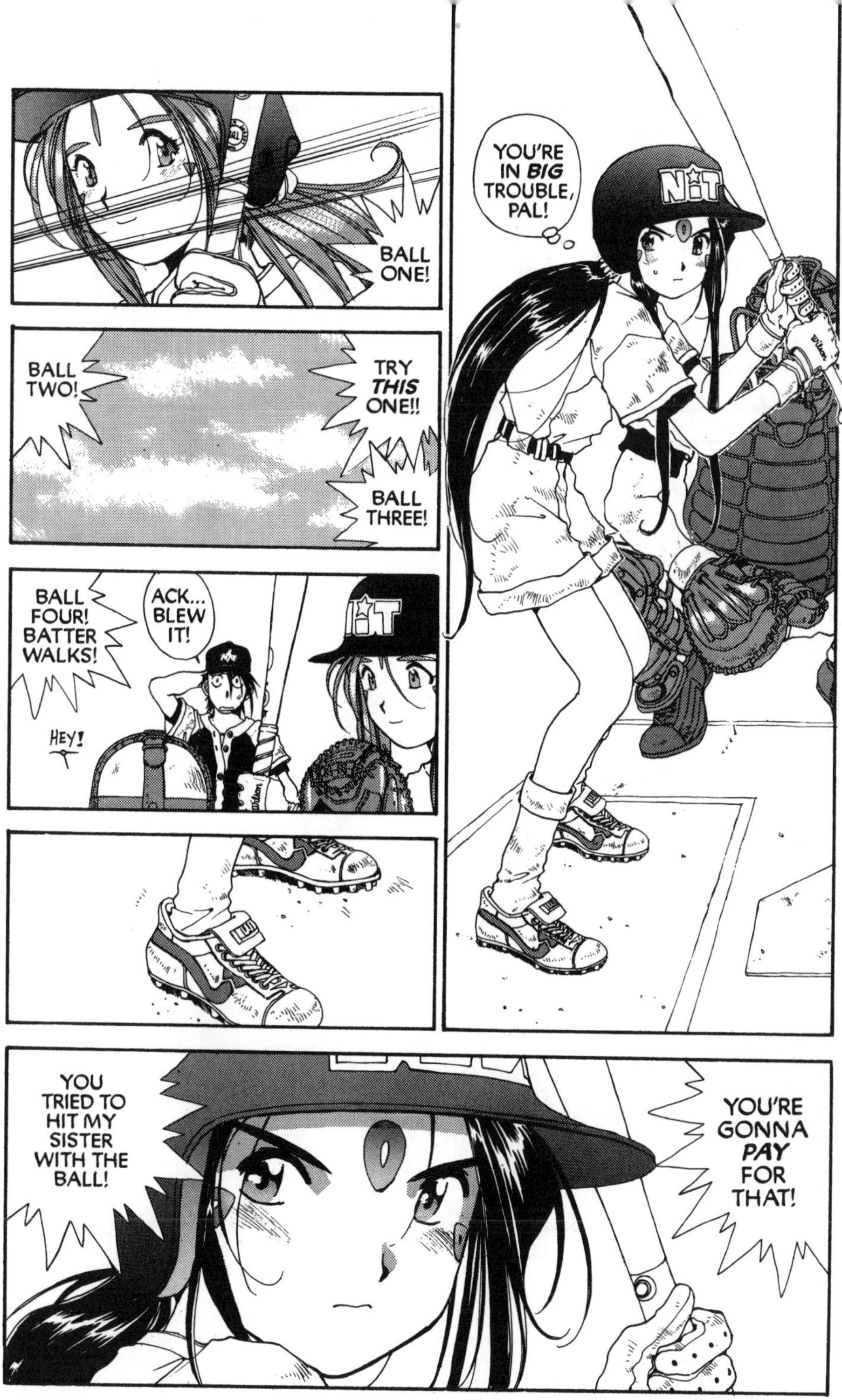
BALL ONE!
BALL TWO!
TRY *THIS* ONE!!
BALL THREE!
BALL FOUR! BATTER WALKS!
ACK... BLEW IT!
HEY!
YOU'RE IN *BIG* TROUBLE, PAL!
YOU TRIED TO HIT MY SISTER WITH THE BALL!
YOU'RE GONNA *PAY* FOR THAT!

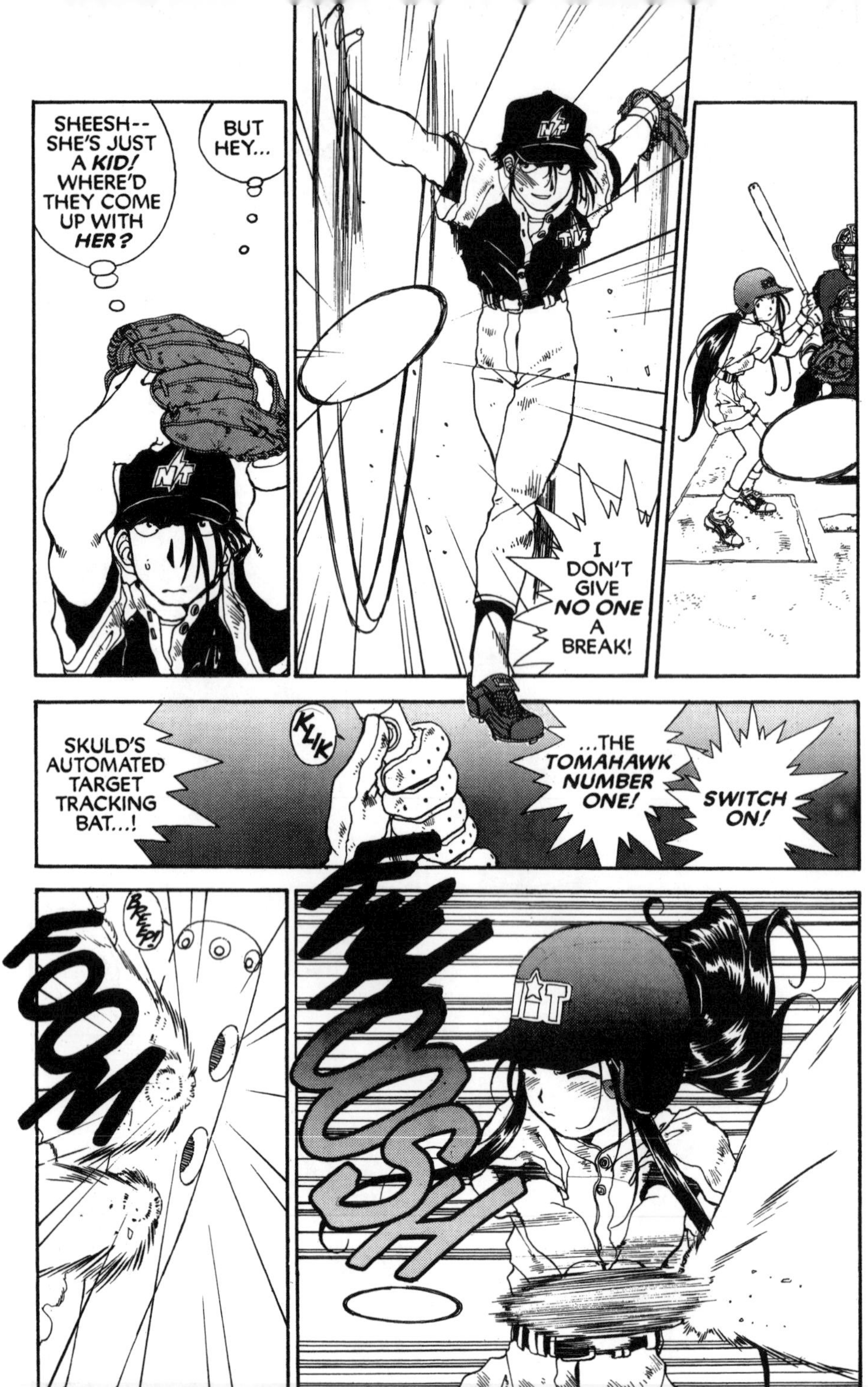
SHEESH-- SHE'S JUST A *KID!* WHERE'D THEY COME UP WITH *HER?*
BUT HEY...
I DON'T GIVE *NO ONE* A BREAK!
SKULD'S AUTOMATED TARGET TRACKING BAT...!
KLIK
...THE *TOMAHAWK NUMBER ONE!*
SWITCH ON!
BREEP!
VOOM
FWOOSH

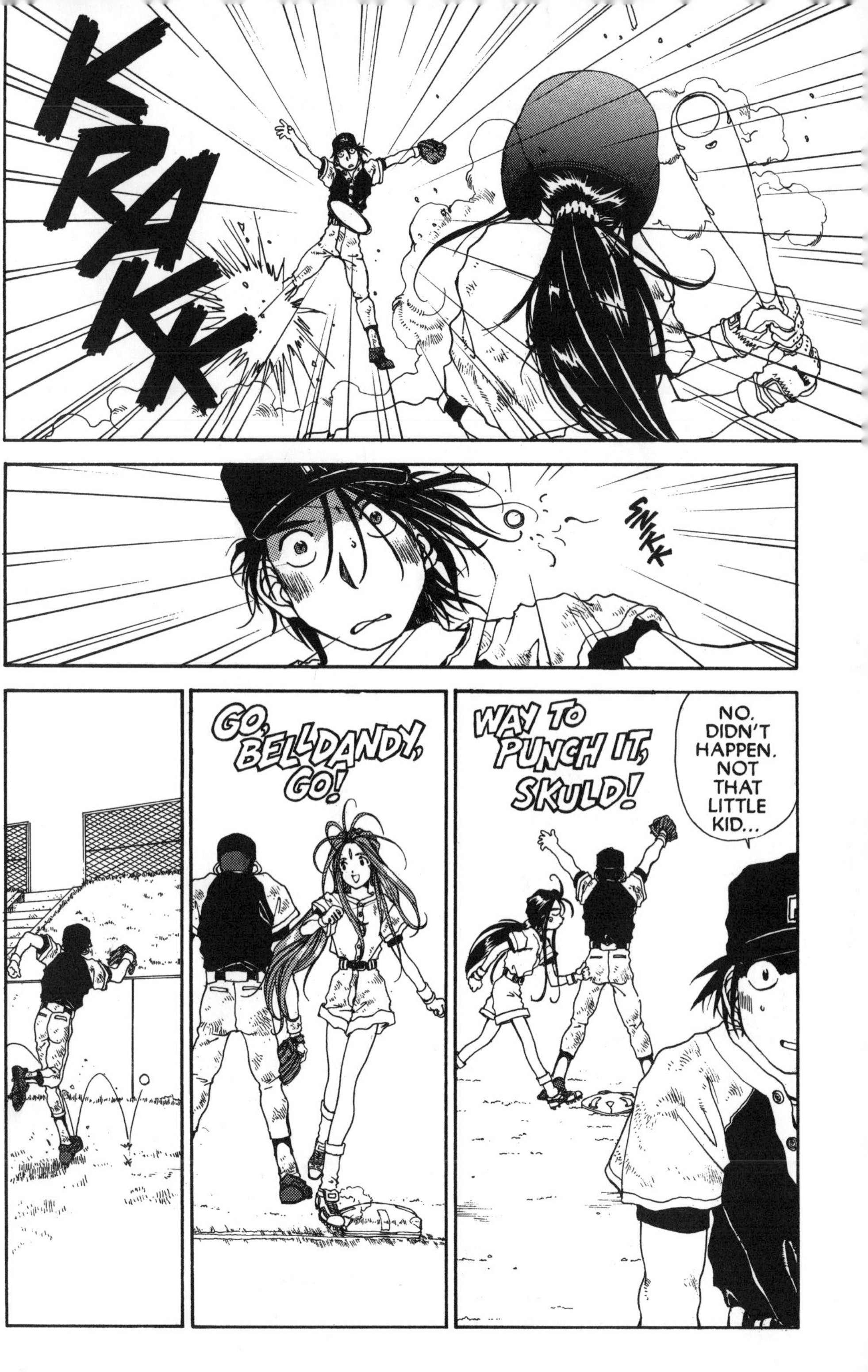
KRAKK
SNIKK
GO, BELLDANDY, GO!
WAY TO PUNCH IT, SKULD!
NO. DIDN'T HAPPEN. NOT THAT LITTLE KID...

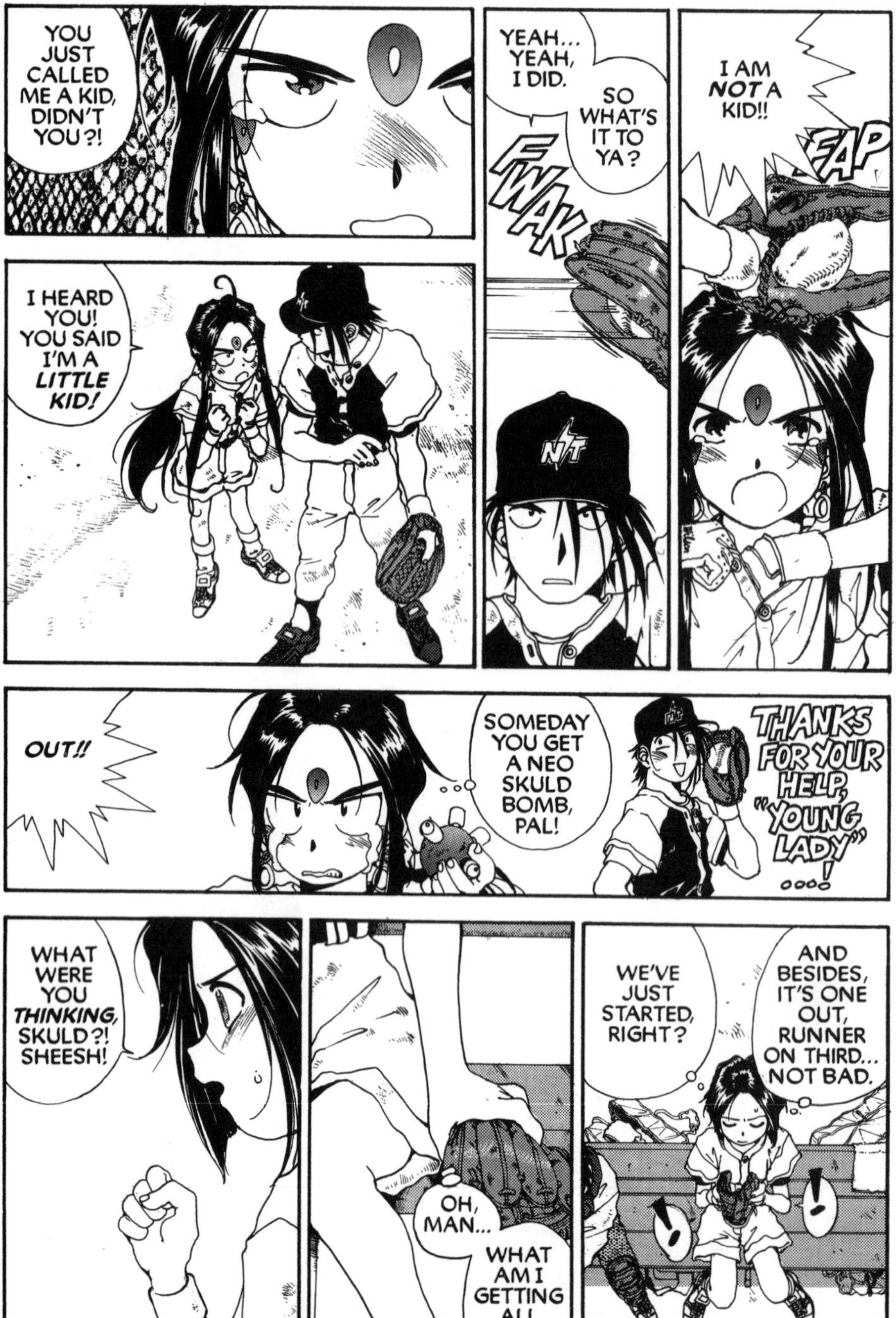
YOU JUST CALLED ME A KID, DIDN'T YOU?!
I HEARD YOU! YOU SAID I'M A *LITTLE KID!*
YEAH... YEAH, I DID.
SO WHAT'S IT TO YA?
FWAK
I AM *NOT* A KID!!
FAP
OUT!!
SOMEDAY YOU GET A NEO SKULD BOMB, PAL!
THANKS FOR YOUR HELP, "YOUNG LADY" ooo!
WHAT WERE YOU *THINKING,* SKULD?! SHEESH!
OH, MAN...
WHAT AM I GETTING ALL UPSET FOR...?
WE'VE JUST STARTED, RIGHT?
AND BESIDES, IT'S ONE OUT, RUNNER ON THIRD... NOT BAD.

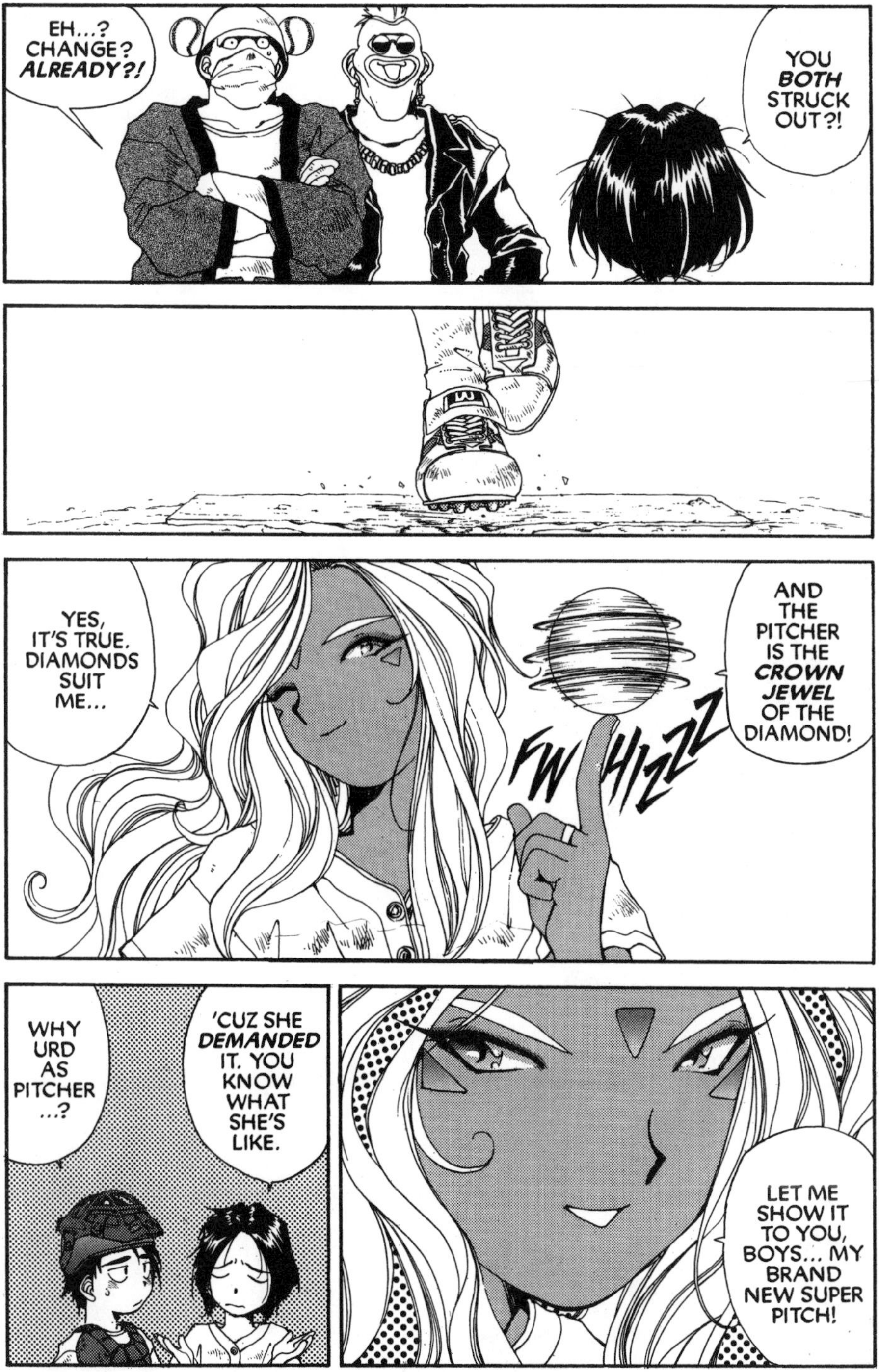
EH...? CHANGE? ALREADY?!
YOU BOTH STRUCK OUT?!
YES, IT'S TRUE. DIAMONDS SUIT ME...
FWHIZZZ
AND THE PITCHER IS THE CROWN JEWEL OF THE DIAMOND!
WHY URD AS PITCHER ...?
'CUZ SHE DEMANDED IT. YOU KNOW WHAT SHE'S LIKE.
LET ME SHOW IT TO YOU, BOYS... MY BRAND NEW SUPER PITCH!

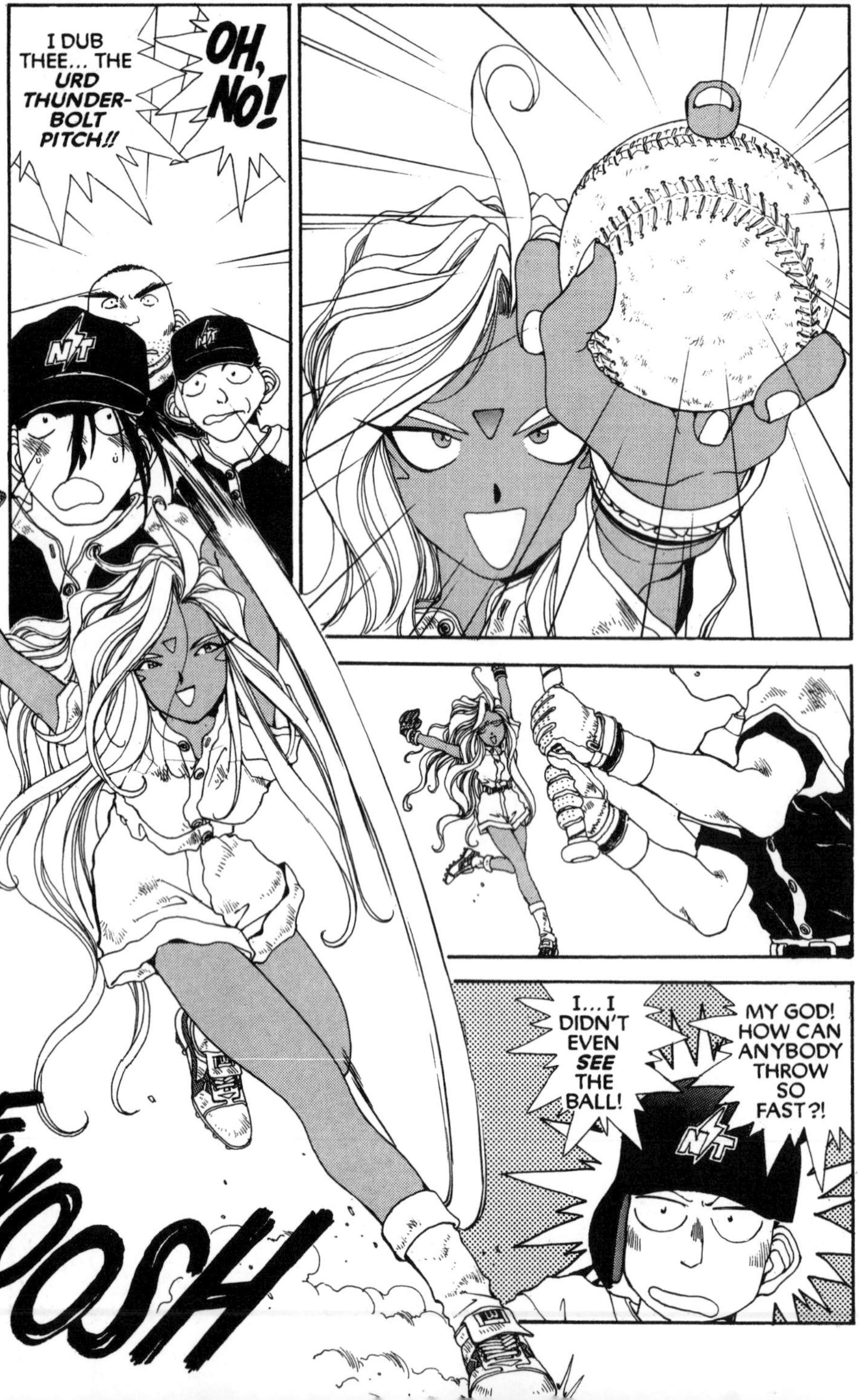
I DUB THEE... THE URD THUNDER-BOLT PITCH!!
OH, NO!
FWOOSH
I... I DIDN'T EVEN SEE THE BALL!
MY GOD! HOW CAN ANYBODY THROW SO FAST?!

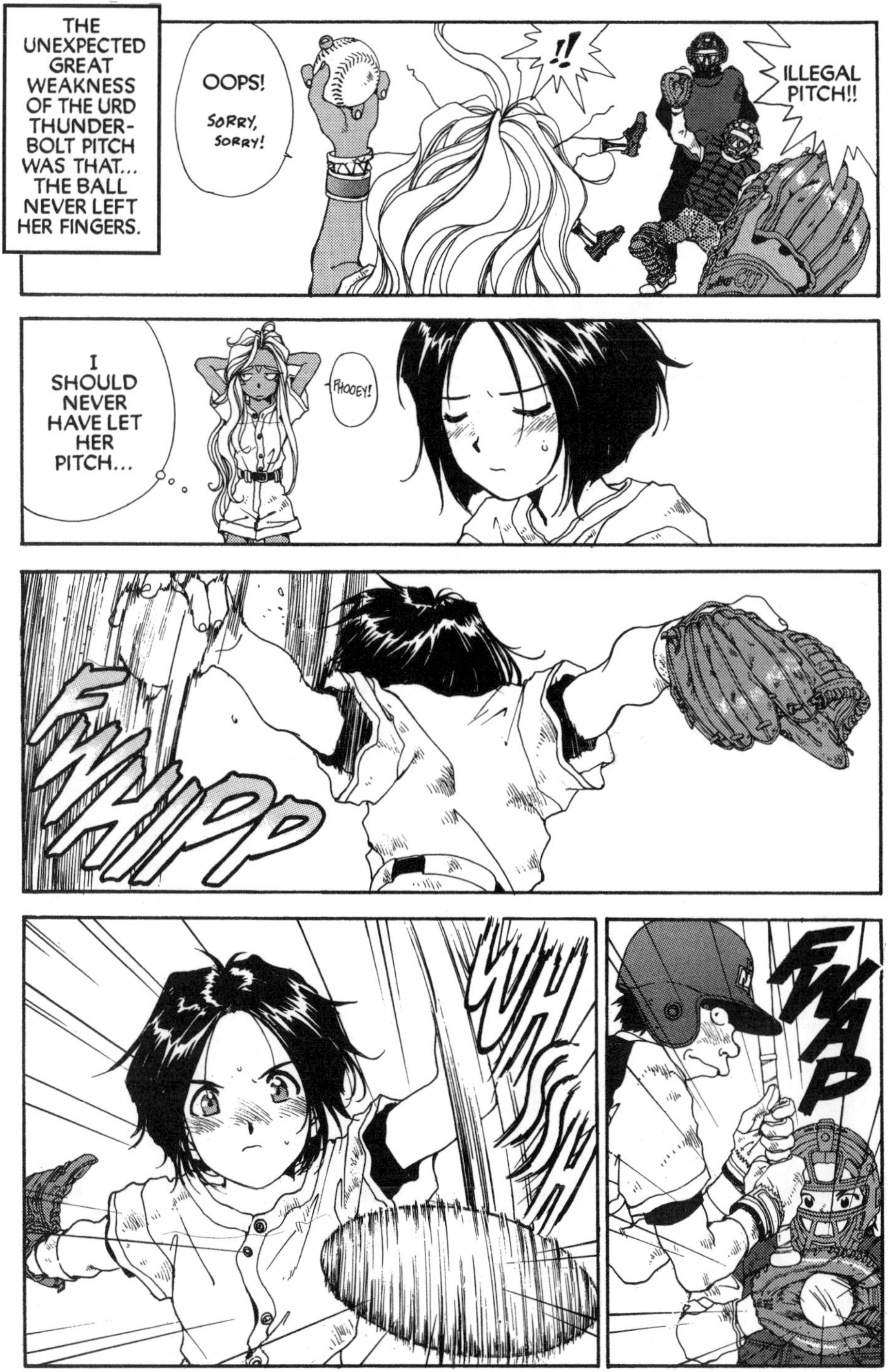
THE UNEXPECTED GREAT WEAKNESS OF THE URD THUNDER-BOLT PITCH WAS THAT... THE BALL NEVER LEFT HER FINGERS.
OOPS!
SORRY, SORRY!
!!
ILLEGAL PITCH!!
I SHOULD NEVER HAVE LET HER PITCH...
PHOOEY!
FWHIPP
FWAP

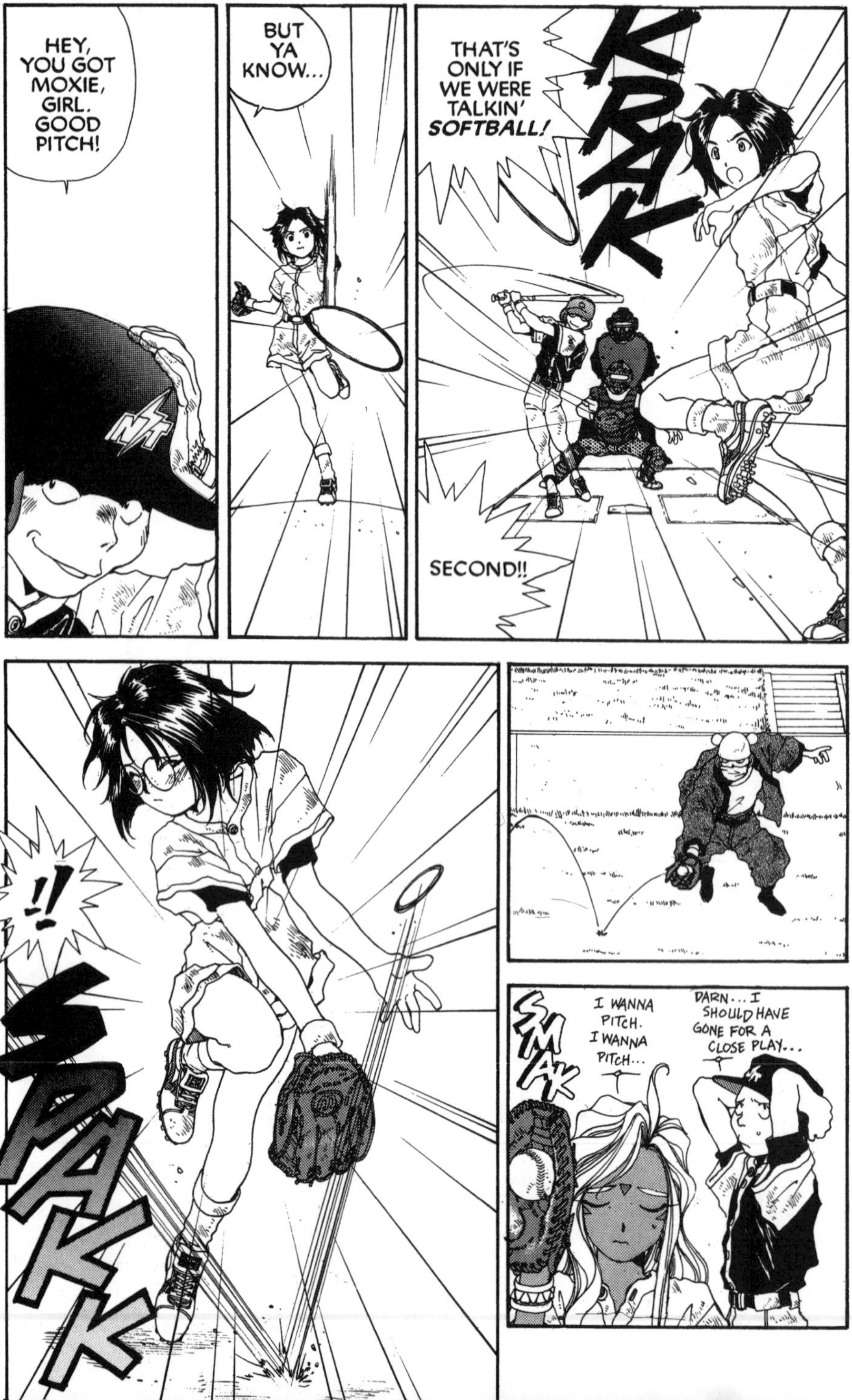
HEY, YOU GOT MOXIE, GIRL. GOOD PITCH!
BUT YA KNOW...
THAT'S ONLY IF WE WERE TALKIN' *SOFTBALL!*
KRAK
SECOND!!
!!
SMAK
I WANNA PITCH. I WANNA PITCH...
DARN... I SHOULD HAVE GONE FOR A CLOSE PLAY...

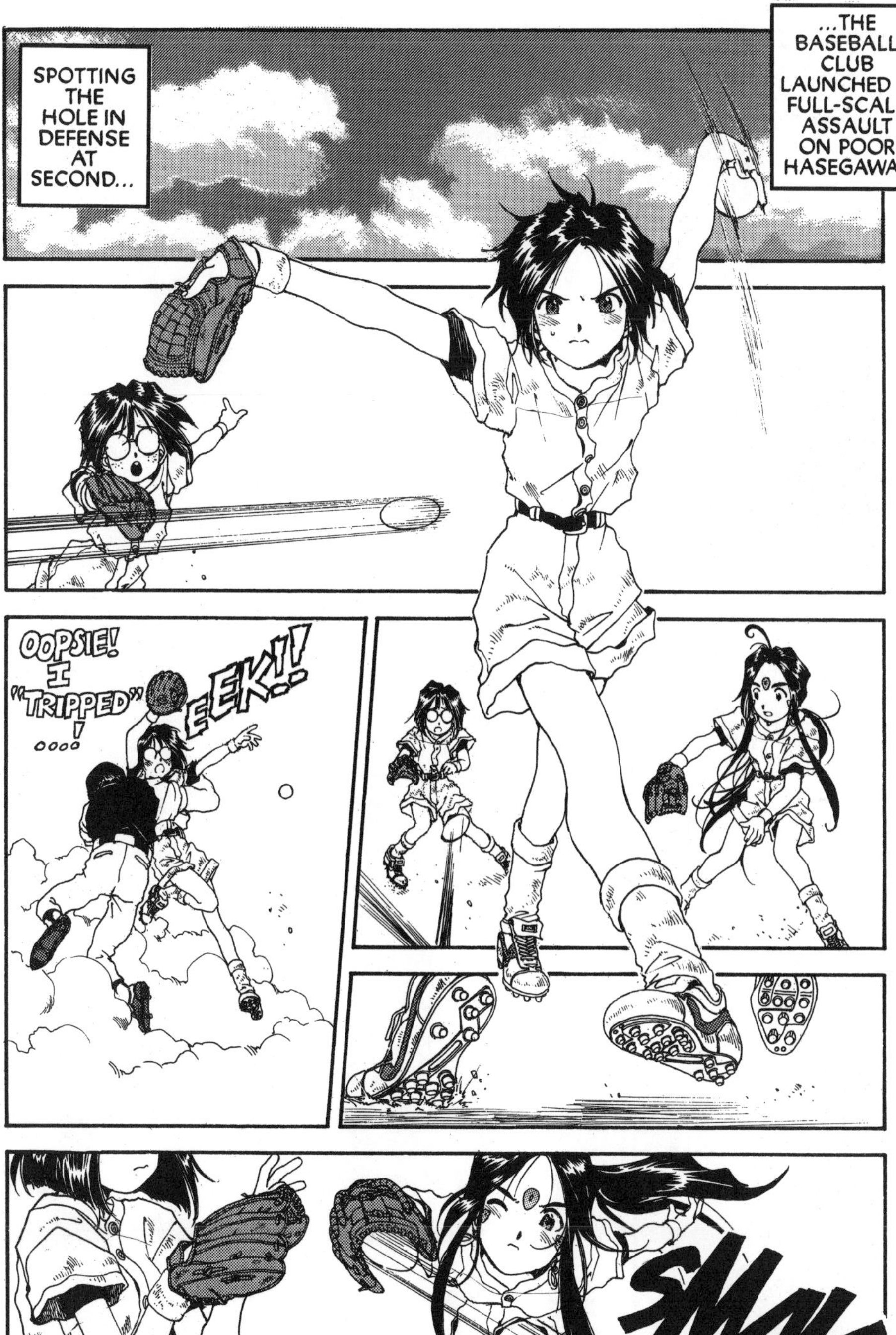
SPOTTING THE HOLE IN DEFENSE AT SECOND...
...THE BASEBALL CLUB LAUNCHED A FULL-SCALE ASSAULT ON POOR HASEGAWA.
OOPSIE! I "TRIPPED" ...!
EEK!!
SMAK

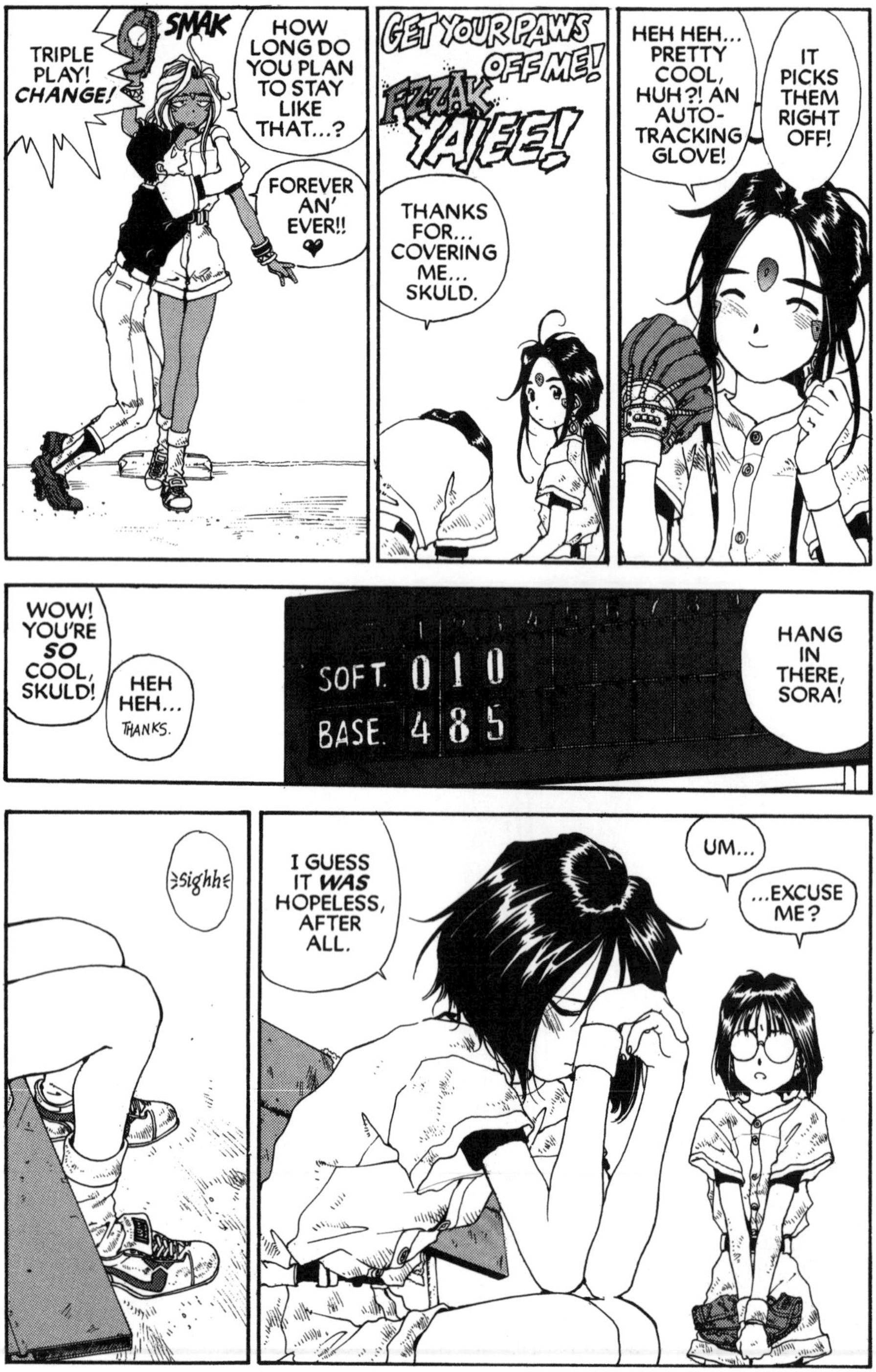
SMAK
TRIPLE PLAY! CHANGE!
HOW LONG DO YOU PLAN TO STAY LIKE THAT...?
FOREVER AN' EVER!!
GET YOUR PAWS OFF ME!
FZZAK
YAIEE!
THANKS FOR... COVERING ME... SKULD.
HEH HEH... PRETTY COOL, HUH?! AN AUTO-TRACKING GLOVE!
IT PICKS THEM RIGHT OFF!
WOW! YOU'RE SO COOL, SKULD!
HEH HEH... THANKS.
SOFT. 0 1 0
BASE. 4 8 5
HANG IN THERE, SORA!
≡sighh≡
I GUESS IT WAS HOPELESS, AFTER ALL.
UM...
...EXCUSE ME?

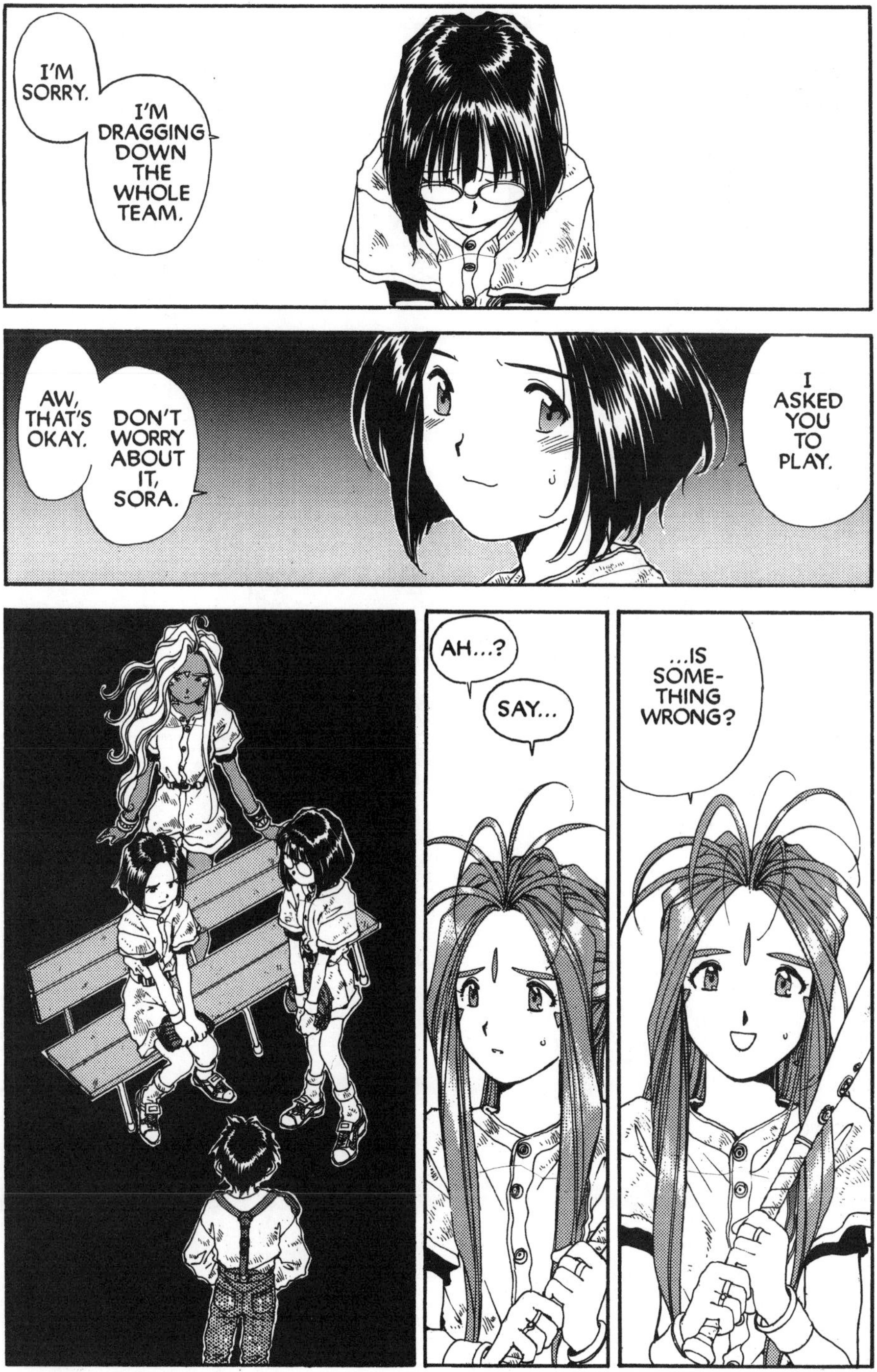
I'M SORRY.
I'M DRAGGING DOWN THE WHOLE TEAM.
AW, THAT'S OKAY.
DON'T WORRY ABOUT IT, SORA.
I ASKED YOU TO PLAY.
AH...?
SAY...
...IS SOMETHING WRONG?

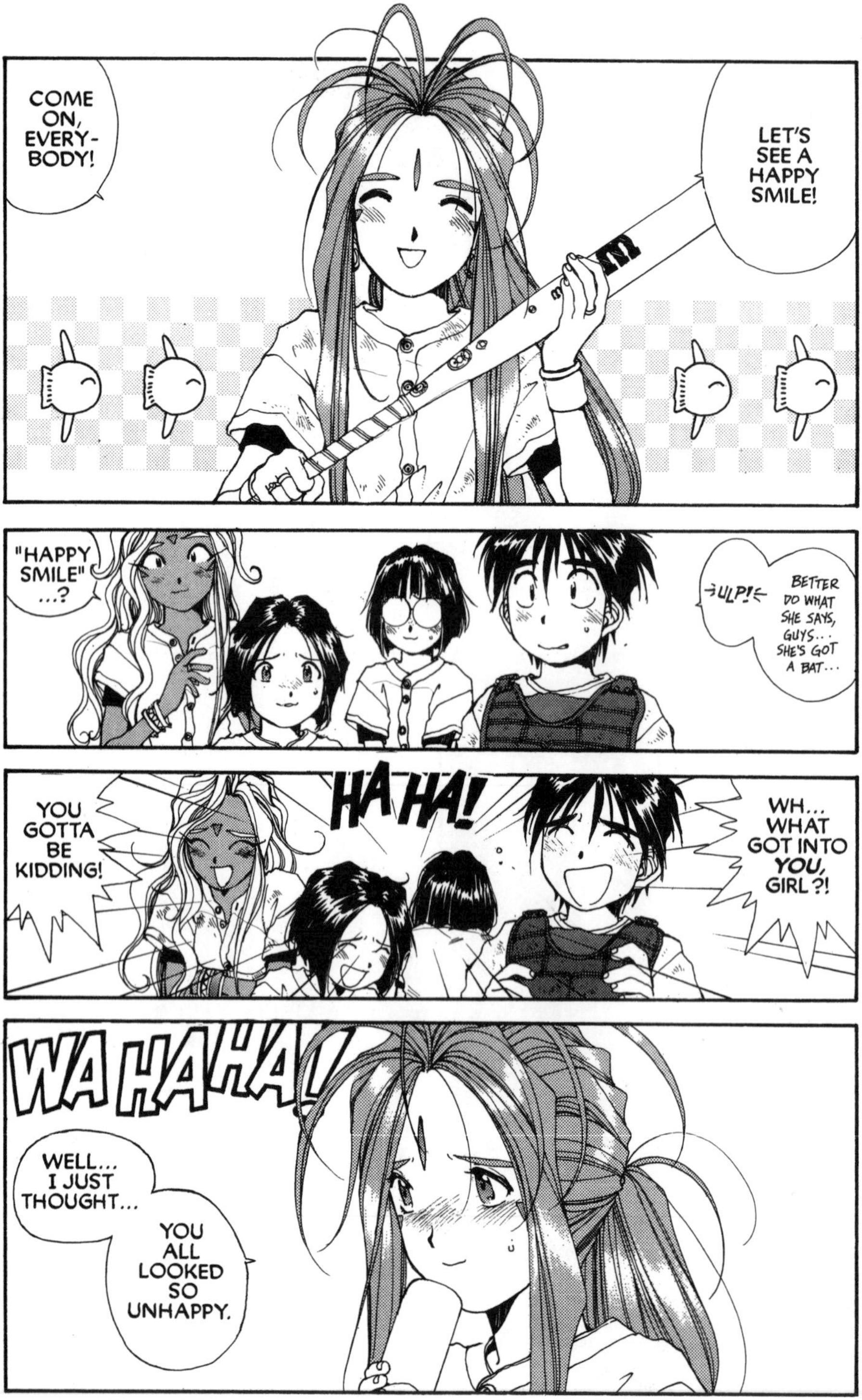
COME ON, EVERY-BODY!
LET'S SEE A HAPPY SMILE!
"HAPPY SMILE" ...?
ULP!
BETTER DO WHAT SHE SAYS, GUYS... SHE'S GOT A BAT...
YOU GOTTA BE KIDDING!
HA HA!
WH... WHAT GOT INTO YOU, GIRL?!
WA HA HA!
WELL... I JUST THOUGHT...
YOU ALL LOOKED SO UNHAPPY.

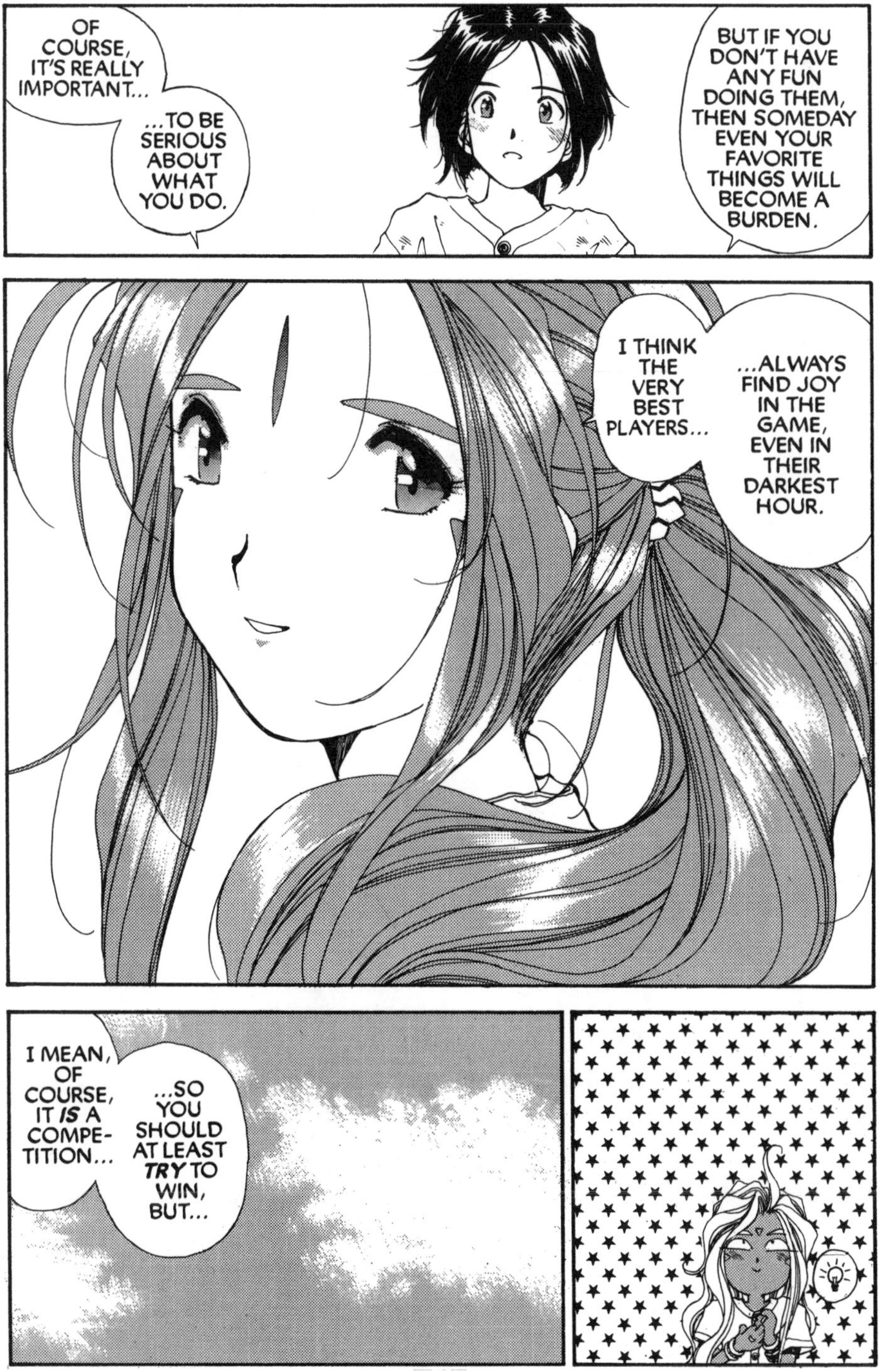
OF COURSE, IT'S REALLY IMPORTANT...
...TO BE SERIOUS ABOUT WHAT YOU DO.
BUT IF YOU DON'T HAVE ANY FUN DOING THEM, THEN SOMEDAY EVEN YOUR FAVORITE THINGS WILL BECOME A BURDEN.
I THINK THE VERY BEST PLAYERS...
...ALWAYS FIND JOY IN THE GAME, EVEN IN THEIR DARKEST HOUR.
I MEAN, OF COURSE, IT *IS* A COMPETITION...
...SO YOU SHOULD AT LEAST *TRY* TO WIN, BUT...

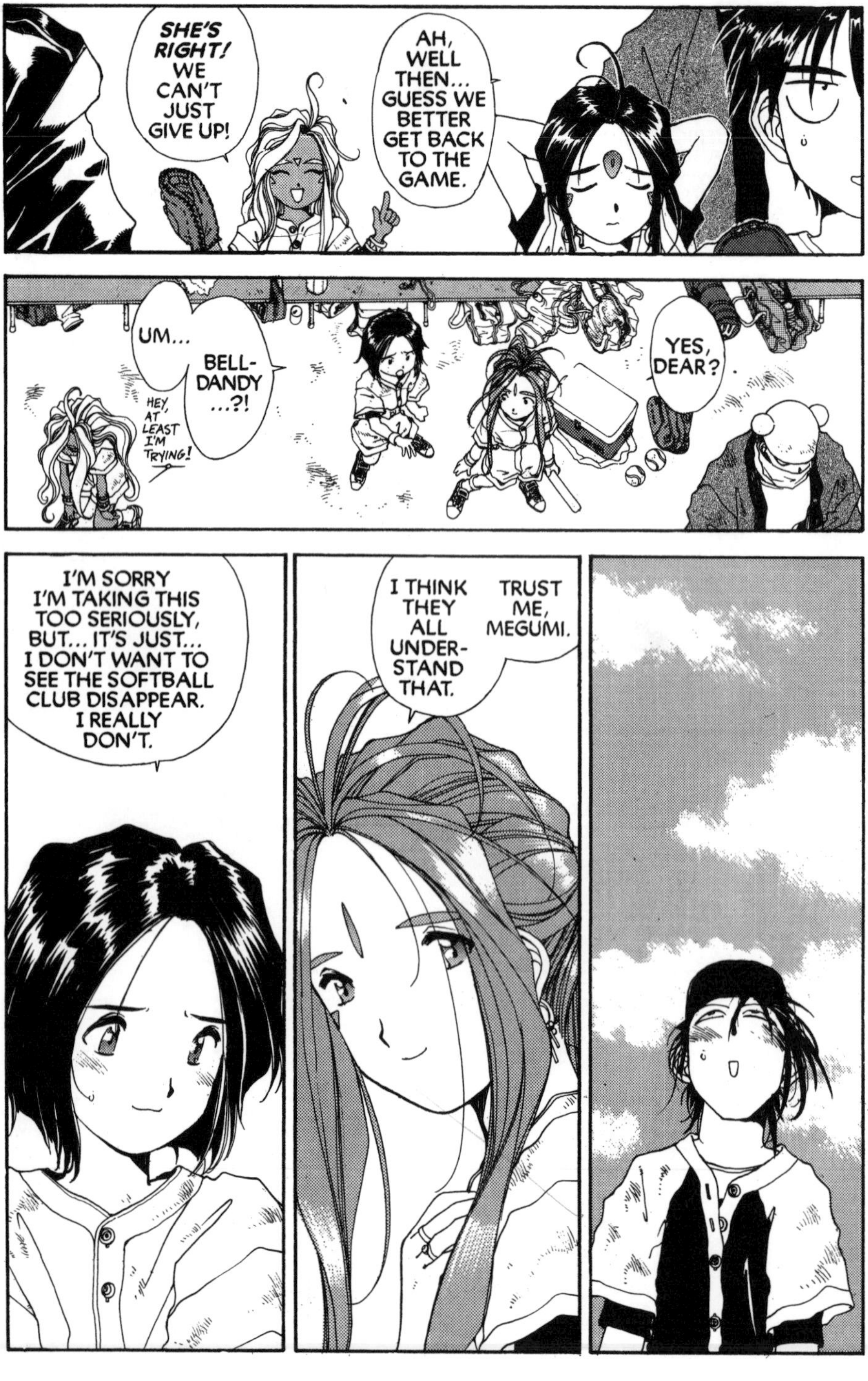
SHE'S RIGHT! WE CAN'T JUST GIVE UP!
AH, WELL THEN... GUESS WE BETTER GET BACK TO THE GAME.
UM...
BELL-DANDY ...?!
HEY, AT LEAST I'M TRYING!
YES, DEAR?
I'M SORRY I'M TAKING THIS TOO SERIOUSLY, BUT... IT'S JUST... I DON'T WANT TO SEE THE SOFTBALL CLUB DISAPPEAR. I REALLY DON'T.
TRUST ME, MEGUMI.
I THINK THEY ALL UNDER-STAND THAT.

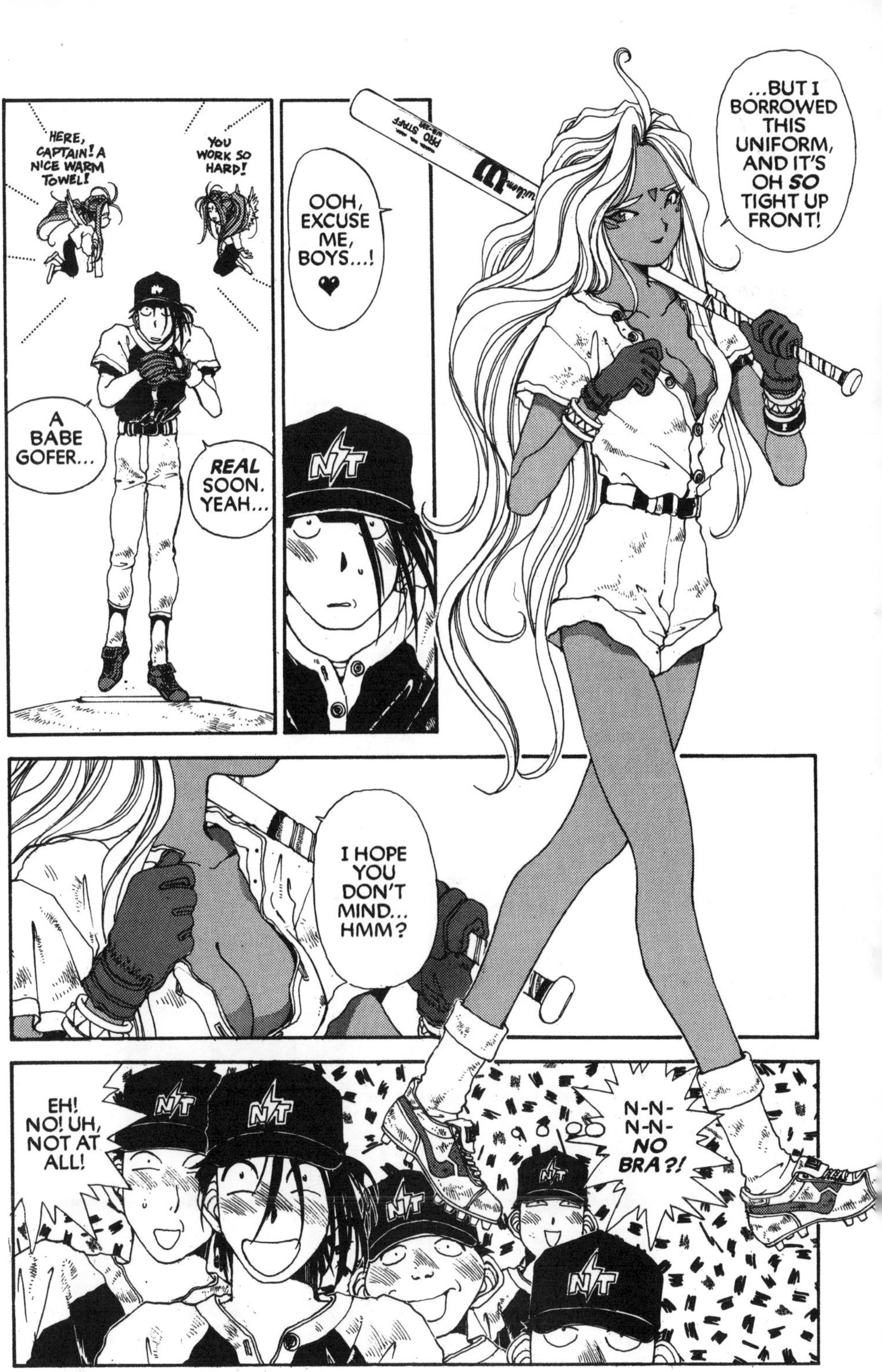
HERE, CAPTAIN! A NICE WARM TOWEL!
YOU WORK SO HARD!
A BABE GOFER...
REAL SOON. YEAH...
OOH, EXCUSE ME, BOYS...!
...BUT I BORROWED THIS UNIFORM, AND IT'S OH SO TIGHT UP FRONT!
I HOPE YOU DON'T MIND... HMM?
EH! NO! UH, NOT AT ALL!
N-N-N-N-NO BRA?!

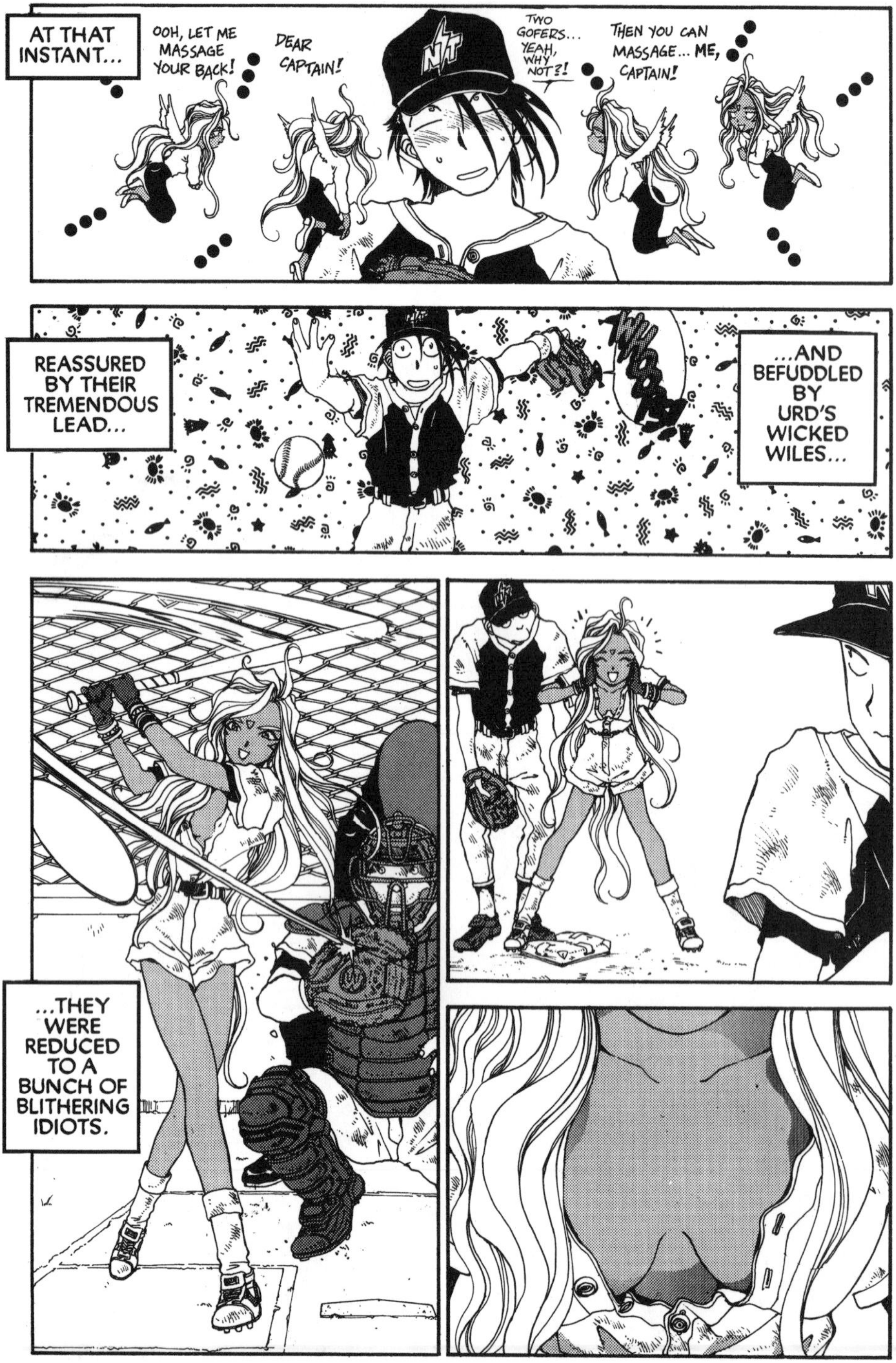
AT THAT INSTANT...
OOH, LET ME MASSAGE YOUR BACK!
DEAR CAPTAIN!
TWO GOFERS... YEAH, WHY NOT?!
THEN YOU CAN MASSAGE... ME, CAPTAIN!
REASSURED BY THEIR TREMENDOUS LEAD...
...AND BEFUDDLED BY URD'S WICKED WILES...
...THEY WERE REDUCED TO A BUNCH OF BLITHERING IDIOTS.

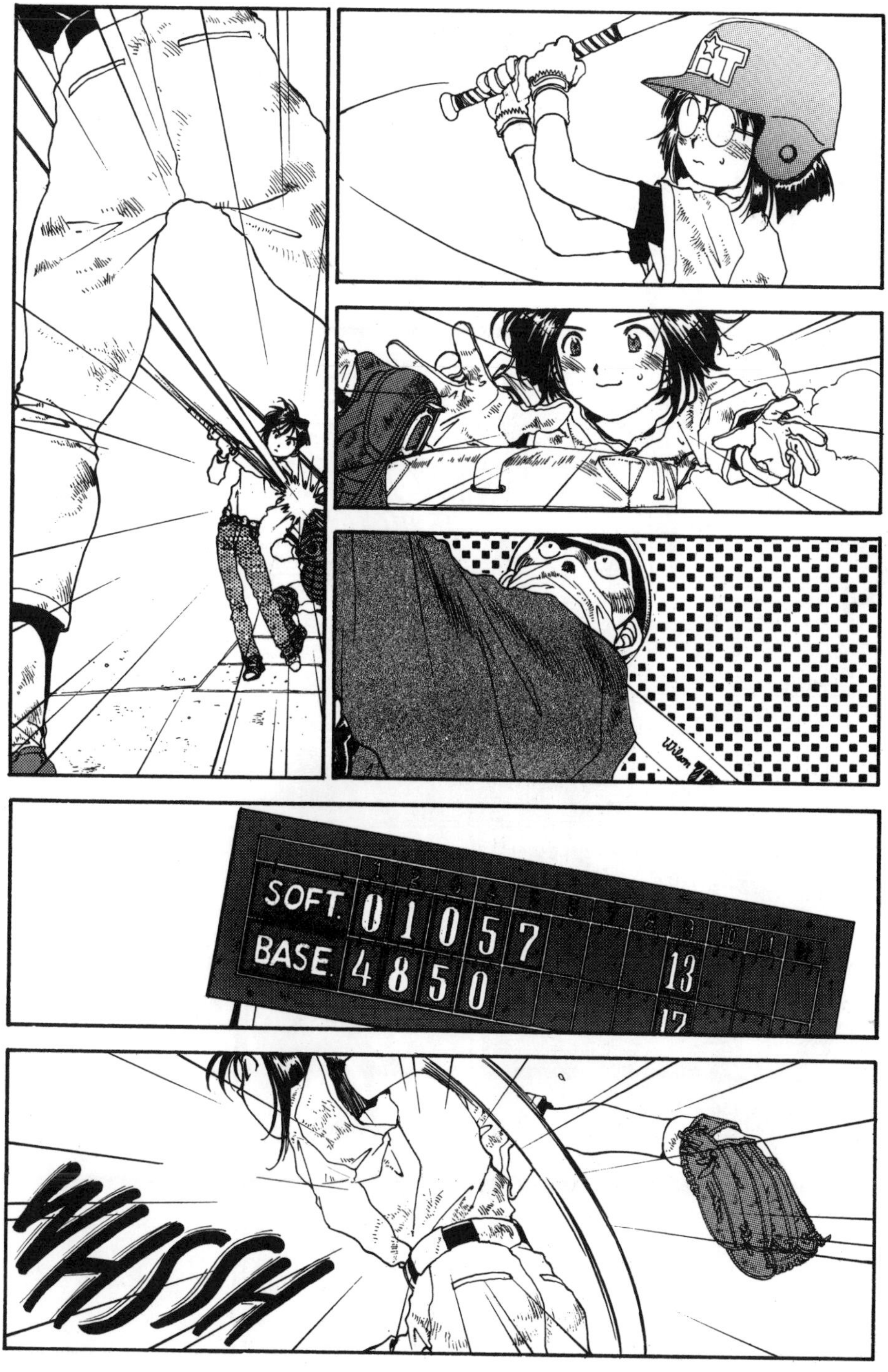
SOFT. 0 1 0 5 7 13
BASE. 4 8 5 0 17
WHSSH

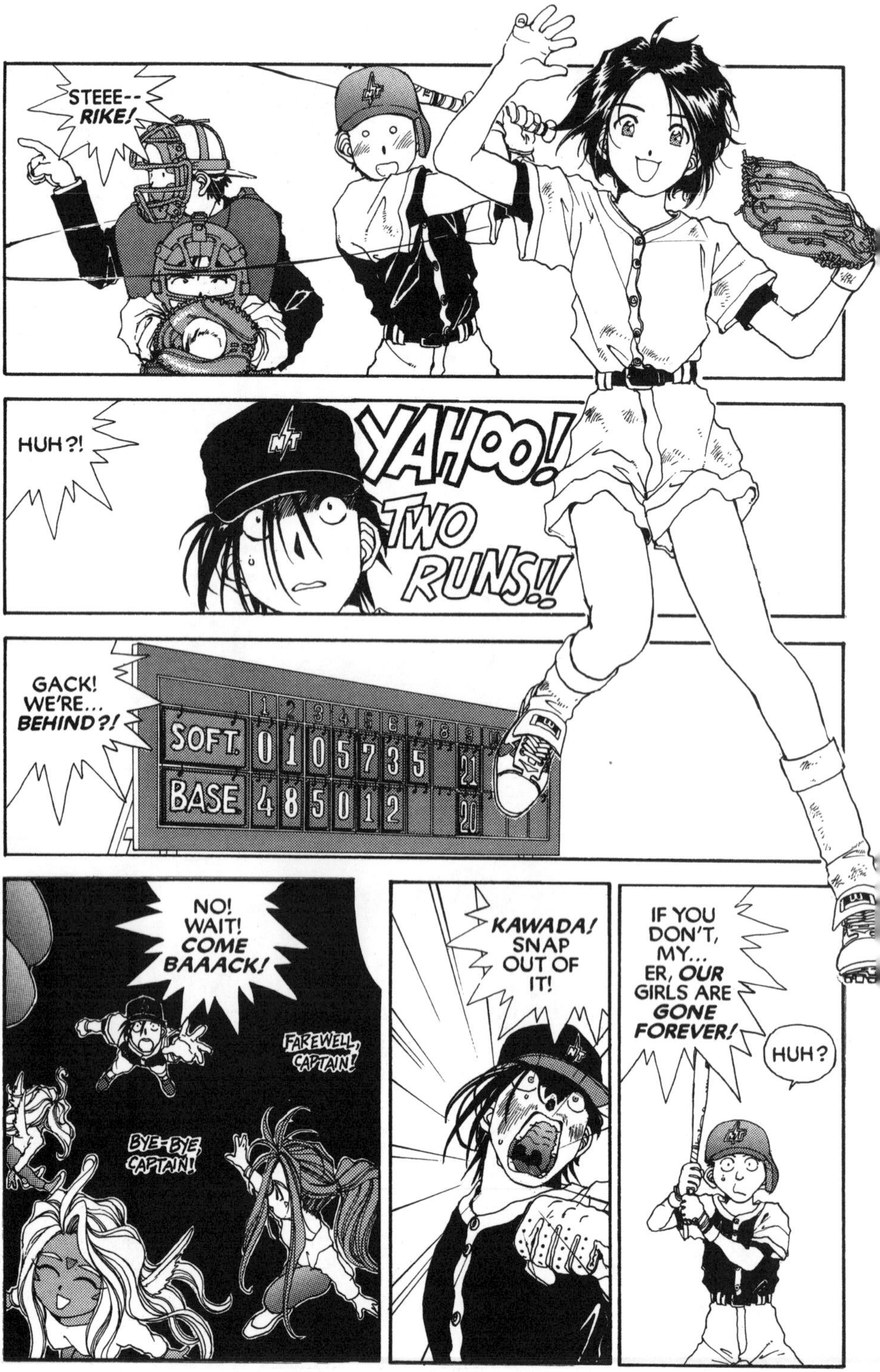
STEEE-- RIKE!
HUH?!
YAHOO!
TWO RUNS!!
GACK! WE'RE... BEHIND?!
SOFT. 0 1 0 5 7 3 5 21
BASE 4 8 5 0 1 2 20
NO! WAIT! COME BAAACK!
FAREWELL, CAPTAIN!
BYE-BYE, CAPTAIN!
KAWADA! SNAP OUT OF IT!
IF YOU DON'T, MY... ER, OUR GIRLS ARE GONE FOREVER!
HUH?

OH *NO!* RIGHT BETWEEN FIRST AND SECOND!

SKULD CAN'T COVER HER!

SORA?!

HEH...

SO MAYBE I'M GOOD FOR SOMETHING, AFTER ALL...?

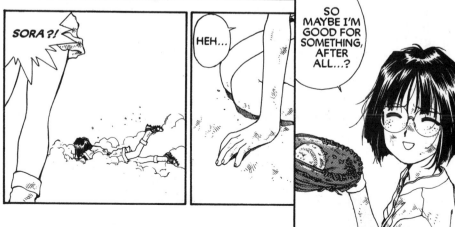

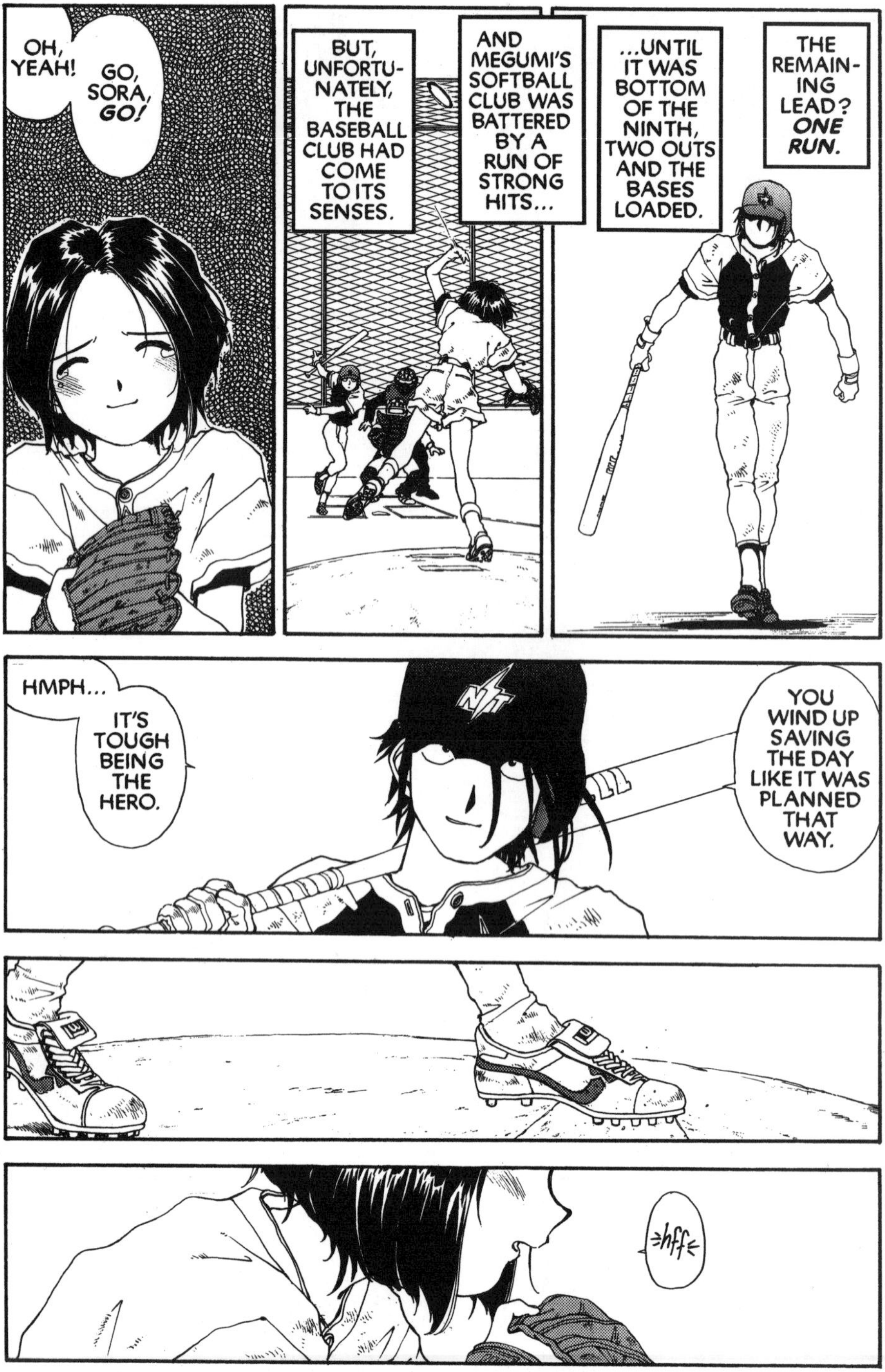
OH, YEAH!
GO, SORA, GO!
BUT, UNFORTUNATELY, THE BASEBALL CLUB HAD COME TO ITS SENSES.
AND MEGUMI'S SOFTBALL CLUB WAS BATTERED BY A RUN OF STRONG HITS...
...UNTIL IT WAS BOTTOM OF THE NINTH, TWO OUTS AND THE BASES LOADED.
THE REMAINING LEAD? ONE RUN.
HMPH...
IT'S TOUGH BEING THE HERO.
YOU WIND UP SAVING THE DAY LIKE IT WAS PLANNED THAT WAY.
hff

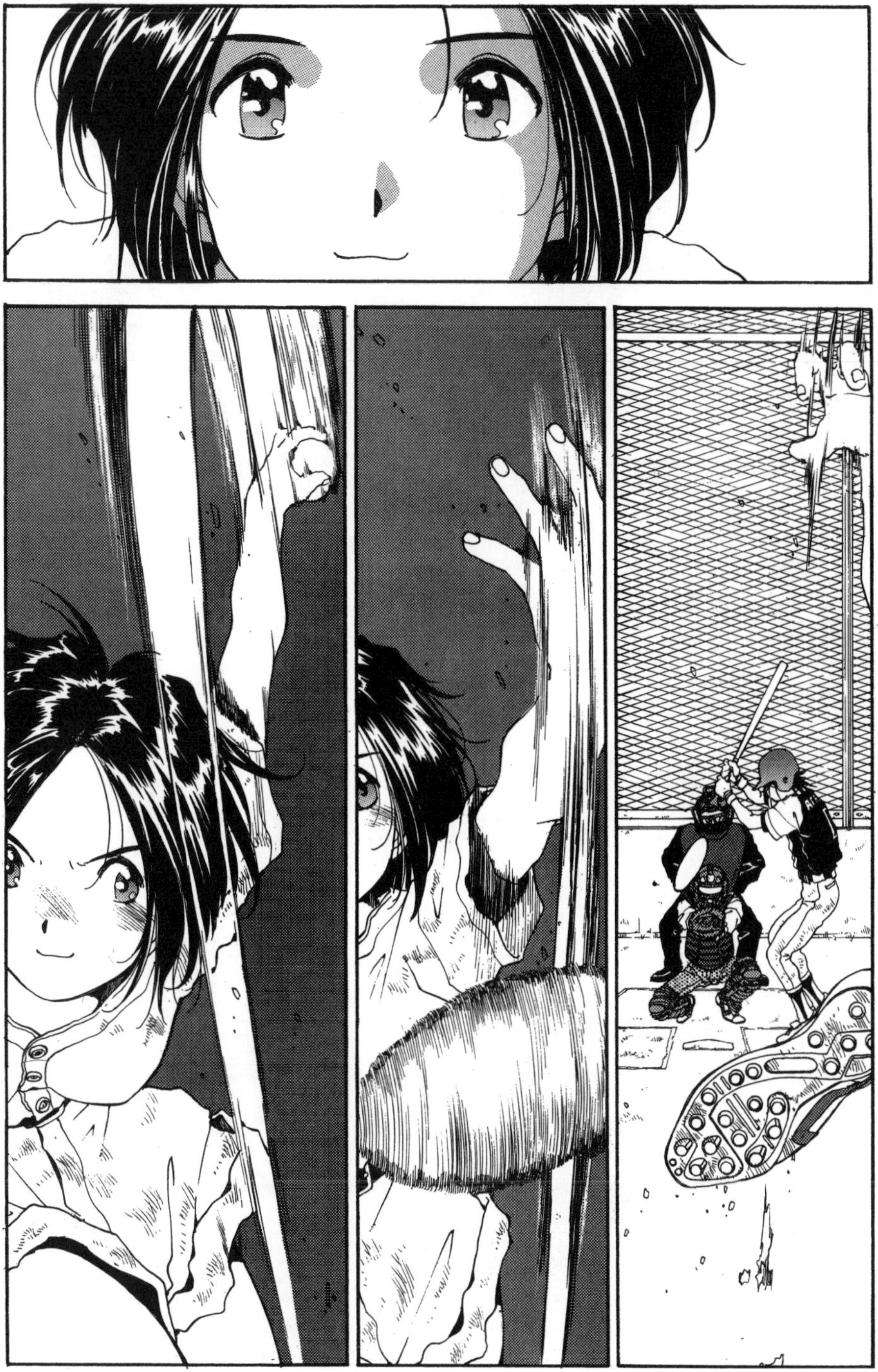

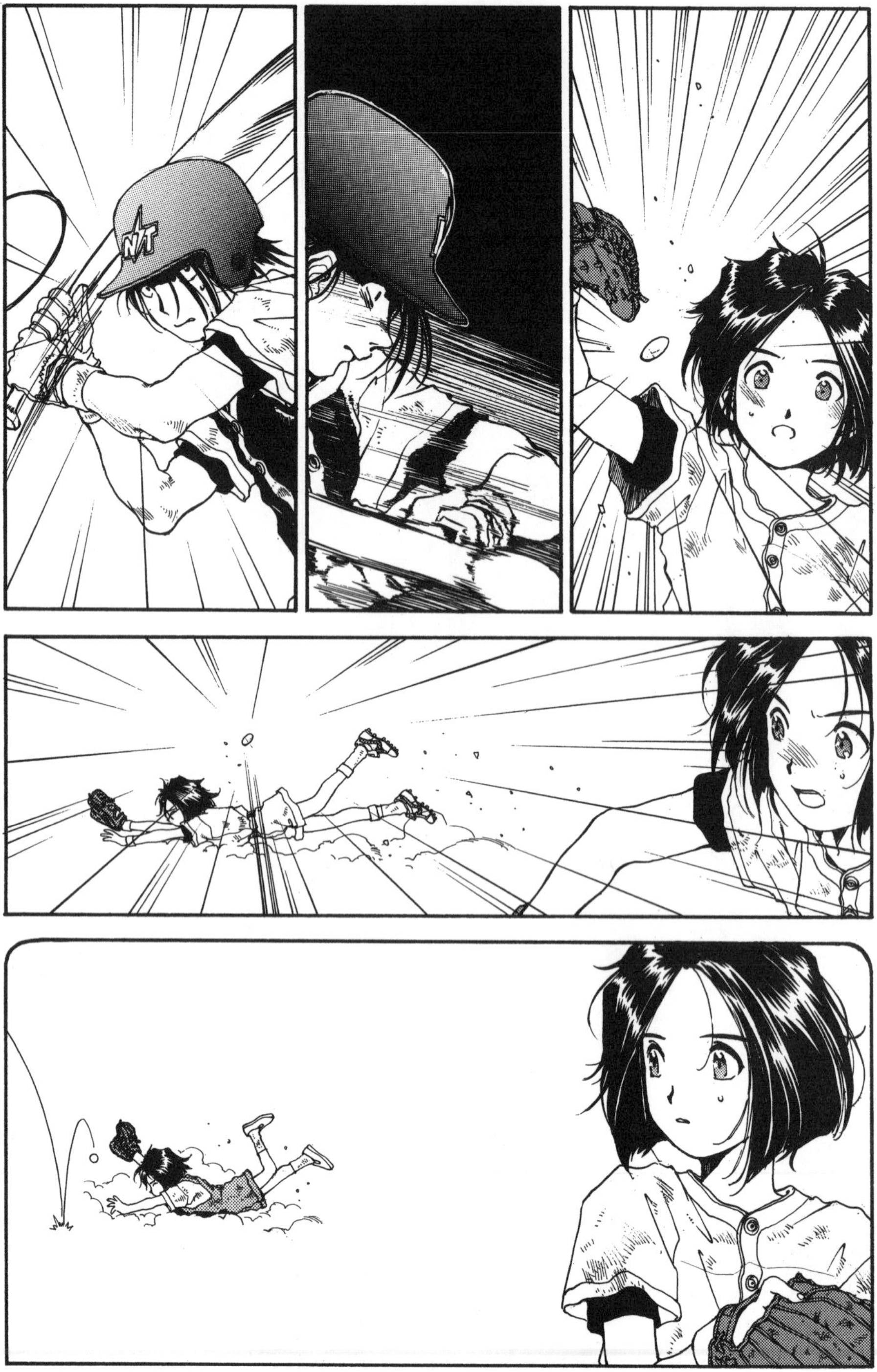

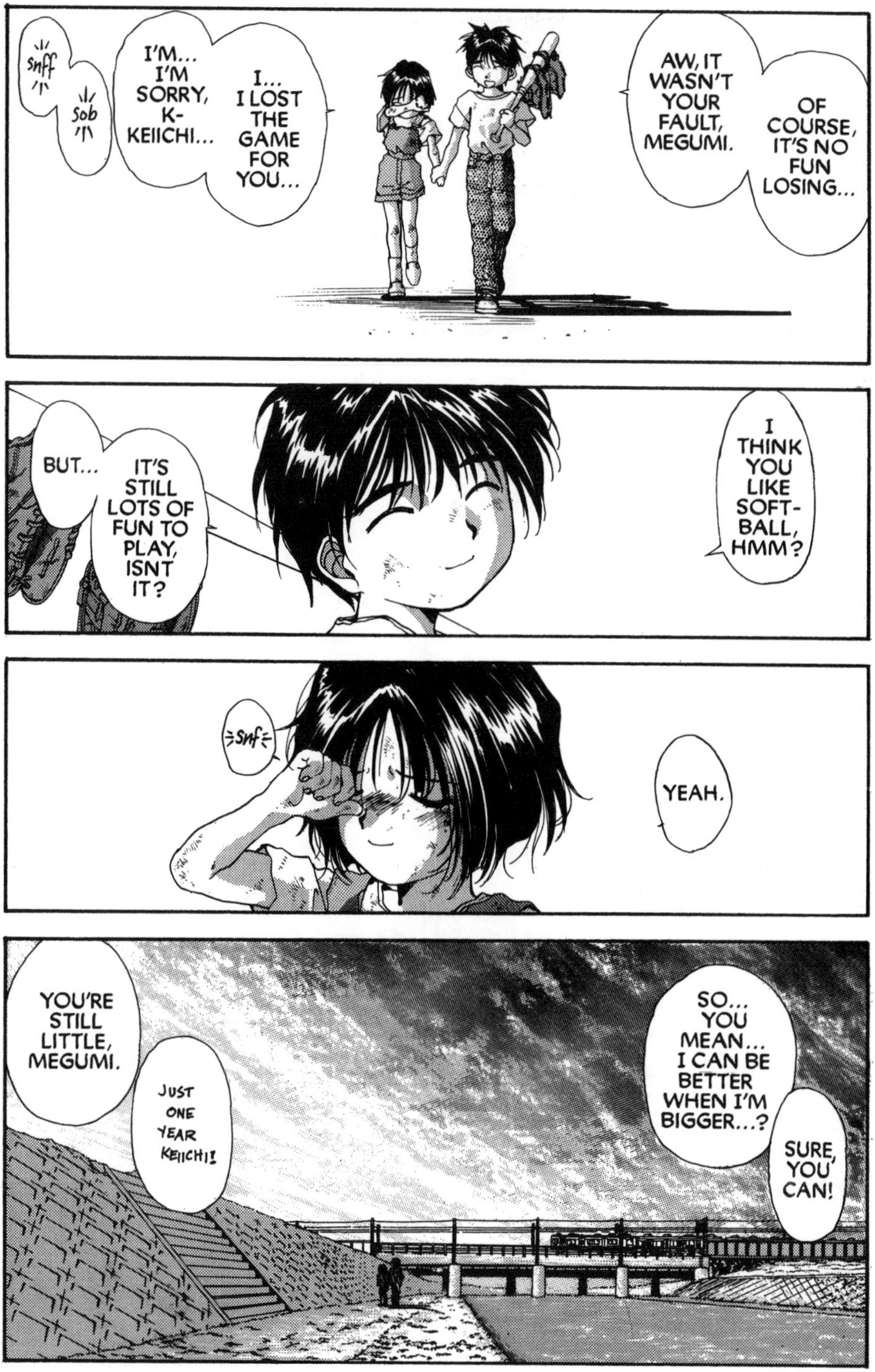
snff
sob
I'M... I'M SORRY, K-KEIICHI...
I... I LOST THE GAME FOR YOU...
AW, IT WASN'T YOUR FAULT, MEGUMI.
OF COURSE, IT'S NO FUN LOSING...
BUT...
IT'S STILL LOTS OF FUN TO PLAY, ISNT IT?
I THINK YOU LIKE SOFT-BALL, HMM?
snf
YEAH.
YOU'RE STILL LITTLE, MEGUMI.
JUST ONE YEAR KEIICHI!
SO... YOU MEAN... I CAN BE BETTER WHEN I'M BIGGER...?
SURE, YOU CAN!

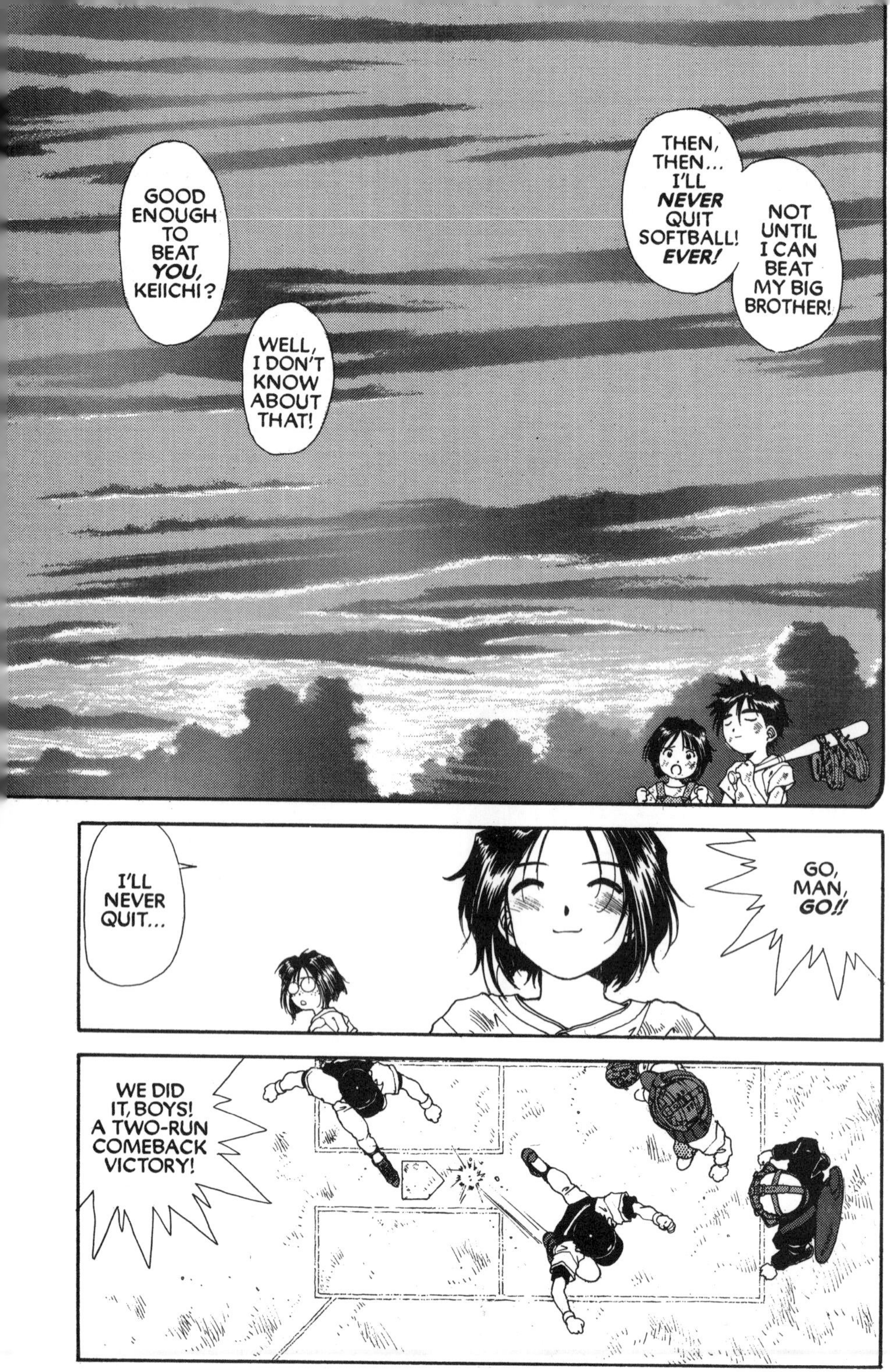
GOOD ENOUGH TO BEAT ***YOU,*** KEIICHI?
WELL, I DON'T KNOW ABOUT THAT!
THEN, THEN... I'LL ***NEVER*** QUIT SOFTBALL! ***EVER!***
NOT UNTIL I CAN BEAT MY BIG BROTHER!
I'LL NEVER QUIT...
GO, MAN, ***GO!!***
WE DID IT, BOYS! A TWO-RUN COMEBACK VICTORY!

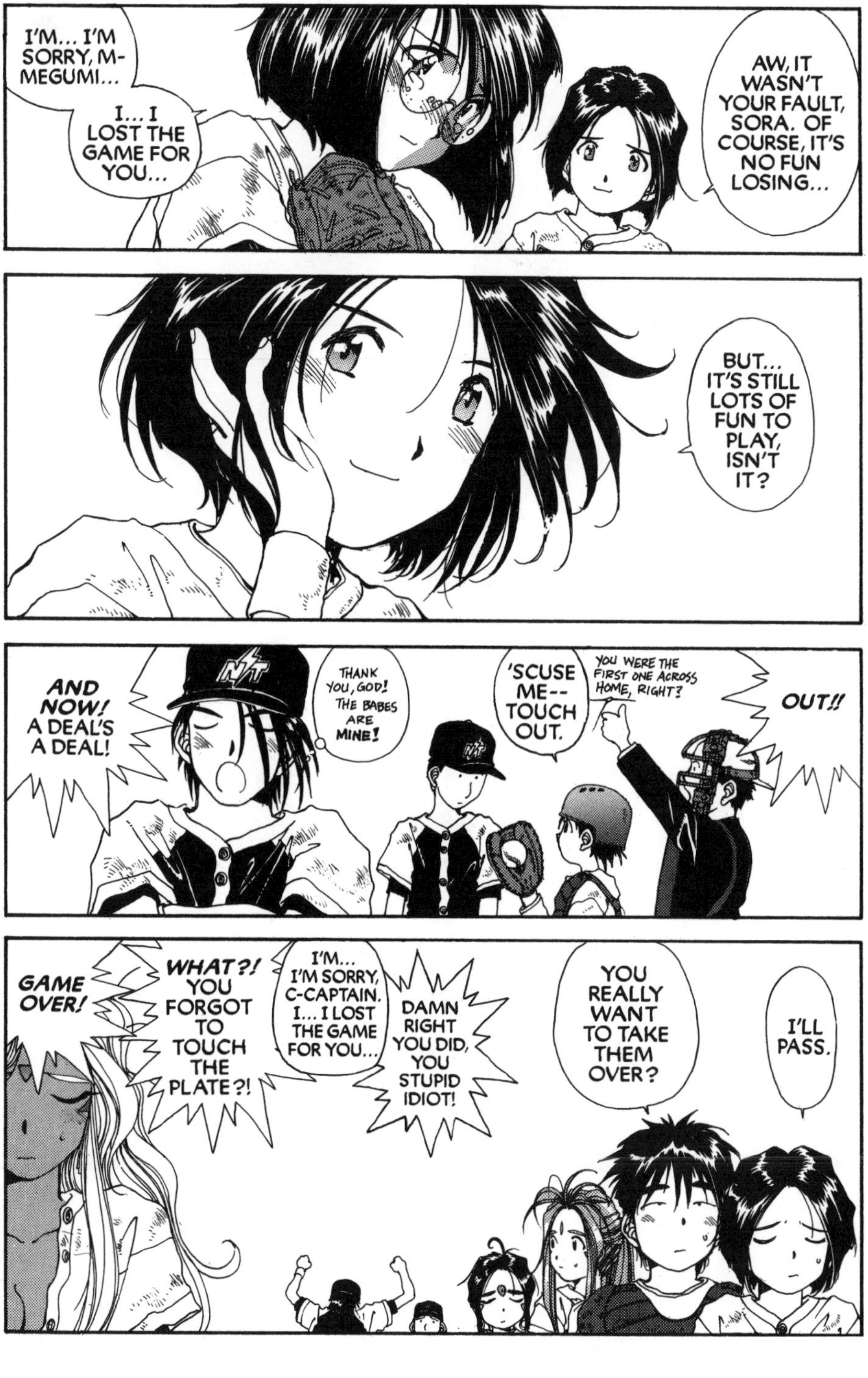
I'M... I'M SORRY, M-MEGUMI...
I... I LOST THE GAME FOR YOU...
AW, IT WASN'T YOUR FAULT, SORA. OF COURSE, IT'S NO FUN LOSING...
BUT... IT'S STILL LOTS OF FUN TO PLAY, ISN'T IT?
AND NOW! A DEAL'S A DEAL!
THANK YOU, GOD! THE BABES ARE MINE!
'SCUSE ME-- TOUCH OUT.
YOU WERE THE FIRST ONE ACROSS HOME, RIGHT?
OUT!!
GAME OVER!
WHAT?! YOU FORGOT TO TOUCH THE PLATE?!
I'M... I'M SORRY, C-CAPTAIN. I... I LOST THE GAME FOR YOU...
DAMN RIGHT YOU DID, YOU STUPID IDIOT!
YOU REALLY WANT TO TAKE THEM OVER?
I'LL PASS.

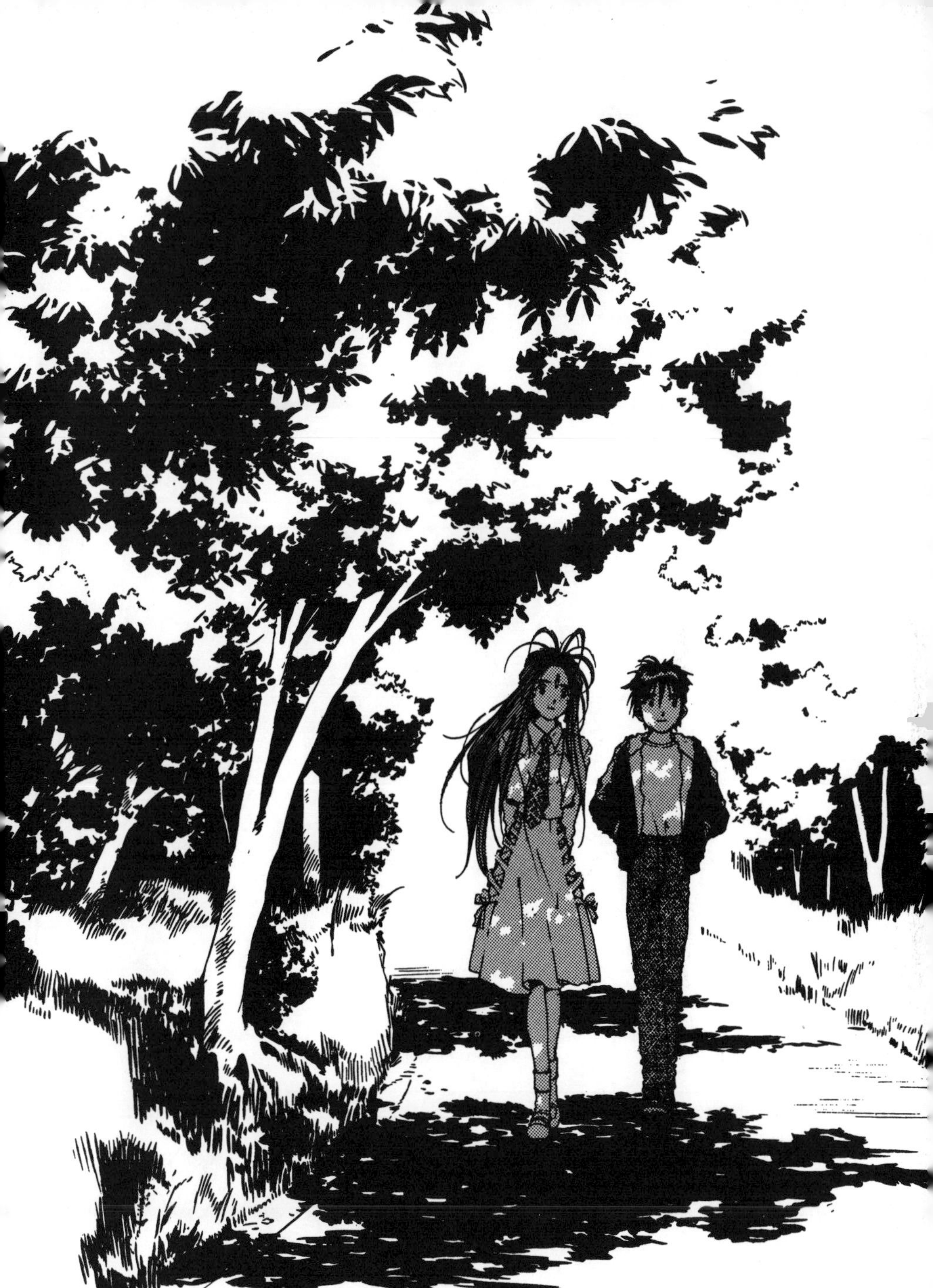

Sorrow, Fear Not

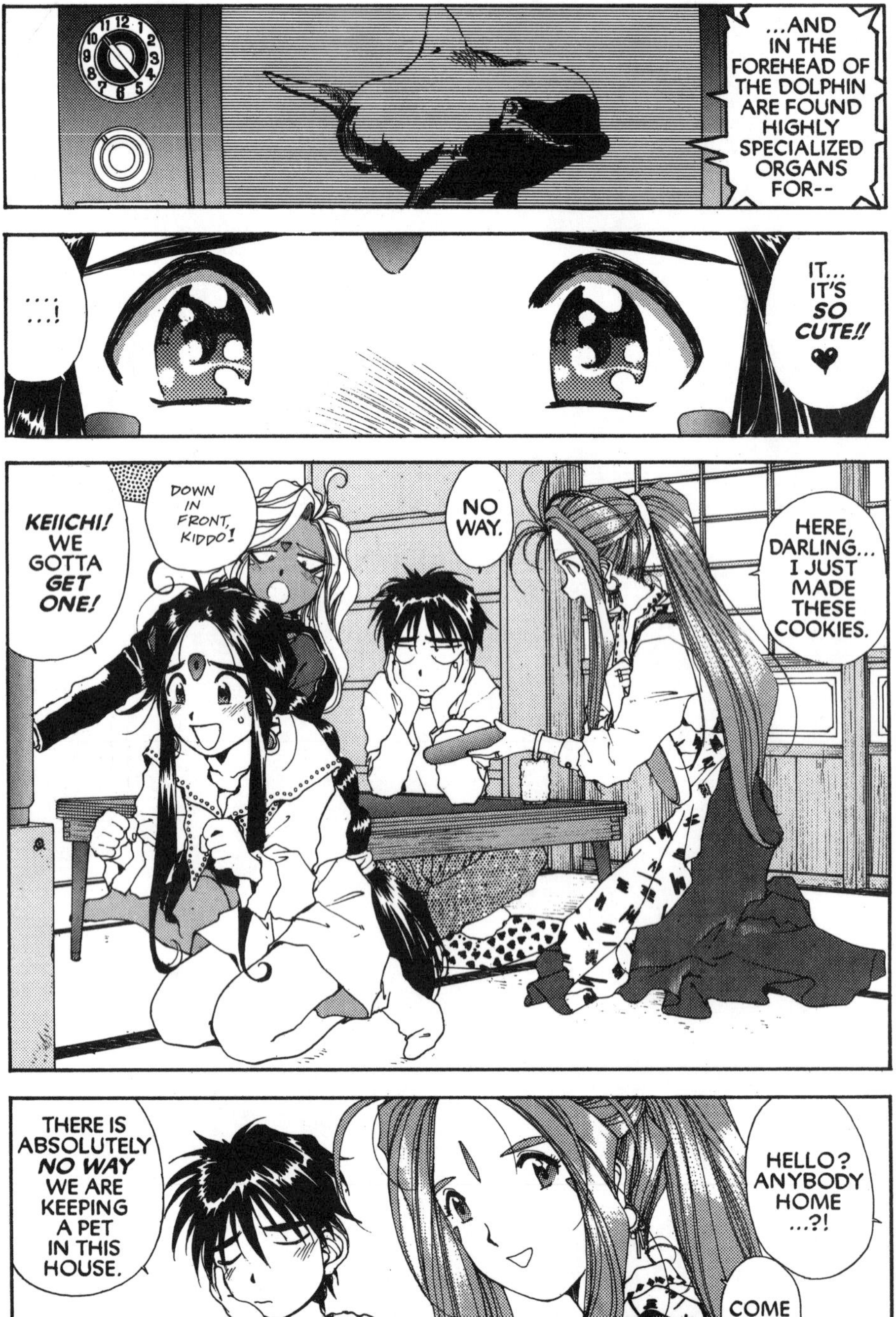
...AND IN THE FOREHEAD OF THE DOLPHIN ARE FOUND HIGHLY SPECIALIZED ORGANS FOR--
...;
...!
IT... IT'S SO CUTE!! ♥
KEIICHI! WE GOTTA GET ONE!
DOWN IN FRONT, KIDDO!
NO WAY.
HERE, DARLING... I JUST MADE THESE COOKIES.
THERE IS ABSOLUTELY NO WAY WE ARE KEEPING A PET IN THIS HOUSE.
HELLO? ANYBODY HOME ...?!
COME IN!

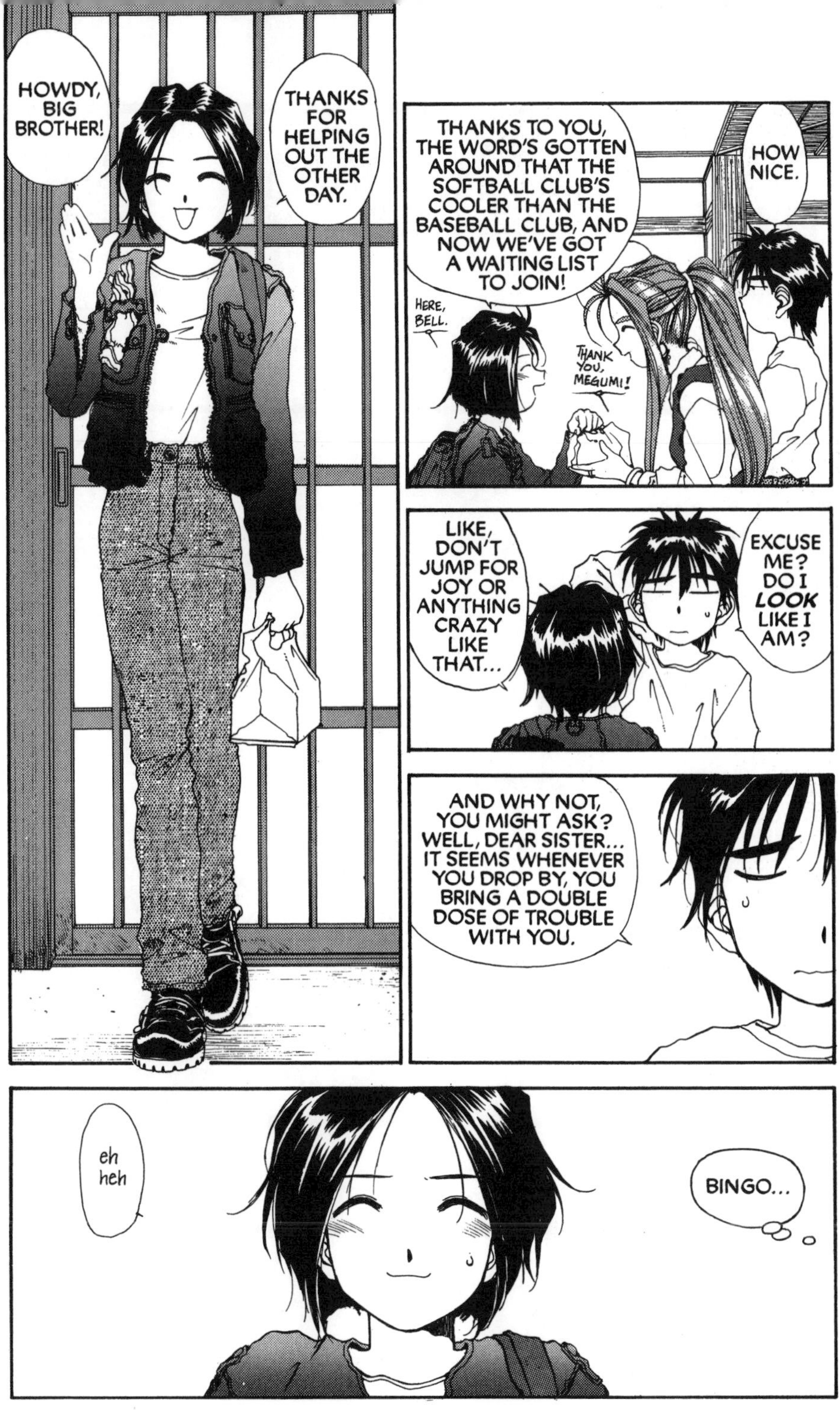
HOWDY, BIG BROTHER!
THANKS FOR HELPING OUT THE OTHER DAY.
THANKS TO YOU, THE WORD'S GOTTEN AROUND THAT THE SOFTBALL CLUB'S COOLER THAN THE BASEBALL CLUB, AND NOW WE'VE GOT A WAITING LIST TO JOIN!
HOW NICE.
HERE, BELL.
THANK YOU, MEGUMI!
LIKE, DON'T JUMP FOR JOY OR ANYTHING CRAZY LIKE THAT...
EXCUSE ME? DO I LOOK LIKE I AM?
AND WHY NOT, YOU MIGHT ASK? WELL, DEAR SISTER... IT SEEMS WHENEVER YOU DROP BY, YOU BRING A DOUBLE DOSE OF TROUBLE WITH YOU.
eh heh
BINGO...

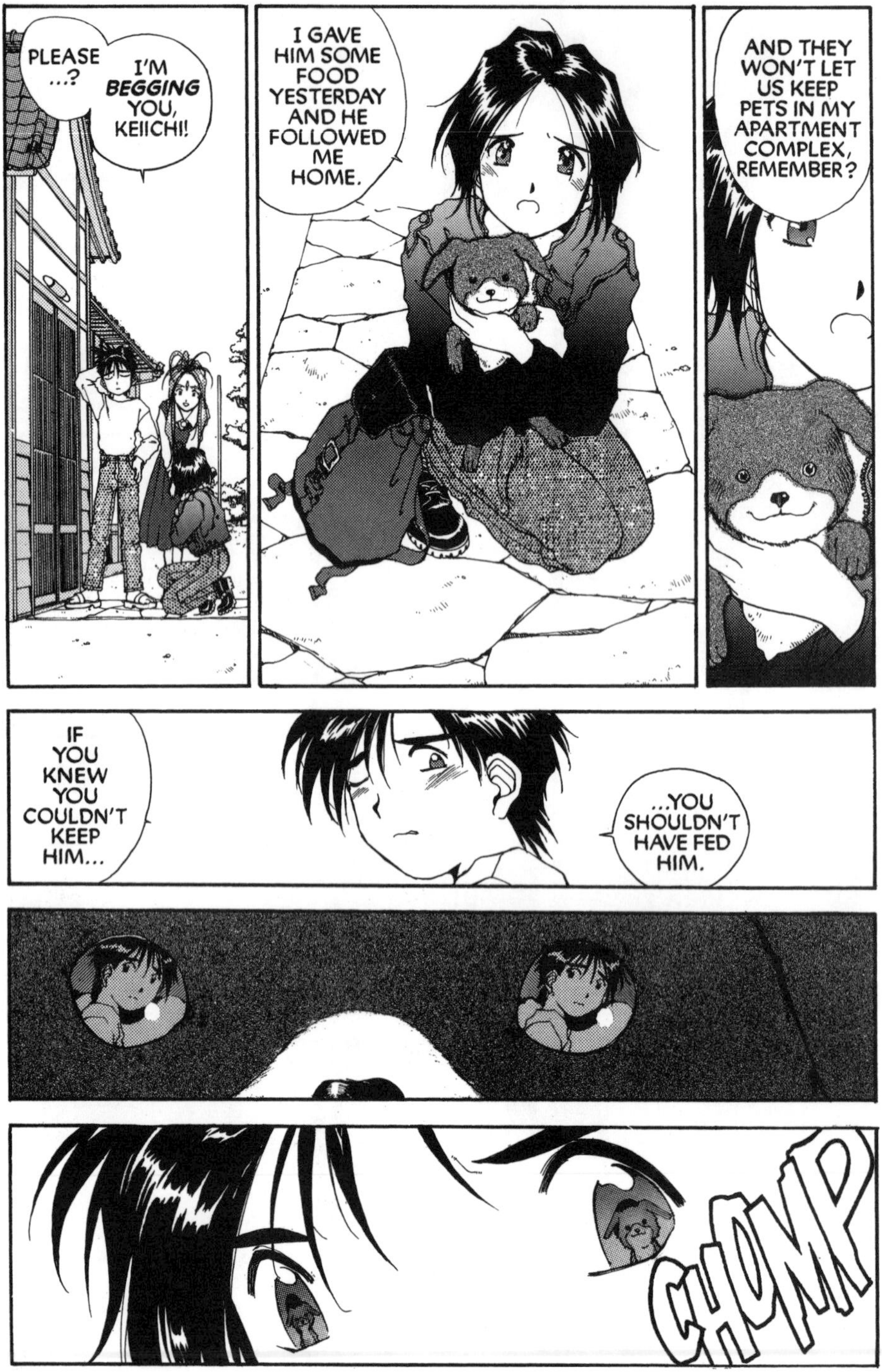
PLEASE ...?
I'M *BEGGING* YOU, KEIICHI!
I GAVE HIM SOME FOOD YESTERDAY AND HE FOLLOWED ME HOME.
AND THEY WON'T LET US KEEP PETS IN MY APARTMENT COMPLEX, REMEMBER?
IF YOU KNEW YOU COULDN'T KEEP HIM...
...YOU SHOULDN'T HAVE FED HIM.
CHOMP

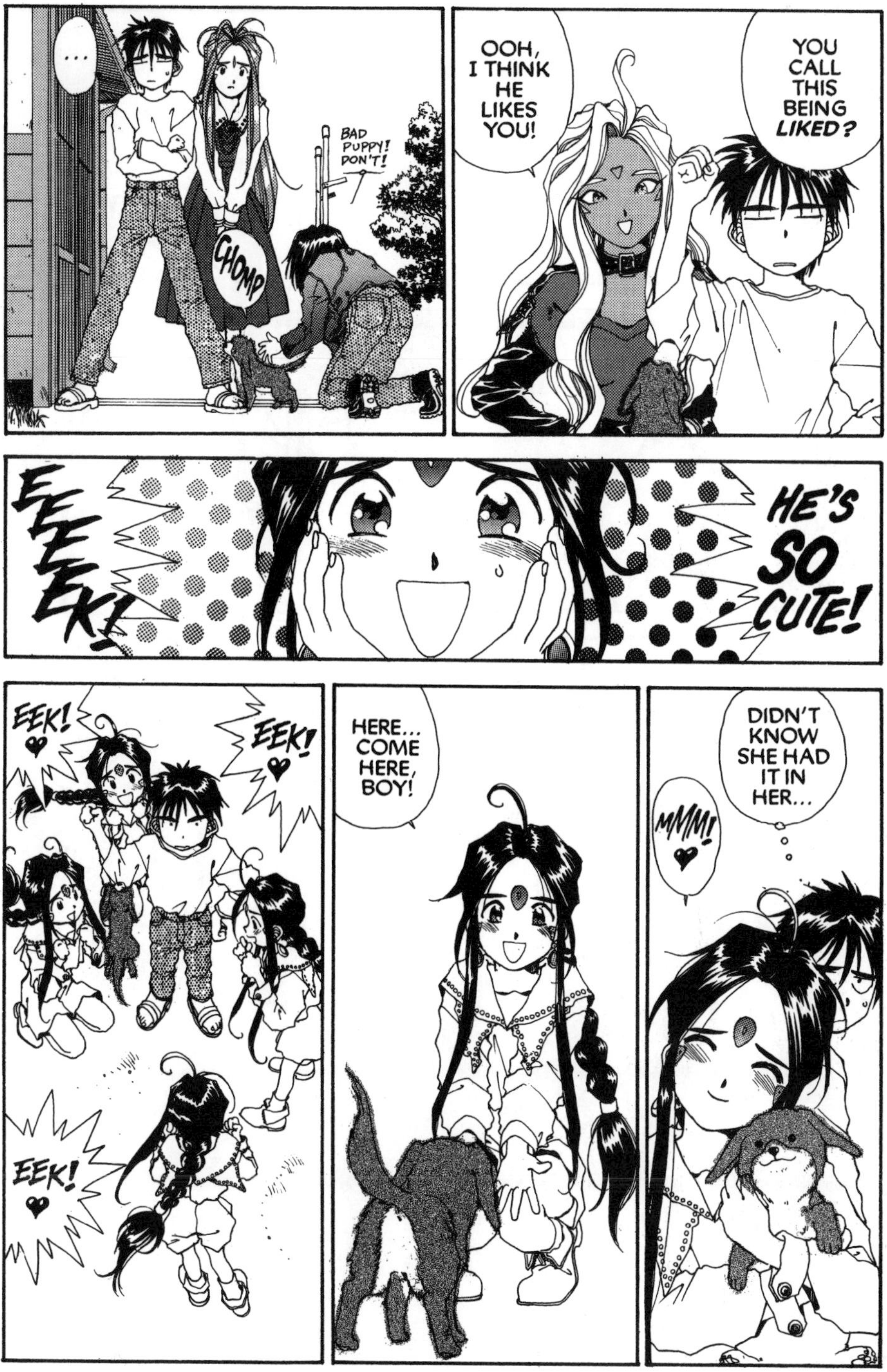
...
BAD PUPPY! DON'T!
CHOMP
OOH, I THINK HE LIKES YOU!
YOU CALL THIS BEING *LIKED*?
EEEEEK!
HE'S SO CUTE!
EEK!
EEK!
EEK!
HERE... COME HERE, BOY!
MMM!
DIDN'T KNOW SHE HAD IT IN HER...

KEIICHI! KEIICHI! HE'S GONNA STAY WITH US FOREVER AN' EVER, RIGHT?!

WRONG. NO KEEP.

OOOH!

WHAT?! NO WAY!! WHY NOT?!

I WAN' HIM, I WAN' HIM!

GEEZ... JUST LIKE A KID...

I HATE YOU I *HATE* YOU!

YOU BIG STUPID DUMMY!!

GOT THE SHIRT, TOO... SHE'S *DEFINITELY* GETTING MORE POWERFUL.

HATE YOU DUMMY

STUPID HATE YOU

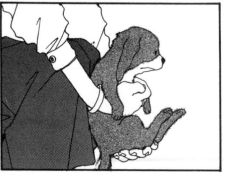

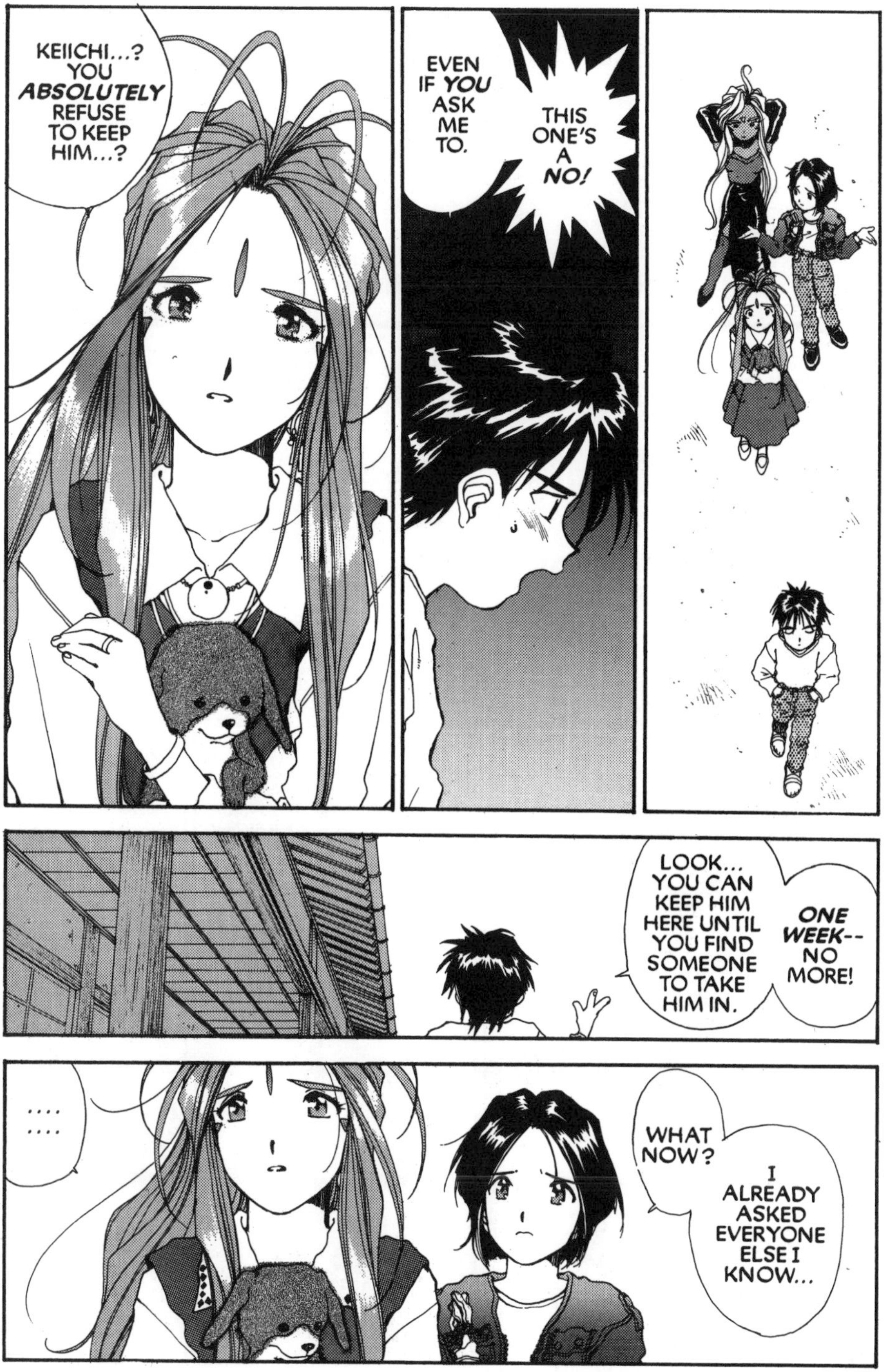
KEIICHI...? YOU ABSOLUTELY REFUSE TO KEEP HIM...?
EVEN IF YOU ASK ME TO.
THIS ONE'S A NO!
LOOK... YOU CAN KEEP HIM HERE UNTIL YOU FIND SOMEONE TO TAKE HIM IN.
ONE WEEK-- NO MORE!
....
WHAT NOW?
I ALREADY ASKED EVERYONE ELSE I KNOW...

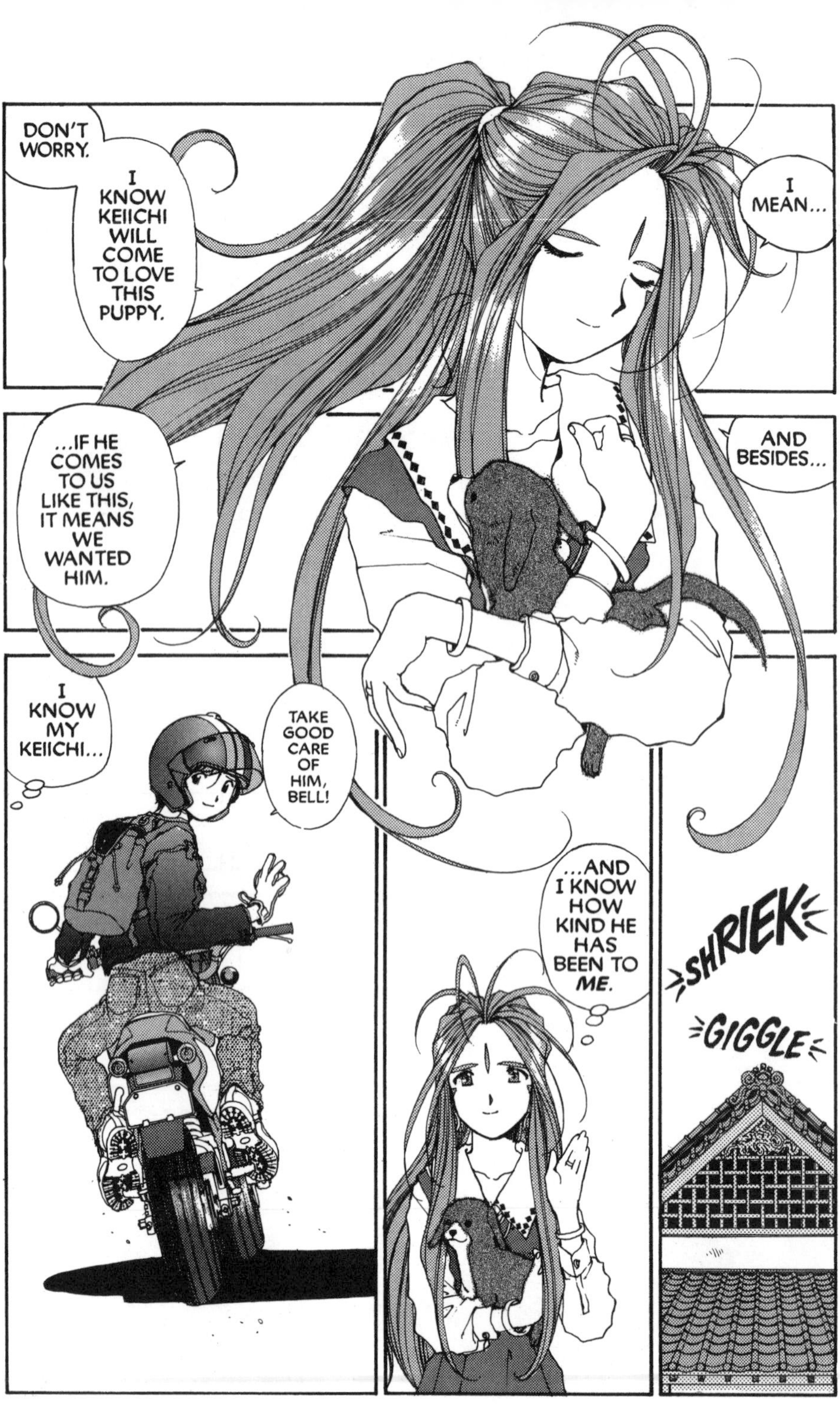
DON'T WORRY.
I KNOW KEIICHI WILL COME TO LOVE THIS PUPPY.
I MEAN...
...IF HE COMES TO US LIKE THIS, IT MEANS WE WANTED HIM.
AND BESIDES...
I KNOW MY KEIICHI...
TAKE GOOD CARE OF HIM, BELL!
...AND I KNOW HOW KIND HE HAS BEEN TO *ME.*
SHRIEK
GIGGLE

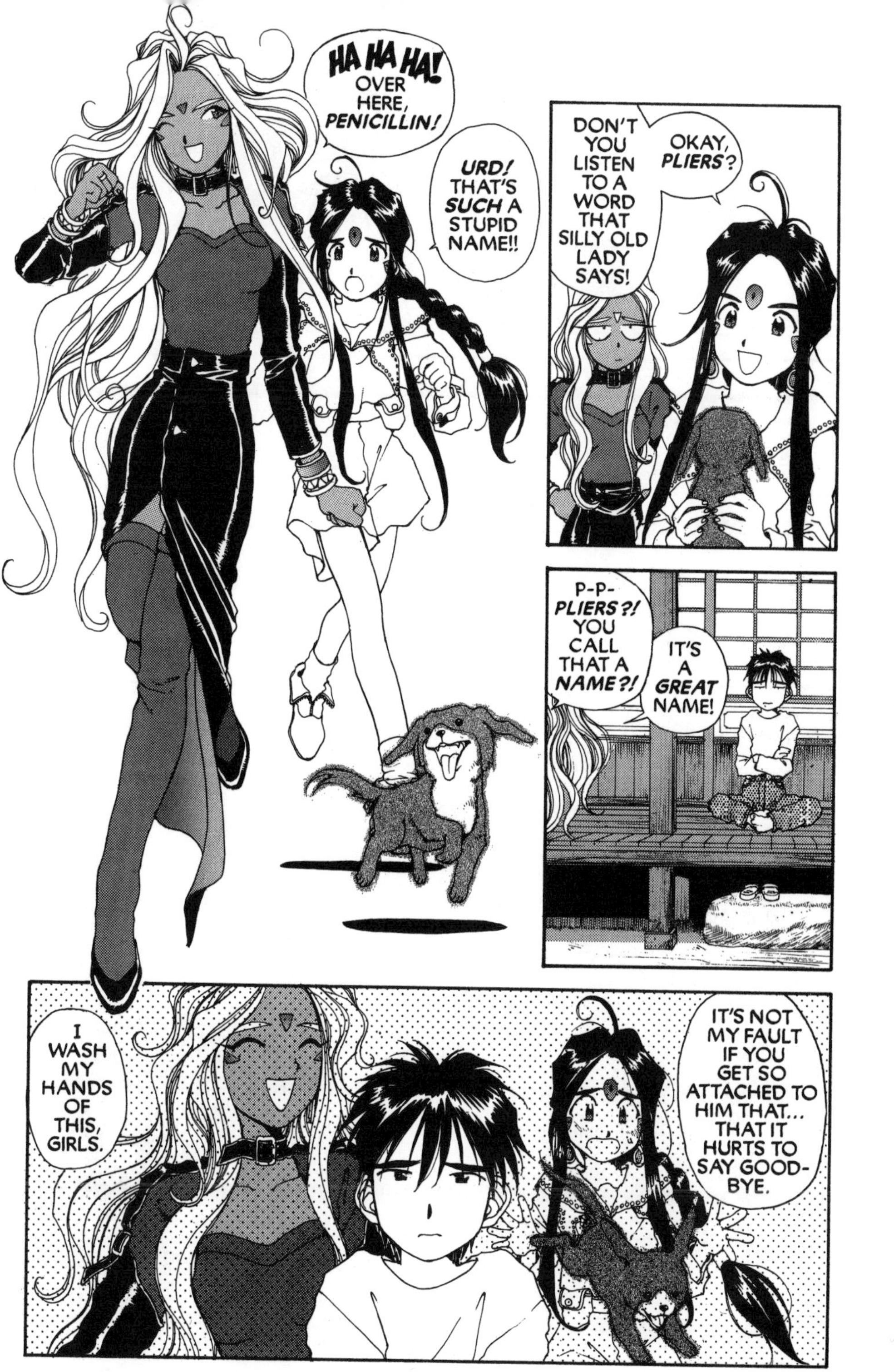
HA HA HA! OVER HERE, PENICILLIN!
URD! THAT'S SUCH A STUPID NAME!!
DON'T YOU LISTEN TO A WORD THAT SILLY OLD LADY SAYS!
OKAY, PLIERS?
P-P-PLIERS?! YOU CALL THAT A NAME?!
IT'S A GREAT NAME!
I WASH MY HANDS OF THIS, GIRLS.
IT'S NOT MY FAULT IF YOU GET SO ATTACHED TO HIM THAT... THAT IT HURTS TO SAY GOOD-BYE.

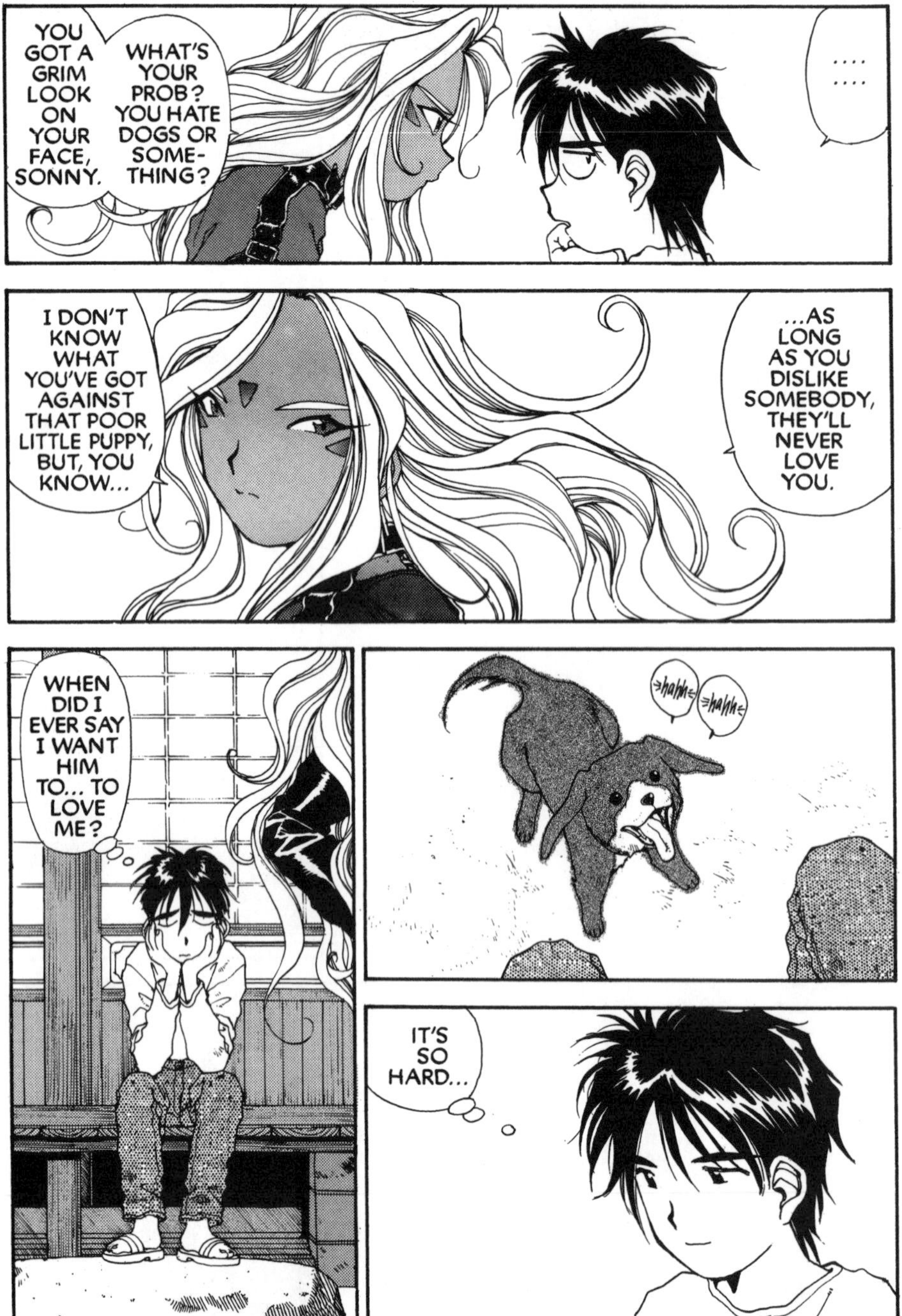
YOU GOT A GRIM LOOK ON YOUR FACE, SONNY.
WHAT'S YOUR PROB? YOU HATE DOGS OR SOME-THING?
....
....
I DON'T KNOW WHAT YOU'VE GOT AGAINST THAT POOR LITTLE PUPPY, BUT, YOU KNOW...
...AS LONG AS YOU DISLIKE SOMEBODY, THEY'LL NEVER LOVE YOU.
WHEN DID I EVER SAY I WANT HIM TO... TO LOVE ME?
hahh
hahh
IT'S SO HARD...

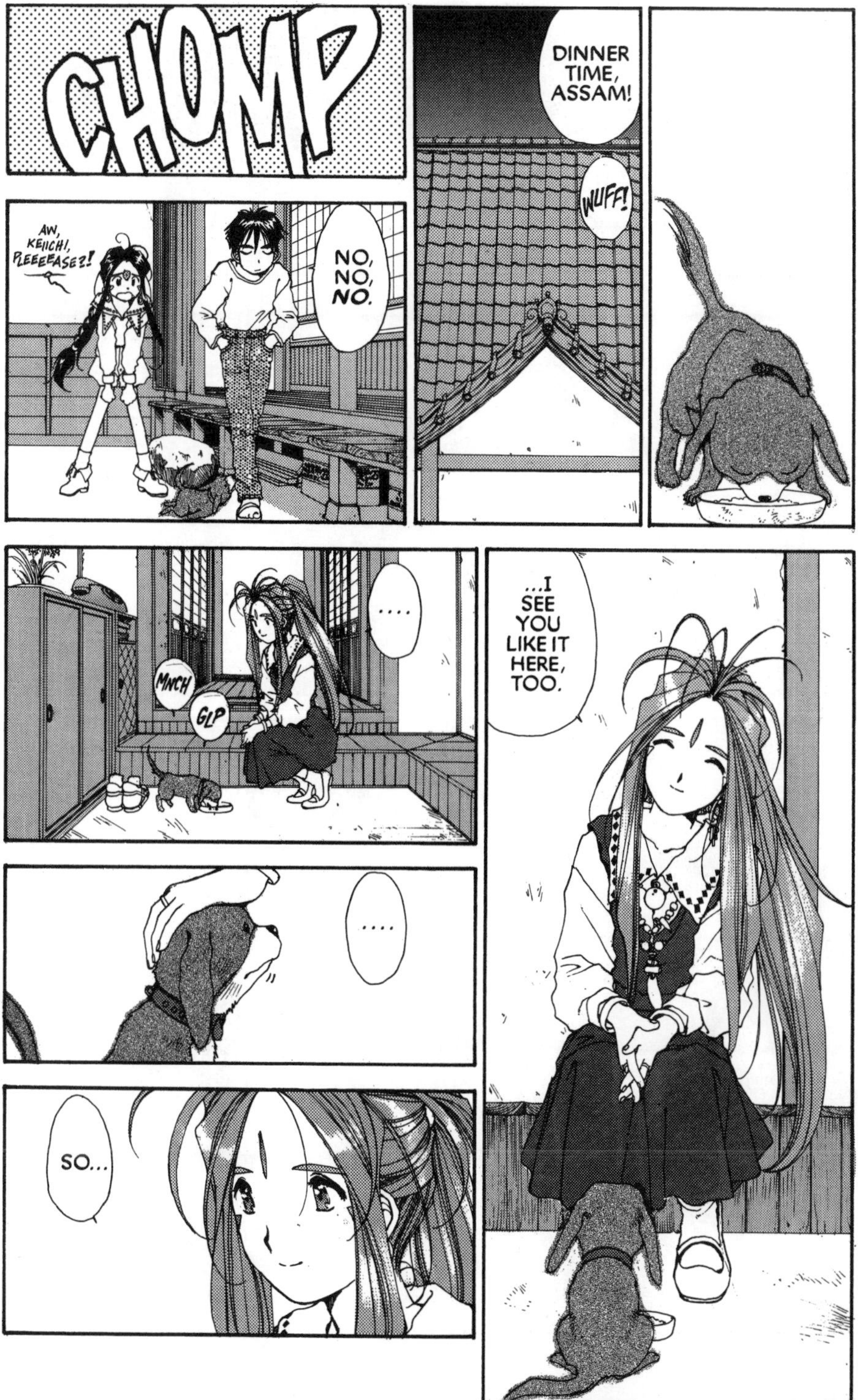
CHOMP
DINNER TIME, ASSAM!
WUFF!
AW, KEIICHI, PLEEEEASE?!
NO, NO, NO.
....
MNCH
GLP
...I SEE YOU LIKE IT HERE, TOO.
....
SO...

I KNEW YOU WOULD.

AND I'M SURE...

...KEIICHI DID, TOO.

...

NO. I ABSOLUTELY WILL *NOT* KEEP THAT DOG.

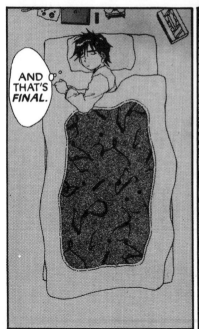

AND THAT'S *FINAL.*

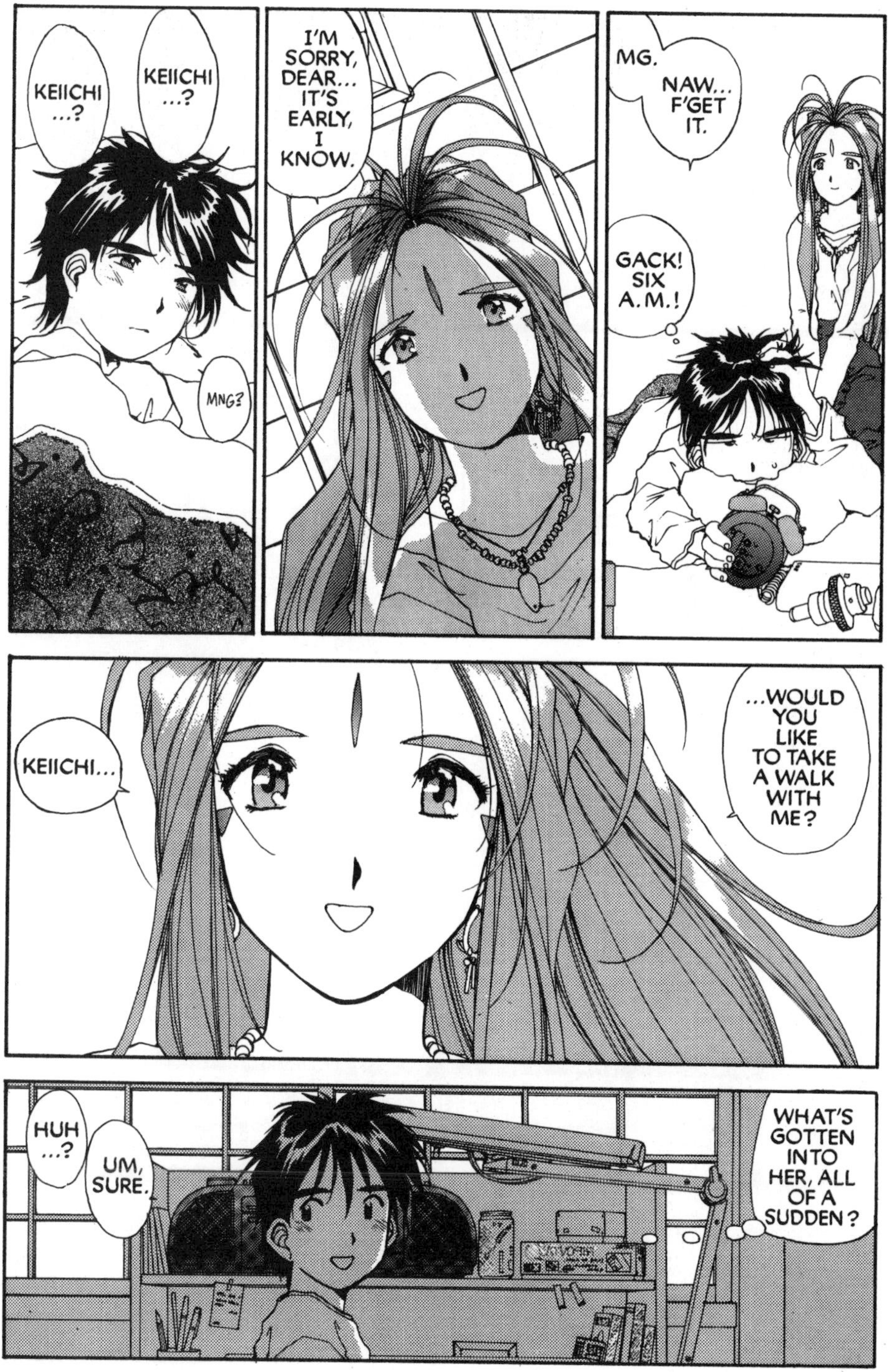
KEIICHI ...?
KEIICHI ...?
MNG?
I'M SORRY, DEAR... IT'S EARLY, I KNOW.
MG.
NAW... F'GET IT.
GACK! SIX A.M.!
KEIICHI...
...WOULD YOU LIKE TO TAKE A WALK WITH ME?
HUH ...?
UM, SURE.
WHAT'S GOTTEN INTO HER, ALL OF A SUDDEN?

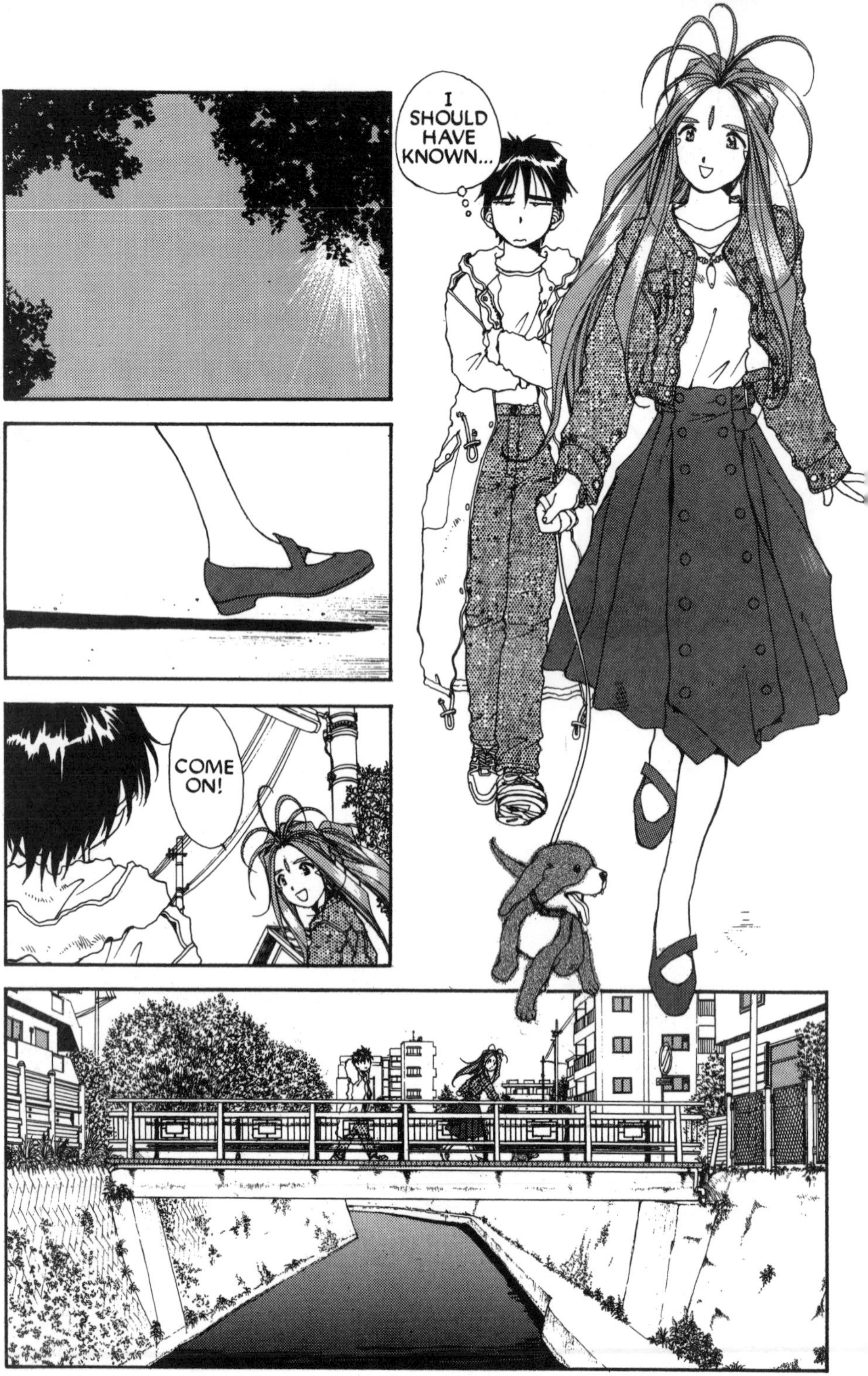
COME ON!
I SHOULD HAVE KNOWN...

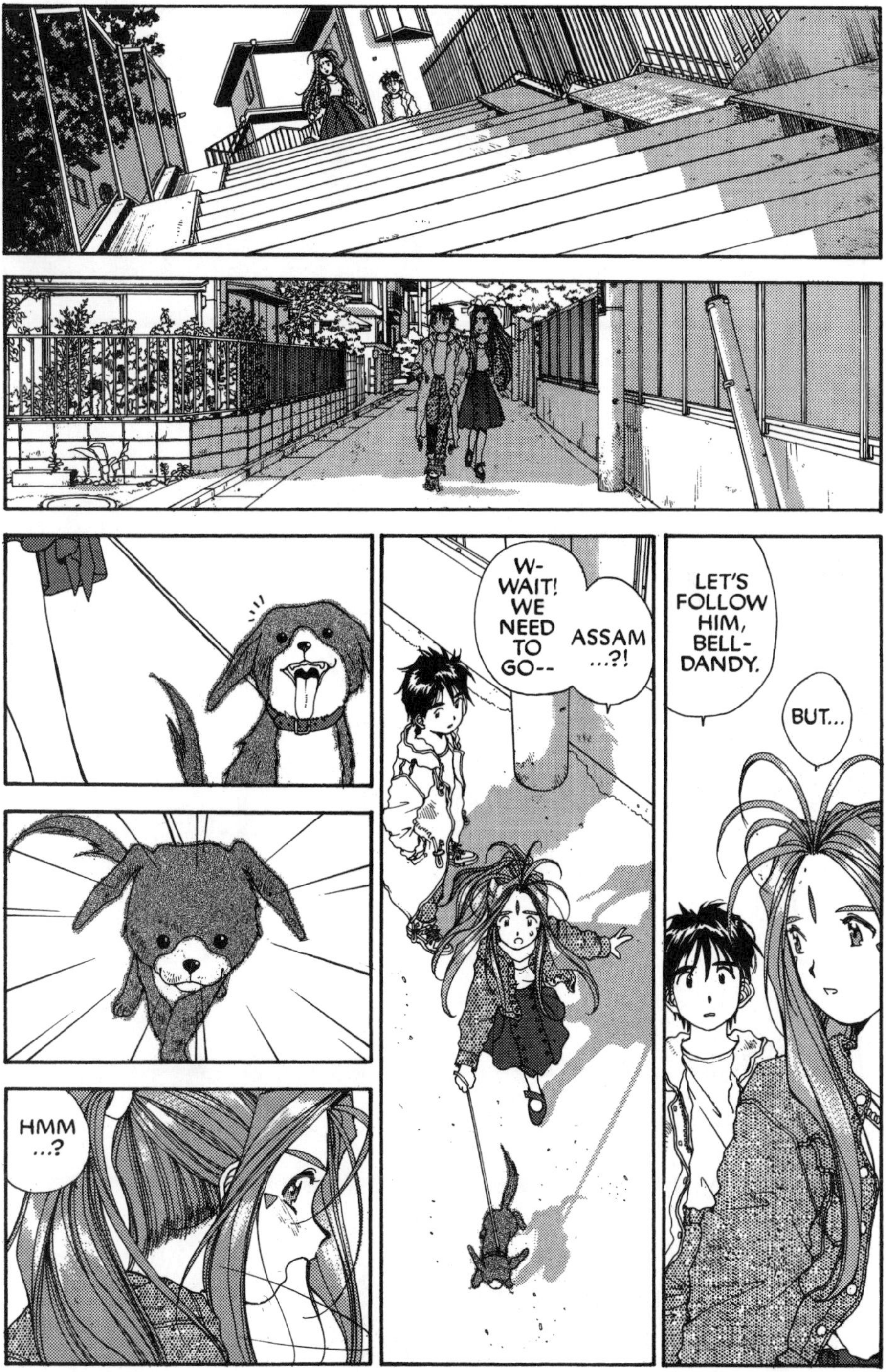
HMM ...?
W- WAIT! WE NEED TO GO--
ASSAM ...?!
LET'S FOLLOW HIM, BELL-DANDY.
BUT...

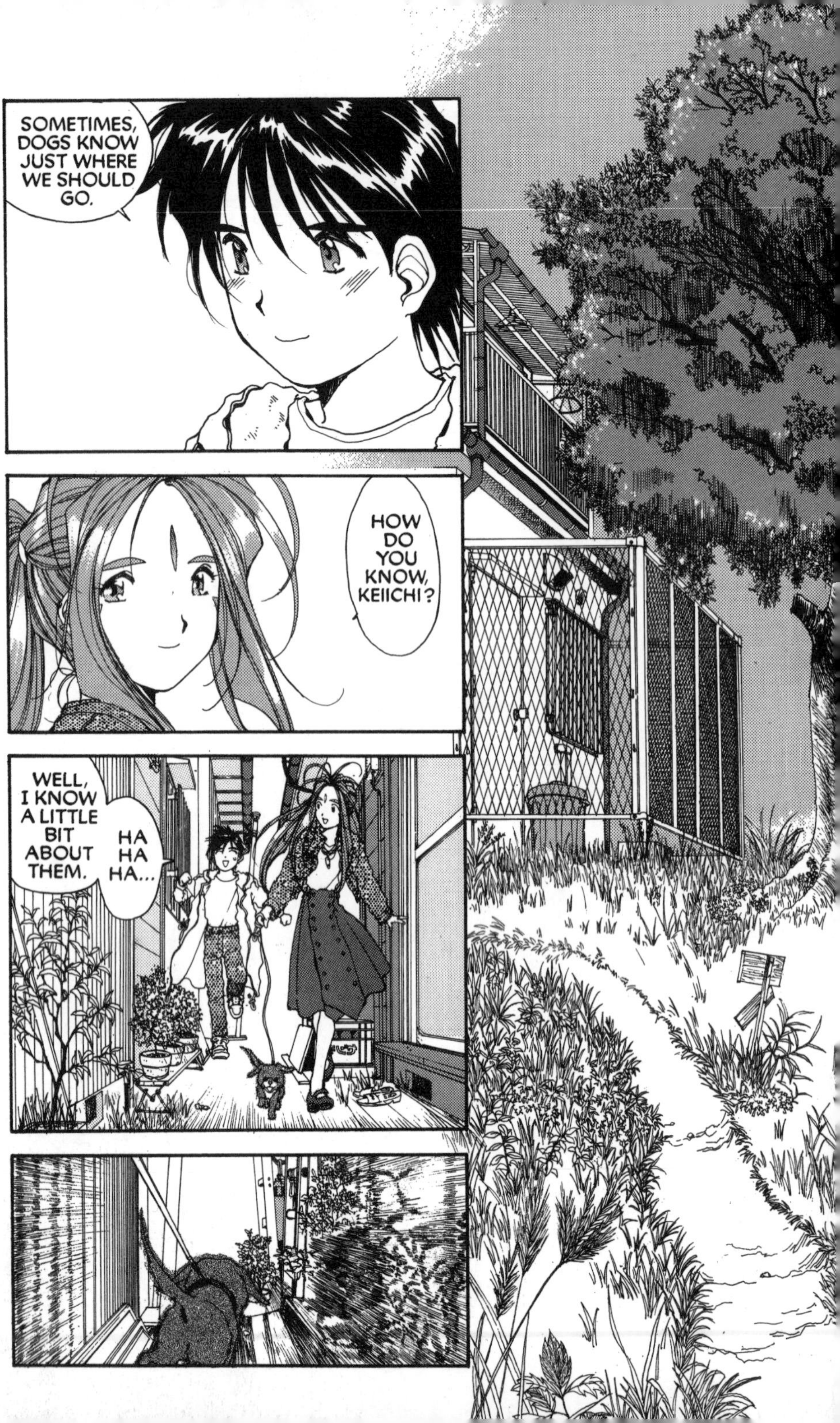
SOMETIMES, DOGS KNOW JUST WHERE WE SHOULD GO.
HOW DO YOU KNOW, KEIICHI?
WELL, I KNOW A LITTLE BIT ABOUT THEM.
HA HA HA...

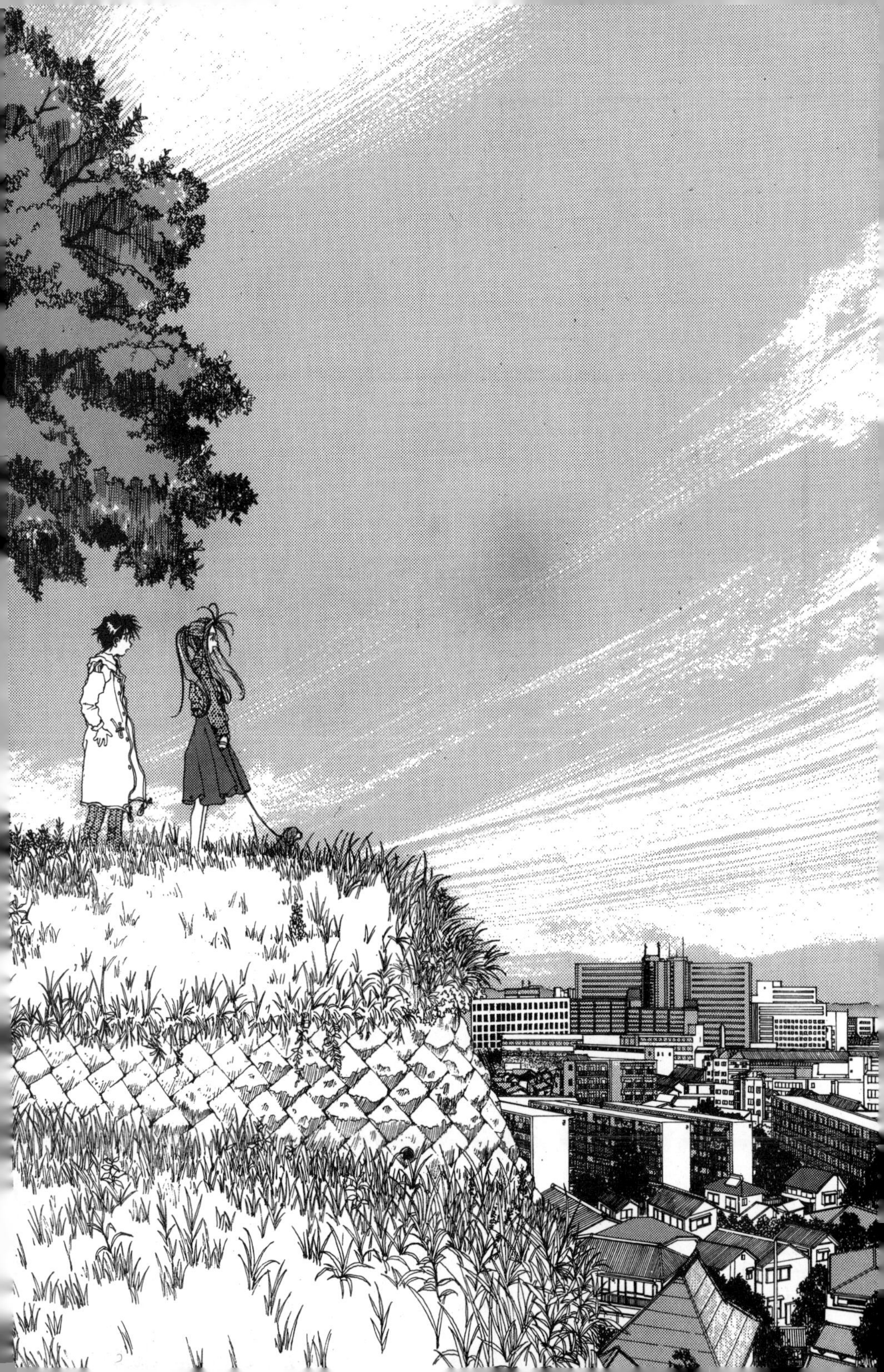

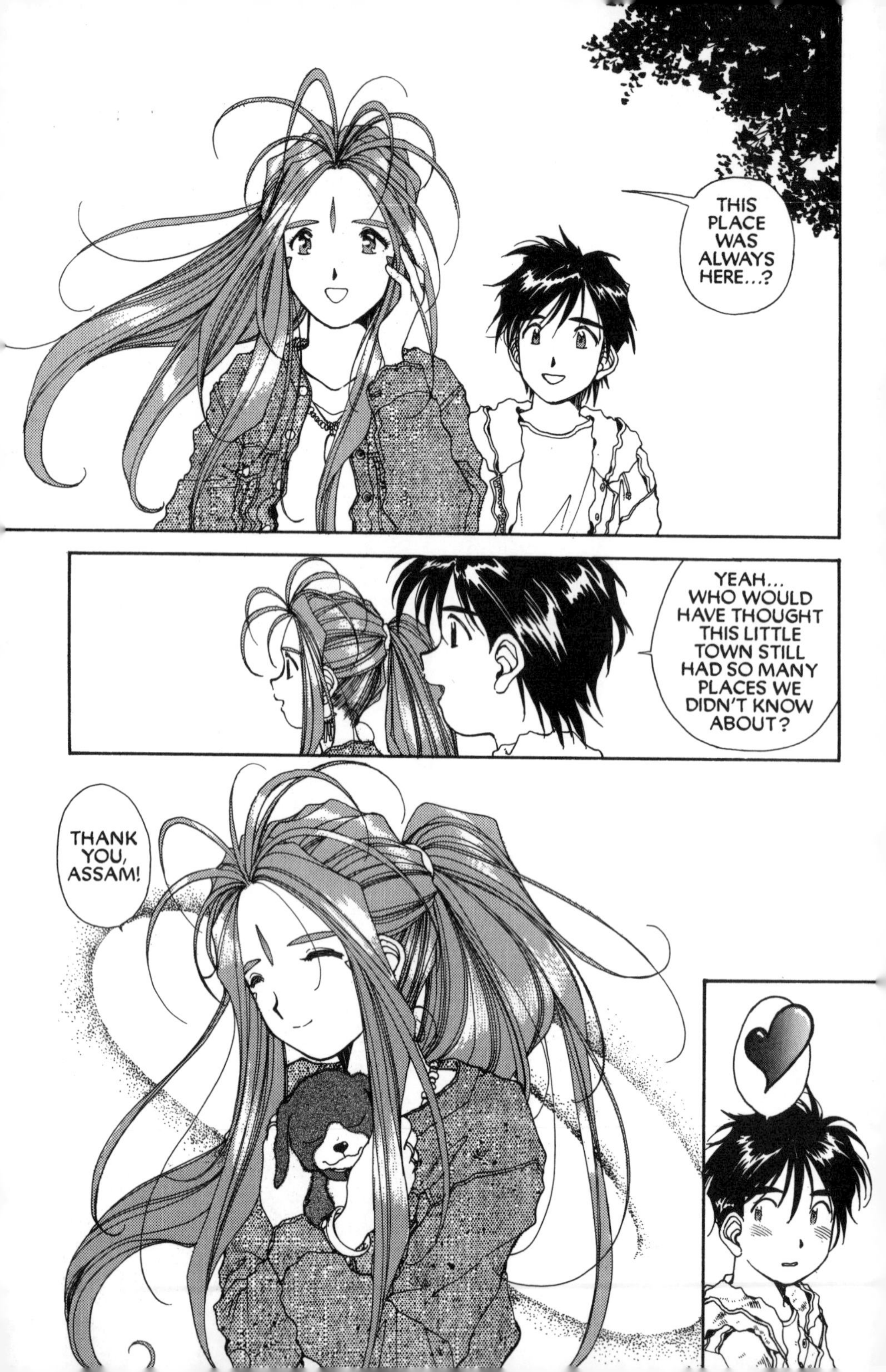
THIS PLACE WAS ALWAYS HERE...?
YEAH... WHO WOULD HAVE THOUGHT THIS LITTLE TOWN STILL HAD SO MANY PLACES WE DIDN'T KNOW ABOUT?
THANK YOU, ASSAM!

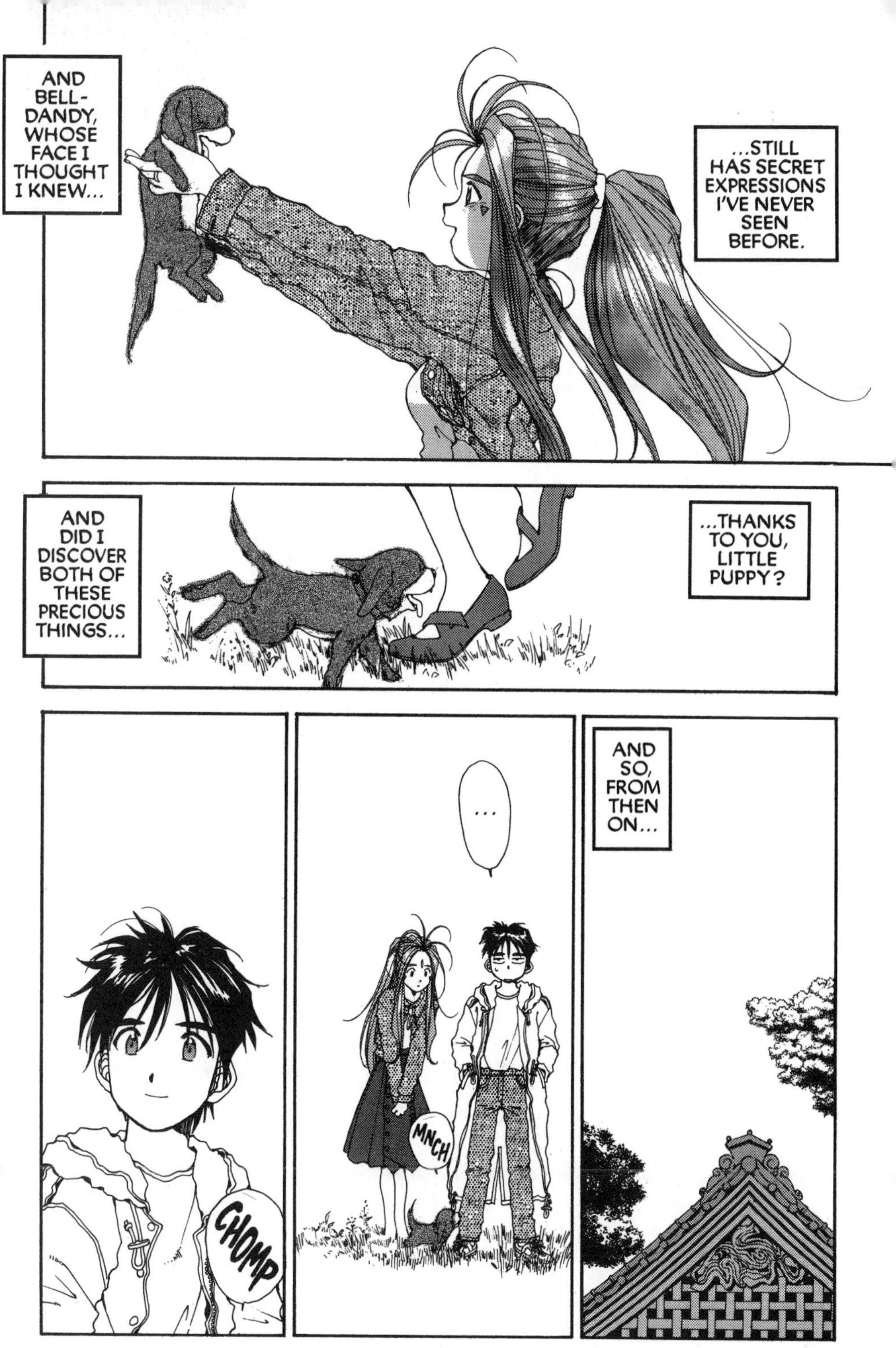
AND BELL-DANDY, WHOSE FACE I THOUGHT I KNEW...
...STILL HAS SECRET EXPRESSIONS I'VE NEVER SEEN BEFORE.
AND DID I DISCOVER BOTH OF THESE PRECIOUS THINGS...
...THANKS TO YOU, LITTLE PUPPY?
CHOMP
...
MNCH
AND SO, FROM THEN ON...

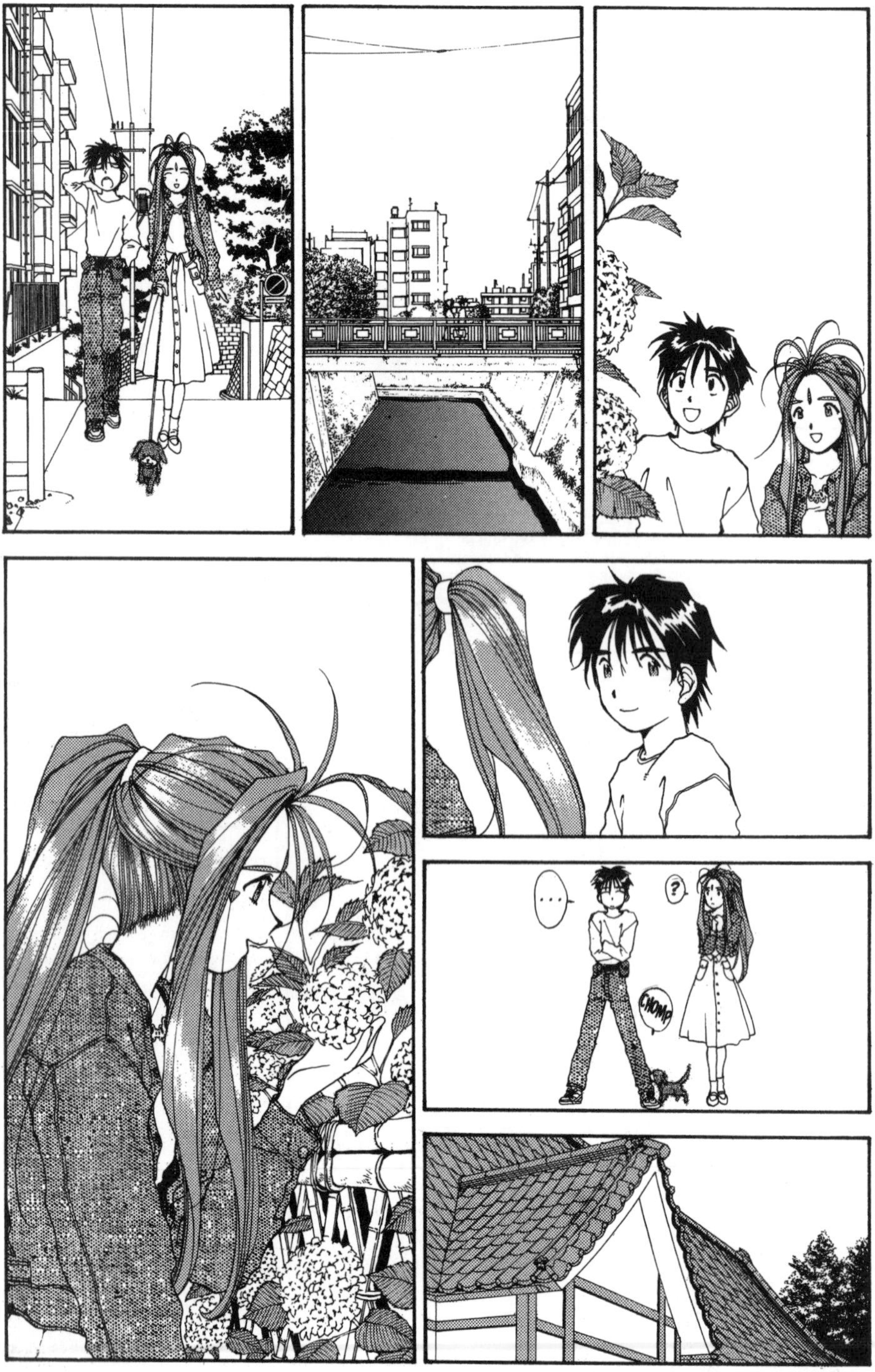
...
?
CHOMP

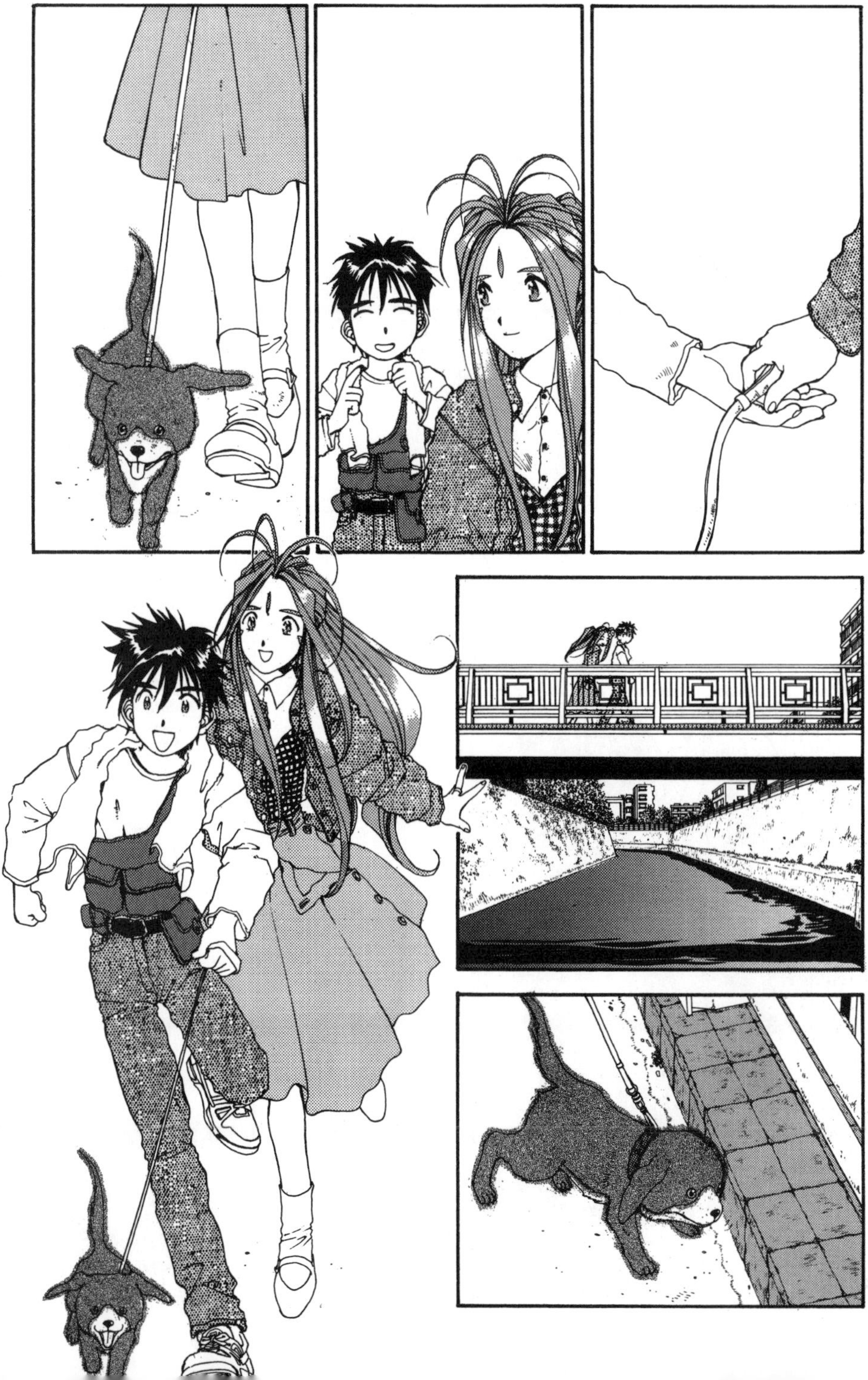

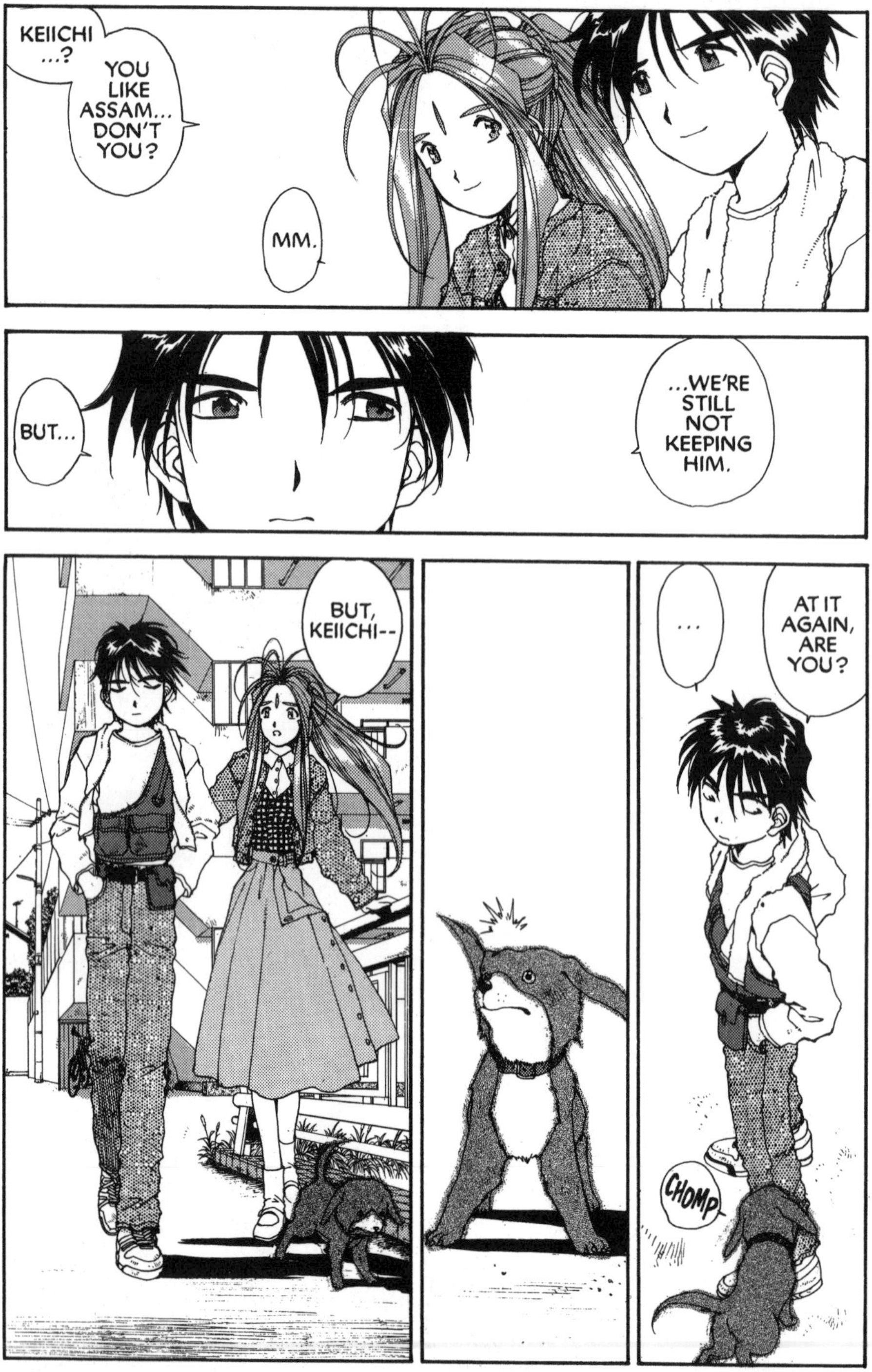
KEIICHI ...?
YOU LIKE ASSAM... DON'T YOU?
MM.
BUT...
...WE'RE STILL NOT KEEPING HIM.
BUT, KEIICHI--
...
AT IT AGAIN, ARE YOU?
CHOMP

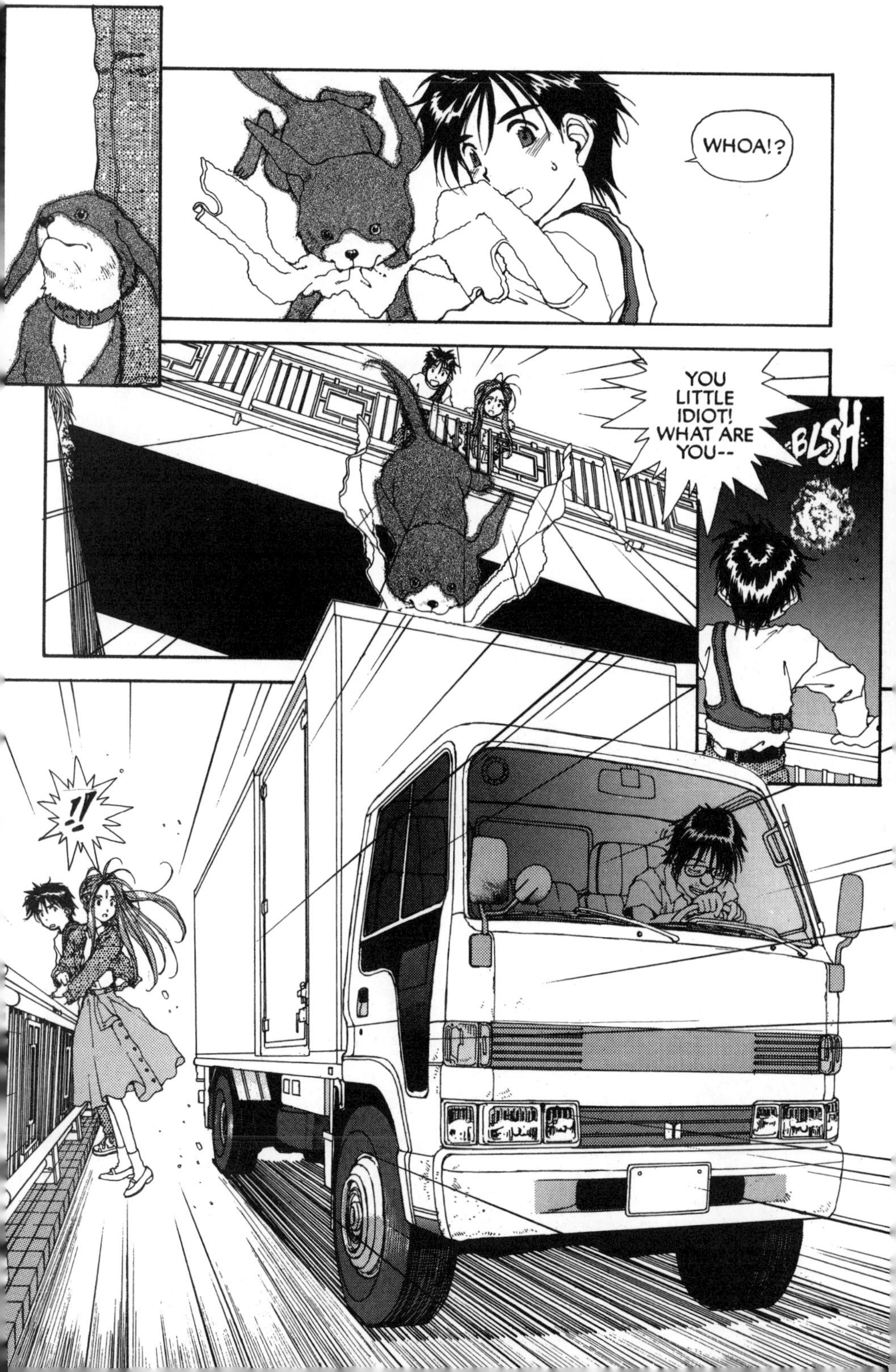
WHOA!?
YOU LITTLE IDIOT! WHAT ARE YOU--
BLSH
!!

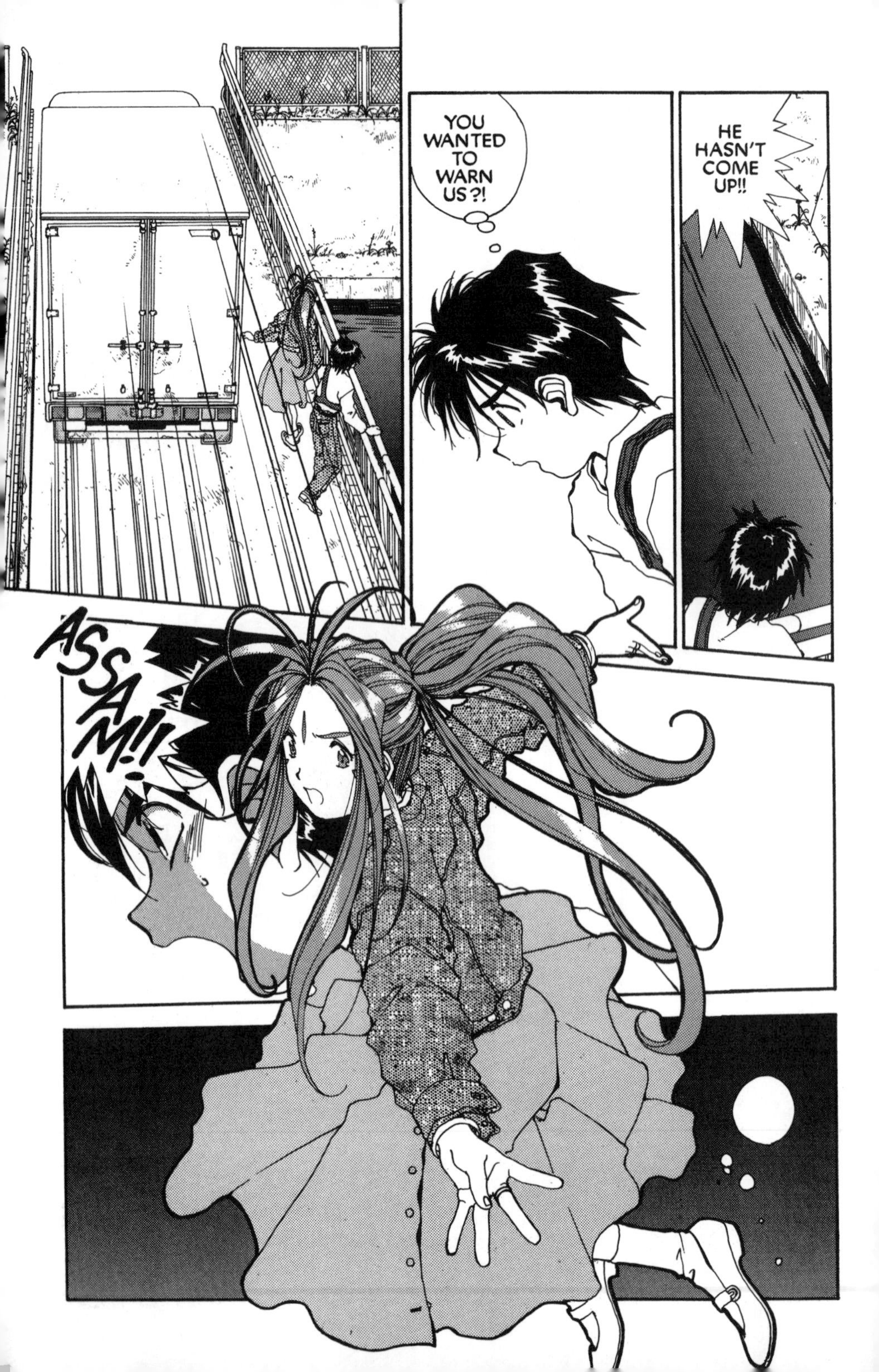
YOU WANTED TO WARN US?!
HE HASN'T COME UP!!
ASSAM!!

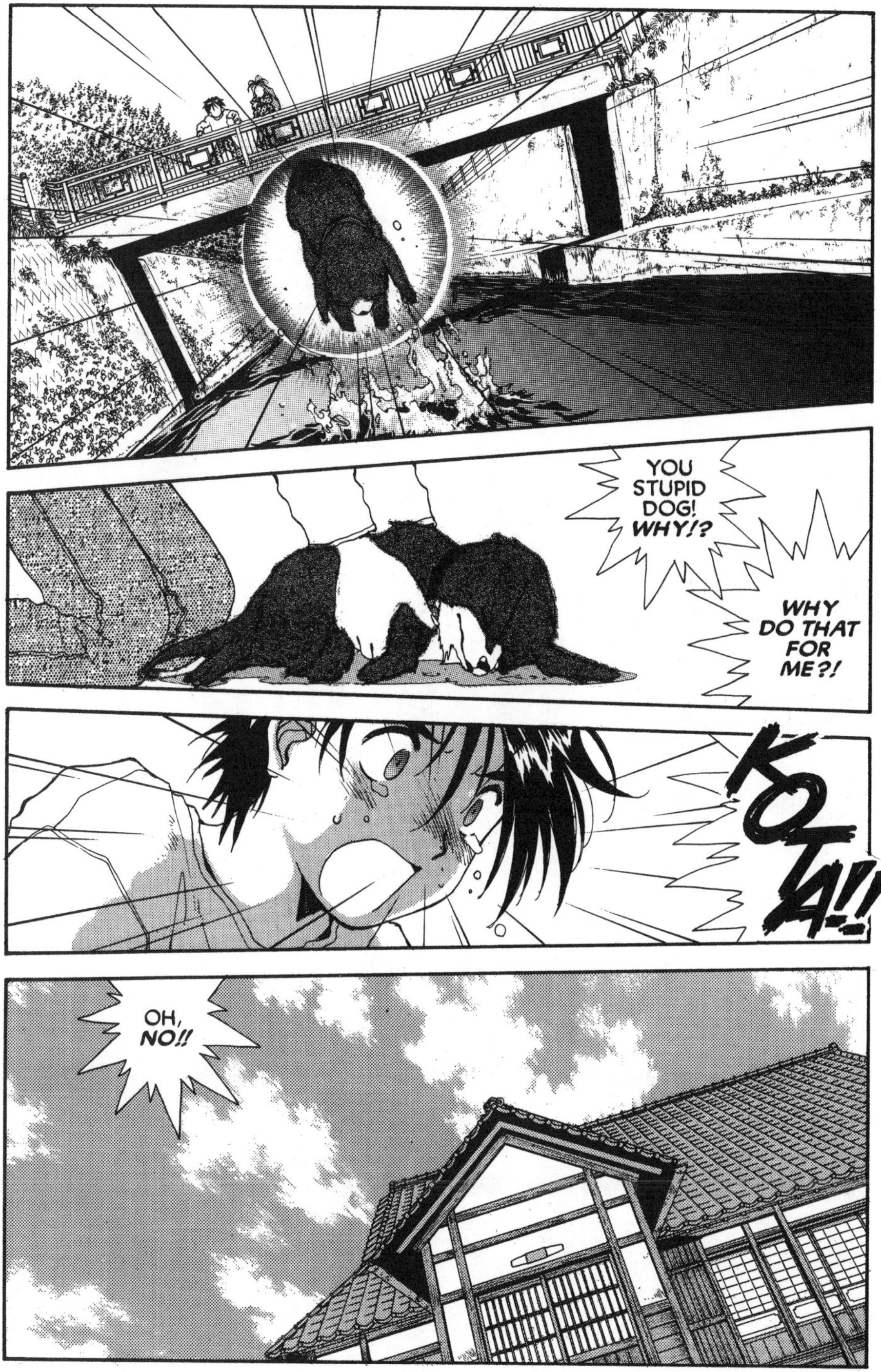
YOU STUPID DOG! WHY!?
WHY DO THAT FOR ME?!
KOTA!!
OH, NO!!

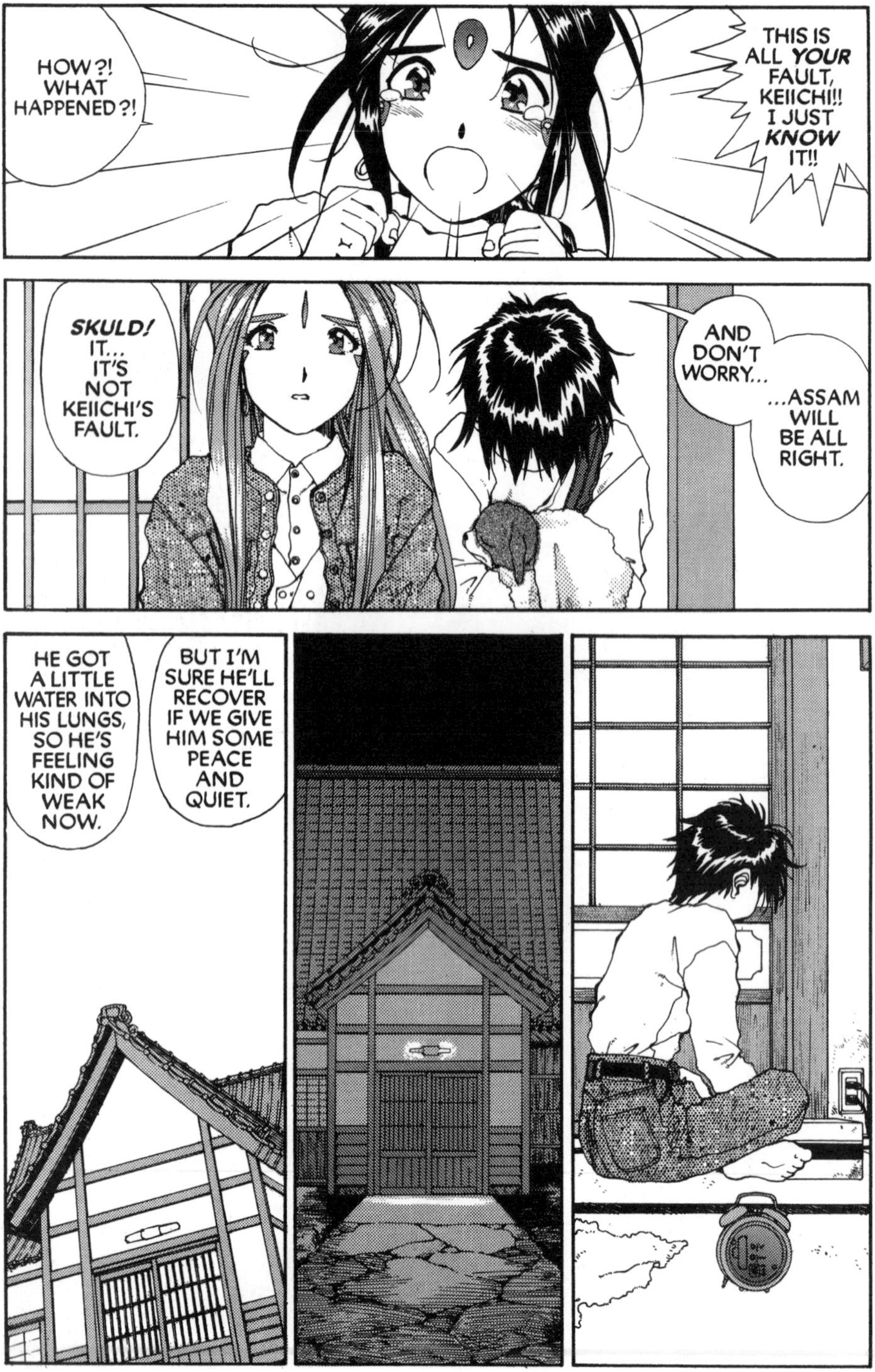
HOW?! WHAT HAPPENED?!
THIS IS ALL *YOUR* FAULT, KEIICHI!! I JUST *KNOW* IT!!
SKULD! IT... IT'S NOT KEIICHI'S FAULT.
AND DON'T WORRY...
...ASSAM WILL BE ALL RIGHT.
HE GOT A LITTLE WATER INTO HIS LUNGS, SO HE'S FEELING KIND OF WEAK NOW.
BUT I'M SURE HE'LL RECOVER IF WE GIVE HIM SOME PEACE AND QUIET.

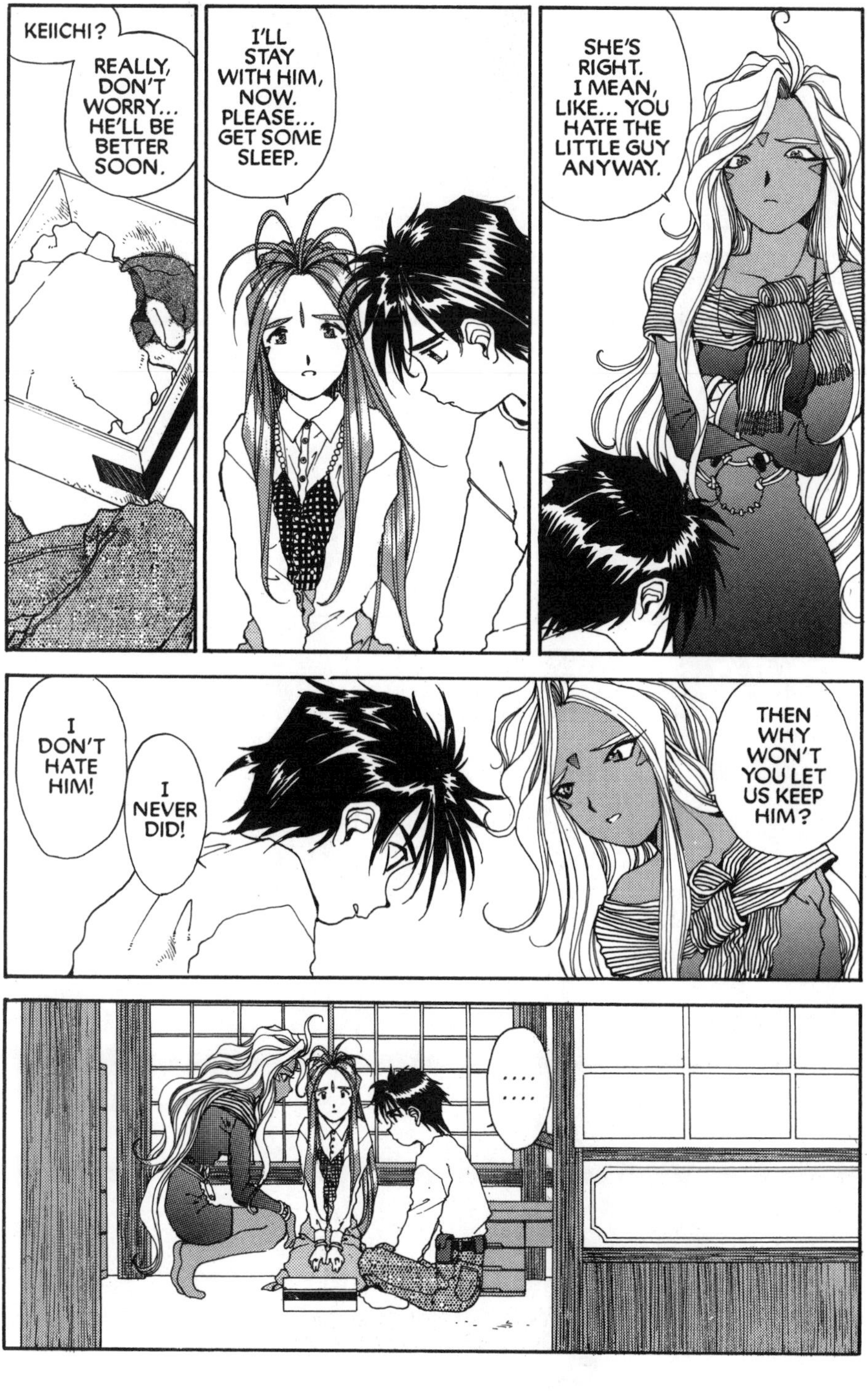
KEIICHI?
REALLY, DON'T WORRY... HE'LL BE BETTER SOON.
I'LL STAY WITH HIM, NOW. PLEASE... GET SOME SLEEP.
SHE'S RIGHT. I MEAN, LIKE... YOU HATE THE LITTLE GUY ANYWAY.
I DON'T HATE HIM!
I NEVER DID!
THEN WHY WON'T YOU LET US KEEP HIM?
....
....

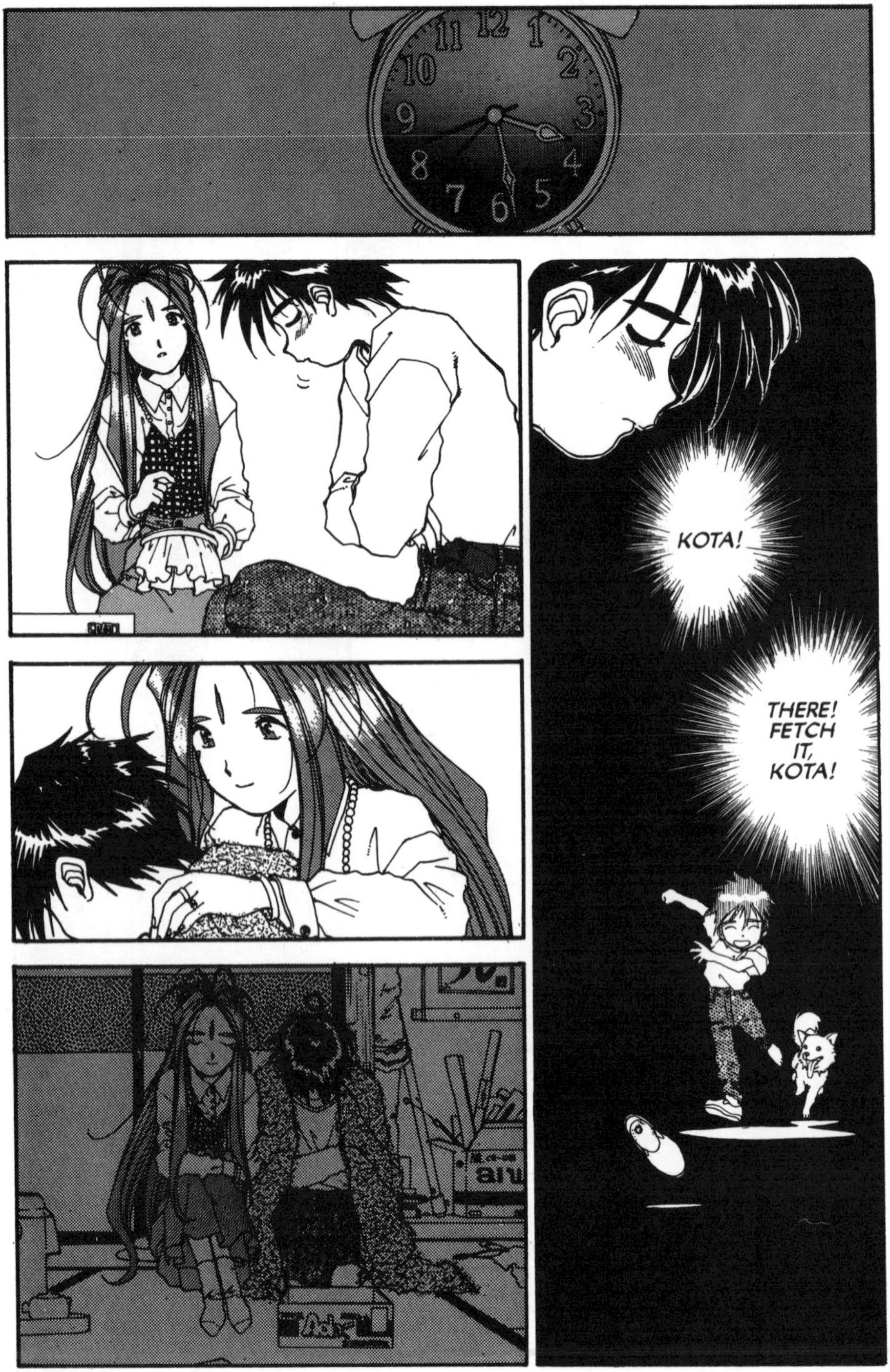
KOTA!
THERE! FETCH IT, KOTA!

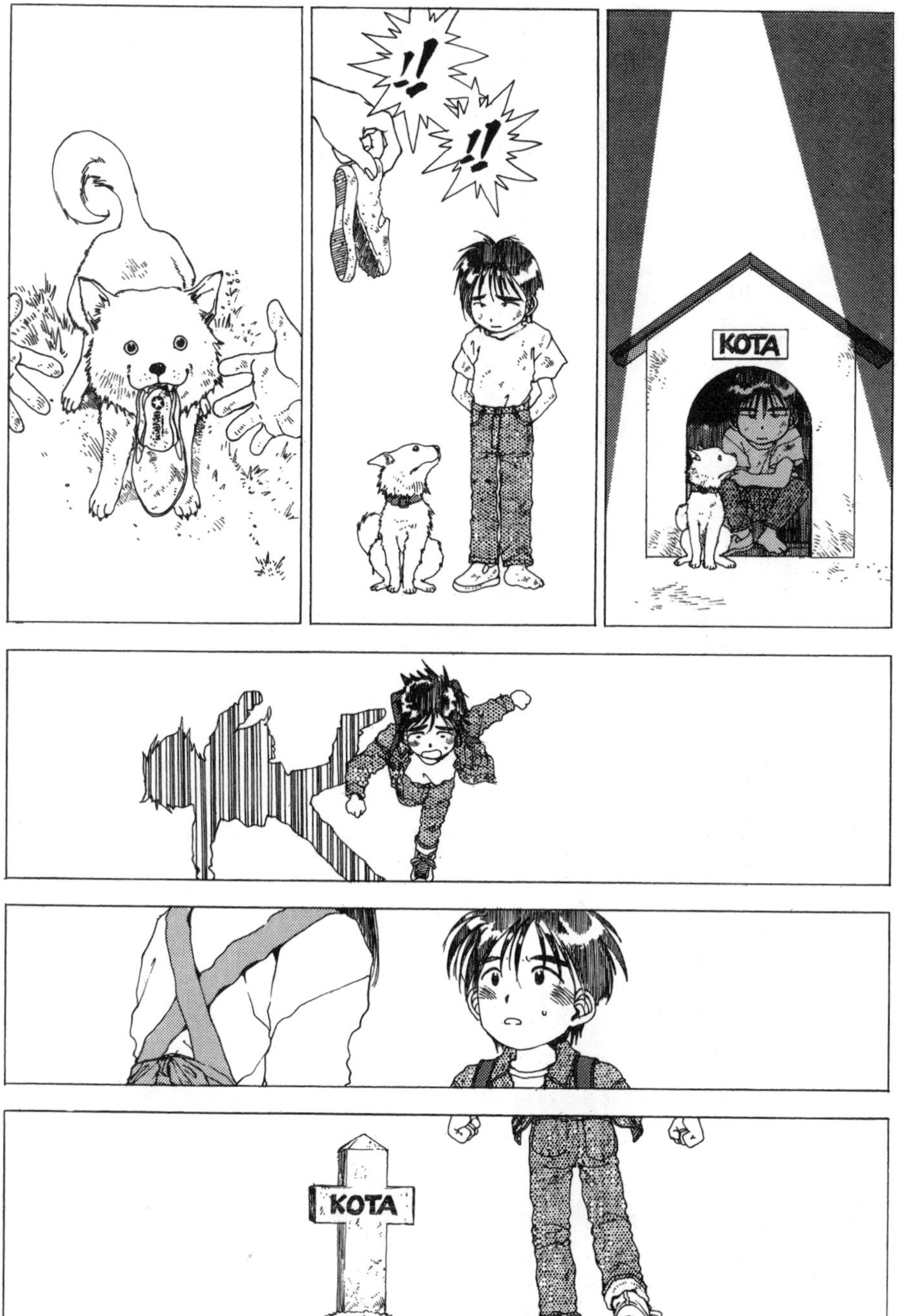
!!
!!
KOTA
KOTA

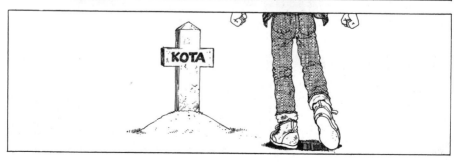

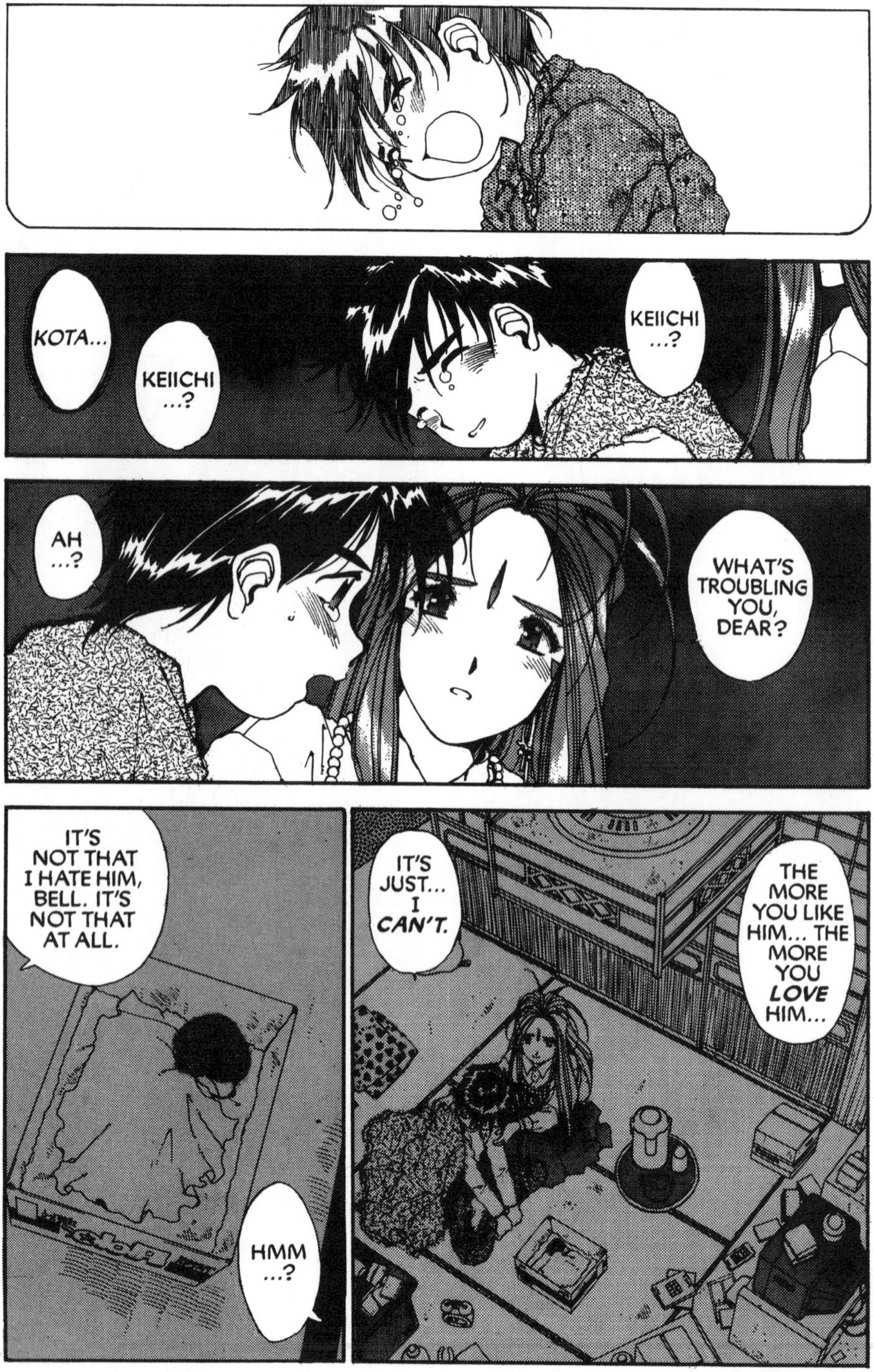
KOTA...
KEIICHI ...?
KEIICHI ...?
AH ...?
WHAT'S TROUBLING YOU, DEAR?
IT'S NOT THAT I HATE HIM, BELL. IT'S NOT THAT AT ALL.
HMM ...?
IT'S JUST... I **CAN'T.**
THE MORE YOU LIKE HIM... THE MORE YOU **LOVE** HIM...

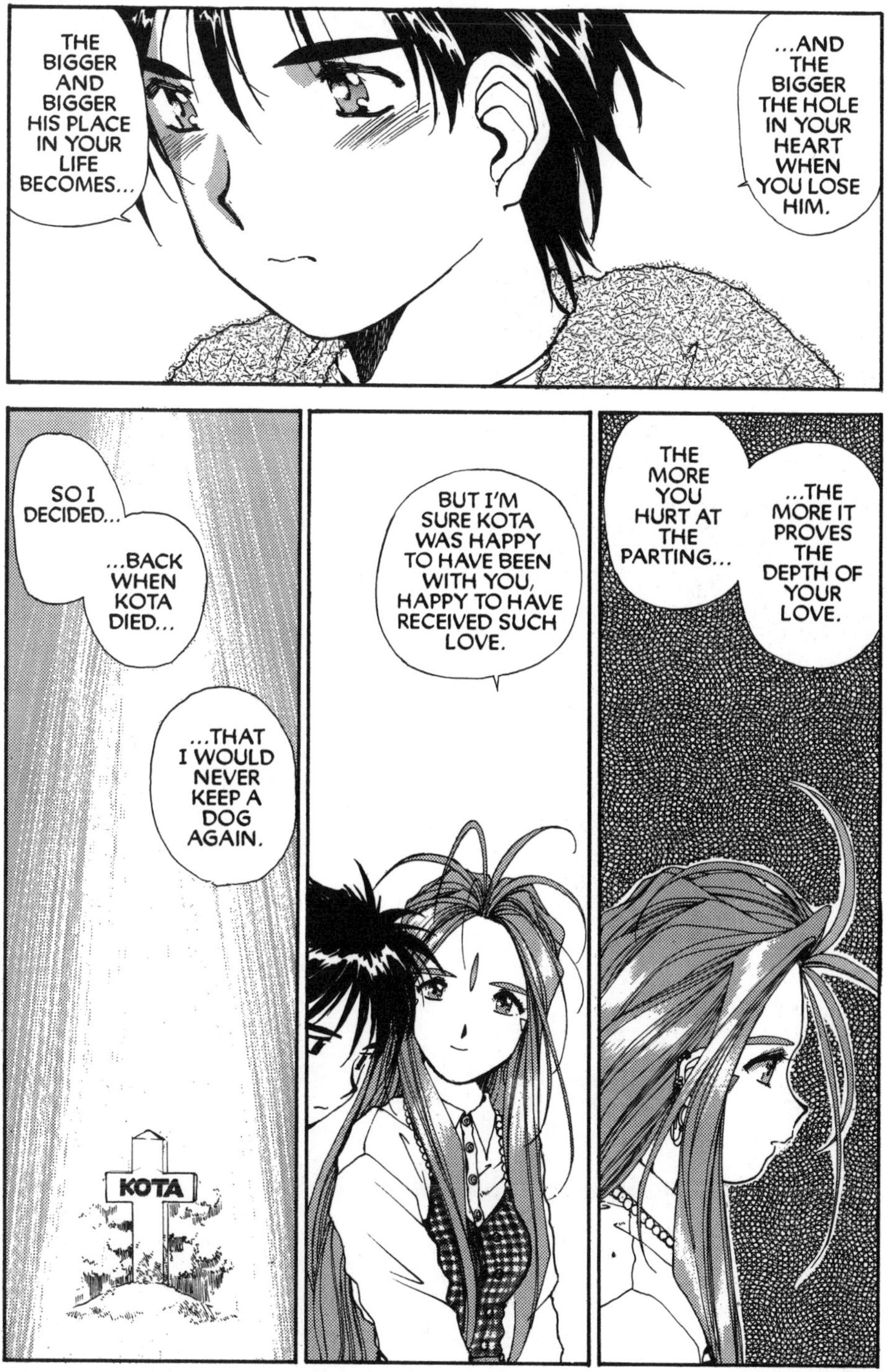
THE BIGGER AND BIGGER HIS PLACE IN YOUR LIFE BECOMES...
...AND THE BIGGER THE HOLE IN YOUR HEART WHEN YOU LOSE HIM.
SO I DECIDED...
...BACK WHEN KOTA DIED...
...THAT I WOULD NEVER KEEP A DOG AGAIN.
KOTA
BUT I'M SURE KOTA WAS HAPPY TO HAVE BEEN WITH YOU, HAPPY TO HAVE RECEIVED SUCH LOVE.
THE MORE YOU HURT AT THE PARTING...
...THE MORE IT PROVES THE DEPTH OF YOUR LOVE.

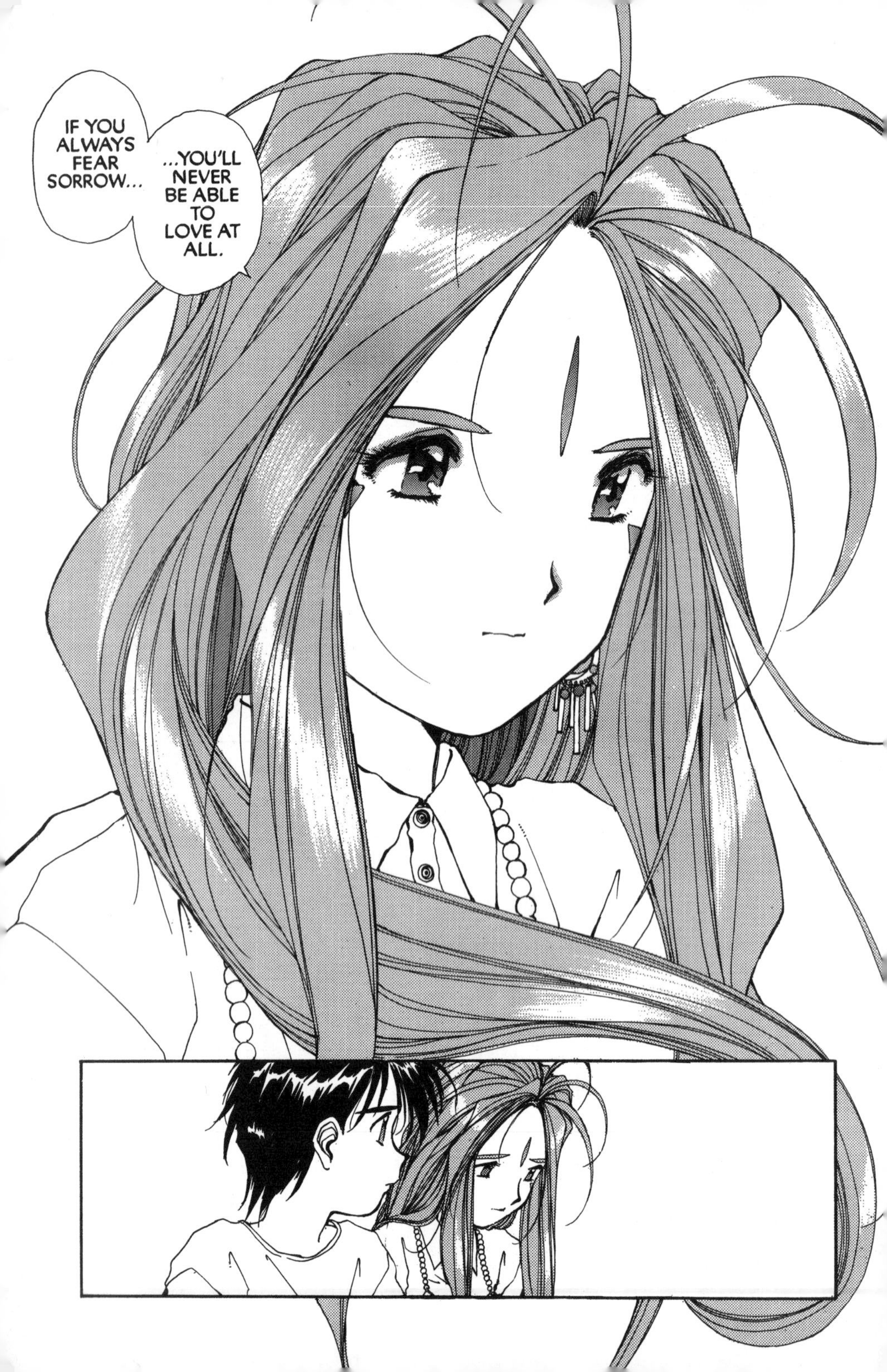
IF YOU ALWAYS FEAR SORROW...
...YOU'LL NEVER BE ABLE TO LOVE AT ALL.

HEY...

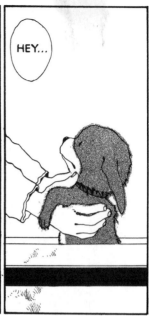

HA HA HA! YOU SCARED US HALF TO DEATH, YOU LITTLE MUTT!

JOY, TOO...

...IS THE PROOF OF LOVE.

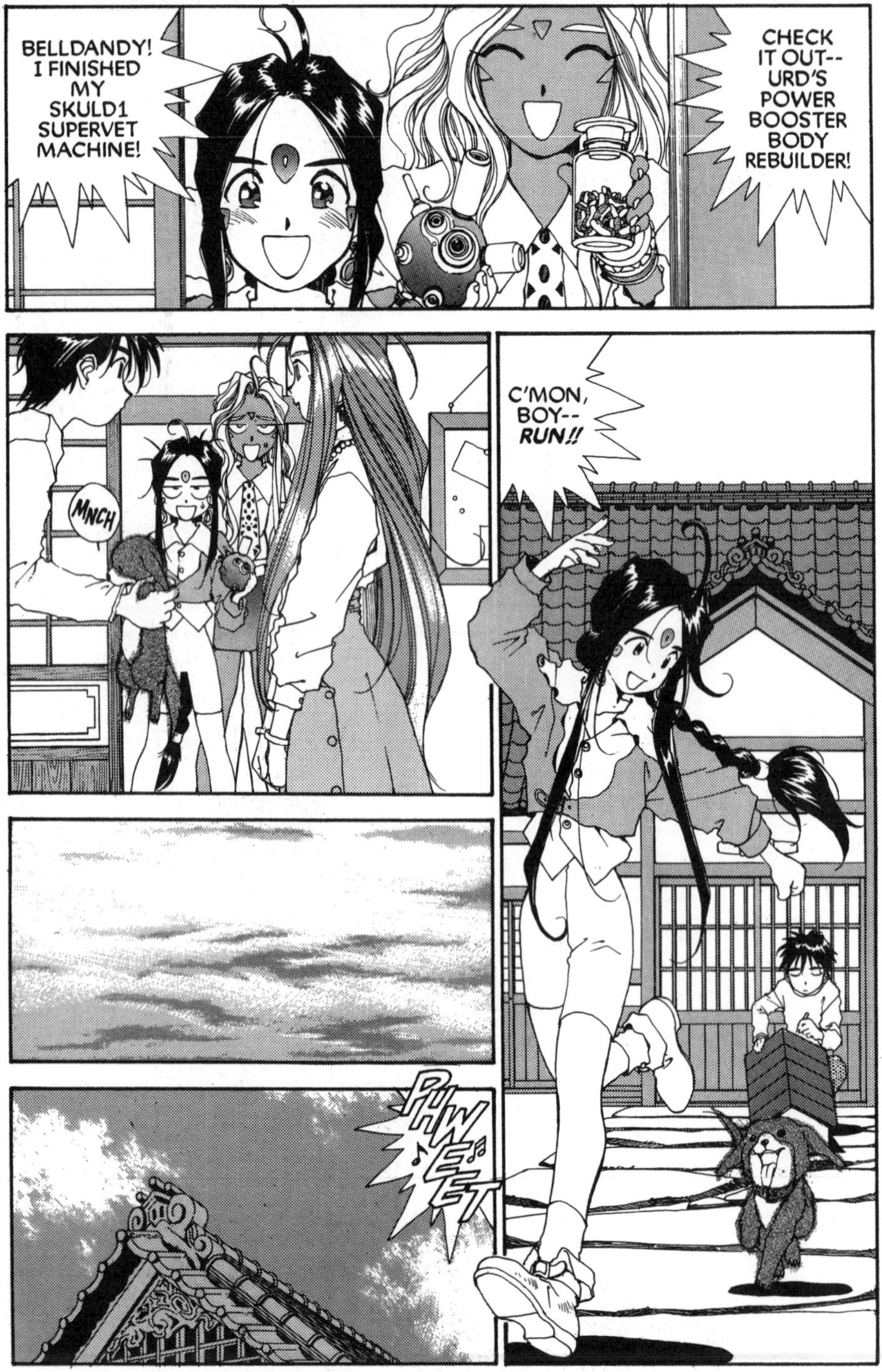
BELLDANDY! I FINISHED MY SKULD1 SUPERVET MACHINE!
CHECK IT OUT-- URD'S POWER BOOSTER BODY REBUILDER!
MNCH
C'MON, BOY-- RUN!!
PHWEET